Also by Gail Sheehy

Middletown, America

Middletown, America

ONE TOWN'S PASSAGE

FROM TRAUMA TO HOPE

——

Gail Sheehy

RANDOM HOUSE | NEW YORK

LIBRARY OF CONGRESS CATALOGING-IN-PUBLICATION DATA

Sheehy, Gail.
Middletown, America : one town's passage from trauma to
hope / Gail Sheehy.
p. cm.
Includes index.
ISBN 0-375-50862-7
1. Victims of terrorism—New Jersey—Middletown.
2. Terrorism victims' families—New Jersey—Middletown.
3. Middletown (N.J.)—Social conditions.   4. September 11
Terrorist Attacks, 2001.   I. Title.

HV6432.S52 2003
974.7'1044—dc21

2003046694
Printed in the United States of America on acid-free paper
Random House website address: www.atrandom.com

2 4 6 8 9 7 5 3

First Edition

Book design by Barbara M. Bachman

To my three angels . . .
Ella, Chris, and Caryn

Preface

A few weeks after the attacks of September 11, I set out to explore the human side of the catastrophe. My subjects are the people who remained *after* the devastation and who are putting their lives back together. This is a book about life going on.

September 11 was both a shared national trauma and a unique private tragedy for thousands of families. Not only were the victims innocent citizens but certain communities seemed to be singled out for death in disproportionate numbers. The toll appeared to be particularly heavy in New Jersey. As Jersey newspapers began collecting names and hometowns of those confirmed dead, one town kept surfacing: Middletown. The name rang a bell. *Middletown: A Study in Modern American Culture* was a famous book that revealed many different aspects of American life in the 1920s through the prism of one small American city in the middle of the country. It occurred to me that we could learn a good deal about American life at the opening of a new millennium through the microcosm of Middletown, New Jersey.

Nearly fifty people were robbed from this middle-class commuter suburb and its sister hamlets on the Rumson peninsula by the terrorist attacks twenty miles away at the World Trade Center—the largest concentrated death toll. Those lost included a gung ho Port Authority Police officer who had raced to the scene, single working moms, beloved sports coaches, and a heavy contingent of traders and brokers who worked in the Twin Towers. Most clicked out of their garages in the dark of early morning, took the train or ferry across the river, and clicked back into their garages after dark. They didn't think they needed to know their neighbors or depend on the community.

I began walking the journey of trauma and grieving with some of the victims' families and survivors, week by week. What would become of the young wives carrying children their husbands would never see, wives who had watched their dreams literally go up in smoke in that amphitheater of death across the river? I remember sitting with a formerly feisty surfer girl, Kristen, as she raked her fingers through her uncombed hair and described a visit to the library. "Where is the book for a thirty-year-old woman with a two-and-a-half-year-old child whose husband was killed by terrorists and who watched it on TV? Where is the book for that?" And yet this same Kristen later channeled her pain into the battle for an independent investigation of the government's failures to protect its citizens—a battle that led her all the way to the White House.

Would the tears ever stop for a middle-aged woman who lost her son only months after her husband walked out on her? Or for the wife so defined by her now-dead husband that the only identity she had left was as the mother of a Down's syndrome child? How would children make sense of an evildoer called Osama with powers greater even than those of his Hollywood counterpart, Saruman in the *Lord of the Rings* movies? Was there any light at the end of the tunnel for widowers who felt like Kevin, the forty-two-year-old construction manager, whose greatest remaining wish was to find his dead wife under the rubble so he could lie down beside her and go to sleep to stop the pain?

I closely followed selected families of Middletown over the better part of two years. It was a tumultuous passage—through disbelief, passivity, panic attacks, sheer survival, rising anger, deep grieving, and realignment of faith—to the shock of resilience, the secret romances, the discovery of independence, the relapses on the first anniversary, the return of a capacity to love and be loved, and, finally, the commitment to construct a new life. I cannot imagine any greater reassurance of the powers of the human spirit, buttressed by faith, to heal itself.

These stories are relevant to many situations less horrific than death by terrorism. We experience many kinds of loss and trauma in life. Within the experiences of the characters I followed is just about every kind of human struggle.

It wasn't only the journey of the bereaved families of Middletown that I wanted to follow. Thousands of witness-survivors were also traumatized, and past experience suggested that they would carry a dangerous burden of guilt. How would religious leaders explain the inexplicable to their depressed flocks? Would mental health professionals accustomed to dealing with "traumas" on the order of divorce and depression be prepared to help people make sense of lives shattered without warning by human missiles propelled out of hate? What would teachers and principals tell their students? Would friends and neighbors emerge to form vital networks of support?

How would the corporate leaders calculate their debt to the bereaved families of their deceased employees, weighed in each case against the dire need to protect the corpus of a decimated enterprise? How would the police be changed by spending months of white nights at Ground Zero picking through body parts to find remains of families they knew? They would not emerge from that pit the same people. Who would look after *their* recovery—an issue that remains a concern? Would the country's leaders demand investigation of this massive failure of government to discharge its basic duty to provide domestic security? Or would they evade, stonewall, cover up, and use 9/11 for their own political ends?

The town itself became a character—a social organism turned inside out. Middletown is like many affluent middle-class American suburbs today, which are not always connected to the cities that spawned them. They appear ideal in good times, but how well equipped are they to absorb trauma?

THE RESEARCH PROCESS

This book follows more than fifty characters. Their stories run parallel and often intertwine. To follow them all on a month-by-month basis required more than nine hundred recorded interviews, as well as many follow-up phone calls and e-mails. But the word "interviews" doesn't begin to convey the trust that had to be earned and the emotional nakedness that was allowed by the people who agreed to participate in this book. Over the months we developed a special kinship. My investment in them extended beyond the writing of a book. I wanted to know their future, at least insofar as previous experience could help them navigate their ongoing passage through trauma and grieving toward a renewal of hope. I went back to interview families and survivors from the Oklahoma City terrorist bombing of 1995, and even further back to families robbed of spouses and children by the terrorist attack on Pan Am 103 over Lockerbie, Scotland, in 1988.

The thoughts, feelings, dialogue, and actions attributed to people in the book were described to me in interviews by the participants themselves. Thoughts and feelings are italicized, but all have been verified by the individuals themselves.

Apart from the Holocaust, there is no clinical study of the families of victims of traumatic mass murder, especially where there are no intact bodies or only remnants. There appear to be no data on what kinds of treatments work specifically for victims of terrorism in the context of living with an ongoing threat. Another vacuum in our knowledge about coping with man-made trauma is how to protect against vicarious trauma. Those in the helping professions who step forward to offer clinical support take on heavy emotional burdens, as do those friends, neighbors, and community volunteers who offer consistent support to people directly affected. In the context of living with the ongoing threat of terrorism, how do we protect the protectors?

The single event that we know as 9/11 is over. But the shock waves continue to radiate outward, stirred up by orange alerts, terrorism lockdowns, and the shrinking of personal liberties we once took for granted. The stories in this book of real people faced with extraordinary trauma, and gradually transcending it, are the best antidote to our fears.

The one indispensable ingredient in coming through any adversity is hope. Once a person has hope, it is possible to mobilize his or her resources, both inner and outer. The families of 9/11 who have already begun constructing new lives point the way to others. Tellingly, these families are the *least* fearful of another terrorist attack. If they could cope with 9/11, they know they can cope with almost anything. Their stories compose a powerful parable for our times. This is a book of hope.

Contents

BOOK TWO

THE REST OF THE STORY

—

Personae

(IN ORDER OF APPEARANCE)

KRISTEN BREITWEISER: widow of 9/11 victim Ron Breitweiser, vice president at Fiduciary Trust; mother of Caroline; leader of the families' fight for an independent national commission to investigate the terrorist attacks of 9/11.

ANNA EGAN: Canadian-American widow of 9/11 victim Michael Egan, AON director and manager; mother of Jon and Matthew.

KENNY TIETJEN: Port Authority police officer and Middletown volunteer firefighter, killed on 9/11.

PAT WOTTON: widow of 9/11 victim Rod Wotton, a Fiduciary Trust technology manager; mother of a post–9/11 baby, Rodney Patrick, and two-year-old Dorothea.

BOB PLANER: survivor of the 1993 and 2001 Trade Center bombings; executive vice president and co-head of equity sales at Keefe, Bruyette and Woods. He lost sixty-seven coworkers on 9/11.

PAULA PLANER: wife of 9/11 survivor Bob Planer and soccer mom of four.

LIEUTENANT BILL KEEGAN: Port Authority police lieutenant who became the night commander of Ground Zero.

RABBI HARRY LEVIN: rabbi of Congregation B'nai Israel in Rumson. A religious conservative and activist who seized on the tragedy of 9/11 to build bridges across religious boundaries.

PARSON JOHN MONROE: pastor of First Presbyterian Church of Rumson.

BOB HONECKER, JR.: First Assistant Prosecutor, Monmouth County.

CHARLES BROWN III: administrator of mental health services, Monmouth County.

MARY MURPHY: widow of Jimmy Murphy, a Cantor Fitzgerald trader; mother of Morgan, Jimmy, and a post–9/11 baby, Meredith.

FATHER KEVIN KEELAN: formerly a priest at Holy Cross Catholic Church, Rumson.

LAURIE TIETJEN: sister of a 9/11 victim, PAPD Officer Kenny Tietjen, and daughter of Janice and Kenneth Tietjen.

EILEEN THEALL: parish nurse at St. Mary's Catholic Church.

KATHY AND FRANK PEZZUTI: lost daughter Kaleen and son-in-law Todd Pelino, the father of two young children, on 9/11.

JOHN POLLINGER: Middletown police chief and commander of the largest police department in Monmouth County.

LISA LUCKETT: widow of 9/11 victim Teddy Luckett, an eSpeed executive; mother of three.

KAREN CANGIALOSI: widow of 9/11 victim Stephen Cangialosi, a Cantor Fitzgerald trader; mother of Peter and Jeffrey; aerobics instructor.

ANTONIA MARTINEZ: principal of Middletown Village School.

SHERRY AND AMANDA McHEFFEY: mother and sister, respectively, of 9/11 victim Keith McHeffey, a Cantor Fitzgerald trader.

ELAINE CHEVALIER: mother of 9/11 victim Swede Chevalier, a Cantor Fitzgerald trader, and of a teenage daughter, Brittany; commercial real estate manager.

RICK KORN: music and documentary producer and community activist in Rumson.

CRAIG CUMMINGS: Cantor Fitzgerald survivor and founder of the Craig and Mary Cummings Scholarship Fund for the education of 9/11 children.

HOWARD LUTNICK: Cantor Fitzgerald chairman and CEO; brother of 9/11 victim Gary Lutnick.

JOHN DUFFY: surviving CEO of Keefe, Bruyette and Woods; father of 9/11 victim Christopher Duffy

KEVIN CASEY: widower of 9/11 victim Kathleen Casey, an equities trader for Sandler O'Neill & Partners; father of Matt; manager with the New York City Transit Authority.

KATHI BEDARD: a substance abuse counselor who became the coordinator of New Jersey family visits to Ground Zero.

JIM WASSAL: founder of the Alliance of Neighbors of Monmouth County; real estate developer.

GINNY BAUER: widow of 9/11 victim Dave Bauer, director of global sales at eSpeed; leader of families' fight for tax relief; mother of three; named head of the New Jersey State Lottery.

ELEANOR HILL: chief of staff to the House-Senate Joint Inquiry on Intelligence; former inspector general of the Department of Defense.

MORGAN MURPHY: four-year-old daughter of Mary Murphy and 9/11 victim Jimmy Murphy.

DANIEL LANE: principal of Middletown South High School.

TERRY COLUMBO: student assistance coordinator at Middletown South High School.

ALLYSON GILBERT, JANET DLUHI, MARY ELLEN RUANE, AND LAURA WILTON: founders of FAVOR, Middletown's grassroots volunteer network.

KEVIN LAVERTY: widower of 9/11 victim Anna Laverty and father of Deena Laverty.

DONNA LAMONACO: president of the New Jersey chapter of COPS.

MOHAMMED MOSAAD: one of the founders of the Middletown mosque.

GABR FAMILY: Abdel, a doctor, and Eklas, a teacher, and their five children.

KENNETH FEINBERG: special master of the Victim Compensation Fund.

RUDY FERNANDEZ: newly graduated Port Authority police officer who oversaw nighttime recoveries at Ground Zero.

MAUREEN FITZSIMMONS: program director of the Monmouth County Behavioral Health Care Division of Catholic Charities; initiated the support groups for Middletown families.

TERRY FIORELLI: widow of 9/11 victim Stephen Fiorelli, a Port Authority engineer; mother of two; secretary and coach at Matawan Middle School in Red Bank.

PAN AM 103 "SURVIVOR GUIDES": Cathy Tedeschi, widow of Pan Am 103 victim Bill Daniels, and Bob Monetti, father of victim Rick Monetti.

"JUST FOUR MOMS FROM NEW JERSEY": activist partners with Kristen Breitweiser: Patty Casazza, widow of John Casazza; Mindy Kleinberg, widow of Alan David Kleinberg; and Lorie van Auken, widow of Kenneth van Auken. All three 9/11 victims were securities traders at Cantor Fitzgerald.

FATHER JEROME NOLAN: priest at Church of the Nativity.

CAROL VEIZER: psychotherapist and director of the New Jersey Center for the Healing Arts in Red Bank.

RICHARD WINTORY: Oklahoma County senior assistant district attorney.

DIANE LEONARD: widow of Oklahoma City bombing victim Don Leonard; activist for victims' rights and peer counseling of first responders.

POLITICIANS: Senators John McCain, Jon Corzine, Robert Torricelli, Joseph Lieberman, Hillary Clinton, Bob Graham, Richard Shelby. Congressmen Dennis Hastert, Chris Smith, Porter Goss, Tim Roemer (former). White House staffers: Jay Lefkowitz and Nick Calio.

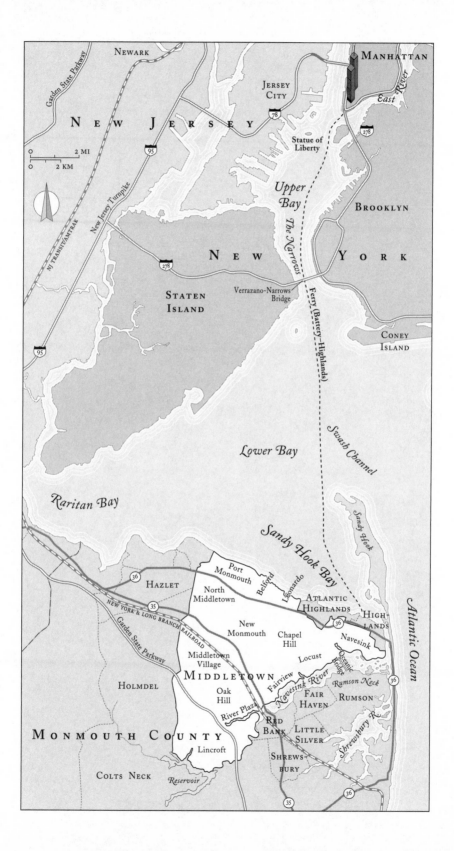

BOOK ONE

SURVIVING TRAUMA

Victims focus on what they cannot change.
Survivors focus on what they can change.

—Chaplain Jack Poe,
Oklahoma City Police Department

Chapter One
———

SIGNS AND WONDERS

KRISTEN AND THE RAVEN

When the glossy black bird dropped onto the lawn outside her kitchen window that August, Kristen felt a shudder go through her body. She called out to her husband.

"Oh my God, there's a raven."

"A what?" he said. Ron didn't know much about birds.

"A *raven*," she repeated impatiently.

"So?"

"You don't understand, that's a bad omen. The raven is the harbinger of death."

Kristen clutched her breast. She had a tumor there, waiting for biopsy. It was in the same place where her mother had found a tumor at the age of thirty-eight. Kristen had lost her mother to cancer a few years earlier. It was a horrible death.

"I'm scared," she told her husband. "I think that's me. I think it's a symbol that I'm going to die."

"You're crazy," her husband said. "It's just a crow."

"I don't want that bird in our yard," she said. Kristen was not usually one to worry. Not this surfer girl from the Jersey shore. This was a tall blond tomboy who grew up with all guy friends. A natural beauty who still had age on her side, being thirty; she didn't give a thought to taming her flyaway hair or painting makeup on her smooth Swedish skin. She was headstrong to the point that she sometimes got in her own way. For instance, she almost missed marrying Ron. Kristen thought she never wanted to be tied down to one man. No interest in marriage. Zero. Hated children.

Her first date with Ron Breitweiser was on his birthday, August 4, 1996. It was the summer of her bar exam, but she found herself far more attracted to this handsome money manager than to the practice of law. Less than six months later they eloped to a Caribbean island. "And I wasn't even pregnant!" Kristen likes to say. "But why waste time?"

The Breitweisers settled in the pleasant land of Middletown, New Jersey, a lush green oasis in the backyard of New York City. Their house was hidden in woods. The two of them became inseparable. She had no hobbies and he had no hobbies because their hobbies were each other. They would watch TV together, read books together; if Kristen got up to take a shower, Ron would follow her into the bathroom so he could keep talking to her. When Kristen brushed her teeth, she would squeeze out the toothpaste onto Ron's toothbrush. They were crazy about their dog, Sam, a golden retriever, whose discombobulated bulk somehow found its way into their bed every night.

They weren't planning to have children. But when Caroline arrived in March 1999, they turned the conversation pit of their living room into a playroom just for her. In late August 2001, when Kristen and her husband went to a cocktail party, they joked that it was the first time in two and a half years they had been out alone, without their daughter. And it was true. They didn't need a social life. They didn't even see much of their own families. In fact, Ron wasn't speaking to his family. They'd had a huge falling-out.

The Sunday before September 11, for some reason, Kristen stopped to read the obituary section. She said to her husband, "Honey, you know, life is so short. Your dad's older. Are you sure you don't want to call them and just suck it up and make peace?" He said no. He just wanted to break with his family.

Kristen had it good, and she knew it. She had graduated from Seton Hall Law School in 1996 and, as she liked to say, left the law at the top of her game—after practicing all of three days. She hated it. Took a leave of absence to care for her mother, but when that duty was done, Kristen showed no enthusiasm for resuming her aborted law career. Her husband told her she didn't have to go back, he could make enough money. He was a whiz at investing. So good, he had been hired at thirty-eight as a vice president by Fiduciary Trust, an investment-management firm for high-net-worth clients. The president, William Yun, had even asked Ron to manage his father's personal money.

But the minute Ron got home from his office in the South Tower at the World Trade Center, he would change into hiking clothes and walk with Kristen and the baby and the dog up the nature trail behind their house. They would gaze across at mountain ridges and muse, "It could be Wyoming." Kristen wasn't a religious person, but as she would reflect later, "We'd notice the birds and we'd notice the deer and we'd notice the beauty in everything. We knew we were blessed. You almost think that's insurance against bad things happening."

On Saturday, August 25, the first day of Ron's two-week vacation, the two were lazing by the living room window with coffee and newspapers. "Look, that bird's back," Kristen said. Again her husband dismissed it. She left the room to look through her English-lit books to try to find the Poe poem. She found a quote in Shakespeare about the raven bringing "warnings, and portents and evils imminent." When she returned, she saw her husband poring over their Audubon birding book.

"You're right," he said, "it's a raven." The book said the predator was nearly extinct in the Northeast. That made the dumb fear crawl in her stomach. That damn growth in her breast. That damn bird.

ANNA AND THE TROPHY HOUSE

The Egan family had just entered the green and blessed land of Middletown—refugees from Connecticut—so that Michael could be closer to the World Trade Center. The commute from Middletown was a breeze; a luxury commuter bus stopped five minutes from his door and delivered him across the Hudson to the door of the South Tower on the tip of Manhattan Island. With two elevator rides he would emerge to the astonishing views on the 104th floor, where Michael Egan commanded his division as director and manager of the multinational insurance giant AON.

Anna Egan was not happy about the move to Middletown. Or the house. She called it a trophy house. Grand in scale and coldly formal with its glass walls and two-story center hall and spiral staircase. Michael intended it to entertain clients and boost staff morale. It was not for Anna that he bought the house, she knew that; he bought it for AON.

But it turned out to be the best of summers for Anna, the first summer she had had her husband to herself in how many years? Not since her first-born son, Jon, who was already flapping his wings in preparation for his flight from the nest to start college in California. Certainly not since the birth of her second son, Matthew, who was sixteen on paper but with Down's syndrome, who could really say? Matthew was away, too, at a special needs camp.

"So here we were in this huge house, just the two of us, no kids, nothing but boxes, and we're like teenagers again," as Anna remembered—cherished—those last seven weeks of the summer of 2001. "We did nothing but spoil each other. It was so long since he'd taken any time off. We'd stay late in bed. He'd go out to lunch and not go back to work. Silly little things, like he bought us both walkie-talkies. 'We need to connect more,' he said. I'd get beeped all the time, even when I was in the shower."

They played chase-and-tickle around the patio, this fifty-one-year-old Englishman and his wife, who, at forty-seven, was petite but voluptuous. To this proper Brit, Anna with her Sicilian background and slight accent stirred erotic fantasies of Anna Magnani. "You're still sexy after all these years," he would say, looking into her large, dark Mediterranean eyes. Over and over he would tell her, "I love you, darling."

But there was a little flutter in Anna's stomach that wouldn't go away. "I was scared and I didn't know why." It wasn't the move. She had moved so often, she was a pro. She always dove right into the community and made friends and opened their home to her sons' friends.

When she thought back on it, there was an eerie element about her husband's behavior that summer. He bought her a PalmPilot and beamed into it the phone numbers of all his associates, even old ones. "Why, Michael? I don't need this," she'd protest. "You never know," he'd say. He always carried in his briefcase the keys to the family house in England, but one day he entrusted them to her. "Why?" "Just in case I might lose them," he said. He called her all the time: from the office, from the train, even from watering holes in the city when he was out entertaining clients. "Let's get this straight," he'd tell the clients. "She's not Italian. She's Sicilian. She's the best. Say hello, Anna."

Then there was the freakish conversation on the night of September 10. Michael's sister Christine had come down from Canada, at Anna's urging, to stay with Matthew, so the couple could get away to Bermuda to combine a business trip with a celebration of their twentieth anniversary. Christine Egan had never been to the World Trade Center; she was excited about seeing Michael's office way up on the 104th floor.

It was warm for the weekend after Labor Day. Still felt like high summer. Michael grilled kebabs. Anna lit the pool and uncorked the Chardonnay. They all three took a last dip after supper. Playing, ducking each other under the waterfall, Michael was such a Peter Pan. He could always make Anna feel young and carefree. They sat at the table, sipping a little more wine against the incipient shivers of deepening evening. Michael propped his bare feet on the table and wrapped his arms around his big chest. It was exactly a year since he and Christine had mourned the death of their mother. They talked about the wonderful memorial they had held for her after her death on September 10, 2000. Then out of the blue Mike turned around to his sister and said this thing that Anna will never forget:

"Christine, if you were to go puff"—he snapped his fingers—"if you were to go puff, up in smoke, where do you want to be buried?"

Anna and Christine both laughed. "God, Michael, of all things to say," Anna chided gently. But that was Michael with his zany sense of humor. Christine, who was pretty deft with comebacks for her brother, said, "Well, it's going to be cheap—there won't be anything to be buried!"

They all laughed again. Then Michael said, "No, seriously, if something happened to you, where do you want to be buried?" Christine debated aloud between Canada, where she had spent most of her life, and Hull, England, where their parents were buried. "We do have one more spot there," she said. "Now it's going to be a fight between you and I who gets there first!"

The next morning Anna waved Michael off in his Jag, laughing with his sister on the way to the commuter bus. As they disappeared from sight and left Anna alone in the trophy house, her mind was free to think of the small things she needed to do that day.

KENNY THE FIREFIGHTER

Kenny Tietjen always had to be first at the fire. He was unbeatable, even by grown men. As a kid coming up in a proud blue-collar section of Middletown, he kept a scanner in his bedroom. The minute he heard a report of a fire, he'd streak out of the house and jump on his moped and race to the address. Whereas the firefighters, who boasted of belonging to the largest all-volunteer fire department in the world, would be delayed by the necessities of getting to the firehouse, climbing into their turnout gear, taking their places on the truck, and traveling to the scene. Little Kenny was always there first, waiting for them—a damn fourteen-year-old.

"That kid!" the grown men would growl.

They groused that Kenny's moped was blocking their fire truck. They threatened that if he didn't back off their fires, he would be kicked out of the

Fire Explorers, Post 911, where he became a charter member at the age of sixteen. They chased him away from the firehouse: "Get outta here, you're too young! Pain in the ass." But it was really the ego wound that hurt; Kenny always beat the firefighters to the fire.

"That kid!"

The funny thing was, Kenny had been scared of sirens as a very little boy. "Petrified," recalled his sister Laurie. "Firecrackers, any loud noises, but especially fire and police sirens terrified him." And as a child he was on the runty side, short and skinny and shy. He had to content himself with "torturing" his younger sister. For example, the "spit torture." Laurie giggled. "He would tackle me on the ground, sit on top of me, and—this is so disgusting, I can't believe I'm telling you this—he would spit into drool, so it was hanging just over my nose, and then he'd suck it back up."

"Don't tell Mom," he would order. Their mother, Janice Tietjen, was a devout Catholic, a pillar of St. Mary's Church.

The way Kenny Tietjen dealt with fear was to go toward the very thing that scared him. "He was just so gung ho," said Janice. "He had to be the first one in." As soon as he came of age, he became a volunteer in Engine Company Number 1 in Belford, a briny section of Middletown where the fish factory was and where firefighting was one of the noblest occupations. Kenny moved closer to the firehouse. His mother was shocked upon reading a newspaper account of her son's participation in his first fire. It was a propane tank that might have exploded, but who was the first one on the hose? Kenny.

"That kid!"

Within his first few years in the company, Kenny Tietjen bulked up and more than proved himself. At a large electrical fire in a lumberyard, one young firefighter opened a door and was knocked unconscious by a flash. Kenny ran in behind him and with another volunteer dragged the man out of the smoke-filled shack; saved his life. Kenny's helmet melted, but he suffered no injuries.

"When my brother wound up being a fireman and then a police officer, the whole family, we couldn't believe it," said Laurie. As a member of the Port Authority police force, Kenny wore a smile almost all the time. He loved his job, blossomed in it. "We called ourselves the Regulators," said Mike Ashton, who worked with Kenny in a sector car at the Holland Tunnel. "We were both active cops, we went out looking for it. We called it 'playing.' " The two spent every working night together, ate their meals together, shaved their heads together. Ashton saw more of Kenny than he saw of his own wife. They backed each other up.

One night Kenny pulled over a stolen car with three bad actors suspected of just having committed a murder. Normal procedure would be to hold off the suspects with a sidearm and wait for backup. But Kenny didn't like the way the men in the car were moving around. So he pulled out a shotgun and held them off until Ashton arrived. As the two young cops led their suspects away, one of the bad actors said to Kenny, "Man, this is your lucky day. We were ready to shoot your fuckin' head off, but with the shotgun, you coulda taken all three of us."

In the summer of 2001, Kenny was reassigned to the PATH trains, the deepest of New York's commuter subways. Mike Ashton was heartbroken about losing his partner. But Lieutenant Bill Keegan was delighted. Keegan was a cop's cop, and having supervised Kenny, he knew him to be the kind of cop who was always ready to back somebody up. "The guys at PATH looked forward to him coming down there, because that was a dangerous precinct," said Keegan. "The radios didn't work well. We'd had a couple of guys killed down there. You wanted guys who would be willing to help you. And we weren't getting good people. But Kenny couldn't wait to get down there."

On Monday night, September 10, Kenny called his mother from the job to ask if his grandmother, who suffered from Alzheimer's, had made it through another visit by the emergency squad. She had, barely. Janice Tietjen then said to her son, "Kenny, do you know how important God has been in our family?"

"Yes, Mom," said the dutiful son. He was only thirty-one and divorced.

"Kenny, if anything bad ever happened, would you know enough to call out to God?"

"Yes, Mom."

"Kenny, I love you very much, honey."

"I do too, Mom. Now will you leave me alone?"

PAT THE PREGNANT WIFE

At any given time, it seemed that half the women of Middletown were pregnant. This was a source of both promise and pain for Pat Wotton. God knows the Wottons had tried for more than one child. They had shopped around Middletown, looking at sixty-five houses before finding the perfect nest, a ranch in the rolling Oak Hill section. They bought it in 1996 with the idea of having a bunch of kids gamboling over the generous backyard. But

Pat's pregnancies came hard. Miscarriages, drugs; one baby dead in utero at six months. She relied on her strong Catholic faith, together with fertility treatments, and finally, on Christmas Eve 1998, when she was in her late thirties, Pat conceived twins. Then she lost one. But in early October 1999, the Wottons went home with a healthy baby, a girl, Dorothea Jean.

Pat had grown up feeling gawky and insecure, always searching for some way to make her mark. As a woman she was pretty enough, with waves of coppery hair and delicate Irish skin, but her inner image hadn't much changed. One could see it in the big, sad blue eyes that almost swallowed the rest of her pale face and seemed to be pleading. Pat had started as a secretary at NBC and at one point held the notable position of manager of sports research, which made her feel competent at least. But after she spent ten years of nomadic single life working in New York, the glamour of a dead-end career lost all luster. She was twenty-nine when she met her future husband for their first date, in a Bennigan's bar. Rod Wotton, like Pat, was itching to start a family.

With the birth of her first child, Pat was all too happy to "retire." Now she would make her mark as a devoted mother and homemaker. She disconnected completely from that unfulfilled career-girl self, even stopped reading the sports pages. She joined two garden clubs and let herself become more and more dependent on Rod. Truth be told, her husband wished he could be the one to stay home with the baby. But since he was making more money than Pat, she said triumphantly, "I won."

Not that there was anything lax about Rod's work ethic. His buddy Mark Ebersole, knowing him to be smart, ambitious, and a computer whiz, lured Rod to work with him in the technology group at Fiduciary Trust, a global investment-management company. Fiduciary stretched from the ninetieth to the ninety-seventh floor of the South Tower. Rod was awestruck by the lofty views.

When the company offered a four-day workweek as a perk to hold on to its new mothers, Rod took advantage of it—never mind that it might inhibit his rise among the sharp-elbowed competition, other men in their thirties looking to make their fortune on Wall Street before they hit fifty and burned out.

Pat loved to watch Rod give Dorothea sink baths. His big, strong hand could balance the baby in one palm, like a soap bubble. In the summer of 2001, Pat was pregnant again, and, miracle of miracles, she had made it through the eighth month. A cesarean was scheduled for September 19. Pat had never been so nearly completely happy.

Rod's company had recently been taken over by Franklin Templeton, a California-based global investment-management company. Ironically, Fiduciary's technology group had scheduled a meeting that very morning to go over its "disaster recovery plan." Fiduciary lived or died by the silicon brain that held all its data. Since Rod had been newly designated the manager of Web services, he would be a key member of the contingency team charged with backing up that data in the event of a critical incident.

Rod and Mark, the young bloods, had been working on a "hot backup solution" in which they could flip a switch and create an electronic carbon copy of the primary financial database. They had done mock recoveries and were confident the technology worked. That was a relief, because they all had been trained in the first rule of any disaster recovery: Get yourself and your staff out of harm's way.

On Tuesday morning, the eleventh, Rod went in early. Pat was groggy when her husband left for work, and so very pregnant. She held on to him tight. Many times she had begged him to give up the commuting and find a job in New Jersey. He said he couldn't make as much money in New Jersey.

BOB THE '93 TERRORISM SURVIVOR

On September 11, Bob Planer also went in on the early ferry from Middletown to Wall Street, the 6:20, feeling good, especially good. It wasn't because the market was up; in fact, the pants had been slipping on the economy for over a year now, since the dot-com bubble had burst. Planer's company, Keefe, Bruyette and Woods (KBW), a boutique investment firm specializing in research and mergers and acquisitions for small banks, had not been busy of late. Planer was a trader, and traders being fire walkers by personality, the most painful state for them was inertia, usually relieved by playing practical jokes on one another. But talking big picture, Planer would tell his wife, it didn't really matter a damn whether the market was off or the economy in a downturn. KBW had enjoyed its best-ever year in '98, when the employee-owned firm made a profit of $30 million on $155.5 million in revenue. And today, this very day, the deal was going down by which his company would be bought. By tomorrow, he assured his wife, everybody in it would be looking at more money, fatter stock options, and a shortened tenure until retirement.

Bob Planer was a handsome guy with pewter hair parted in the middle and eyes set deep, but he was no longer young. He had seen the last of his forties. Bob and his wife, Paula, had four children, one in college and three more to go. If not for the buyout of KBW, Planer might have faced growing old there. But in another day or so, the trader and his family would be free to pursue their dream of finding a sweet spot in western Ireland and coasting toward an early retirement.

Planer loved the ferry ride to Manhattan in late summer. Walking the long dock in the fresh morning air with gulls squealing and waves lapping at the hulls of sleeping pleasure boats, he felt content. The water commute from Atlantic Highlands was a glide past the long arm of Sandy Hook and eighteen miles due north into New York Harbor—just enough time to swallow a coffee and skim *The New York Times* and *The Wall Street Journal* before the ferry nudged the pilings at Pier Eleven, the Wall Street stop. The Fast Ferry was a comfortable lounge on a high-speed catamaran, where a fraternity of grown men sat with their cronies, trading can-you-top-this jokes and trusting that when they shared beers on the ferry ride home after five, they would all be a little bit richer.

The longest ride of the day, it seemed, was the six minutes in the express elevator up to the seventy-eighth-floor Sky Lobby, then out, a wait, and into the local, which would take him up to the eighty-ninth floor of the South Tower. Planer was anxious to get to the morning meeting. He was on the group equities desk, where all his accounts were institutional—JP Morgan, Allstate, Morgan Stanley Dean Witter—and they were not happy accounts at the end of summer 2001. But the morning meeting of his group was crowded. And cheerful.

"Great to see everybody again!" somebody said. They were all back from vacation and pumped. Fifty people all sitting around an enormous table, giving out ideas, trading industry gossip, speaking in the adrenaline-high staccato of Wall Street. Windows wrapped around two sides. Sun streaming in. High above the clouds, above the weather copters, above the grid of city streets and webs of suspension bridges, higher than just about everything. It was a magnificent feeling.

And it was such a spectacularly clear day, Planer was thinking he might go out and take a walk at lunchtime. Ordinarily he ate at the trading desk; it took too long to go all the way back down in those elevators. And he still had a slight phobic hangover about elevators.

During the 1993 bombing of the Trade Center, Planer had spent five harrowing hours trapped in the express elevator. He'd stepped on at the seventy-eighth-floor elevator bank and was on his way down to lunch. As floor number nine lit up, the occupants felt a jolt. The elevator stopped. There was

grumbling about an energy problem. Somebody joked, "Oh, they've probably just screwed things up again." No one dreamt it was a bomb. Suddenly
their iron cage lurched and the counterweights yanked it back up to somewhere between the sixteenth and seventeenth floors. Still, no one acted too
concerned. These giant people movers frequently acted up.

Then lights flickered on and off and smoke began pouring in. Black
smoke; they had to breathe through their sleeves. "When my boss goes running across the elevator and starts banging on the intercom, you knew it was
bad," recalls Planer. He was trapped with a dozen people, one a claustropho-
bic, another a spastic delivery biker; only two others remained calm enough
to help Planer coordinate their escape efforts. Every fifteen minutes they
would take their sleeves away from their noses and yell: "SEVENTEENTH
FLOOR—WE NEED HELP!"

The only response was a disembodied voice over the jammed intercom
that repeated: "We have heard your request, we will be with you in a moment." It was Bob Planer's first experience of total helplessness.

After more than four hours, they thought they heard voices. They faded.
Planer yelled louder. Time passed and the voices started up again. Then the
sound of pounding against steel. Planer was saying his prayers. "I had this
feeling I wasn't gonna die in an elevator, so I never was really that concerned even though smoke was pouring in," he said. "I figured God had a
better purpose for me than to die in an elevator." His faith was confirmed
when three Port Authority police officers broke through the floor and created
an opening.

"Slither through," called an officer with a gentle voice. One by one the
survivors dangled their legs into the dark tunnel of Sheetrock, some squealing like little animals trapped behind a wall. As each pair of limbs appeared,
the officer with the gentle voice cried, "We've got you!" and dragged the survivor through, feet first. Planer was one of the last.

The memory of total helplessness, hour after hour, was something
Planer made every effort to forget. He telescoped the terror of that day until
it shrank down to a bizarre little video of somebody else's life, at which he
was merely a spectator, amused and anesthetized. The only portent he had
of a recurrent attack came from his daughter. She was twelve when she saw
the TV-movie reenactment of the first World Trade Center attack. At the
end, they showed a guy taking off in a helicopter vowing, "We'll be back
again."

"Dad, do you really want to be in that building?"

He told her it was only a movie.

LIEUTENANT KEEGAN

Billy Keegan has one of the most dangerous jobs in America. He is a police officer with the Port Authority of New York and New Jersey. Keegan was raised in Jersey City, a gentle Irish-Catholic boy with a soft curl of a smile and a deceptively small build. But somewhere in his chromosomal soup he got an extra helping of leadership ability, which made him feared on the football field and respected on the force.

He grew up watching the Twin Towers being built from his high school playground across the river in Jersey City. He graduated from police academy in the Towers, worked in the Towers, knew just about every stairwell in the Towers. So it was a very personal injury when those towers were bombed in 1993. The blast blew open a crater five stories deep.

Keegan was off duty, but he got an urgent phone call from his partner's wife. "There's an explosion at the Trade Center and Tommy's there [her husband]. Can you find out if he's okay?"

That was all Billy Keegan needed. He sped through the Holland Tunnel and was on the scene in twenty minutes. He reported to a fire department commander. They threw a twenty-pound Scott Air-Pak on his back. Being a police officer, he had never actually been involved in a fire rescue. The equipment was unfamiliar to him. He knew the pack had all kinds of bells and whistles that would go off to warn when you were running out of air, and gauges to alert you if you were about to lose the pressure that keeps the mask tight against your face. *I hope I remember how to use this thing,* he was thinking as he rushed into the tower. People with blackened faces were being helped out by EMS professionals and their civilian coworkers. Keegan had a moment of doubt:

What are we going to do when we get in here? Where do I start?

Thick jets of smoke were shooting up through ventilation and elevator shafts, producing havoc and fright among thousands caught on the upper floors. But as Keegan began walking up the stairwells in the haze of rising smoke, he was amazed to see men still at their desks, working. When he asked them to leave, they refused. They were traders.

"No, no, this isn't a request," he said firmly. "You have to go."

"Listen, I got business to do here," one said. "There are other people you need to go get."

"This is an order. Go!"

Still, some wouldn't get up. "Hey, the market's still open, there's money to be made here."

Bizarre. By then, the rescuers were quite certain that this was not a matter of some generator that had blown up. The explosion was way too large. This was terrorism. The blast had rocked all the surrounding buildings; these men at their desks had felt it, but still they wouldn't get up. Keegan almost laughed out loud. He would have to use the "universal language." When handcuffs come off a belt and people hear the click, they know they are up against force.

"You're going out of here, one way or the other," Officer Keegan said.

After evacuating the occupants from Tower Five, he began moving underground to the South Tower. Climbing up floor by floor, feeling the weight of the Air-Pak and his gun belt, he smelled the dangerous odor of smoke. All at once, in the fourteenth-floor stairwell, a blackened face came out of the dark at him. The face emitted a whoop of joy. It was his partner, Tom McHale, the man he had gone in to look for. Having grown up together, the two men had always imagined themselves connected beyond the normal energy fields. And here in this mad exodus of people, they had found each other. They embraced and enjoyed a laugh.

"Where's the most pressing need?" Officer Keegan asked his partner.

"I'm going up," his partner said. The two Port Authority police officers climbed a couple more floors. They heard banging. It seemed to be coming from inside an elevator stuck between floors. They ran into two more police officers, who said they had heard voices. It was by then past 4 P.M. The occupants had already been trapped for almost four hours. But the police officers had no rescue tools.

Keegan and his partner searched the floor until they found a couple of axes. They began chopping through a thick drywall until they were stopped by the clank of steel. They were up against steel cross-members. Once they smashed through the studs, they hit another drywall. But now they could see that the elevator was above them, stuck between floors, so they would have to chop higher to create an escape hole. It was close to five when Billy Keegan was able to see the first feet dangling. "Slither through, we've got you!" he shouted. He and his partner began catching survivors as they slid down the hole and bringing them out to safety.

This was the first rescue of the kind that Officer Keegan had ever done. "I was just a patrol officer, more of a handcuff-the-bad-guys officer," he would later say. "It really felt great to get those people out. They were trapped and terrified, thinking they were waiting for the fire to get to them."

Among those Officer Keegan saved that day in 1993, in the express elevator stuck between floors sixteen and seventeen in the South Tower, was Bob Planer.

For Planer it was a day of ignominy he tried everything to forget. For Keegan it was a day of pride, one he liked to remember. Six people died. But everyone else was evacuated. But after the '93 bombing, the specter of terrorism at home became real to Billy Keegan. It was a tough existential leap to recognize that there were people living right across the river—in his hometown, the Muslim followers of Sheik Omar Abdel Rahman, whose mosque was in Journal Square, Jersey City, not more than a quarter mile from where Keegan went to high school—who hated America so much they would plan and accomplish this horrible thing.

Officer Keegan had followed with acute interest the news stories about Sheik Rahman. In June '93, Rahman's Jersey City apartment was raided after the arrest of eight of his followers, all Muslims of Arab extraction who followed Rahman's murderous interpretation of Islamic doctrine. The cop took note when the sheik was later convicted of a conspiracy to wage a "war of urban terrorism" against America. Its central element was to have been a cataclysmic day of terror in New York City. Powerful homemade bombs like the one that shook the WTC were to blow up the George Washington Bridge, the Lincoln and Holland Tunnels, and the United Nations Building. That was when Billy Keegan began to think about his men as holding among the most dangerous jobs in America.

"Three of those four sites are ours," he would remind his men on the Port Authority police force. "When you listen to intelligence reports, it's not a question of if, but when, they're going to hit us again. I think they'll always target for the highest media impact. We've already been victimized by a bombing at the World Trade Center in '93. Those buildings belong to us. We built them. We guard the airports, the seaports, the Port Authority Bus Terminal. Targets with international American name recognition. *We* are the favorite targets of terrorism."

There was one thing about which Officer Keegan felt secure: He and his circle of Port Authority officers who did rescue duty in '93 made it their business to learn more about the actual structure of the Twin Towers. The PA engineers didn't mind boasting that they had designed a very special building. "Those towers were built to withstand anything—a bomb, even a plane," they assured Keegan. "There is no way they could be brought down. No way."

THE RABBI OF RUMSON

Rumson is little but it's rich. The Rumson peninsula projects from the underside of Middletown, separated by the Navesink River and joined by the Oceanic Bridge. But despite living cheek by jowl with Middletowners, socially Rumsonites live in a different world. New Wall Street money mixes with old WASP Wall Street fortunes, allowing the lawns to stretch up to four or five acres per family. The trees tower and the hedges hide homes that look like hotels, with pillars at the iron gates and split-rail fences surrounding private riding paddocks and man-made ponds decorated with live ducks.

People who enter the magical land of Rumson, and possess it and settle in it, are given, as believers see it, a great heritage. Long-dead Dutch and English settlers left them legends from the 1600s, when they drove out the Indians, and more legends from the 1700s, when Washington's army drove the British army down the King's Road and off the coastal shelf of New Jersey. But like America itself in the new millennium, Middletown and its wealthy sister Rumson probably had celebrated no heroics since World War II and had no true heroes, except Bruce Springsteen, a cultural hero. Instead, these personal castles with their grassy moats of privacy were the stuff of contemporary legends—self-invented legends—promoted by the business media and the post-feminist Martha Stewart cult of domesticity.

There was no temple at all in Middletown although, unbeknownst to most of the population, there was a mosque. The only synagogue around was in Rumson. Congregation B'nai Israel was a small, conservative synagogue that served the five hundred or so Jewish families in the area.

The rabbi of Rumson was new to town. And still a curiosity. For a conservative rabbi and a scholar of the Torah, Harry Levin was a surprisingly youngish forty-eight, not yet all gray. He was a big bison of a man with a huge, meaty handshake; he projected his Brooklyn working-class roots, but then again, he had an intellectual's close-together eyes wrapped with rimless glasses. And he was very hip. Over his black turtleneck he usually wore a jean jacket and under his black pants a pair of cowboy boots—the real thing, from Wyoming, where the rabbi owns a refuge up in the mountains and maintains friendships among the militias, just in case. Jews always have to be ready to disperse.

On the Jewish Sabbath of Saturday, September 8, Rabbi Levin read from the Bible the same lesson heard by all Jews at Shabbat services around the world on that Saturday. The first words were important: *Kee tavo,* meaning "When you enter . . ."

When you enter the land the Lord your God has given you as a heritage and you possess it and settle in it . . .

The text instructed believers how to make offerings and give thanks for having come to such a lovely land, and possessing it. The rabbi read on in Deuteronomy:

> *Moses said . . . as soon as you cross the Jordan into the land the Lord your God is giving you, you shall set up large stones and coat them with all the words of the teachings.*

Meaning, as soon as one crosses into this blessed land, one must make sure to establish an ethical life. The text promised that if the faithful obeyed the Lord their God and observed all his commandments, they would be set high above all the other nations of the earth. Here, Rabbi Levin paused for emphasis—this was the suburban hook:

> *Blessed shall you be in the city, blessed shall you be in the country . . . blessed shall be your comings and blessed shall be your goings . . .*

But—the *but* was implied by the rabbi's pregnant pause—if they did not faithfully observe God's commandments and laws, this is what would happen:

> *Cursed you will be in the city, cursed will you be in the country . . . cursed in your comings and cursed in your goings.*

> *The skies above your head shall be copper and earth under you iron.*

> *The Lord will make the rain of your land dust, and sand shall drop on you from the sky until you are wiped out.*

> *The Lord will put you to rout before your enemies. You shall march out against them by a single road but flee by many roads. . . .*

> *You shall grope at noon as a blind man gropes in the dark.*

> *If you pay the bride price for a wife, another man shall enjoy her.*

If you build a house, you shall not live in it.

You shall be helpless.

These were the words, taken from scrolls and set down in Deuteronomy, read to or by Jews around the world on September 8, 2001. As Rabbi Levin later reflected, their relevance was glossed over.

Chapter Two

———

IMPACT

R on Breitweiser was at work on the ninety-fourth floor of the South Tower when he called her. It was 8:52 A.M. Kristen the sturdy surfer girl tucked the kitchen phone under her chin; she was halfway out the door with her hands full, one guiding their toddler daughter while the other tugged on the collar of their golden retriever. She answered brusquely: "Hello?"

"Sweets, I'm fine. I don't want you to worry."

How odd—her husband seldom called at this time of day. Thinking he was concerned about her upcoming biopsy, she said, "Good, fine. I'm feeling okay. Today." He told her he had sat down at his desk and all of a sudden his ear felt very warm. "I looked over and saw this huge fireball."

"What are you talking about?"

"Don't worry. It's not my building." He sounded so calm.

"Sweets, okay. I'm glad you're all right. Caroline and I are just rushing to—"

"You don't understand. There's people jumping out the windows." Now his voice broke.

"What are you talking about?!"

"Turn on the TV."

She tuned in to the *Today* show just in time to watch the top of his building explode—right where she knew he was. Her insides dissolved into jelly and she fell, screaming, onto her knees. Her daughter began wailing. Kristen has replayed that scene hundreds, thousands of times in her mind. A few weeks afterward she said, "I just pray he didn't see his own death." She shut her eyes and replaced the image. "I just know he immediately turned to ash and floated up to the sky."

Every night since the eleventh, once the struggle was over to settle down her two-year-old daughter, Kristen had found it impossible to sleep. The nights yawned like endless caverns of memory and longing. To comfort herself, Kristen went back to the nightly ritual of her married life. She took out her husband's toothbrush and slowly, lovingly, squeezed the toothpaste onto it. Then she would sit down on the toilet and wait for him to come home.

ANNA'S SELFISH MOMENT

Michael, you made it!"

Anna Egan exploded with joy upon hearing her husband's voice over the phone. After seeing the first tower hit, she had stood frozen before the TV, going crazy.

"No," he said. "We're stuck."

In the South Tower, Michael had apparently made one or two trips to shepherd his staff down from the 104th floor to the seventy-eighth-floor Sky Lobby, where scores of office workers were waiting for the express elevators. But that's as far as he got himself. He was approached by security guards. "You need to go back up, sir," they told him. "There's nothing to worry about." Relaying this to Anna over an office phone, his voice was calm and reassuring. Hers was hysterical.

"What do you mean, go back up! No, Michael! You can't go back up! We need you!"

"My selfish moment" is how Anna describes it now. "Then I got a grip on myself and asked about his sister. 'Where's Christine? Is she with you?' "

Michael didn't know; they had been separated. The last call Anna had from her husband, he had led people up a floor higher, to 105, hoping it would be better. It wasn't. They tried to take the elevator, but it was stuck. The heat was unbearable, he said. The sprinkler system wasn't working. The alarm system didn't go off. Windows had blown out. "Things don't look good," he told her. He was with fifteen people, lying on the floor. "We just can't breathe up here," he said. And then, while she had the phone to her ear and her eyes on the TV, the second plane showed up on her screen. Sailing toward the South Tower.

She sucked breath. *No, no! This was not possible!* She reached toward the TV and tried to grab him out. She heard Michael gasp, "Oh, God." He must have seen it, too, because his next words came in a rush: "I love you, darling. Kiss the boys—"

Then the line went dead.

KENNY THE KID

Kenny Tietjen, the gung ho Port Authority police officer and volunteer firefighter, was down in the bowels of the PATH subway station when he heard about the first plane. He raced up to the ground level at Thirty-third Street, but it was morning rush hour and traffic wasn't moving. He was grounded. Adrenaline pumping, stomping up and down in the street, he put through an urgent transmission to his New York sergeant, Marty Duane, asking if his unit could respond. The message came back: Affirmative.

Kenny had to be first on the scene. He commandeered a taxi. His new partner, Joe Shipansky, a rookie with only a year on the job, likes to say that Kenny politely placed the driver in the backseat. Then Kenny drove as if in an action movie, humping over sidewalks and swerving through alleyways with the cabbie in back screaming bloody murder and Shipansky muttering, "You're crazy, man." They got as far as they could before they had to stop to avoid the fleeing escapees. Just then an Emergency Services Unit vehicle drove by and they jumped on and rode down Church Street.

That kid!

All of twelve minutes after the first plane had hit, Officers Tietjen and Shipansky arrived at the disaster site. They ran into the North Tower, where Sergeant Duane had already set up a command post in the lobby. Kenny was stepping into his firefighter's role now, and his partner noticed that he wore a big smile on his face. Kenny asked for a Scott Air-Pak. He knew how to use it. His young partner did not.

The two Port Authority police officers carried burn victims out from the lower levels of the North Tower. Before they had finished that work, the second plane hit, gouging the South Tower from the seventy-eighth to the eighty-fourth floors. They raced toward the second tower, but there was only one Air-Pak. That silver cylinder is an extra set of lungs, so to speak, filled with oxygen that feeds into a firefighter's face mask. At best, the extra air lasts only fifteen to twenty minutes under the heavy exertion of climbing stairs in full turnout gear and inhaling a lot of smoke.

Kenny grabbed the one Air-Pak and smirked at the rookie. "Seniority rules," he said. Shipansky followed him into the concourse. But Kenny was revved up to run deeper into the burning tower. The last time Shipansky saw him, Kenny turned around and gave his partner a big thumbs-up and a smile mixed of guile and gallantry. Then he plunged deeper into the burning tower.

"Were you scared?" Kenny's sister would later ask.

"I can promise you," Shipansky told her, "your brother wasn't scared."

From the outside, Shipansky heard no creaking steel, no groaning studs, saw no leaning tower, no nothing. One minute the tower was up. The next minute it was not.

PAT THE WOEFUL WIFE

It was surreal on the ninety-seventh floor of the South Tower. The noise of the explosion in the North Tower felt like TNT bursting in one's ears, followed by streams of paper and smoke. *A ticker-tape parade? But paper doesn't fly up ninety-seven floors. What gives?*

Rod Wotton, husband of the very pregnant Pat Wotton, ran over to the windows and looked north toward the Empire State Building, mouth agape. "Holy shit," he said. His buddy Mark Ebersole nudged close. From the damage in the North Tower, the two men could see an exit path of something significant. "Let's get the fuck outta here," Mark said. They both ran back to their desks to grab their bags and Mark ducked into the men's room. "It's New York, think about it," he would explain later to incredulous people who didn't know about the lack of public rest rooms in the city. It was in the men's room that Mark heard the fateful announcement by the Port Authority, which oversaw the Trade Center and had a public address system installed in every office for emergencies: "We have a situation in the North Tower. Please do not evacuate the South Tower. The South Tower is secure."

It was about 9 A.M.

"I'm standing there for a split second, but it seemed like an eternity," Ebersole recalled. "The doors to the office open and one of our coworkers, Jason Jacobs, runs out, very agitated. He shouts, 'Ed said everybody back inside, we have to do disaster recovery.' " Rod Wotton's boss, Ed McNally, another Middletown area resident, was known to be a die-hard company man. In the '93 bombing of the World Trade Center, the man had escaped by walking down ninety-seven flights carrying his computer.

"I don't think so, Jason. I'm leaving," Ebersole said.

Jacobs got more agitated. "No! Ed said everybody back inside. We have to meet over at the Financial Center." The existing plan for any disaster was for the technology group to assemble in the Winter Garden of the nearby World Financial Center and await further instructions. The three senior executives invested with the authority to issue that order were all out of the office that day. It had fallen to Ed McNally to make the decision.

Ebersole told Jacobs, "I don't think you're going to get to the Financial Center from here." He and Rod had already seen the catastrophic damage. "Oh, yeah, right, I have to go tell Ed," Jacobs said.

When Jacobs opened the office door to reenter, Ebersole saw Rod Wotton. He called to his friend to come out, but Rod was leaning in to look at something, maybe a computer screen, and he held up an index finger—*wait a moment*—then the door closed. The doors of the elevator opened. It was empty. Ebersole rode the elevator down, holding his breath. The doors had no sooner opened at street level than the terrible sound of TNT exploded in his ears again.

It was Pat Wotton in Middletown with a TV on who had to tell her husband that the noise was a big plane that had smashed into his building. Rod started asking lots of questions: Where did the plane hit? What floor? Pat handed the phone to her father, Brendan Greene, who was calmer. Rod went into a long recitation of all the things Pat's parents had done for them, for him, for their daughter, Dorothea, thanking them. He gave his father-in-law a solemn charge: "Take care of Pat for me." Then he asked to speak to his wife once more.

"I'm not going to make it out," he said. His voice was deathly calm. "Pray for me."

"What do you mean? We're going to have a baby next week," Pat wailed. "Who are you with? Can't you take the stairs?"

"There's no way out," he said. "No one here to help us. Please stop asking me so many questions."

BOB THE 2001 TERRORISM SURVIVOR

At 8:48 Bob Planer was back at his trading desk in the South Tower, fidgeting, waiting for the market to open. Suddenly he heard a roar, not a big explosion, just a muffled sort of roar. The president of the firm ran out of his office shouting, "What the hell is that!" Bob looked across at the windows. Papers were flying around like snow in a paperweight. Everyone in the room ran over to the north windows. The tower next door, ten floors above them, was belching fire.

They couldn't see what caused the fire. "It's a bomb," somebody said. "It's a plane," somebody else said. It sounded like a Superman movie. Bob climbed up on a ledge and looked below, but he could see no wreckage. He was thinking, *This doesn't make sense.* It was an instinct left over from the '93 bombing, when he had been trapped in an elevator shaking and bouncing for five hours. He had vowed then he would find a deeper purpose in life. That bombing had been a wake-up call. But like most of us, he had put it on snooze alarm.

Phones were jangling at every desk. Planer was like most of the traders: they rarely got up from their desks for fire drills. It was part of the boy code. Only wimps worried about fire drills. He couldn't just run. He needed a rationalization.

A boss shouted, "Hey, you guys, get back to your desks! Answer the damn phones. We gotta keep the business going!"

"The hell with that," Planer muttered, being the sort who hates to go in the same direction as everybody else. Having trained long ago as a paramedic with a first aid squad, he thought maybe he could help somebody out. He looked over at his group and said, "Hey, I'm going to run downstairs for a few minutes, anyone want to come with me?" No one budged. Paula, he thought, Paula, his wife, had a sixth sense. He punched in his home number on the console and in seconds he heard her soft voice. He reported calmly, "The other building just got hit by something, a bomb or something, turn on the TV."

"Bob, something's really wrong," Paula said. "Get out of your building now. Get out of that city."

Planer hemmed and hawed a little. Paula came back at him with her all-business voice.

"Bob, just leave everything there and *get out.* I have a bad feeling. I'm hanging up on you right now. *Just go!*"

That was enough to push him out.

As he left the trading floor, he passed the office of Michael McDonnell, KBW's young comptroller. McDonnell was the company's fire warden, and he took the job very seriously. He was on the phone trying to contact the fire department for instructions on which elevators or stairways to use to get the staff to safety. Planer kept on going, out to the local elevator on the eighty-ninth floor. Somebody shouted down the stairwell to the company's receptionist on eighty-eight, "C'mon Frannie, we gotta leave!" Frannie's voice sang back, "No, we're fine on this floor. It's the other building, not us."

When Planer stepped off the elevator on the promenade level and glimpsed the outside, it looked like a war zone. Cars on fire, mangled fire trucks, debris everywhere, but no people. It still didn't make sense.

Security told the escapees to go down to ground level. Bob heard a couple of *boom-booms*. Everyone started running, panicking. He ran in the opposite direction from the crowd, heading for the exit under the subway. He came up across the street from the South Tower, but there wasn't time even to turn around and look. The police were propelling everyone up the street. Bob ran a block up Broadway before he turned back and his eyes filled with horror. The South Tower was a mass of fire.

He groped the phones in a street phone bank. Tried to call his wife, his company. Phones were dead. Then, above, he saw a human figure with all four limbs splayed out, falling from the tower like a huge bird. He thought: *I can't stay around here watching this.* He ran toward the East River. Along the way he passed a man he knew who had a laptop over his shoulder. "Could you e-mail my wife I'm all right?" he asked. The man looked too frantic to take anything in. The late ferry was just pulling into Pier 11 at Wall Street, ready to disgorge another glut of Middletown commuters. Most cowered in shock. Before them was an island shrouded in what looked like an atomic cloud. Ash-covered commuters were piling back on the ferry, mute with fear.

"Pull down the life vests," somebody shouted as one ferry departed. Another commuter smashed through the slats holding extra vests and began handing them out. A cooler head finally said, "Hey, we're not sinking!"

Planer sat belowdecks, still as a stick. Another trader he knew began complaining because they wouldn't let him off the ferry: "Damn, and I had a big deal going down today." Bob felt sick. He went up to the observation deck to get air. It was ten minutes before ten. The ferry was just about to slip under the Verrazano-Narrows Bridge when he saw his building go down. The words slid out of his mouth:

"I just lost half my firm."

THE RABBI AND THE REVELATION

Rabbi Levin is always chasing after an understanding of the nature of revelation. He looked back at the Shabbat text he had read on the Saturday before, and it took his head off. It predicted everything. Exactly.

Cursed you will be in the city, cursed will you be in the country . . . cursed in your comings and cursed in your goings . . .

(The commuters in his flock, cursed in their comings and goings to and from New York.)

The skies above your head shall be copper and earth under you iron . . .

(What was he seeing on TV? Coppery flames of fuel in the sky, twisted iron of cars and fire trucks lying on the earth.)

The Lord will make the rain of your land dust, and sand shall drop on you from the sky until you are wiped out . . .

(Buildings raining down debris and thousands of people turned to dust, wiped out.)

The Lord will put you to rout before your enemies. You shall march out against them by a single road but flee by many roads . . .

(People fleeing on foot across bridges, on ferries, by many roads.)

You shall grope at noon as a blind man gropes in the dark . . .

(Darkness at noon, survivors groping.)

If you pay the bride price for a wife, another man shall enjoy her . . .

(How many men would leave widows?)

If you build a house, you shall not live in it . . .

(All those trophy houses.)

You shall be helpless.

Chastened, the rabbi went back over the second reading from the Shabbat, verse 43 in Deuteronomy:

A stranger in your midst shall rise above you higher and higher, while you sink lower and lower . . . The enemies of the Lord will let loose against you.

Rabbi Levin didn't need to wait for confirmation that the terrorists were Muslim jihadists. It disturbed him deeply to think that fanatics might have hijacked the Muslim faith as a mask for their own agenda. The rabbi had a long history of friendship with a Muslim imam and scholar, Dr. Mokhtar Maghraoui. In the early nineties they had worked together in upstate New York. A hate-radio jockey was spewing anti-Semitic remarks and the two religious leaders embraced him and educated him. Ultimately the general manager of the station, WRPI, turned over the hate-radio show to the religious leaders and it was renamed *The Rabbi and the Imam*. As Levin understood the complex interplay between the faiths, the Jews believe that revelation happened once—on Mount Sinai—and the explication, the hunting for those secrets, goes on forever. Essential Muslim teaching respects the revelations of Jews and Christians but asserts that Mohammed's revelation supersedes all others. "They perceive themselves as the ones God has sent to a society that is not keeping God's laws," said the rabbi. And the shocking thing was, in rereading the biblical text, he saw the prophecy was right there:

> *The Lord will bring a nation against you from afar, from the end of the earth, which will swoop down like the eagle . . .*

(What did those jetliners look like? Like silver eagles, swift and fearless. The terrorists even stole the image of our nationhood.)

> *. . . a nation whose language you do not understand, a ruthless nation that will show the old no regard and the young no mercy. . . . It shall shut you up in all your towns throughout your land . . .*

(What happened? The government shut everything down—roads, bridges, tunnels, subways into and out of Manhattan. All air traffic was grounded. Americans were shut up in their towns or kept out of their country for three days.)

> *. . . until every mighty towering wall in which you trust has come down.*

A truly chilling prophecy. Those towers were the tallest structures in New York City, among the tallest structures in the whole world. Many Middletowners set their inner clocks by the sun on the Twin Towers. Those giant reflectors were in their "backyard." People marked the start of their morning by the icy blue reflection of sunrise on the Towers' faces and confirmed the end of their day by looking over to see the sun bronze the Towers as it slid, floor by floor, into the river. Those Towers had become part of people's inner landscape. How could they be gone? Were they really gone? Maybe it was just a nightmare.

This was a mute mass murder. Those of us outside the buildings or the planes heard no screams. We saw no evident death. No bodies in the rubble. We didn't even see a falling tower. One moment the Towers were there, wounded, belching smoke and fire like the breath of great dinosaurs that could never be felled, and the next moment—to be precise, all of ten seconds—the first one was gone. Twenty minutes later, another shimmy of melting steel, and in a matter of seconds the North Tower, too, was gone. Vaporized.

Some Middletowners later beat themselves up for not remembering the exact color of the light on the Towers. "We just took them for granted," Bob Planer said. The profile of the Twin Towers to them *was* New York: strength, power, possibility, aspiration. The fact that people from a ruthless nation whose language Americans don't understand had the motive and the power to bring down the steel walls of those towers they had learned for twenty-eight years to trust as immutable—they say they will never get over it.

Chapter Three

WHAT IS MIDDLETOWN?

REFUGEES

While Ground Zero is in downtown New York, the emotional "ground zero" is in the suburbs. The largest group of victims in New York City was concentrated on the Upper East Side—forty-four people killed. But most of the families of those who died lived outside of Manhattan. Certain suburbs were randomly singled out by the death that showed no mercy.

The newspapers of New Jersey kept scrambling to compile the names and total numbers of those lost in Monmouth County. The uncertain figure was ultimately placed at 138. But glaringly, the notoriety of the largest casualty list in one township belonged to a place with a name that is quintessentially American: Middletown. Nearly fifty people never came home to Middletown and environs after September 11.

There is no middle in Middletown.

That's the first thing one discovers. That is, unless you count Route 35, the dizzying four-lane highway that splits the place down the middle and spawns countless copycat shopping centers. When farming and fishing were the lifeblood of the place, it was a scattering of quaint villages, until they were collected into the forty-one-square-mile township that today is the largest in both size and population in Monmouth County. Its old-timers have been outnumbered by what the real estate mavens call "relocatees"—mostly Irish and Italian families who deserted the big, brawling cities.

If the Middletown of today has any center, it is the train station. Around those tracks, spread out like a starfish, are the thirteen separate sections of

Middletown. Each section has its own name and most have their own jeal-ously guarded zip code and post office. Each one boasts its own elementary school. And with the exception of one, all have their own fire company, which allows Middletown to boast of the largest all-volunteer fire depart-ment in the world.

Among the lost Middletowners were young Port Authority police, like Kenny Tietjen, proud of being local and living in one of the four blue-collar enclaves that string along the coastline, known as the bay-shore area. In Belford and Leonardo, Port Monmouth and New Monmouth, you will find rough-bearded lobstermen and ferrymen and tradesmen of all types, men who work with their hands the same way their fathers and grandfathers did. The houses in these areas are mostly small, single-story former beach cot-tages that sit on tiny patches of land. The center of social life is the churches, where the women volunteer to help the sick and less fortunate, and the fire-houses, where young men like Kenny Tietjen learn the ropes from an older generation, and where the volunteers take their breaks from paying jobs in the trades to hang out with one another. Families like the Tietjens are defi-antly blue-collar. They aren't necessarily looking to "trade up" to one of the pricier sections of town.

A heavy contingent of those who never came home belonged to New World money: traders and brokers who worked in the Twin Towers for great financial institutions. Rarely did these men go to Harvard or Yale or even necessarily business school; they didn't have to. There was so much raw op-portunity on Wall Street in the bull market of the nineties, anyone had a chance to make money and rise fast. And so these men mostly came out of small Catholic colleges like Seton Hall and Villanova or state universities like Rutgers, and moved out to Middletown to raise their families along the 1950s model. The dream of these upwardly mobile Americans was to park the wife and children snug and safe in a virtually all-white suburb while the husband battled in the high-stakes, macho world of Wall Street. They might start off with a three-bedroom in the Fairview section, where the av-erage income in 2000 was $86,832, and trade up to one of the four high-income, high-status sections of Middletown: Oak Hill, Lincroft, Locust, or Navesink, where sale prices of homes range broadly from $90,000 to over $10 million.

Given its Indian name, you might guess that Navesink is the oldest sec-tion, and one of the richest. The sprawling estates along Navesink River Road sit astride plump lawns behind peanut stone pillars and slope down, on the river side, to sweet lagoons. On the other side of this rolling road are the remnants of vast horse farms. Some homes here date back hundreds of years, a few still inhabited by descendants of the early English settlers.

Celebrities began discovering Middletown about fifteen years ago. Bruce Springsteen, who grew up rough in Freehold, New Jersey, was the first, followed more recently by Jon Bon Jovi, who tore down an old house and built a turreted stone chateau for $11 million on Navesink River Road. TV personalities Geraldo Rivera and Connie Chung and her husband, Maury Povich, used to live here, but they sold their fantasy houses and moved on. CEOs and high-flying entrepreneurs top one another by building mansions with slate roofs and screening rooms and employing small armies of Latino landscape workers to keep their grass uniform and their gardens rotated by season. A mansion along Navesink River Road was recently bought by Derek Jeter, the star shortstop for the New York Yankees.

What passes for middle-class in Middletown would be considered upper-middle most anywhere else in America. Take a couple like Bob and Paula Planer. When Bob first went to work as a trader for Keefe, Bruyette and Woods, he was a laid-back guy content with a middle-class life in a middle-priced house in Middletown. But by 2000, middle-class in Middletown meant an average income of $98,000. As Planer's bonuses fattened along with the historic swell in the stock market, he and Paula moved out to the peninsula and entered what could be called "a Rumson state of mind."

Rumson is a sister community. It is located on a luscious green peninsula, the Rumson Neck, that juts out from the mainland of Middletown like a bejeweled finger. Three little jewels sit on this finger, Rumson being the wealthiest, but Fair Haven and Little Silver only marginally less so. The three jewels are surrounded on all but one side by two broad rivers—the Navesink and the Shrewsbury. Rumson has been a chosen refuge for Wall Street figures going back to the early twentieth century. Jacob Schiff, the legendary German-Jewish chairman of the investment firm of Kuhn, Loeb, purchased a 375-acre estate on both sides of Rumson Road in the early 1900s. Together with the sons of the powerful financier Jay Gould and the great-grandfather of former New Jersey governor Tom Kean, among other notables, these men founded, in 1910, the Rumson Country Club. In the twenties, the club was the scene of elegant summer polo matches. After hours, couples could enjoy raucous relaxation of the Prohibition laws. But after Schiff passed on, the Rumson Country Club was not hospitable to Jewish members.

Today Wall Streeters dominate life in the three little hamlets, and many are Jewish. "Rumson is very affluent, probably the top of affluence," said

Bob Planer. "Most people feel Rumson's pretty snooty, and I wouldn't argue with that." He gives a little chuckle of false modesty. "I'm part of the problem now, too. You don't even talk to your neighbors."

At some point, most Middletowners ceased to function as citizens and became strictly taxpayers. Reluctant taxpayers at that. They didn't think they needed community, and few of the newer residents showed much interest in community building. The commuters can click themselves out of their garages in the dark, drive or take the train or the ferry over to Manhattan, and click themselves back in after dark, without seeing a neighbor for months at a time. They were living the ultimate suburban dream: to buy or build one's own domain with enough land to create a moat of privacy and live with the illusion of total self-reliance. And safety.

That was before September 11, 2001. But what happens when tragedy hits? "It's like a bomb dropped right in the middle of our towns," said Rick Korn, a music producer from Rumson. "It devastated this place."

THE FORGOTTEN HISTORY

Most New Yorkers haven't a clue where "this place" is, and they might not find Middletown on a map. (Because it's a township, maps usually feature only the names of its different sections.) Middletown sits due south of the tip of Manhattan. But it is partially hidden by a long, narrow curve of barrier beach known as Sandy Hook. Let's say you were on board Henry Hudson's tall ship the *Half Moon,* back in 1609, and exploring the vast bay waters beyond the southern tip of New York. Your vessel would sail between the blunt shoulders of Brooklyn to the east and Staten Island to the west, through the Narrows and out into the Swash Channel, where the bay is exposed to the mighty Atlantic and its capricious winds would test your seaworthiness. Soon you would see a blur of headlands bulging out from the shoreline of New Jersey. Once you slipped inside the welcoming arm of Sandy Hook, you would be amazed to see bluffs rising up two hundred feet from the water, so close to the ocean they support spectacular views yet are sheltered by the curl of seashore. This would come to be called the Highlands, welcome mat for Middletown.

"A very good land to fall with and a pleasant land to see," was the journal entry of Hudson's shipmate Robert Juet on board the *Half Moon* in 1609. Your ship would round the Highlands and easily find the mouth of the broad

Navesink River, banked with rolling hills. Game and fish, clams and lobsters would be plentiful in such a place, and it was destined to attract farmers and fishermen. Much later, when some of New York's most successful business-men sought a nearby resort area where they could cool off and pleasure themselves in summer, Middletown and the Navesink River area became a luxurious second home to them.

Nearly four hundred years after Henry Hudson, the commuter ferries would make the same eighteen-mile voyage between Wall Street and the Highlands—in less than an hour—many times every day. But few of the re-locatees could be expected to know much about their forebears. Middle-town has always been a secretive place, perhaps a natural protective covering for a place of refuge. The oldest settlement in New Jersey, it lured Dutch and English in the 1600s and became a Tory stronghold. But once the British army was driven out, the place became a refuge for settlers de-scribed by one historian as "the wickedest people and the best people in the world."

Enlightenment came early to Middletown. The first white settlers, the Dutch, appeared as early as 1613. But once English refugees—mostly Bap-tists and Quakers being persecuted in New England and Long Island for their religious beliefs—migrated to these shores, they made a compact with the Indians to acquire their birthright to the land, fair and square. They forged a famous legal document, the Monmouth Patent. Once they persuaded the sachem of the Lenni Lenape Indians to mark his *X* on the document, the set-tlers took it to New York and there, in 1665, the British governor signed it and created the township of Middletown.

This remarkable document guaranteed the settlers freedom of worship, the right of assembly, and the right to elect their own town officials—an ex-traordinary eruption of independence within the confines of a provincial British stronghold. What was even more enlightened was the provision for settling one hundred families seeking religious freedom along the King's Highway, on one-acre lots. Thus was Middletown Village born as a housing development. The real center of Middletown, then, is a linear stretch along King's Highway that holds the oldest deeded land, the oldest Baptist church in the state, and a quilting of private family burial grounds.

Middletown has always been an outpost of raw individualism. It not only guaranteed freedom of worship to Baptist refugees but, equally, free-dom of piracy to Captain Kid's brigands. When a confessed pirate was found guilty in 1701, villagers sympathetic to freebooting locked the court offi-cials, including the governor, in jail and freed the prisoner. Young lads used

King's Highway for horse racing. Informed of the "waywardness" of this rural population, the Church of England sent small armies of missionaries. Despite the individualistic strain, older Middletowners had to make common cause—and live in real community—at least until the late 1950s, because for most of the nineteenth century Middletown was all farming and oystering. It was also fiercely homogeneous, or, to be blunt, totally WASP. The dominant Protestant church—Tower Hill Presbyterian, where General Washington once slept—enjoyed in the early 1960s a respectable membership of about 2,800. Today, it has dwindled to 1,600.

"Since the sixties, it has gone from being totally WASP to becoming a strong Roman Catholic area," says Reverend John Musgrove, pastor of Tower Hill Church. "It's the upward mobility of the Romans as their second and third generations continue to move down the coast from Staten Island or urban blight." Forty years ago, when the chairwoman of the Landmarks Commission, Mary Lou Strong, first settled here, the commute to New York was by train, through Hoboken, and it took two hours to get to Wall Street. The automobile changed all that.

As exits off the Garden State Parkway spliced the area into the circulatory system that pumps into the heart of New York, Middletown began to attract Italian and Irish families who were able to leave cramped quarters in Brooklyn, Queens, and Staten Island and find in Middletown affordable housing with room for large families. Even before the second public high school was finished in 1976, the township had become the largest in Monmouth County, and already, a quarter century ago, it was overwhelmed with growth. It had swelled from a sleepy agrarian area of fewer than 10,000 inhabitants in the 1950s to 67,000 by the end of the century.

Today, Middletown is a conglomerate of every suburban town in America. Along with the bedrock of blue-collar stock and old rich, butting up against newer Wall Street money and celebrities, is a newer contingent. AT&T Laboratories, which used to be fueled by the Protestant Midwest, began in the nineties to bring in people from all over the world. The corporation became the major employer in town. That set off another population explosion: Muslims from the Middle East and Indian and Asian professionals. These newly affluent settlers mostly congregated in Holmdel, next door to Middletown, where they built huge, showy American dream homes on a checkerboard of tiny lots. The Muslims have become such a large, if mostly unnoticed, presence that they have built an enlarged mosque.

Middletown Township has been built out to 85 to 90 percent. That explains why, even on small plots across from the train station, new homes sell for $400,000 to $500,000.

What you won't find here is many black people. Since farmhand work dried up, less than 2 percent of the population is black. The town has very few people who would be considered poor. The only local social service organization is called, tellingly, Middletown Helps Its Own, which means volunteers put together Thanksgiving and Christmas baskets for two hundred to three hundred families.

But it's not all affluent. And even the affluent are not content. In fact, Middletown is known for its contentiousness.

"There's a town-and-gown mentality," said Mary Lou Strong of the Landmarks Commission. Randall Gabrielan, the only living writer of the town's history, described Middletown as "a municipality lacking a single identity." Many, possibly most, of its residents identify first with their neighborhood and second—or not at all—with the municipality. Gabrielan predicted, "That kind of division, which has deep historical roots, is not going to be remedied or removed by the aftermath of any tragedy."

Beneath the beauty, then, Middletown, by September 11, had become a place too large, too divided, perhaps too upwardly mobile to behave with a sense of community. How many communities have seventeen public schools? And despite the usual stated intention of new relocatees—that they wanted to move to where their children would be guaranteed a good public school education—the aspirations they bring with them to this suburb express a different hierarchy of values.

The giant share of taxes goes to Middletown's schools—64.18 percent. Yet the state of public education in Middletown is, to be kind, sorry. School principals and superintendents come and go on a revolving-door basis. The PTA's are not very active. And over the years, when Middletown South High School has offered programs for parents to educate them on techniques for coping with their adolescents, the results have been dismal.

There is no civic life to speak of in Middletown, apart from occasional neighborhood meetings at which residents bang on about taxes, development, and congestion. Here again, Middletown is a microcosm of the outer suburbs of America in the new millennium. As Robert Putnam demonstrated in his enlightening book *Bowling Alone,* social connectedness of all kinds— from helping the neighbors to having people over for dinner—has been in decline for the last thirty years.

The strongest anchor in Middletown is the Catholic church. Many residents attend Mass regularly in historic churches that now have standing room only. Beyond the Catholics, there is probably more active church membership than in many communities. The only other obvious social interaction comes through children's sports activities and membership in the beach and country clubs. This is where bonds of friendship and networking are formed by families who work for newer, expanding financial institutions, like Cantor Fitzgerald.

THE CANTOR FITZGERALD FAMILY

Bob Feeney was one of the Pied Pipers who brought traders to the area from the Cantor Fitzgerald firm. "Towards the late eighties, the brokers found out about Middletown through word of mouth. Prices were reasonable. Taxes were reasonable. Close to the city. Close to the shore. It offered a lot."

As the Cantor firm expanded aggressively, it began hiring young girls right out of high school or community colleges as support people and clerks. But it was definitely a high-testosterone environment. Whoever yelled loudest in the trading room became the first buyer. Same thing on the sell side, everyone scrambling to "hit the button" first and register the trade. Profanity was the lingua franca. It was a very physical world. Anti-intellectual. Traders followed the boy code to a T. "You just had to be quick on your feet, aggressive, and have a lot of confidence—it was like a really high-speed game," said Feeney. "If you had three or four accounts and you did a million dollars' worth of business, you'd be paid from $250,000 to $300,000."

But under all the bluster, the men and women traders and brokers became unusually close—almost like police and firefighters, who often spend more time with their coworkers than with their spouses. "No matter how big the trading room grew," said Feeney, "you needed each other."

Once the financial markets became global, the business was twenty-four-hours-a-day with lots of pizza at the desk and a couple of nights on the town to entertain customers. It was exciting but hard-living. Most men left the Street before they hit fifty or burned out. So they were necessarily in a hurry to make their bundle. Bob Planer at KBW was one of the unusual ones who stayed on; he was coming up on the fifty mark. But Planer had a large family and an expensive stake in Rumson. He and his wife had a plan: two more years and he would have enough to leave the Street and do something to give back—to merit his survival of the '93 bombing.

Some of the women at Cantor were pulling down six-figure commissions in their twenties. But they were also in a position to meet and date the ambitious money managers who were on their way up at the Wall Street firms. And most of the women seemed only too happy to "retire" before they turned thirty, marry one of these brash men, and set their sails for a home on the shoreline of Jersey. "Then when they made the decision to have a family, the wives decided to stay home," said Feeney. "It became a tradition."

And it wasn't only Cantor families who harked back to a 1950s configuration. The minimum number of children per family seemed to be two, but a noticeable number of young families have three and four. Sociologists have shown that in periods of unusually high prosperity, Americans in the family-building stage tend to have larger-than-average families. In an outer suburb like Middletown in the booming 1990s, the future looked better and better every year. "There aren't many day-care centers for career mothers in Middletown," offered Norma Frushon, director of the Academy Preschool. "Our families don't want sitters, they want to be *with* their children." She granted that many families have "live-ins," but pointed out that "the live-in is there to take care of the mundane things of life. To allow the moms free time to spend with their children. I have never met a more loving group of parents." A certain degree of smugness seeped through such statements, which glossed over the fact that these moms had more time to be loving because the dads were making enough money that only one of them needed to work.

MIDDLETOWN POST–9/11

For a few weeks after the catastrophe across the river, Middletown drivers were more polite. Road rage was absent even as people spent their Saturdays foraging for spaces in one of the thirty-odd shopping centers. Shoppers in long checkout lines were more likely to give way to a mother balancing an infant on her hip. Attendance at the churches swelled, but within a month dropped to a little lower than before the national tragedy.

"The main issues for Middletown *before* 9/11 were taxes, development, and congestion," said historian Gabrielan. "The main issues for Middletown *after* 9/11 were taxes, development, and congestion."

Something else didn't change after September 11. Real estate prices in Middletown continued to spiral upward. Top realtors like Sherry Villano, who were perpetually low on stock, saw their listings dwindle to no more than a half dozen in any price category. Oblivious to the deep psychic wounds of this pleasant land, more people were looking to Middletown for refuge. It's far enough away from the City—as relocatees call New York—to have three golf courses, but close enough to watch the sunset reflect off the backs of the Twin Towers.

Or it was.

Chapter Four

FIRST RESPONDERS

For Middletowners, the terror at the World Trade Center on September 11 did not just happen on television. It happened in their front yard. It was personal.

To a seagull soaring over the ferry dock at the Highlands in the late morning of September 11, the scene might have looked like a summer excursion. Cloudless blue sky, sparkling ocean, bright green grass, packed ferries nudging into the pilings and hundreds of people spilling off—men in short sleeves, many of the women shoeless—all scanning the gathered crowd for the glimpse of a loved one. But on the ground, the scene was more like disembarkment at a port of foreign immigration.

A SECOND TRAUMA

A massive law enforcement presence was positioned at the two ferry docks within an hour of the second plane's attack. Fifty men and women in uniform were there to meet and process the survivors fleeing Lower Manhattan. Thousands of residents of Middletown and environs had been witness to the horror; they were walking to work, or in the midst of their semiconscious commute, or just sitting down at their desks and stirring their coffee, when their collision with history instantly turned them into refugees. Stunned and disoriented into passivity, they now filed off the boats, many covered in glass and ash, only to be run single file between yellow lines and dispatched to detectives to have their identities checked.

But, Officer, I was just sitting down at my desk. I mean, I left my wallet—but I'm an American!

If they had left or lost their wallets or purses in flight, somebody had to vouch for them. Then they were herded onto buses and shipped ten minutes to another ferry station, where men shrouded in white hazmat suits herded them into a big tent and hosed them down, head to toe, most with their clothes on, to decontaminate them.

It was the second, if necessary, trauma.

"We didn't know if there might be some escaping terrorists hidden among the victims, or if they were carrying any kind of chemical or biological contaminants, and we weren't taking any chances," said Bob Honecker, Monmouth County's senior assistant prosecutor. He was charged that day with authority over all law enforcement personnel—an outpouring of police, fire, emergency, medical, and mental health people who were the first responders. It was a huge leap for Honecker, who looks less like a tough prosecutor than a young dad with a dimpled chin who likes best spiraling a football to his sons. "When you think about emergency management, you think about what we used to be involved in: hurricanes, snowstorms, power outages, political demonstrations," he ruminated. "And now, suddenly, we're involved with weapons of mass destruction."

Honecker was bracing for something much more lethal than the asbestos they found mixed in the soot and debris covering the survivors. The FBI was warning the prosecutor's office to be prepared for a secondary attack. Reports about attacks on the Pentagon and an aborted attack on the White House had just come in. Once all the emergency management forces in the county were gathered at one command center, the terrorists might attack there to take out all those personnel. "That's what had just happened at the World Trade Center," said Honecker. "When the emergency personnel responded to the first plane's hit, they never really expected that second plane to hit. So when it did, you had all those emergency workers and police and firefighters entrapped at that location."

All sorts of other nightmare scenarios were flickering in Honecker's mind. Early projections from New York said to expect in the neighborhood of ten thousand victims. He had emergency trauma rooms mobilized in all five of the county's hospitals. A contingent of New York police was dispatched to Riverview Hospital in Middletown, ostensibly to take evidence from victims. Those officers spent the next twelve hours nervously walking around the hospital parking lot in circles, with nothing to do but yearn to be up at the site trying to rescue their own. By early afternoon Honecker was advised to set up a temporary morgue. One of the ferries was being stripped down to carry bodies out of the boiling ruins and across the bay to Sandy Hook. Fifty doctors and nurses were poised to do triage with the casualties.

And then no casualties came. Oh, a smattering of people with cuts and bruises. Burn victims were kept in New York. But nothing required urgent response by any of the dozens of ambulances lined up at the shore's edge. It was another bizarre aspect of the whole scene. As subsequent waves of survivors disembarked on the Jersey shore, the medical professionals became more and more dispirited; they faced a crisis of marginality. The fact gradually seeped in: one either walked out of the Twin Towers with barely a scratch, or one didn't come out at all.

None felt more superfluous than Charles Brown III and his emergency response team of behavioral health professionals. As Monmouth County's mental health administrator, Brown commands a team of sixty-five volunteers, all licensed clinicians, who are used to being called for drownings or natural disasters such as fires and hurricanes. Here they were observing literally thousands of emotionally traumatized people coming out of the jaws of hell, and they had nothing to offer.

"What people wanted to do was only one thing: connect with their families," said Brown. "There was tremendous relief for those who hit the shore and were able to hug a family member—beautiful moments." But a number of people were far from home, from other counties or even other states. Brown acknowledged, "The basic attitude toward us was: 'If you can help me get home, great. If you can't help me get home, then get out of my way.' "

Cell phones were the Holy Grail. Honecker's men handed them out, but their circuits were mostly overwhelmed by the volume of chaos. So Honecker provided a global communications van, police radios, wireless communications, whatever it took to connect people with someone who made them feel safe again.

Bob Honecker had to think fast. Calls were coming into the county prosecutor's office from other potential trouble spots. Fort Monmouth, the FBI's regional computer center, sat smack in the middle of town with a sleepily guarded entrance. It is one of only four regional sites in the United States through which all the FBI information filters. An engineer from Naval Weapons Station Earle was on the phone. Earle, too, occupies a huge portion of central Middletown, and sends out its bombs on a railroad track astride a long, skinny finger of land that reaches into the bay and is notched with berths for navy ships to load up the weapons. What could be done to guard the pier? Honecker knew the coast guard would respond from New York only on an as-needed basis. He also had to worry about some of the country's top defense contractors that were located right there, in Middletown: AT&T and Lucent. And God knew how many malls and schools in Middletown would make attractive venues for suicide bombers.

All at once, Bob Honecker began to see his town with the eyes of an infrared camera—as chock-full of potential terrorist targets.

RAPTUROUS SCENARIOS

Pastor Scott Harris's first thought was a thrilling one: *It's the beginning of the Rapture.*

As an evangelical Christian, Pastor Harris believed that just before the end of the world, Christ would return and collect the true believers—both living and dead—draw them up and out of this world and into heaven. If suddenly there were no pilots in those planes, maybe they were the first ones to be pulled up, "raptured," and oh, how he wanted to believe it. That would mean the second coming of Christ the Savior!

"The mind was not able to wrap itself around an evil so great," he realized later. "So it fills in the gaps with something more familiar, or at least less threatening." How many people told others they had seen a small plane, or a Piper Cub, or a stunt pilot, hit the tower by accident?

Harris is the pastor of Middletown Reform Church. "Reformed from what?" is the most common question he gets. "Reformed meaning from the corruptions of the Catholic Church in the Middle Ages," he said, describing his nearly two-hundred-year-old church on King's Highway as Calvinist in its theology. When Pastor Scott was informed of the raw brutality of the attacks, his usual implacability faltered. He was at a loss. He passed on the information to the headmaster of the church's preschool, Richard Frushon. The headmaster turned white as a ghost.

"This is your gig," the headmaster said finally. "I don't know what to do."

"All right, give me fifteen minutes to get my act together," said Pastor Harris. The next quarter of an hour may have been the longest in his life. "Here I am, a clergyperson for a religion that says, 'Love your enemies and pray for those who persecute you.' And so I found myself in a position where I had to make a choice. I could choose the dark hatred and die inside, or I could choose to do something positive and life-affirming. I made the choice to put my anger aside for right then, and just pray for strength. I would concentrate on these kids and their needs and their feelings."

Pastor Harris decided to keep the children incommunicado until a family member picked them up. "If need be, we'll make meals for them, or sleep them here on cots." He had until the next day to compose advice for his teachers on what to tell the returning children about death. Pastor Harris would make a point of picking up his own son early from elementary school that afternoon. "*I needed to hug* him."

At 11 A.M., the children of the Academy Preschool were enjoying circle time and singing a song about the color red when the headmaster called his wife, Norma, out of her kindergarten class. "You've got to be kidding," she gasped. But she knew from the way he was shaking that he was not joking. Norma Frushon began to cry. She had to compose herself. She thought about three of the children whose fathers worked for Cantor Fitzgerald. Two of them were only four years old.

Just then, the mother of one of the four-year-olds, Morgan, came to pick up her daughter. Mary Murphy had come early with homemade cupcakes. It was Morgan's day to celebrate her birthday at the school. Ordinarily, Mary Murphy bounced into the school, her pale blond hair bobbing out the back of a cap, one of those slender, shapely women who at thirty-five, even though a few months pregnant, still look like teen prom queens. But this day Mary was moving as if in a trance. Totally numb, disbelieving, disembodied. She felt as if she were watching a movie; this couldn't possibly be *her* life.

MARY MURPHY'S MOVIE

Maybe it was just a replay of 1993, when she and her husband, Jimmy, had been working together at Cantor Fitzgerald on the 105th floor of the North Tower. When the bomb went off in '93, she panicked. Not Jimmy. He wrapped a scarf around Mary's nose to block the smoke and together they walked down 105 floors. It took them an hour and a half, but once outside they kept walking as if nothing had happened. They took a subway home and scraped off the black film, changed clothes, and rushed right out to a wedding. When they returned to work, they were given mugs with the message: *Welcome back to the World Trade Center.*

Mary joked, "I'd rather have a gas mask."

But that bombing was an aberration, she told herself; lightning never strikes in the same place twice. It never occurred to her to give up her great job in the Trade Center. She had started working for Cantor as a lowly sales clerk right out of college, and she had done very well. By the time she was twenty-five, Mary's compensation had soared from $17,000 to $100,000.

Life was pretty much a lark, living in New York and entertaining clients at fancy restaurants and Broadway shows.

The best part was working cheek by jowl with "my guys." That's what she called the men on her trading desk. She was one of the only females in mortgage-backed securities, one lissome blond beauty with a trickling laugh surrounded in a horseshoe by forty or fifty giant gonadal Irish extroverts, warriors all, each one shouting out his competitive bids and taking turns teasing Mary for comic relief. They all sat so close—practically joined at the hip by chairs that touched—it was impossible to have a private conversation. Everybody knew everything. After work Mary socialized with "my guys"; they entertained her; they protected her. On the weekends they golfed together, played tennis and racquetball together. The guys even took vacations together in Ireland to play on the famous course called Lahinch in County Clare. Only Mary didn't go to Ireland with them, because by then, she had been singled out by one Jimmy Murphy.

He had been spying on her for a while, he admitted, tipped off by his buddies on the mortgage-backed securities desk. Just look for a long, lanky platinum blonde with a body made for bikinis, he was told. He caught up with Mary at a pool bar in Spring Lake. She was surprisingly reserved, owing to her Midwestern Scandinavian stock. Before long, Jimmy Murphy brought her home to his big, boisterous Jersey Irish family. Eight brothers, all over six feet, and a very close-knit clan they were. "It was a bit overwhelming at first," Mary told her guys, "but nice. The Murphys just scooped me in." Once Mary reached the twilight of her twenties, she was ready to give up working and living in the city. Following the Pied Pipers of Cantor who had found Middletown an ideal place to raise a family, the couple made the move. Mary had happily settled into the much slower pace of Middletown and easy pregnancies.

By now they had two beautiful children, Morgan, four, and Jimmy, two, both towheaded little replicas of Mary but with the signature blue eyes and curly black lashes of the Murphy family. One night the contented family was out for dinner at Danny's Steak House and enjoying the exquisitely histrionic Italian opera music Danny played on Monday nights when Mary felt the telltale fluttering in her heart. The extra beat every few seconds. She knew what it meant. It meant she had enough blood flowing for two.

Jimmy couldn't wait to get on the phone and spread the news to his mother and his aunts. He hardly noticed Mary sitting on the kitchen floor, sobbing. "Hey, this is a *good* thing," Jimmy tried to tell Mary when he saw how upset she was. "Pull yourself together."

"When I found out, I was hysterical," she remembered. "He's the one who wanted more children. He's like a big kid himself, and he loved to take them outside and play. With my other two pregnancies, I was just thrilled. This time, I fell apart."

It *was* a good thing, of course, and she herself had been mystified by the dread that settled on her once the pregnancy was confirmed. Now here she was, five months away from delivery of their third child. And where was Jimmy? Again, terrorists had attacked the building where her husband worked. That was the preposterous news she was getting from her father over the cell phone as she was driving to Morgan's school on the morning of the eleventh. Mary froze. A movie of someone else's life began running on a split screen in her head.

The terrorists who wanted to take the world back to the Dark Ages were techno-savvy enough to pull off an act of visual violence that outdid Hollywood's finest. They knew how to hit Americans where we spend most of our downtime—in movie fantasies. They were creating images on the backdrop of a perfect cloudless sky that they knew would be recorded by the New York media and replayed ad infinitum until nothing could ever erase them from our collective cortex.

Mary felt cursed. "I couldn't understand why I was so upset about getting pregnant this time," she would muse later. "Now I think I know why. Somehow, I knew."

THE BLACK HOLE

Pastor Harris was hardly the only cleric to be overwhelmed by the demands of that awful day. Several Catholic parishes were hit so hard, the priests themselves were reeling from the battering of faith. As men trained to comfort the sick and dying under normal circumstances, several priests later acknowledged that they struggled with how to answer the hardest question: *Where is God when terrible things happen to innocent people?*

The parish of St. Mary's in the New Monmouth section of Middletown was a small, historic church with an overflow of membership—five thousand—by far the largest Catholic parish in the four counties of the Trenton diocese. When the bishop's office called Father John Dobrowsky to find out how many of "our people" were lost, the priest couldn't say for sure. Somewhere in the neighborhood of twenty-three or twenty-six souls. Unthinkable.

Father John's phone began ringing nonstop. Distraught families wanting information, pleading for pastoral visits. Father John, new to the parish and seen by some as young and arrogant, made himself scarce. "Our administration was rocked, I was busy talking to them about procedures," he said later. But he was not scarce to the media. Parishioners suddenly saw him with his flyaway hair and bulby nose all over TV and quoted in the newspapers. Father John Dobrowsky was apparently savoring his fifteen minutes of fame.

Pat Wotton, the woeful wife of Rod Wotton, who had asked her to pray for him, found some comfort in meeting with Reverend Monsignor Rebeck at St. Catherine's in Holmdel. Twelve parishioners were missing at that Catholic church. Pat, like so many wives and parents, was in absolute denial of death. Their loved ones were "missing," or "hiding," or "lying in some hospital without ID." Monsignor Rebeck, an avuncular priest with a long tenure in the Middletown area, quickly realized, "It isn't the words. It's presence. Being there. Whatever they want to talk about—how wonderful their loved one was, the last words with a spouse, just walking the walk with them."

Pat Wotton refused to pray for her husband's soul. She prayed for his return to her.

The younger, popular priest at Holy Cross Catholic Church in Rumson, Father Kevin Keelan, was stranded in Ohio. Planes were grounded. He hitched a ride as far as Indianapolis and found the last rental car in the airport, paid an exorbitant rate, and sped off. Once Father Kevin settled behind the wheel for the fourteen-hour drive back to Middletown, time collapsed. It became more than a trip. It was a passage through his own past traumas. He had been introduced to death as a child. Both his grandparents had expired in his family's living room. He had lost his father to a sudden heart attack while they were working together. The most recent loss was so grotesque, he was still struggling to recover from it: the previous summer his sister had ended her own life at the end of a rope. Father Kevin passed his long night of the soul trying to compose homilies rather than surrender to the darkness.

"It was like I was being pulled into a black hole," as he later recounted his thoughts. "That's the darkness. And you have to tell yourself to turn toward the light. There is nothing helpful in the darkness. Kelley, my sister, is in the light. So are the loved ones who were lost on 9/11. The pain is gone, they are with God. They are at peace. That's what I need to tell the families—turn toward the light."

Somewhere in the dark of Pennsylvania, Father Kevin was pulled over for speeding. The state trooper looked at his clerical ID.

"Okay, but take it easy, Father," the trooper said. "We've had enough death today."

It was four in the morning when he turned off at the Long Branch exit. Almost missed it, the fog was so thick. He smelled burning rubber. He pulled over to check the engine. Then it hit him. This wasn't fog. This wasn't an engine burning. This was the effluvia blowing over from the World Trade Center. Father Kevin realized he was just a baby, only thirty-nine, and he had never been exposed to anything of this sort. He said aloud:

"This must be what war smells like."

WAITING WIVES

I was so cold."

Paula Planer never heard whether her husband, Bob, had heeded her warning that he drop everything and get out of his office at KBW and out of the city. As she saw the second plane slice through her husband's tower, a silent *I told you so* flitted across her mind. But had he listened? She was on the phone with her sister, who was starting to panic. Being the oldest of three girls, Paula was looked upon as the rock. She didn't want her baby sister to hear what was about to come out of her throat. "I gotta go."

Paula ran outside and fell on her knees in the driveway and screamed up to the heavens, "Oh my God, what am I going to do?" She was shivering. So cold. She ran back inside and found the scotch and took a gulp, but still she was cold, as if her blood had turned to ice water. She ran for blankets and wrapped them around her. Then she called her mother. "You gotta get up here, I'm going to need your help." The woman was seventy-five, but right now, Paula felt like a needy child. Friends began to call: What did Paula know? Nothing. They were coming over.

What does a woman do while waiting to hear if her husband is dead or alive? Paula started cleaning house. Setting the cushions out on the porch. Pulling out the vacuum. Oh my God, what did she have in the house to serve people? Nothing. Today was shopping day. A girlfriend arrived, one who had sat with Paula through the daylong vigil of the '93 bombing.

"You said in '93 that you felt his spirit alive," her girlfriend reminded her. "What do you feel now?" Paula closed her eyes and searched the farther shores of consciousness.

"I just see Bob in a tunnel," she said. "I don't see life and I don't see death. He's absorbed in darkness. He might make it and he might not."

Bob Planer, at that time, was fleeing through a subway tunnel.

In a half hour her mother and father drove up, dressed in mismatched stripes and plaids. "He always listens to you," her mother said. That gave Paula some comfort. Another hour dragged by. Paula talked to each of their four children. Then she went out again into the driveway, and that was when the glad apparition appeared.

Bob Planer had survived. Sooty, shaken, barely able to speak. But he had survived. He would later give credit to Paula. "She has a sixth sense. She knew."

THE UMBILICAL

As the afternoon wore on, Charles Brown dismissed his behavioral health emergency team. Around three o'clock, Bob Honecker took off his chief law enforcer's hat and turned for the moment into a father. He collected his thirteen-year-old son, Zach, and Mariah, his eleven-year-old daughter, at their schools and drove them down to the beach. They could see the navy pier jutting out into the bay on one side and the graceful arm of Sandy Hook on the other, just like always. Behind a swell of dunes was a breathtaking view of Lower Manhattan. Now it was quite literally breathtaking.

A double funnel of gray smoke stretched across the bay. The funnels connected the tip of Manhattan with the beachfront just outside Middletown as clearly as a pair of outreaching arms. But even through the greasy sky, the children could see what Honecker wanted them to see. The great gap. The bleeding sky where the towers they had grown up with used to stand tall.

"Take a look," the father said to his children. "Now they're gone. This is something you will remember for the rest of your lives."

"What's going to happen next?" his son wanted to know. "Are we all right?"

"Don't worry," Bob Honecker told his children. "We're okay."

But he didn't really know if they were.

By late afternoon, the ferries were coming back empty.

Chapter Five
___

RISING TO THE OCCASION

THE REVEREND AND THE RABBI

With the sky falling and souls swirling in the fog, most of the traditional authorities people look to for direction and consolation in crisis were, themselves, at a loss to help members of the Middletown community. Dealing with mass trauma was not in their professional playbook. The exceptions were a few visionaries.

When the pastor of Tower Hill Presbyterian Church heard about the buildings coming down, his first thought was, Where is my son? Reverend John Musgrove's son worked in the Trade Center. Like most Middletowners, Musgrove could not get a call through to New York. So, like most Middletowners, he could get no answers. His next thought was for his parishioners, one third of whom work in Manhattan. He called the Presbyterian ministers in the immediate area and, in a flush of ecumenism, he called an Episcopal priest and also the rabbi of Rumson. He asked them all what they thought should be done. The group decided to hold an open service that evening. Reverend Musgrove turned on the carillon.

The bells of Tower Hill Presbyterian Church played all day long. People heard and they came out, hundreds of them. As Middletowners streamed into the sanctuary, Reverend Musgrove saw in their faces shock, deep fear, excruciating tension. So many of them didn't know about their loved ones.

He called upon another Presbyterian minister, Reverend John Monroe from Rumson, a tall, lean man with a long, pointed nose that twitched at the end when he held back his tears. To strike the theme of oneness, Monroe quoted from a New Testament passage, Romans 8: "Nothing can separate us from the love of God. Neither tribulation nor distress . . ." He extemporized, "Muslim, Jew, Christian, Hindu—we're all one in this experience. We have been reduced to the deepest level of our humanity." Monroe asked for moments of silence to pray for those who had been killed, "or lost, or those we haven't heard from." He invited people to lift up names.

Haunting. Names began floating up from every pew. Suddenly, lost souls were rising out of the dust and claiming presence in the sanctuary with the living. Each of the seven ministers then gave homilies, and each one finished with a consoling psalm. Then Rabbi Levin took his turn.

Levin is a charismatic, conservative rabbi, a scholar of the Torah with countercultural leanings. He saw in this night of terror a teachable moment—a golden opportunity to reach out and try to draw this assemblage of affluent strangers into something like real community. When this big bison of a man stepped forward, his voice was swollen with passion.

"Have any of you seen in your life a cataclysm of this magnitude?" he demanded. "This *is* the moment you have been prepared for. In all your religious schools. In all your church services. In all your moments of private meditation. *This is the moment for which you are alive.*"

He startled the flock, which was his intention. Now he softened a little and spoke to the raw faces in a more accessible Brooklynese:

"We could go home tonight and turn on the television again. What are you gonna see? You're gonna see that same image that you've already watched, what, a hundred times today? Two hundred times today? How many times can you see this? There are going to be voices speculating and other voices speculating *about* the speculation. Our strength must not be dissipated in speculations which only deepen what is irrational or beyond the grasp of reason. So I'm asking you *not* to go home and watch TV. You know what happened. Instead of squandering the precious and fragile resources of your emotional life, *marshal* your emotions."

Now his voice built to a commanding high:

"Knock on the door of your neighbor tonight, or tomorrow, and say, 'You've lived in this house for five years. I've lived in this house for ten. I've never said hello. Tonight we share something so deep, I had to say we need each other.' "

Then he stroked them a little. "Are you ready to learn a little Hebrew that we can all take together into the streets of our towns?" Murmurs of assent. He instructed them that *el* means "God"; *nah* means "please"; *refah* is not a request, it's a command, meaning "heal." He explained, "We Jews recognize the humility of our position in this world. Yet at the same time we know that we can stand and talk directly to God. We can say, 'God, please heal!' " Then the rabbi got the fearful people to stand. Six hundred people rose up in the Presbyterian church and chanted together:

El nah refah nah lah, El nah refah nah lah, El nah refah nah lah . . .

The chanting kept up. To some it felt like the roof of Tower Hill Church were coming off and the strange words coming off their tongues were rising up into the empty sky. The rabbi ended by calling the people to go into the streets: "That's the tone that should dominate our neighborhoods tonight. Go into the streets. Speak from your heart. Speak the language of faith. Use your energies to heal those hundreds of people down the block, the thousands of people across the river, and the millions of people whose hearts are broken tonight."

For the next few weeks, every house of worship in Middletown and on the Rumson peninsula was packed to the gills. Rabbi Levin and Reverend Monroe sensed that something powerful was happening. In ordinary times, a progressive rabbi from Brooklyn might not have discovered the kindred progressive spirit in a Southern Christian who presided over a staid Presbyterian church. But John Monroe had been educated at Princeton, and he and Harry Levin talked the same language. "The closeness we're feeling is the one light in all this," Monroe observed. Levin shared that view. Both spiritual leaders found that it was suddenly easy to hug their parishioners and talk about significant things, and not just with fellow worshipers but with people they would see on the street.

"Do you feel it? For once, we are a *community* with each other," Monroe said. "Let's don't lose this."

Levin was galvanized. Looked at as a spiritual wake-up call, the tragedy could be seen as a gift. He told Monroe, "Now it's up to us to figure out how to sustain the sense of community."

GET THEE TO A NUNNERY

In addition to the visionary clerics, the people who rose to the occasion in the early days were mostly amateurs, people who, not by training or experience, spontaneously and selflessly seemed to know what to do. They were there for desperate families like the Tietjens.

Kenny Tietjen's mother, Janice, felt it in her gut the minute she saw the flames on TV. There was no question that her boy would have moved heaven and earth out of the way to get to the Trade Center on that terrible morning. He wore a Port Authority police uniform, but he also had the instincts and know-how of a firefighter.

At least seventy firefighters who were not on duty or under anyone's orders that day rushed to the scene to throw themselves into the effort to save lives. In the chaos, few were under any superior's command. With old-fashioned radios that functioned poorly and no communication between police commanders and fire chiefs, most of the rogue firefighters were operating blind and deaf.

That's how the Tietjen family was feeling as they looked for some place of consolation in the middle of that long, dark night. They couldn't speak, couldn't eat or sleep. Janice Tietjen was one of the most tireless volunteers at St. Mary's. She might have been comforted by a visit from their priest, but Father John Dobrowsky was living up to a reputation for being brusque and insensitive. Some loyal members of the parish who had called that day asking for a visit from the priest were told no, and given no reason.

The Church of St. Mary looks more like it belongs in a small Italian village than on a traffic-choked avenue of Middletown, where it serves as one of the major centers of Catholic religious life in Monmouth County. With more than a hundred years of history, it is so oversubscribed that most Sundays there are standees—for all nine Masses. They may appear in Capri pants or jeans, but one can easily tell that the parishioners of St. Mary's are faithful from the elaborate choreography around the communion ceremony. Everyone knows which rows move first and last. Hundreds of people file down the center aisle, pausing for a split second to accept the wafer—no wine—and back up the side aisles with the exquisite precision of ants building a hill without evident supervision. The entire church finishes commemorating the Lord's Last Supper in a record fifteen minutes.

But where to go in the middle of the night? The Tietjen family remembered that the Adoration Chapel was kept open all the time. The whole family stumbled in at four in the morning, like lost souls. There wasn't a seat left. The hundred-seat chapel was full of people praying, moaning, rocking, some crying hysterically. Janice Tietjen knelt and prayed for her son, only thirty-one, not enough years even to give her a grandchild. After a while she was overcome by nausea.

Laurie Tietjen, Kenny's sister, was a slender, graceful, girlish woman in her late twenties with a B.A. in communications and an important corporate job. She left the chapel to look for some water for her mother. Wandering down a long hall, she found only row upon row of tiny dormitory rooms. The building had once been St. Mary's Convent and housed forty nuns. But these days, young novitiates were scarce in the Church. Then Laurie saw a light. She entered a comfortable lounge and was scooped into the arms of a small, tulip-shaped woman.

"C'mon in, dear. Have a hug and a cup of coffee."

These were the basic tools of Eileen Theall, the parish nurse, who had risen to the occasion to offer consolation for the community of St. Mary's. Within hours after the second attack, a pastoral assistant had called her to report that people were converging on the church and needed some guidance. Theall, being a retired acute-care nurse, was accustomed to responding to the unexpected. She dashed over and saw in the rows of empty nuns' bedrooms perfect nooks for spiritual counseling. She called fifteen or so people to help her—nurses, substance abuse counselors—and within an hour she had a crisis center set up right outside the Adoration Chapel.

Sister Sharon, the director of religious education, joined Nurse Eileen and added a more astringent style of spiritual guidance. A Franciscan nun, Sister Sharon drapes her impressive stature in full nun's habit and follows the strict rule of orders set down by Saint Francis. Together, the two women got the lounge filled with pillows and blankets and tables piled with food. The place became the busiest crisis center in Middletown. People wandered in at all hours, day and night.

"Absolutely bewildered, devastated, traumatized," recalls Nurse Eileen. "We were as scared as they were, because we didn't know any more than they did. But here we were, telling them everything's going to be fine." One good-looking young man came in crying. The coworker in the very next cubicle to him had been killed, and that man had five children. "I'm a no-good bastard," moaned the survivor. "Why did God leave me and take him? How do you answer that?"

All Nurse Eileen could say was, "God obviously saved you for something. You've got to listen and let God speak to you. He's not going to pop it down in front of you. It may not come to you for years down the road, but He's got something in mind for you."

The Tietjen family came back to the crisis center often. "Eileen Theall was an absolute angel," says Laurie Tietjen. "We were in terrible shape at first. One night my dad started talking to Sister Sharon about playing spoons. Next thing, my dad and Sister are singing together, 'I'll be down to get ya in a taxi, honey . . .' My dad needed so badly to laugh."

Nurse Eileen would stay all day at the center, slip home around 9 P.M. to grab a few hours of sleep, then be back up at 4 A.M. to wait at the chapel for the night wanderers. There was no time even to give the center a name. Her ministrations went on for several weeks. One night she walked into her house and her husband looked up blankly. "And you would be . . . ?"

REACHING OUT TO "NOT OURS"

Father Kevin, the young and popular priest at Holy Cross in Rumson, made it back to Middletown in time to be inundated by the needs of bereaved families. Some were "not ours," as the bishop would say, but Father Kevin eagerly accepted anyone who asked for a priest to do a memorial or a funeral.

"We had fourteen families to do, so Father Hughes and I divided them up and took seven each," said Father Kevin, still somewhat dazed a few weeks later. He began naming the deceased, stopped, and said, "How many is that, that's five, isn't it awful? I can't even remember them all."

The Pezzutis needed a double funeral. Kathy and Frank Pezzuti had lost their twenty-eight-year-old daughter, Kaleen, and their son-in-law, Todd Pelino, whose death had left their older daughter with two little children. The parents were being pulled down into the black hole with which Father Kevin was only too familiar, the black hole from which he had had to turn away, toward the light, after his sister's suicide. Frank Pezzuti had worked at the same company, Cantor Fitzgerald, and in the same tower where his child and his other child's husband were murdered. *Why them, not me?* The father had retired a few years before. So intimately did Frank Pezzuti know the Cantor offices, he told Father Kevin he kept picturing the fire sweeping through and the children's last moments. The priest kept urging the father, "Turn toward where they are; they are with God, they are at peace."

One woman referred to Father Kevin, Christine Spencer, had lost her thirty-five-year-old husband; she also had a new baby, not yet baptized. Her friends kept telling Christine how strong she was. She told the priest she was tired of hearing it. "Truth? I feel like shit."

She asked Father Kevin if he would conduct a funeral and baptism in the same service, so that the acknowledgment of death could be followed by a celebration of life. He told her it might be the first time in two thousand years of the Catholic Church, but he would be happy to do it.

Holy Cross in Rumson was standing room only for the first few weeks after the attacks. Father Kevin struggled to answer the big question: *Where was God?* The image offered by the young priest, who had lost his own father to an untimely heart attack, was that of God as the ultimate parent. "A parent knows children must be free to do certain things, like playing football, even though they risk getting hurt. The parent can stand on the sidelines and be there for comfort if anything happens, but can't prevent it. God allows us free will, and in the game of life, anything can happen. That doesn't mean God isn't there. It's just the way life works. The key is to believe that God is very much there."

BOB AND THE SIN OF SURVIVAL

Bob Planer was nominally a member of Holy Cross, and he liked Father Kevin, but he was acutely aware that he hadn't been personally close to a priest since his college days. That was a lapse he vowed to remedy.

He couldn't confess his sin of survival, but he couldn't sit at home, either, and take one more call saying, "So glad to hear you're all right." He called the Hartford office of Keefe, Bruyette and Woods and asked for his company's Christmas list. At seven in the morning of September 12, Bob Planer set out in his car to visit all the wives he could and tell what little he knew.

He gave no warning of his visits. When the first wife opened the door, Planer simply walked in and announced, "I'm Bob Planer from KBW."

"Oh no," the wife wailed. "Are you here to tell me he's dead?"

"No, no, that's the last thing I want to do!"

He felt so bad, he turned to leave. The woman's children begged him, "Oh no, don't leave." So he stayed and told her the story: "Here's the last we know. I've talked to one guy who got out. He was on the sixty-sixth floor. As far as I know, nobody who was on a floor above where the plane hit . . ." That was all he could tell them, except to give them hugs and say, "We're praying with you, there's still hope."

MUTINY IN THE MAKING

Chief John Pollinger commanded the largest police department in Monmouth County. He liked to be called Chief. Tall, trim, and loosely bolted, he had the John Wayne lope down pat. He believed in projecting authority through his persona, and part of that was costuming: hence his blue shirt was perfectly tailored, his silver hair center-parted, and his eyes usually hidden behind wraparound Ray-Bans.

Notwithstanding, the Chief had a mutiny on his hands during the chaos of those first few days after the eleventh.

On the first day he had taken a calculated risk, sending his entire EMS unit and his detective bureau to Ground Zero. With freelance foot soldiers from all the boroughs streaming to the site and no command structure set up, all Pollinger's twenty-five men could do was traffic and crowd control. Yet the next day they insisted upon going back. By the thirteenth, the Chief expected his officers to report for duty in Middletown. When he found out that his chief of detectives had taken a half dozen of his police officers up to Ground Zero on the thirteenth without his authorization, the Chief resolved to play it cool: "I wasn't going to let anyone go AWOL—I didn't want a martyr on my hands." The next day he had a little talk with the detective.

"You're leading men who aren't trained for rescue and who don't have the proper equipment," the Chief pointed out.

How much training do you need for a bucket brigade? the officer countered.

"You're not covered by insurance if you get hurt off duty," the Chief warned. "A career-ending injury doesn't help your family."

"Half the country is up there!" the cop shot back. "The John Pollinger of ten years ago would have gone."

That hurt. The Chief told his staff officer, "You are probably right. But not now. No matter what the noble purpose is, I still have a responsibility for sixty-seven thousand people here in Middletown."

The detective was adamant. He was going up on the fourteenth, and he was taking a dozen cops with him. He turned his back on the Chief and stormed out.

The National Guard had been mobilized by the twelfth. Farm boys from upstate New York who had never set foot in the Big Apple were all over downtown Manhattan, carrying rifles and wading through thick curds of concrete dust in their combat boots. Urban search-and-rescue teams were pouring in from all over the country. Civilian personnel from Port Authority and long-retired New York cops and firefighters were begging to join the bucket brigades. Pollinger needed his police at home more than ever to respond to calls from the county prosecutor's office for extra security around Fort Monmouth and Naval Weapons Station Earle, on the ferries, at the train stations, around electrical generating plants.

"What we try to avoid in our business is freelancers," said Assistant Prosecutor Honecker. "We didn't want police officers and firefighters going over there to a dangerous rescue operation, on their own, without any organized structure. Because that in and of itself leads to confusion and disorganization."

The same phenomenon had complicated the work of first responders at the Oklahoma City bombing. "You're caught between your personal need to rush to the site to help, as opposed to staying in your official role in any helping agency—just *being there,*" recalled Tim O'Connor, director of Catholic Charities and Community Mental Health Services in Oklahoma City. Oklahomans gave the phenomenon a name—"donor panic."

By Friday, the Middletown police chief had to draw the line. He sent a letter to all his staff officers, informing them that the NYPD had wired area police departments *not* to send any more volunteers. They were saturated. He gave the insubordinate bureau commander of detectives ten days to come to him and apologize. When he refused, the Chief had him transferred. That set off such a furor that statewide radio stations talked about the troubles in Middletown. The dispute ended with the Patrolmen's Benevolent Association suing the Chief. At first, Pollinger shrugged it off. This sort of stuff had gone on for decades. But his dissenting officers were solicited, over the Internet, to refuse to attend a memorial service the Chief had planned.

"It got that bad," the Chief admitted. Dryly. He wasn't a man who trusted emotion, his own or anyone else's. Pollinger was almost fifty. He tried to shrug it off. Anytime after the Fourth of July, 2002, he could take a walk into retirement and go fish for bass.

RISING FROM THE PILE

The media began calling it Ground Zero. But truth be told, most New Yorkers had been blasé about if not outright dismissive of the Twin Towers, a real estate gambit from the 1970s that had intruded on a skyline beloved for a congenial group of skyscrapers in Midtown. It took a gang of messianic Middle Easterners to recognize the Towers' value as the apotheosis of American capitalism. Only when the terrorists emptied the New York skyline of those towers did they become icons around the world, and New Yorkers felt the hole with the belated ache of a parent whose upstart child has run away.

Billy Keegan kicked himself for not being able to get to the Towers in time to perform rescues. He was now a lieutenant with the Port Authority Police Department (PAPD). Given his experience in doing rescues in the '93 bombing, there was no question in his mind how he would have functioned. Lieutenants are the leader–foot soldiers who make critical decisions at disaster scenes and offer the steadying influence of experience. "I would have grabbed five men—Kenny Tietjen first if I'd seen him—and said, 'Come with me, I know where there's an exit stairway and a hose connection.' "

But the morning of the eleventh, Keegan and his wife were focused on a tragedy closer to home. Their daughter. Eight years old and still not speaking. The Keegans had waited months for an assessment by the neurological experts, hoping some way could be found to stimulate the child to speak. The little family had just pulled into the hospital parking lot when Keegan's sister-in-law, who works in the New York Stock Exchange, reached his cell and told him a plane had just flown into the Trade Center. "But they think it's a small plane," she added.

"Oh my God, how stupid is that," Keegan said. The little family walked into the hospital. The cell again. Another plane. Keegan knew then: "This is war. We're being attacked." He knew there would be death and destruction and his men would be heavily involved. But the family had waited months for this assessment. His wife wanted it. "Okay, I'll do this and then I'll go over there," he said, adding, to reassure himself, "They're trying to knock down those buildings again, but they're using small planes, so it won't work." After the appointment, he drove his wife and daughter home, changed cars, sped through the Holland Tunnel, and faced an experience for which nothing in police training had prepared him.

Arriving at the Trade Center about 1 P.M., Keegan began debriefing other police officers and brass who had been in the buildings when they collapsed, trying to develop some intelligence about what was happening beneath the dissolved towers. "What's good and what's not good?" Their responses told a singular story: it was all bad.

No one knew exactly how many Port Authority Police Department officers were trapped in the voids or buried alive under gooey steel girders that would continue to burn for weeks. The PAPD force of 1,400 was much smaller than the New York police force, and in proportion its losses already looked to be staggering. Lieutenant Keegan was determined to stay as long as it took to find his lost brothers and sisters. That night, however, his new commander had different ideas.

"Aren't you supposed to be working the Staten Island bridges tonight?" he was asked by the inspector, who by virtue of mass deaths was suddenly the four-star chief of the Port Authority police.

"Yes," Keegan said. "But—"

"Billy, you gotta cover those bridges."

Keegan looked at the chief—*New York is burning and I'm going to be exiled to Staten Island?*—but he didn't complain.

"I know," the chief said, "but, Billy, I need you to go there. They're having near riots out in Jersey. People want to get home to Staten Island and the bridge is closed. *All* our bridges and tunnels are closed."

Keegan nodded. Then a wonderful thing happened to him.

"When you come back, Billy," the chief said, "you're going to run the command post at night."

BECAUSE THIS WAS a building collapse, the New York City Fire Department was in charge of the "incident" and insisted upon calling the shots. New York firefighters wanted to be sure nobody else found their victims. Not New York police, not Port Authority police. Belonging to the Port Authority Police Department of New York and New Jersey rated about as much recognition as belonging to a farm team. When a plane crashed at Kennedy or La Guardia or Newark airport, it was Port Authority police officers who were first to rush into the wreckage and pull out burn victims and dig for bodies. But by the time the media arrived, the hero footage would usually show the later-arriving New York police and firefighters.

"It was frustrating in the beginning to get the fire department to understand that we could be really helpful to them," said Keegan. "But they'd lost so many, their whole command structure was shot up, and their emotions took over. In their disorganization, they froze up and shut people out."

Lieutenant Keegan's voice is soft, but his eyes have the power to search your soul. He saw the misery in his men's eyes—men who had brothers and sons and partners down there in the burning ovens beneath seven stories of pulverized concrete. When he heard reports that the FDNY and NYPD were finding bodies, he couldn't sit still. Some of those bodies might be PAPD officers. "They belong to us."

Keegan knew when to use diplomacy and when to slip under the radar and do what one had to do. Around the time that Chief Pollinger's freelancing Middletown police were trying to penetrate the site and find something useful to do, Lieutenant Keegan was negotiating with the top brass of the fire department to welcome his men into their outposts on the perimeter of Ground Zero.

"My cops know this place like the back of their hands," he cajoled. "You don't have to worry what's behind a door—they know. When you can't get under the collapsed subway, my cops will know another tunnel to get you under and up to where you want to go." This strategy worked, to an extent.

When it didn't, Keegan moved his forces into the disaster site with the relentless determination of General Eisenhower in his final push into Germany. Keegan had somewhere between three hundred and four hundred volunteers, mostly active men and women police officers, but there were also retired cops and civilians, women with staff jobs at Port Authority who had worked with Kathy Mazza, a missing police captain. As a lieutenant, Keegan was expected to set up a leadership tree and assign tasks. He divided his people into teams and set up a rotation—each team would be allowed on the site for an hour at a time—and they would work all night until relieved by the day shift.

Thus, on the night of September 12, Billy Keegan found himself in the bombed-out ruins of those grand towers he had watched being built as a kid. Towers where the Port Authority Command Center had been housed. Towers that had swallowed the lives of some of his best friends and ablest officers—all 220 stories of the two towers incinerated and compacted into a seven-story mountain of fiery ruins.

Faced with the enormity of it, he sat down on a bent sword of steel by West and Vesey streets and stared at the skeletons of those mighty towers. He looked out at two-ton beams of steel twisted like someone had curled them into ribbons for a Christmas present. He knew this vast crematorium was pocked everywhere with invisible voids. No commanding officer wanted to wind up telling a dozen widows, "Well, jeez, I made a mistake and sent the men in when it wasn't structurally secure." Suddenly, Billy Keegan found himself unable to move, unable to think straight.

What do I do? How do I lead men whose brothers and fathers and best friends are buried in there? If this is Ground Zero, where is the ground? Nothing left is stable. Where do we start?

Suddenly he flashed back to an earlier experience of trauma. As he later described it: "I remembered sitting with our daughter on my knee in the specialist's office. She was a year old, but she wasn't developing normally. He gave her a test. She failed miserably. When the doctor said the words 'mentally retarded,' it felt like a physical blow. A knockout punch. I swear I could taste the blood in my throat. I started talking nonstop, no idea what I was saying, like a fighter who's out on his feet but still swinging."

On his first night at Ground Zero, Keegan felt the same sense of helplessness numbing his limbs, the same strange chemicals flooding his brain and paralyzing him. First he denied it—all those good officers couldn't be dead. Then came the blood-in-the-mouth anger. Then he tried to negotiate with God—the Lord certainly didn't expect Billy Keegan to make this right, did He?

Then he had an epiphany. He had moved through the same cascade of emotions when faced with his overwhelming helplessness to reverse a blow of fate against an innocent child. But after several weeks, he and his wife had pulled themselves together and said, "Okay, we gotta start small, let's put together a plan." They pursued a proper diagnosis and learned that their daughter had Rett syndrome.

On this occasion, it took a fraction of the time for Keegan to clear his head and make an assessment. He could barely make out the silhouettes of bobbing heads on the bucket brigades. Looking at those tiny human figures dwarfed by the mountains of destruction, he was thinking, *You don't remove that with buckets.* He stood up and addressed his team with a plan:

"Awright, here's what we're gonna do," he said. "We're gonna start right here. Start small. You can't just all run up on top of the mountain and work with your hands. We're gonna start removing things. So we can get some bulldozers in here. Get a board in here. Clear this one little area. Let's just start."

They were looking at 1.7 million tons of destruction.

"Okay, maybe that night we only moved a couple hundred pounds, but we got a command center set up," Keegan said later. "A tent. With a desk. So the next day we'd be ready to start tackling the mountains of debris."

Chapter Six

THE NOT KNOWING

The pain of each death is unique. The hole left in each heart breeds a lonely and singular grief. A few weeks after the attacks, Kristen the sturdy surfer girl was visited by two local police officers. They told her New York had notified them that her husband's remains had been found. Or rather, remain. Later, she learned it was his left hand. With his wedding ring. Unmelted. That blew wide open the story she had told herself about him turning to ash and floating painlessly up to the sky. She became consumed with the "What if's." She remembered the raven.

"The bird! When he called me on the eleventh, why didn't I remember that damn bird? It just didn't click in my brain until later. Someone, something, sent that raven to me as a symbol. I should have told him to get out!"

Kristen blamed herself. In the first wave of shock and horror, survivors almost always do. It would be months before Kristen could take in a rational argument: had she told her husband to get out, he probably would have said, "Forget it, I've got work to do." He was dedicated to his work.

Kristen alternated between despair and rage. A few weeks after the atrocity, she said, "Look at my little girl." Caroline, two and a half, sat with her pacifier in her mouth and her blanket, watching Barney on TV. Caroline wasn't speaking much yet; her speech therapist would arrive soon. "She's so happy," said Kristen, morose. "She's too young to know what happened. When I was a child, I would look toward the future and picture myself at thirty years old, and it all came true. That's all gone now. It's totally and utterly gone. All of our dreams, our future . . ."

Kristen wept, raking her fingers through her uncombed hair. "No. I can't turn into this miserable depressed person. I'm only thirty. And I'm a widow. I went to the library. Where is the book for a thirty-year-old woman with a two-and-a-half-year-old child whose husband was killed by terrorists and who watched it on TV? Where is the book for that?"

She looked at her child in silent futility.

PAT AND THE SHOCK OF BIRTH

When the pool boy rang Pat Wotton's bell the week after 9/11, he walked away saying, "She came to the door, man, I never saw such red eyes." Pat's big, sad, pleading Irish eyes had taken over more of her face but found no focus.

On the eighth day after her husband's murder, Pat, a woman whose entire identity was wrapped up in her commitment to being a devoted mother, was taken to Riverview Hospital for a cesarean birth. Still in shock. She had begged to have the date moved up, not wanting this child of misfortune to live inside her deep trauma any longer than necessary. The doctor had declined, saying he didn't want to risk a premature delivery.

Pat's spirit was not present for the birth. It was in the smoking pile across the river, searching for her husband.

Once the baby boy was extracted, his cries sounded to Pat as if he were in agony. The neonatologist said, "They all do that." But even after they cut the cord the baby remained blue. Before Pat could touch him, he was rushed to a neonatal unit in acute lung distress. She was now in danger of losing the last thing she had together with her husband. She named the newborn Rodney Patrick and hoped. Normally, being a strong Catholic, she would have prayed. But her faith in a just God had gone cold.

The infant's respiratory problems were so severe, he had to be moved to a more specialized hospital. Only after much finagling was Pat permitted to transfer with him to Jersey Shore Hospital. She asked one psychiatrist if she couldn't be in postpartum depression. "No," he told her. "You went right into depression." Once she healed from her cesarean, she was told, there was only one way she could remain near her baby: she would have to be admitted to the psychiatric unit. Marie Varley, director of the northern New Jersey offices of Church World Service, who tried to advocate for Pat, interpreted that suggestion as saying, "Be crazy and you can stay with your baby." Varley believed that had a profound effect on Pat. Rather than risk the stigma of a psychiatric record, Pat went home empty-handed.

ANNA AND MATTHEW

Anna Egan received a clipping from the *Sunday Mirror* in London:

> *British-born businessman, Michael Egan, vice-president of AON's New York offices in the World Trade Center, shepherded his staff to safety in the tragedy and is thought to have paid for his heroism with his life. . . . And in a tragic twist of fate his sister Christine, 55, who was sightseeing in the tower, was also believed to have died.*

Anna's private hell was knowing, for sure, that her husband *had* died. Died a hero. That was great for the newspapers back in England, but for her? For his sons? The recurrent nightmare for Anna was seeing her husband in terror, in agony, *knowing* the face of the horseman galloping to devour him, and his sister, and his staff.

Survivors of AON sent letters to Anna Egan thanking her for what Michael had done to save them. It wasn't much comfort to a wife whose thoughts ran to *Dammit, Egan, you should have just gotten yourself out.*

It didn't help that a week after her husband was murdered by terrorists, Anna was at Kennedy Airport to see her son off to college when they evacuated the terminal. Bomb scare. For seven hours she and Jon were kept in the parking lot. Anna looked at the sea of cars: the bomb could be in any of them. She looked at her beautiful elder son and thought, *No! He's too young to go. It's not fair! Not again!* Helpless. Traumatized for the second time in a week. Then she thought of Matthew, her mentally handicapped son, left home with neighbors she hardly knew. She panicked. Lost it. Lapsed out.

A few weeks later, Anna stopped in a local delicatessen after church, and again she lapsed out. Another of the Middletown widows happened to be in the store—Karen Cangialosi, an aerobics instructor whose husband, Stephen, had also been killed. Karen recognized that look. The lost look.

Karen approached Anna and started talking to her. Gratefully, blindly, Anna spilled her story to this total stranger: how she'd lost her husband and how her son was retarded and how she didn't know a soul in town. Karen gave Anna her phone number and urged her to call. Being well grounded in the community, Karen went out of her way to hook up Anna with a support group at St. Mary's Church. That support group would become a lifeline for both of them.

Over the next months Anna tried to force food down, but so violently did it come back up, she stopped trying. Tired, so tired. Once she saw Matthew off to school, she stayed mostly in bed, but there was no rest. She kept replaying the last conversations with her husband. Or moving about mechanically, like a zombie, in physical pain. Or fighting off panic attacks after she attended memorials in the city. Matthew, sweet, uncomprehending soul born with an extra chromosome clamping down his brain and labeled a Down's syndrome child, would come home from ninth grade at Middletown South High School and make her tea.

"You okay, Mom? Don't worry, Mom. I'm man, I take care of you."

Anna worked at maintaining a smiley face until she had tucked Matthew in at night. "I was so afraid to break down in front of him." But the boy sensed his mother's misery. Matthew would come to her bed at two in the morning and pull her covers up. "You okay, Mom?" he'd say. Every day he asked for his daddy. And every day Anna would tell him, "Daddy's up in heaven." They sent balloons up to heaven with messages for Daddy. Anna helped Matthew do drawings of what had happened. He drew a tower with people falling, a sun trying to come up, Michael in the sky with sunglasses. Anna wished she could open up the boy's mind and read it. She made a scrapbook filled with pictures of Michael and news clippings about the disaster, believing it was important to help the boy grasp and accept the reality.

"Hey, Matt! Look at this," she would say, holding up the scrapbook. "Where's Dad and Auntie Chris? Where's Daddy now?"

"Sick," said Matthew.

"No, he's not sick. Matt, Matt, where is Dad?"

"Sick."

"No. Remember, he's an angel. Where?"

"Heaven."

But some days Matthew was adamant. " 'Nuf heaven," he'd say. "I want Daddy home. Now."

THE HEROIC PHASE

By Friday of the first week, the count of missing people from Middletown was roughly thirty-five. From the Rumson Neck, with its three little hamlets of Fair Haven, Little Silver, and Rumson, the toll was thirteen—all men, all living similar lives with similar dreams. Their cars still sat in commuter parking lots being dusted with ash and specks of memo paper blown over from the vanished Trade Center. Given the numbers being guesstimated on TV—maybe five thousand missing or dead—the numbers missing from this one area in New Jersey were a mere jot on the calculator. But to the relocatees who had chosen Middletown to plant the roots of their American dreams, and to the closely knit families of the Neck whose offspring had returned to propagate there, the missing fathers and mothers and aspiring adult children left gaping holes in their landscape. And a sense of violation.

For a time following the terrorist attacks, people's usual behavior changed dramatically. Middletown's drivers and shoppers couldn't show enough kindness to strangers: "Oh, please, you go ahead of me in line." The traditional virtues of faith, hope, and charity, as demonstrated in teamwork, leadership, and love, were noticeable almost wherever one looked. This is what the bereavement counselors call "the heroic phase." It is the first phase following the shock of a shared trauma, when everyone is on his and her best behavior.

The heroic phase is usually short. It is followed by the disillusionment phase, when people's anger often shows in outbursts of irritability: "You've got eleven items! What the hell are you doing in this ten-item line?"

Many Middletowners clung stubbornly to the vision of themselves as somehow insulated from the horror of the world. Those who lived on the cliffs of the bay shore had grown so used to seeing the sinking sun turn the Towers sparkling bronze, they kept peering through the funnel of smoke hoping it was just a joke. Rich entertainers like Bon Jovi, and luxury-car dealers like Ray Caetano, whose castles commanded views of both the Navesink River and the Atlantic, hung out gigantic flags as if to challenge the suicide bombers to fight. The police chief of Fair Haven, Rick Towler, vowed at a memorial, "We'll give up hope when they clear the last bit of rubble. Then, it's over. Not before."

Streams of neighbors began cutting across lawns bearing trays of food to those whose loved ones were still "missing." They needed desperately to help, needed to bring flowers and offer to do the laundry and watch the children and walk the dogs. It was part of the whole dance around violent death, a way to propitiate their own dumb luck. The widows and widowers and paralyzed parents who sat inside their houses, stiffened with shock, tried to rouse themselves to appear properly grateful. Accepting "help" was not in the playbook for most of these suburbanites. *They* helped *others.* An important part of their identity was to know themselves as good givers, who joined the Junior League and helped plan charity events like the Monmouth Ball and even the annual foxhunt, where, for those who could afford a thousand-dollar contribution, couples would dress up in gowns and black tie and hire a car with friends to pull up in front of the country club like royalty. Suddenly, they were the recipients of the charitable response. They had to let themselves be helped whether they wanted it or not.

Then, the sanctification of the victims began.

In the aftermath of the shocking losses, *The New York Times* extolled the victims' most endearing idiosyncrasies. Coworkers spoke of them with the hyperbole of guilty survivors. Priests and rabbis praised them to the skies. The civilian workers had not gone into the office that day to become heroes, but whether they would have chosen it or not, they were now symbolic as well as real victims of this atrocity against America. And they were going to be sanctified.

Pictures of them were enshrined in makeshift public memorials, votive candles flickering beneath their beatified faces. Poems and songs were written for them. Wives and husbands laminated their likenesses and put them on cords around their necks. Later, both Kristen and Pat would wear their husbands' recovered wedding rings on chains where before they might have worn holy crosses.

Where was the room in all of this reverence for a smidgen of messy human reality? Were there no troubled marriages or unhappy families? Surely there were women in Middletown, as in any affluent suburb, who fought frantically against moments of solitude in their sprawling homes by telephoning friends and filling their days with book and garden clubs, tennis and lunch dates, committee work; women who shrank from the prospect of spending an intimate weekend alone with their husbands but who panicked at the possibility of divorce.

Right from the start, a number of the widows struggled with their anger at their husbands. Of course, it was something they had to keep to themselves. Anger at a dead man? Bizarre, irrational, unspeakably selfish. Nonetheless there was this free-floating anger at . . . at . . . what? At being abandoned.

Actually, it is quite natural to target the very loved one who has disappeared, even when it was a good marriage. Suddenly, one is bereft of a life partner in whom one has invested a great deal. To "be reft" is an old English phrase meaning to be robbed. These women were robbed not only of a husband but also of the father of their children, the breadwinner of their family, the one who did the driving on long road trips and made the investments and fixed the things that go bump in the night. These are what the trauma literature calls "secondary losses."

LISA AND TEDDY

For some widows there was another secondary loss, not so obvious from the outside. These were women at a particularly sensitive stage of life to lose a husband—at the threshold of midlife passages of their own.

Lisa Luckett was suddenly another Middletown area widow. But she is also a realist. Lisa has the All-American girl look, with the golden coloring of homegrown corn. Tall and husky with a big toothy grin, freckly skin, and tassels of natural blond hair, she is full of infectious energy. She meets you head-on with her take-charge voice, and you know right away that she is accustomed to controlling her environment. On the Rumson Neck, where she grew up, Lisa could walk to school and ride her bike in the safe streets. And like many girls who had grown up in that idyllic place, after her sojourn as a single working woman in New York, she brought her new husband back to the tight little bastion on the shore. She didn't have to persuade him to settle down in Fair Haven. It was filled with financial executives like him.

Big, tall Teddy. A big bear hug of a guy. Life of the party. Great sense of humor. Troubles rolled off his back. Lisa was the designated worrier. She took care of the bills and made sure she knew where all their important documents were. She worried constantly about Teddy's health: "My husband's working on Wall Street, thirty pounds overweight, he's a walking heart attack waiting to happen. *What if . . . ?*"

After eleven years together, Lisa and Teddy still slept together like two spoons. They had two beautiful children, Jenn, seven, and Billy, four, whose joint oil portrait hung over the fireplace. *So, fine, we're finished,* she had thought, itching to pick up her career again after the long emergency of motherhood. Lisa had sold advertising in the New York radio market for fifteen years.

Then poof! On her fortieth birthday Lisa learned she was pregnant again. Her third child would be born in the summer of 2001.

It was that September that Lisa turned forty-one, a birthday she found depressing given that she was now overweight, lactating, leaking, and juggling sibling jealousies. Four months after the birth of her third child, the novelty had given way to the throb of fatigue and flares of postpartum depression. Sleeping like two spoons wasn't all that romantic when the wife had to go to bed fully clothed in button-down-the-front pajamas and a nursing bra. She knew exactly what she was in for and how long it would last. Forty-one was too old to have her sleep interrupted four times a night by a newborn who screamed for her breast and still wake up fresh enough to feed her other children and drive them to school. It irked Lisa that her husband was not inconvenienced in the slightest by their midlife surprise.

"Sidelined." That was how she put it in the vehement confrontation with her husband the night before September 11. Teddy had come home depressed. Twenty eSpeed people had been laid off that day. Lisa was caught up in her own problems. "My life is hugely sidelined for at least two years," she told him, "but you, your life just keeps going forward."

This was not exactly true. Teddy Luckett was just as unsettled as his wife. After a successful fifteen-year run on Wall Street, he had moved into a volatile new business—eSpeed—recently launched by Cantor Fitzgerald, which was going through growing pains as it tried to wean accounts from bullish voice traders onto the cool medium of an electronic trading platform. Ordinarily, when one of the Lucketts was down, the other was up. The summer of 2001 had produced not only a newborn but waves of uncertainty that knocked both of them off their usual stride.

Only weeks before, Lisa had had a nightmare and woke Teddy in the middle of the night, crying hysterically. "I dreamt you were gone, you didn't love me anymore, you left me, you had someone else." She sounded truly frightened. "I'm so sorry if I've been a bitch." Teddy calmed her down until they both could laugh.

Perhaps that was why, on the morning of the eleventh, Lisa had not sent her husband off to work at the Trade Center with the usual bromide: "Have a safe trip to work." She wanted to make things right after having given him a rough night.

"I love you," she told him. "You're my soul mate."

A few hours later, Lisa's house in Fair Haven had filled with maybe forty or fifty people: shaken wives and neighbors, as well as soggy husbands who had run for their lives and come off the ferries only to be doused by decontamination hoses. They didn't look much like the macho men of Manhattan's money world whom Lisa was used to seeing ride the ferry with her husband. She asked them all, "Teddy—have you heard from Teddy?"

She didn't cry. She had to hold up. By afternoon, when the ferries were coming back empty, Lisa knew she would never see her husband again.

BOB AND THE "IF ONLY'S"

All sixty-seven people who perished out of the 125 Keefe, Bruyette and Woods New York employees came from Bob Planer's floor. As far as he knew at that point, he was the sole survivor from his company on the eighty-ninth floor. (Later, the CEO estimated that eight or ten others had survived.) Planer hated thinking about the numbers, just as he resisted counting the number of memorials and funerals he would attend in the coming months. Three or four every week, double and triple a day on weekends.

"I don't count them, I don't want to keep count," he grumbled when friends would ask. "It's a little obnoxious people going around saying, 'I've been to seventeen funerals.' "

Bob Planer was not himself. Normally, his emotional temperature seldom rose above neutral. But after September 11, it took very little to set him off. And one of the first things that set him off was the insensitivity of other employees on his floor. One salesman in particular, who worked within Planer's earshot and knew the same victims, begged off working late by telling the boss he had so many funerals to attend.

"I have a real *problem* with you," Planer sneered at the salesman one day.

"Yeah, why?"

"You're begging off overtime, and you haven't been to *one single service.*"

The salesman said he didn't deal well with death.

Planer restrained himself from saying something really rude, like "Well, get used to it, buddy, because I don't think you're immune." Instead, Planer sucked it up and seethed inside.

"What set our company apart, we really were a family," he said. "Granted, I didn't do a lot of socializing with my coworkers on weekends, but we really were friends. I lost my train of thought. . . . Oh yeah, so . . ."

The earliest and almost ubiquitous signs of post-traumatic stress are forgetfulness and difficulty concentrating. The mind is so absorbed with the "what if's" and "if only's" and the actual physical pain of loss, one is apt to lock the keys in the car, miss a birthday, forget the names of friends, and lose a train of thought so many times in a day, it feels like the brain is made of Swiss cheese.

THOSE KENNY LEFT BEHIND

On the Friday after September 11, Father John Dobrowsky held a mass for the twenty-six families at St. Mary's whose loved ones never came home. Laurie Tietjen made a point of asking the reporters huddled in the church hall before the Mass to be sure to give the families privacy. But after the service the families emerged from the church, most of them half blind with tears, into the prying eyes of telephoto lenses. Who had invited the press?

Laurie and her father hurried across the parking lot, but her mother stopped to share a hug with a friend. Laurie spotted a photographer rushing at her distraught mother for a close-up. She shot out of the car: "Please, leave my mom alone!" The photographer said he'd have to defer to the reporter, who ignored the request. Disgusted, Laurie drove her parents home and returned to confront the priest. She found Father John laid out on a lounge chair in the rectory. He did not stand up or shake Laurie's hand or offer so much as a word of comfort.

"We asked you to give us privacy," Laurie said.

The priest admitted that he was the one who had invited the press, but he had no apology. In fact, the reporter was waiting to interview him at that very moment.

"That's it!" Laurie told her parents. "I'm never going back to that church again."

Mike Ashton was wrestling with his own demons. He had bonded with Kenny Tietjen when the two had worked together on the Holland Tunnel and shaved their heads together and called themselves the Regulators. Ashton had never had such a good friend. In fact, Tietjen was one of the only men he had ever trusted enough to call a friend. Ashton was a street boy.

"A guy like me, I grew up in orphans' homes and foster homes in really tough neighborhoods," he said. "So I'm used to being around the dregs. I don't trust nobody. That's my nature. I don't talk to nobody. But Kenny and me, we could sit and talk about our personal life. Law enforcement work was exciting to us. When Kenny and me would be playing, doing foot chases or car chases or anything that puts your life in harm's way, you get an adrenaline rush. So much is going on, you don't have time to be scared."

On the afternoon of the eleventh, when Ashton walked into his command and overheard Lieutenant Keegan saying that Kenny Tietjen was missing, he started to cry. He couldn't believe it. The prospect of losing his friend scared the hell out of him. He began babbling, "Hey, maybe Kenny is buried somewhere with a bunch of other cops, just sitting there, maybe in a good air pocket, waiting for us to rescue him—" As soon as he could, the night after, Ashton maneuvered his way onto a bucket brigade at Ground Zero.

"The night I was digging, it was quiet," he said. "The fear was in everyone's eyes. You could see it."

There was good reason for fear. The earliest rescuers were surrounded by still-standing towers that had been part of the Trade Center complex. Through the fog of swirling concrete dust, those huge black hulking buildings were only dimly lit by spotlights or the miner's lights on the rescue workers' hard hats. They looked to Ashton like they were swaying, leaning, *breathing*. Every fifteen or thirty minutes, warning whistles would shriek and everyone had to scramble. "You didn't know if any of those buildings were going to come down on your head while you're not looking," said Ashton. "I was scared. That was legit fear."

But it was worse being off the pile. Especially being home in bed. Trying to sleep. Seeing the buildings coming down, and coming down again. Waking up and knowing that Kenny was underneath it all, maybe breathing his last. Ripping himself up and down for not being with his friend on that day of days.

"I feel like I should have been there. I put a guilt trip on myself for not being there. Would I have died with him?"

Ashton stopped and ran the tape through his head again.

"Would I have changed the course of things if I'd been there and stopped him? 'Cause there was only one tank of air. I probably would have argued with him about going in with just one tank. The rookie who was with him didn't go in as far as Kenny did, because Kenny had all the apparatus and he didn't. God knows what I would have said to him if he'd tried to pull that seniority stuff on me. You can pull that stuff on a young guy. But I probably would not have listened."

Ashton stopped and changed the tape in his head before he ran it again, and again.

"Knowing Kenny, he would have gone in anyway. And I would have went in with him. I wouldn't have let Kenny go in alone."

The hardest part of the aftermath for Mike Ashton was the night he had to visit the Tietjen family. Every missing officer was assigned a liaison by the Port Authority, and being such a close friend of Kenny's, Ashton was messenger to the Tietjen family. After two weeks of digging, he came off the pile late one night, filthy black, and he forced himself to drive straight back through the Holland Tunnel and down to Middletown to the home where Kenny had grown up. Janice and Kenneth, the mother and father, and Cindy, their twenty-five-year-old daughter, and Laurie, their married daughter, had been sitting around the parents' house night and day, literally waiting for the phone to ring.

Not knowing.

They were so happy to see Ashton, even at midnight. He sat down at the kitchen table and Janice Tietjen brought him a beer. He held up his hand; it was shaking from muscle fatigue. Janice said to him, "I'm going to hope until you tell me there's no hope left."

Ashton looked down. Laurie knew he didn't want to answer.

"Is there?" Janice's voice was a whisper now. "Any hope?"

Mike Ashton dragged his eyes upward and forced them to meet the eyes of Kenny's mother. He said, "There's no more hope."

Was knowing better than not knowing? Laurie told herself it was. She told herself that this would give the family some closure. Cindy said she was relieved, at least, not to be in limbo. The girls felt touched by the guts and love that Ashton had shown that night, to be able to tell them the truth.

Now, at least, the family could plan a funeral.

Oh no. There could be no funeral. They had no body. Should they wait until Kenny's body was found? What if he was never found? What if they found just some little part? What if they waited and held a funeral when they found just some little part, and then a month later they found another part?

They were back to not knowing.

THAT OCTOBER 4, Kenny Tietjen's memorial was about to begin. At the end of the block in a blue-collar enclave, two fire trucks met in the middle of the street, their ladders fully extended to form a steeple with a huge American flag hanging from it. A flotilla of motorcycle police began the procession, their engines at the gentlest purr. Then the honor guard marched with flags flying past a block-long, triple-deep line of Port Authority police, Middletown police, and their brothers and sisters from across the country, all in dress blues with their brass buttons sparkling in the sun of a beautiful Indian summer day. At least a thousand firefighters and police had turned out, including Chief John Pollinger. Many faces glistened with tears.

The bagpipe corps was led by two sinewy men lifting their white-spatted boots in unison. The doleful drum. The squealing pipes. What followed was a fire truck bearing, not a casket, but a bunting festooned with big bright sunflowers. That's all.

Now out of limousines spilled the fiancée, wiping her eyes. And the sister Laurie, drawn but stoic. And the mother Janice, her lips moving, this deeply religious woman, as she told herself over and over, *He's at peace, he lived his life fully, God allowed him that because his life was going to be so short, I just know my baby is in a better place.* Mike Ashton, and Kenny

Tietjen's many brothers among the volunteer firefighters of Middletown, filed in behind the family to fill a small modern Catholic church to bursting. They were deprived even of the honor of being pallbearers. The aisle of the church held, not a casket, but a pillar supporting a folded military flag.

An unidentified man approached Kenny's grandfather. He said he had read in the newspaper about the memorial service and he wanted to come and tell the family what their Kenny had done that day. He said a police officer dragged him out of the building. He didn't see his face because of the officer's mask, but he did see his badge. The name was Tietjen.

"I just came to tell you that your grandson saved my life."

And with that, the man turned and left. Kenny's ninety-one-year-old grandfather tried to catch up with him to learn more, but the survivor disappeared. The family did not even know his name. Kenny himself would never know the name of this man, or any of the others, for whom he gave his life.

Janice had asked that "God Bless America" be played. When the priest had given her a hard time, she went all the way to the bishop and told him she'd call the pope if she had to; the anthem was played. The eulogies stuttered out of Kenny's fellow officers and firemen, fighting to hold back their tears. When his sister Laurie spoke, however, she was beautifully poised. Her job, as vice president of corporate communications for the travel-and-residential-real-estate-services giant Cendant, lent her polish. But there was a more intimate reason:

"My brother used to tease me if I cried, and I kept thinking if I cried while I spoke at his memorial, he's going to come down and kick my butt!" In their anguished family, Laurie had taken upon herself the role of the Strong One. Once all the tributes were given, the bagpipers burst into the tiny church and wheezed down the aisles and their music shook the very saints in the stained-glass windows. Laurie cried, but joyfully:

"It was like the heavens opened and Kenny was right there with us."

CHIEF POLLINGER

Middletown Police Chief John Pollinger was among those who stood in the long blue line on that sad day. "Right after the Kenny Tietjen memorial service, I lost it. I broke down on the phone. I had to close the door to my office." The Chief started to well up as he was recounting this a day later. "I've always tried to separate my job from who I am. You have a persona, right?"

Looking at this tall, trim, crisply tailored poster boy for a police chief, one could only agree.

"Well, I realized that I was kidding myself. I'm not going to retire and go fish for bass. I am not going anywhere. This is me. I love this town. We have to pull together now." His heart was suddenly evident on his sleeve. "For me to complain or to say I have problems does a disservice to all the people who died on the eleventh. Every one of them who died, every one would trade places with anyone like me in a minute."

The Chief wiped away a tear, without shame.

"It's totally changed my perspective on life."

Chapter Seven

THE KNOWING

WHO WILL TAKE CARE OF THE MOTHERS?

Sherry and Kathy and Elaine are all attractive women in that stage of life when a little alchemy is required to keep blond hair from tipping into gray. Each of them is a mother of adored grown children. Each is further bonded by friendships made at Cantor Fitzgerald, where their husbands worked elbow to elbow shouting one another's names all day; on the weekends they would take their wives to the weddings and christenings of their Cantor colleagues. Sherry McHeffey and Kathy Pezzuti and Elaine Chevalier live only a fraction of a mile from one another in Middletown, Rumson, and Fair Haven, respectively. They all belong to the same clubs.

"But the club we're in now, nobody wants to get into," said Kathy Pezzuti.

Sherry and Kathy and Elaine have all been robbed of their children.

SHERRY'S ABANDONMENT

How death invades your life. You're just taking the lid off the coffee at your desk when the girl next to you says she heard a plane hit the World Trade Center. You are flip: How blind does a pilot have to be to hit the World Trade Center? You sip your coffee and take the first phone call of the day.

"Yes? Sherry McHeffey speaking." Sherry was at her secretarial desk at Monmouth College Career Services, a half hour from her home. The caller was her son's girlfriend. "Oh, no, Keith couldn't be in the World Trade Center, he was supposed to be . . ."

That instant before fear strikes. Fear like a bucket of ice emptied into the veins, starting from the top of the head. Your brain throws up a barrier of facts: *But Keith just started working at Cantor Fitzgerald; he followed his boss, Mike McCabe, and the deal was they were supposed to open a brand-new office in the suburbs, in fact, around the corner from Middletown, in Shrewsbury, and they wouldn't have to commute and Keith would be around home even more and it was going to be wonderful, so why would he be in New York?*

Then Sherry remembered. Her son had told her he was going in to the New York office to get acquainted until their suburban office opened. She had put it out of her mind; she didn't like heights.

Hours passed in less than the three frantic minutes it took to fly out to her car. She didn't dare turn on the radio for the half-hour drive from work back home to Fair Haven. She just kept repeating, *He's so smart, he'll get out, he's so athletic, he'll get out, he's so young, only thirty-one, HE HAS TO GET OUT.*

SHERRY'S SON KEITH MCHEFFEY was No. 39 of the bodies recovered. *White male, age thirty-one, intact.* He was taken to St. Vincent's Hospital. Sherry never saw him again. The medical examiner refused to allow her to see his autopsy report or picture. His father was the one to identify him. It was an unnerving experience, he reported; although the young man was not burned, his body was crushed. Sherry juggled that oxymoron around in her mind—*crushed, but intact*—and it left her even more unsettled. Thinking, *He must have been on the move, he was probably almost out. Was he frightened? Hopeful? Is he really not ever coming back?*

Sherry McHeffey is a lithe-bodied suburban beauty with silvery blond hair who looks eternally girlish in her big Irish cable-knit sweater and skinny pants. One would never guess that she was walking around with an open wound for nine months *before* the terrorist attack robbed her of her only son.

"My husband left me for another person nine months ago," she confessed. "I didn't expect it. It was a major abandonment thing. Apparently, abandonment is a primal fear that we all have. It hit me, big time. But Keith, my son, had stepped right in when my husband left. He told me, 'Don't worry, Mom, I'll take care of you. We'll be fine.' "

After his parents' separation, Keith became the new "Dad." He took an apartment near his mother's home and dropped in to see her every night. Keith's presence in his mother's life made her forget for a while the feeling of being a discard. Because she bore him when she was only twenty-two, mother and son had almost grown up together. Keith was her little buddy, grown big and handsome and fearless and very, very funny. His younger sisters, Amanda and Leigh, looked forward to his nightly visits as much as his mother did. He would tease them and blow holes in their cockamamie schemes: *You're not going to do that, and I'll tell you why.* Leigh said she looked to her brother as more of a father figure than her own father.

The three McHeffey women rushed through plans for a funeral a week later, before they had time to fall apart. They carried it off like seasoned actors. Eight hundred mourners passed in front of their faces, which were locked in polite smiles. At one point Leigh excused herself and gazed down upon the scene from a balcony. There were all Keith's young, hip friends and his still-young family, and Leigh was thinking: *This is a party, bizarre, it's my brother's funeral party!*

Amanda, soft, angelic-looking nineteen-year-old Manda, took to the sofa after the funeral and did not get up for the next three weeks. She was an emotional amputee.

Sherry returned to her job, in body only; she wasn't there. She was invited to a support group, but all the other women were widows. Their grieving was a world apart from hers. "I feel a different sense of loss than those women who lost their husbands," she said ruefully. "They are grieving terribly, too, but they will go on with their lives. They're young, they can make another marriage. But I'll never have another son. He's my only son."

THE PEZZUTIS' DOUBLE BLOW

Kathy Pezzuti lies a little about her height—she's less than five feet tall—but everyone sees her as larger than life because of her warmth and caring. She is a nurse and a natural mother. "We've been so lucky our whole lives and so blessed," she said. "We've done everything right." The rewards were her children: her beautiful twenty-eight-year-old daughter Kaleen, who worked for Cantor Fitzgerald, and Kaleen's boyfriend, who also worked for Cantor. Her brilliant older daughter, Megan, was married to another Cantor trader, Todd Pelino. The whole tribe of young people would come back from the city on weekends and pile in on Mom and Dad and together they would play golf and go to the beach and have a cookout.

So it was natural for Kathy Pezzuti to keep a vigil for Kaleen and her boyfriend, and for her son-in-law, Todd, all of whom were among the missing. "Kaleen was blown out by a fireball, or she's under a beam somewhere, just waiting to be rescued," Kathy told everyone the first week. "She's so strong, she's just waiting to be saved." Hadn't her daughter backpacked all over Europe? And she had those sturdy hockey player's legs. Every time the phone rang, Kathy jackknifed. Before she could compose herself to answer, she prayed: *Please do not find just* part *of her.*

But Kaleen Pezzuti was one of the early ones found. Her mother had to confront a deformity of the natural life cycle: parents are not supposed to die *after* their children. On top of that, she had to comfort her older daughter and her two grandchildren, who had lost their father and their godmother, Kaleen. The holes in her heart left Kathy, quite literally, breathless.

A grief counselor was called to come to the Pezzuti house. Kathy told him she was overwhelmed with answering all the condolence calls and cards. The counselor told her this was one time when she could get away with saying no and "I don't want to" and "I can't." She shouldn't try to please everyone; it would only wear her out. The counselor's next question took her by surprise:

"Who fills you up?"

Kathy sat there, silent. She had never thought of filling herself; she was a mother and nurse; she took care of others. She mentioned a woman friend and her older daughter, Megan. "I felt guilty that I didn't say 'Frank fills me up, my husband,' " but Frank had retreated into a mute rage.

"You can't expect Frank to fill you up, and you can't fill him up," the counselor said. "You both need to be filled up by someone else."

Kathy thought that was good advice. She determined to look for someone or something in the day that would fill her up.

ELAINE AND THE VISION

Elaine Chevalier is a small blond wisp of a woman, but in her faith she is strong as a pillar. A believer in God signs, she was waiting for a sign to tell her where, in the imponderable between earth and heaven, she might locate her son, Swede.

Like so many women found guilty by their husbands of growing into middle age, Elaine was faced with the upheaval of her marriage and relying on her son as her rock. Her only son, Swede. Her big, strapping, bursting-with-confidence son, Swede. He was only twenty-six, not yet ready to marry or give her grandchildren. But that was fine by Elaine, because her son was back living with her and his little sister at home. In a home where he was the only man of the house. He was overprotective of them.

Having graduated from Cornell University, Swede was breaking into the high-rolling world of Wall Street finance as an assistant equities salesman at Cantor Fitzgerald, but his heart and mind were not in money; they were in making things grow. Flowers. Shrubs. Trees. Swede had started his own landscaping business when he was only sixteen years old. He had started with a little dump truck spreading mulch for homeowners, and his personality and love of growing things had made him popular. His business grew to cultivating flowers and trees. He had kept it up during summers all through college and even after he started working full-time in the financial world. His successful business, Holly Hill Farms, was named for the former estate on which his family had bought an old brick Georgian. Situated on a hillock over Navesink River Road, from the upper floor of the Chevaliers' house one could see the broad river and, beyond it, the ocean. The estate was called Holly Hill.

Mornings, Elaine loved to stretch in front of her window and look out upon the holly trees that stood like stanchions all around the house. Swede and his mother had nursed them from ordinary trees to glossy giants. There was no need for the artificiality of Christmas lights at the Chevalier house. The hollies, under Swede's loving care, gave forth a splendor of red berries that lit up the winter. That September, Elaine took pride in looking out on the flats upon flats of brilliantly colored chrysanthemums that Swede was cultivating for the fall gardens of his clients. Many of those clients were the senior brokers he worked with at Cantor. He couldn't wait to get home to Middletown after a frenzied day on the equities desk and plunge his hands into soil.

Elaine felt close to her only son in a new way. He was a grown man now with a degree in business administration, and she was preparing him to join her in her business. Elaine might look like a small blond wisp of a woman, but she bought and sold and managed big commercial buildings. To have her strong, strapping son as a partner on her next buy, that was the dream of a lifetime.

On the morning of the eleventh, Elaine heard her son start the car and thought of running down to kiss him good-bye, but instead, she said a little prayer. She prayed to the angel Raphael, whose domain was healing and to whom she had often turned when suffering from migraines. But this morning, she made a specific request for Swede.

"Go with him."

———

SWEDE'S BODY WAS FOUND, intact, several days after the tower in which he worked disintegrated. Thus Elaine was one of the few family members who knew, and knew early. She knew the literal truth—that her son would no longer live with her in this world—but where was he in the imponderable between earth and heaven?

She waited for a sign.

The following Monday, six days after the disaster, she had a vision. In that apostrophe between sleep and awakening, she *saw* the angel Raphael. He was standing just behind Swede, looking upon her son with an incandescent tenderness. Swede stood, whole of body, beside a stream banked with white chrysanthemums, smiling at her. His yellow Lab was beside him—the dog he adored, and who had died only a few months before. In Elaine's vision, her son and his dog turned and followed the angel Raphael.

Fully awake, she cried with relief. She knew now. The angel had heard her prayer. He *had* gone with Swede that morning. Now that she reflected on it, she understood that Swede's dog had gone ahead, as dogs do. The angel had lifted Swede out of the tower and spared him suffering and led him and his Lab to "pass over" into the garden of all gardens.

Later that day, Elaine walked through the woods where Swede had found wild chrysanthemums. To encourage their root systems, he had clipped off the buds and left them to mulch. Elaine gasped. Another God sign. The buds, with no grounding, had opened and lay with their white faces fully open. It was as if Swede were speaking through the flowers he loved, to offer her a message of comfort.

Elaine sat down in the woods and prayed for guidance. When she was finished, she knew what she needed to do. This sadness, borne alone, would be inconsolable. And not just for her. What about Sherry and Kathy and all the other mothers and wives? Elaine would start a group for the mothers and widows of Middletown dedicated to recovery through spiritual guidance.

Chapter Eight

THE MONEY NIGHTMARE

oney in America is seen as the great green salve. Whatever ill or setback we suffer—from whiplash to divorce to business failure—our
anger seeks its first outlet in the demand for money: someone has to pay for
our misfortune. Similarly, the compassionate response to those whose misfortune is clearly undeserved is to comfort them with cash. In the case of
people whose loved ones were ripped out of their lives by a stupendous act
of barbarism, would money even begin to salve their wounds?

MIDDLETOWN HELPS ITS OWN?

he talk across America was of unity and community. These were vesti-
gial values in a large township like Middletown, which places a pre-
mium on privacy. There is only one townwide event in the year, Middletown
Day. This year it fell on a Saturday only two and a half weeks into the gray
of our post-attack world.

The townspeople were still walking wounded, the holes in their souls
made manifest each time they drove past another house with a family member still missing. The mayor of Middletown, Joan Smith, passed the word
that people should come out for Middletown Day. "Just come out for a few
hours and try smiling again," she urged. "See how it feels. Because you have
to start getting back into life again." By late morning families began to appear. The tragedy had not robbed them of their physical vigor.

In the magical township of Middletown, everyone was thirty-five—or so it seemed. (In fact, the average age of Middletowners lost on 9/11 was 37.5.) These were suntanned, sports-crazy, health-conscious Americans, the men working out to maintain the muscularity of their varsity days, the women fighting to preserve bikini-worthy bellies; far too young to have given a thought to mortality. Even those in their forties, fifties, possibly sixties appeared to be what one might call "youthful."

But there was a striking difference in the way Middletowners used space and time that morning. They moved in the bright September sunshine like sleepwalkers. Slowly, as if testing the ground beneath them. Wives with toddlers were noticeably shaken; these were women whose bargain with life was to forfeit careers to marry ambitious young men, some of whom had busted out of high school or halfway through college to get a foot in the door on Wall Street in its glory years. Many of these families had been moving up dizzyingly fast, confident enough to have a third child, or a fourth, because the sky was the limit on affluence and comfort. Fathers, too, came out for Middletown Day, the ones left, holding on to their restless little boys and clingy little girls. They watched local firefighters demonstrate mock rescue operations.

"It's only pretend," the parents had to reassure their children.

Everything had changed. Less than two weeks after America's homeland was attacked, Middletowners were struggling with the idea that their shores, less than twenty miles from Lower Manhattan, were now a potential battlefront. They needed a homeland army. It would be composed of their volunteer firefighters and their public health nurses and their urban search-and-rescue teams and now, perhaps, even their teenage sons, who could volunteer on EMS and hazmat teams, and their smart daughters, who would still bravely commute to big jobs in Manhattan. Even some grammar-school children now felt they had to be little men and women to take the place of a missing parent. Anybody and potentially everybody had been transformed into civilian combatants and thrust into a surrealistic war against shadowy fanatics armed with weapons beyond imagination and a suicidal hatred that seemed to cloak them with supernatural powers.

Middletown's people were canaries in the mine shaft of the New Normal.

The media kept reporting on the fabulous sums of money being thrown at the Red Cross, United Way, various funds and concerts, but it didn't look like any of it was coming in the direction of the widows and widowers of Middletown, New Jersey, anytime soon. On top of the loss of their life partners, the widows and widowers now felt their way of life mortally threatened. How to pay the mortgage? Get the car repaired? Cough up school tuition?

They looked for compassion from the companies for which their spouses or children had worked. Some firms were quite humane, appointing a personal liaison for each family to answer questions and maintain contact. Other companies were initially quite brutal about getting back to business.

KRISTEN, PAT, AND THE FIDUCIARY FIGHT

Kristen Breitweiser and Pat Wotton, and other families whose loved ones worked for Fiduciary Trust, were notified by Franklin Templeton, Fiduciary's new parent, that their health insurance would be terminated by the end of October. This caused near panic. (When some families protested, the cutoff date was later extended to the end of November, then April, and finally, to the end of 2002.) But in the short term, Pat, the Irish-eyed postpartum mother, was frantic: Who was going to pay for all the support services and emergency interventions that she would need to keep her new post–9/11 baby alive?

She would have to beg.

Shockingly, Middletown itself raised no money for its families. Other communities read about the victims and made efforts on behalf of towns like Middletown. A teenager in upstate New York raised $1,000 and sent a check to the police chief. Pat Wotton read about this act of generosity and called the Chief to ask if she could get some of it. It was humiliating.

Kristen the surfer girl's china cabinet was filled with three-ring binders bulging with all of the paperwork that described her new circumstances. The labels were "Crash File," "Charity File," "Govt Fund File," "Fiduciary File." She had demanded that Fiduciary Trust send out a representative to discuss her financial situation. She reminded them that the firm's president, William Yun, had asked her husband to manage his father's personal money. When the representative showed her the compensation package it planned to offer, rage seethed through her whole body.

According to Kristen, the company was promising little beyond the insurance benefit and workers' compensation that would have kicked in with any death. "There's little children across America selling lemonade and giving their pennies away for the families of 9/11, and here my husband worked for you," Kristen said to the company rep. "He died at his desk because he was there at eight in the morning. What you're doing in my opinion is really paltry. It's shameful."

Some of the widows refused to enter the general grousing about money from the companies or the charities. "It's a no-win conversation," Lisa Luckett said. "If you get less money than you think you deserve, you'll feel bad. If you get more, you'll feel guilty."

Families whose breadwinners had worked for the insurance giant AON were said to be pleased with the hands-on attention they were receiving from contact persons assigned to stay in touch with them. Anna Egan of the trophy house was not so enthusiastic. Although her husband, Michael, had been a senior executive at AON and a hero in attempting to save staff members on September 11, Anna was bogged down with immigration issues. She was a Canadian. "Not being a U.S. citizen, I face all kinds of tax problems in getting benefits," she told me. Her voice broke. "I can't think about that now. But I do need to protect myself and my boys." One son was just off to college; the other was a teenager with Down's syndrome whose medical and psychological needs were constant, and prevented her from returning to work. It was a shock to her to realize "I have to do it all on my own."

THE SPRINGSTEEN EFFECT

Rick Korn, a music and film producer and a bushy-browed, boyish-looking father of three, had planned a concert to benefit world hunger for the weekend after September 11. Obviously, it had to be canceled. Or did it? Bill Ayers, the originator of World Hunger Year, said why not redirect the concert to help the families of Monmouth County? Korn's neighbor Bruce Springsteen and Bruce's bass player, Garry Tallent, agreed: *People are going to need music, let's get up a charity, but we want to be sure the money goes to the families.* Rick called the owner of Danny's Steak House, the closest thing to a town center in neighboring Red Bank, and Danny Murphy went over to talk to the mayor of Red Bank, Ed McKenna, and those two hefty Irishmen decided to turn the concert into a real Jersey night—a benefit for the friends and neighbors they had lost.

An hour and a half after the two concerts were announced, they had sold out. They would easily gross a million dollars, but the infusion of energy and hope sent out into the hearts of Middletowners a month after the tragedy would be an even greater gift. This was going to be a real grassroots Jersey night. Invitations were extended personally to each of the families. They were promised a private audience with Springsteen.

Karen Cangialosi, an aerobics instructor and vivacious young mother, was a devoted Springsteen fan. But having lost her husband on September 11, Karen was still in shock. She was a painfully thin, pretty, tense woman with long waves of honey-colored hair, a generous mouth, and eyes as big and blue as morning glories, and her first reaction to the tragedy had been to run around trying to please everybody. She agreed to go to the concert, but only for the sake of her two young sons, about whom she worried obsessively. Jeffrey, ten years old and trying hard to be a little man, had dreams of himself in a Superman role. "I want to be something that can fly," he said, "so I can take Daddy off the top of the Towers."

Jeffrey always had tried to emulate his father, who had coached the boy's baseball team and taught kids how to play ice hockey on the neighborhood pond. As a pitcher, Jeffrey was unusually composed on the mound. His printing was letter-perfect. All the neighborhood mothers said that Jeffrey was the perfect son. He proved it again at the Mass for his father, Stephen Cangialosi. Jeffrey had stood up with his glasses on and his face scrubbed and his little tie straight and read what he had written:

A couple of days ago I realized a hero doesn't have to be a baseball player or a soccer player, actor, or movie star. A hero can be someone who is sitting right next to you. This person could be your hero because they love or did something nice for you or even just being a friend. . . . My hero is my dad, Stephen Jeffrey Cangialosi. . . . Before I went to sleep every night, he said I love you. He always spent lots of time with me, like checking my homework, playing catch and having snowball fights in the winter. I'll remember him when I play baseball, tennis, and swim. I also have lots of pictures of him to remember him. My dad is an American hero.

The priest said Jeffrey helped set the tone for people to accept what had happened. But his mother said, "I worry about him holding it in. His father did the same thing."

On the night of October 18, Rick Korn had to practically drag the widows out of their houses, some for the very first time, and down to the Count Basie Theater in Red Bank to meet with Springsteen. He was a reassuringly familiar face with whom they had grown up, a working-class Catholic Jersey boy. The gracious superstar hugged the widows and signed old LP albums for their kids. Meanwhile, musicians were pouring into the creaky old vaudeville theater from Nashville and Arkansas, legends from every musical era of the last half century: Sun Records stars Sonny Burgess and D. J. Fontana, who played backup for Elvis; Felix Cavaliere, who played with the Rascals in the sixties; the eighties punk rocker Joan Jett. Max Weinberg, Springsteen's drummer and a Middletown dad, was starstruck himself. Then the music started, and it was fabulous. The baby-faced Jon

Bon Jovi, who lives with his two kids in Middletown, knocked them out with "Wanted Dead or Alive." And finally the icon himself, the Boss, brought everybody a foot off the ground singing "Land of Hope and Dreams."

Young Jeffrey Cangialosi was up in the balcony when Karen was called onstage as representative of Middletown's widows to receive a check for $50,000 from Geraldo Rivera. Karen said the right words and made the crowd feel good. But as the freshly minted widow walked up a side aisle, she spotted another mother who had worked at the Trade Center, for the Port Authority. "Thank God you weren't there!" Karen exclaimed. The woman fell into Karen's arms, trembling, and the two women rocked each other, clinging and sobbing. No one else heard them. The crowd was chanting "Brooose, Brooose, Brooose," while Springsteen ripped his guitar and commanded to God and audience: *Stand* by me, stand *by* me, stand . . . by *meeeee.*"

That was little Jeffrey's job now. How would he and his mother fare over the next year?

The side aisles were jammed with standees—firefighters and rescue workers and Port Authority cops—and tears ran shamelessly down their faces as Springsteen sang the prescient lyrics of "My City of Ruins." At the chorus, everyone stretched up their arms and swayed and sang with the Boss, "Rise up, come on, rise up," reverent as a meeting of religious witnesses. By the time he called out all the stars for the finale, the audience was dancing and crooning. Backup singers from the local gospel choir embraced two youngsters who had lost their fathers and everybody joined in singing "Stand by Me."

The music touched the survivors, most of whom belong to a generation that bonded around music. But for some of the widows, the concert was bittersweet, stirring up memories of better times when they might have danced on the beach with their husbands while Springsteen played pickup with a bar band. *What am I doing here?* Lisa Luckett caught herself thinking. *Why am I dancing only weeks after my husband died?* She told herself it was okay, there is music that allows you to cry and music that allows you to feel joy. But she wasn't comfortable about feeling good.

THE POP HEALERS AND AMATEUR ACTIVISTS

A concert wasn't enough. In a heartfelt effort to circumvent the tedious paperwork and overhead that were holding back payments from the big-name charities, the kid-faced Korn got several of Rumson's movers and shakers to jump in and help create their own ad hoc social agency. The idea was to hand out fast cash to strapped families. Korn also realized that Middletown and Rumson families were struggling with issues that couldn't be solved by money. The friends and relatives helping them out would eventually have to go back to their lives. These families needed plumbers and accountants and insurance advisers and baby nurses.

Seven days after the attacks, a grassroots network called the Alliance of Neighbors of Monmouth County had been incorporated. Within a couple of days, seventy-two Middletowners had volunteered to offer their services, free, including a team of trial lawyers who could look over the settlements being offered to the victims' families. Korn approached the principal of Rumson–Fair Haven Regional High School, Pete Righey, to involve the schoolkids. The day after the concert they staged a Day of Remembrance—a street fair that pulled together every high school in the county to sell whatever it could make.

That day Springsteen cruised the booths along Front Street in Red Bank with his two little girls, like any other neighbors. When people approached the legendary musician to thank him for the concert the previous evening, he smiled, the jagged saw of his bottom teeth jutting over his top ones. The concert had touched him, too, he said. "All these musicians who came in from Nashville and around, it was great workin' with them." Asked if he felt moved, as a citizen of the Middletown area, to write music inspired by September 11, his expression became serious. "We've lost so many people, whatever music can do, we'll do."

Shortly thereafter, the brother of a resident killed at the Trade Center saw Springsteen driving by and shouted, "Hey, Bruce, we need you!" Springsteen knew exactly what the man was talking about. The fifty-two-year-old multimillionaire, who believes in the human spirit, set about writing the music that would mark his comeback as America's national bard in our time of need.

Korn invited a lunch group to Danny's Steak House in Red Bank to brainstorm about how to expand the mission of helping the families—beyond giving them aid from the $750,000 grossed by the concerts. Halfway through the meeting, the widow Lisa Luckett burst in, threw her keys on the table, and began grousing in her big, take-charge voice. "I find the people around here are so sad. My friends come over and speak to me in hushed tones. I go to the store and they speak to me in hushed tones. Everybody's being so careful not to bruise my sensitive feelings. But you know what? I feel much better than I thought I would. Really strong. Maybe I'll crash later on, but right now I feel pretty good, and I—"

A spasm of sobs locked up her throat in midsentence. She had glimpsed an image of the Twin Towers being used in the Alliance's press kits. Tears leaked down her face. Lisa was completely unaware of the disconnect between the verbal and emotional territories of her mind. Composed again, she carried on as if there had been no interruption.

"I can't cry. I'm not interested in joining some support group for wives where they sit around holding each other's hand and cry," she said. "I want to help others," she insisted. "What can I do for the Alliance?"

Danny Murphy, the owner of the restaurant, came over with an urgent warning of new terrorist threats. "I talked to the guys at Fort Monmouth. They say stay out of the terminals and off the ferries." Lisa scoffed, "I don't have that fear anymore, because the worst has already happened." She folded her arms over her still-puffy postpartum waist. "I'm nursing a five-month-old, so nature is protecting me. And my kids are small enough that I can slow down the train wreck for them."

But her own words came as fast as a train. In the conversation and body language of the new widows, there was a great hurry. They were pushing the moments. It is a sign of grief, wanting to rush through the day, but then night comes and it's worse.

Word of mouth spread about the Alliance of Neighbors of Monmouth County. Widows were told simply, "Call Rick. He's cutting checks." Korn would show up at the door, usually in shorts, having just come from coaching lacrosse or the Pop Warner League, and cut a check for $10,000 the very same day. "No questions, no forms—amazing," marveled Kristen Breitweiser when one phone call produced her check.

But the rush to play Good Samaritan glossed over many sensitivities that were certain to cause problems. To begin, these men hadn't a clue how to play social worker. Korn was nonplussed at his first home visit. The attractive young widow of Little Silver who opened the door said, "You know, my husband would kill me for accepting any kind of charity." Korn knew from local gossip that the woman was behind on her mortgage and in deep need financially. He tried pulling back the check with a joke: "Hey, look, if you don't want it, I'll keep it." That loosened things up.

Another of the originators of the Alliance was Jim Wassal, a former football coach, who related his "instant freakout" when he knocked on his first widow's door. "I was so afraid. I didn't know what to say." Wassal operated with a coach's MO: create a team, set goals, and call the shots. He saw the mission of the Alliance as providing for the education of the children who had lost a parent. The events of 9/11 had awakened a long-dormant trauma in his own earliest life. "My dad died when I was a year old," he said. "This year will be the fiftieth anniversary of my dad's passing. If this issue conjured up things about my dad, the effects can last in people for a long, long time. They are going to relive it through articles, books, personal memories. So the long-term mission of the Alliance is mental wellness."

One night Korn and Wassal appeared at the door of Pat Wotton. She looked upon these two strange men with fear. They explained that they were from the Alliance of Neighbors. "Pat was the most outwardly devastated widow of all those I'd visited," Korn recalled. "Her little daughter was running around, acting out. The baby was still in the hospital. Pat was in shock. I realized that people were affected differently depending on their stage of life. Here was a woman not only dealing with the loss of her husband, but the life of her newborn was in jeopardy. I left her house incredibly sad and hoping she could pull it out."

THE SHATTERED CANTOR FAMILY

Area Residents Are Gone
Not Forgotten
—*The Courier,* September 20, 2001

Local newspapers tried their best to collect the names and affiliations of the nearly fifty missing in the Middletown circulation area. One company seemed to pop up next to every other name: Cantor Fitzgerald. "I personally knew twenty-five people in the towns around here," said Craig Cummings, an accidental survivor, one of only five members of the equities division on the 104th floor at Cantor Fitzgerald who did not perish on September 11. Craig began to rattle off the names: Mike Tucker, Mike McCabe, Keith McHeffey, Jim Martello, Swede Chevalier, Dave Bauer, Don Robertson. "Glenn Wall was down the road from us. . . ."

Craig lost his composure for a few seconds. His wife, Mary, explained that he had been playing in a golf tournament on the eleventh. Cummings is a tall, trim, handsomely Anglo-Saxon man, normally contained in the emotional arena. Several of his lost colleagues in the equities group were meant to open a new office around the corner from Middletown, in Shrewsbury. They were days away from making the move. Instead, the weekend after the eleventh, the Cummingses were holed up in their spacious home in Rumson, with their twin baby boys mewing in their playpen and their two other small sons wandering in and out of the family room for reassurance that Daddy was still there. The TV was off. One of the boys had said, "It makes Mommy cry."

The Cummingses spoke passionately about a scholarship fund they had decided to set up. "It always seemed to me that whenever anyone would die prematurely, with children left, there was an outpouring of money and love and then it tapered off," Craig said. "My friend Mike McCabe, who died on the 104th, has four daughters. The oldest is only ten. Even if you had a couple million in life insurance, with four children to send to college, how is that family going to manage ten years down the line?"

It was clear that Cummings was relating to his own situation: he had a young wife who stayed home to raise their four children. Suppose his number had been up, instead of Mike's or Jim's or Dave's? Cummings was also hearing plenty of complaints from the wives of his missing Cantor colleagues.

Howard Lutnick, the chairman and CEO of Cantor Fitzgerald, had earned a reputation for being a bloodless businessman well before September 11. He had lost three quarters of his American workforce and his own brother. But four days after the attacks, while most families and rescue workers were still searching and hoping, Lutnick revealed his gut instinct: save the business. He notified families that they had received the last paycheck. Cantor also informed some families that their health benefits would be terminated on September 30. Lutnick knew his insurance company was offering the deceased employees' families two times their salaries—ignoring the fact that a huge share of most of the traders' and brokers' income came from bonuses. He capped life insurance payments at $100,000. In the first days after the attacks, the CEO was seen on national TV sobbing uncontrollably and making his case on *Larry King Live:*

"Wives of the victims call me and say, 'Why can't you pay my husband's salary? Other companies pay their salary—why can't you?' But you see I lost . . ."

(SOBBING)

". . . I lost everybody in the company, so I can't pay their salary."

(SOBBING)

"They—they think we're doing something wrong. I can't pay their salaries."

(SOBBING)

"I don't have any money to pay their salaries."

Larry King asked the CEO, whose net worth has been estimated in the tens of millions, if not higher, "Can America help at all?"

Lutnick recovered his equanimity in time to make a shrewd pitch: "If every money manager and pension fund just gives us a little bit of business, then maybe we'll survive."

Families began calling Lutnick every name in the book; he became more the focus of their fury than Osama bin Laden. The cruelty was in virtually pronouncing all seven hundred–odd missing employees of the firm dead. "It was a desecration," whispered one bereaved mother. "How dare that asshole slobber all over TV and turn around and cut off my husband's paycheck!" "Well, if he's seen screwing over all the families of his dead employees," said another wife in a score-settling tone of voice, "he'll lose all the customer loyalty our husbands built for him." Yes—but that would be cold comfort. If Cantor Fitzgerald were to fail, there would be no benefits for anybody.

Lutnick's disaffected former partners saw an opportunity to stab Caesar in the heart, as long as they didn't have to give their names. "My brother was just about to turn forty, but he was a prisoner of Howard Lutnick, like so many others who died that day," one former partner told me. "Howard came up with this scheme where everybody had to buy into the company, buy a partnership, if they wanted to go anywhere. Guys gave back their stock options, took a second mortgage, scarfed up savings. The higher up they were, the more they had to put up to buy in. When Cantor stock started sliding, after the dot.com bubble burst, they couldn't afford to get out. Howard would offer them ten cents on the dollar."

Lutnick was said to ride the elevators to his office in the Trade Center with a bodyguard on either side. Some in the company joked that the guards were there to protect him from his own employees.

It quickly became apparent that the news media were going to slit Lutnick's throat. Wives were lining up to bad-mouth him on Fox News. Craig Cummings urged Lutnick to come out and talk face-to-face with the Cantor families in Middletown, to put down the mutinous attitude. On the night of October 9, Lutnick left his Park Avenue apartment and boarded a ferry at Wall Street with a couple of advisers at his side. He was overheard arguing with them over how much he would have to cough up. "Where am I going? What's Middletown? What do these people want from me? What am I getting into here?"

The Salt Creek Grille is a popular shore restaurant and bar on the Navesink River with a welcoming fire pit on the porch. I was present and watched the widows enter in little knots, two together, dressed as if for combat in leather car coats or black nylon parkas. Some came on the supporting elbow of a brother-in-law or an attorney. They did not smile or partake of the buffet. Some came with clipboards or big legal pads. Serious. Armed. This was not a day at the beach. The grieving parents were even more gaunt. The fathers sat hunched over their beers, silent. Some displaced their own anguish onto their wives, saying, "She will never be the same."

Kathy Pezzuti, the four-foot-nine nurse from Little Silver, looked smaller than ever. The suffering was all over her face. She sat with her husband, Frank, a retired senior manager from Cantor, whose face was stone still. The Pezzutis planned to go into New York the next day to clean out the West Side apartment of their daughter Kaleen. Twenty-eight years old. "We moved her in and we want to move her out," Kathy said. "She was so beautiful. . . ." Another woman at Kathy's table overheard us. "I always said Kaleen was the prettiest baby in the shopping cart."

Another grief-stricken mother, Sherry McHeffey, talked about her son, Keith, who had been working at Cantor for only a year. Sherry's petite frame was swallowed in a big loose cable-knit sweater. Friends asked why they hadn't seen her around town. "I had to go away, to get away from myself," she said. "I couldn't look inside." Elaine Chevalier, the mother of Swede, put on a brave front. She was already organizing a support group at Holy Cross Church.

Lutnick had been circling the room, sweat glistening on his high forehead, his black hair slicked down into insouciant curls that flipped up over the open collar of his white shirt. He had come out to the burbs in a Wall Street black suit but tieless, the very picture of the casually superconfident CEO. He kept thrusting out his hand and throwing his arms around men's shoulders, trying to act the part of comforter. But the crowd in that room could have sucked the air out of a dirigible.

He jumped up on a riser and brought a hand mike to his lips: "I've made a deal with everybody. I'll stay as long as you want to talk to me. For those of you who don't know my story, I lost my parents when I was fourteen or fifteen. I lost my little brother in the Towers. It's just me and my sister now, and it's not too easy."

More oxygen was sucked out of the room. This crowd had not come to hear about Mr. CEO's woes. But he went on, lugubriously.

"On Tuesday, I had no idea how we would do anything. I was jumpy. But the people I talked to, they're committed to make it happen for yourselves. And that's why I got out of bed on Wednesday morning—I didn't really want to get out of bed—cuz everything that I had in my life that I *thought* was important had been lost—my best friend, my brother, not to say my brother is my best friend but I'm godfather of his four-year-old and his two-year-old. Who's gonna be the daddy there now? Whenever I take my five-year-old out on Saturday morning for breakfast, I go pick up those kids, too. Whoever thought as a godfather you had to *do* anything? I thought you just had to buy presents at Christmas."

Audible groans. Lutnick was getting nowhere with this tack. He talked about giving the families two times the last salary check. "That's about forty million."

No response.

"And we're gonna pay all the bonuses by October twenty-second. A hundred percent of what people received last year! How's that?"

Nothing.

"I've spoken to *sixty* wives, okay? Each and every one swears their husband was havin' their best year ever. Hard to believe Cantor was flat last year, all right?" Now he was calling the widows liars.

Desperate to get any reaction out of this crowd, Lutnick's gruff voice kicked up an octave and he began to sound like an auctioneer. "Here's what I'm gonna do, okay? Cantor is a privately owned partnership, right? I'm gonna commit to share twenty-five percent of Cantor's profits out of the distribution that usually goes to the partners. *Twenty-five percent.*" His pitch was that to get money to the families, the company would have to make money. "Say we make ten million. Seven point five million goes to the partners. We'll take the other two and a half million and set that money aside for assistance to families of the people lost—to pay for *ten years* of health insurance—whaddya say to that?"

Still no applause. Arms remained folded across chests, heads tilted in skepticism. Suddenly Lutnick lashed out, the shine of perspiration making a mirror of his balding forehead: "Don't doubt me! *I got no life.* Give me and everyone else who survived the benefit of the doubt." He whined, "Everybody says I'm a faker. I've been called every damn name in the book. I don't like it! Damn media! I'm sorry, I'm just a person."

(Sobbed)

"No matter what we make, we'll get you a hundred thousand per family. But we need your help. The way it's going now, it's not helping. The news organizations are following me around. We gotta be on the same side." This tack began to resonate.

"Okay, hear this!" he shouted in auctioneer-ese. "For those of you who have stock options in eSpeed, you can have five years to exercise them. Five years!"

As Lutnick's promises became more and more magnanimous, the wives took furious notes. His delivery became rapid-fire double-talk: "Every employee of the company received stock options. Everyone who wanted to convert their option to an eSpeed partnership was allowed to, and all but two or three did. Well, now, if the partnership sells eSpeed shares, right, we'll have a gain that we can distribute to the partners. And twenty-five percent of that money goes into this pool cuz you guys are sharin' it with us. First it pays for health insurance, what's left goes out in cash. So everyone in this room is going to pull for eSpeed to do very well, right? Because Cantor Fitzgerald has more than twenty million shares in eSpeed. And if you think, Wow, Howard's gonna do something funny with that money, he's gonna hide it, let me tell you something: I'm *standin'* here *tellin' you* about it. And if you think I'm a nut case who *stands* here *tellin' you* about it and then *screws you out of it* later, that just doesn't make any sense."

One left that meeting with the distinct impression that Howard Lutnick had given away much more of the store than he had intended when he was ferrying out to some place called Middletown. And in the coming weeks, the much-maligned Lutnick promised to pay all bonuses and commissions by Thanksgiving. He fired his public relations agency and put his sister Edie in charge of the Cantor Family Fund, which was set up to distribute to grieving families 25 percent of the company's future profits for the next five years, minus the cost of health benefits. Under intense pressure from the families and the media, the bloodless businessman began to come through for the Cantor families more generously and promptly than any of the other companies involved.

THE ALLIANCE COMES APART

It's turning ugly—the money thing," Bob Planer told me a few weeks later. People were asking, Who is this Alliance of Neighbors? It was all chiefs, no Indians. Men of action, in such a hurry to play Good Samaritans that they didn't take time to learn how social welfare really works. Why weren't all the families getting ten grand? How long would this Alliance money hold out? There were hundreds of bereaved families in Monmouth County. Why were rich neighbors from Rumson showing up at people's doors and acting like social workers, asking the most personal of questions, *about money?*

"Giving out money in a gossipy neighborhood is not easy," Planer said. "People resent being called by their neighbors and asked, 'What's your monthly nut?' They know that information will leak."

And so it did. Before long, urgent calls and e-mails to the Alliance asking for help were not being answered. The original gush of goodwill on the part of community activists began to turn sour. The great green salve was drying up.

"It's very hard to do good to people" was a mantra of anthropologist Margaret Mead. And Middletowners had very little experience with doing good to one another. They were learning about community as they went along.

Chapter Nine

____

HYPERVIGILANCE

One traumatic event followed another. Weeks of anthrax attacks, bomb threats, and evacuations were followed by the inexplicable crash of an American Airlines jet in a Queens neighborhood—was that terrorism? People could not catch up psychologically.

Although the ongoing trauma was universal, New Jersey remained a microcosm for these accumulating fears. In fact, the Garden State's acting governor, Donald DiFrancesco in a letter to President Bush's head of the newly proposed federal Office of Homeland Security, asserted that New Jersey was the "front line" of the anthrax attacks.

> ### <u>US investigators track anthrax outbreak to New Jersey</u>
> **Investigators are trying to track the US anthrax outbreak back to a New Jersey postal carrier who may have handled the envelopes.**
> *12:11 Friday 19th October 2001*

A jittery governor wanted more money to test all one thousand of the state's postal facilities. Meanwhile, a tough federal judge denied a request from postal workers to close down even a single facility. Workers were picketing the Eatontown mail distribution center, through which anthrax-laden letters had almost certainly passed en route to NBC, CBS, and the *New York Post*.

Every day brought new warnings, new false alarms. Every night in the windows all around Middletown the flicker of television news brought more manipulation of terror for various purposes: political, commercial, psychological. American bombs guided by drones dreamt up by the scientists at Fort Monmouth were pounding Afghanistan. A president who on campaign could not recall the name of the leader of Pakistan was getting a crash course in international relations and looking exhausted. The constant announcement of alerts and warnings to be vigilant cast everyone in the role of combatants. The people of Monmouth County were becoming sick but not from anthrax; they were sick with fear.

Two months into the New Normal of our post–9/11 world, the public health administrator of Monmouth County, Lester Jargowsky, was frazzled by jumping from one FBI briefing to the next anthrax alarm. Hundreds of these reports were coming in every day, mostly false alarms, but he couldn't take any chances. "I am making decisions that can cause my people to die," he said, explaining how dangerous it is to send hazmat teams to examine packages or people suspected of being poisoned with anthrax. "If the anthrax runs out of nutrients and has nothing left to consume, it returns to its spore form and it's ready for its next meal." Jargowsky was suddenly responsible for bringing his pathetically funded public health team up to speed on how to handle a smallpox epidemic, a chemical attack, botulism, all manner of potential pathogens. But his biggest fear was not anthrax, smallpox, or even a dirty nuclear bomb.

"My biggest fear now is for the mental well-being of the residents in Middletown and Monmouth County," he said. "The residents are uptight. The police and firefighters are exhausted and emotionally depleted. The psychological impact of the Twin Towers, the funerals, the anthrax scares—I am really concerned about people reaching their breaking points."

Some people became paranoid, like the woman who set her house on fire because she microwaved her mail. Many refused to fly or to go into New York. Commuters gambled on which mode of transport was least likely to be a terrorist target. Fire Chief Doug Corbett refreshed himself on how to create a "safe" room with sealed windows and stockpiles of water. But anyone looking for pat answers was dismayed.

The federal government wanted an assessment of the impact of the Trade Center disaster on New Jersey before granting any money for mental health support. Monica Endart, a psychologist from the University of Medicine and Dentistry of New Jersey, conducted focus groups in the affected areas. In affluent communities like Middletown, she found a "glossing over." The prevalent attitude was "We're doing okay." "As a psychologist," said Endart, "I know the hardest people to work with are members of the upper middle class, because they have to be perfect. That will be what Middletown will really struggle with," she predicted. "Trauma this great does not follow a descending course. It percolates. It won't even hit, psychologically, until a year or eighteen months from now."

Psychologists like "models." But there was only one disaster trauma model to predict future reactions: Oklahoma City. We tend to forget that September 11 was not the first time Americans were intimately devastated by an act of terrorism. The families and survivors of the Oklahoma City bombing had been on their journey of recovery for six and a half years. But the Oklahoma atrocity had been Out There, and some of the widows of 9/11 admitted guiltily that they had not felt much more than passing shock and sadness at the time. Diane Leonard, an attractive activist who lost her husband on April 19, 1995, when a domestic terrorist blew up the Alfred P. Murrah Federal Building in Oklahoma City, kept shaking her head as she spoke about the newest members of this growing community of grieving:

"They have such a hard time coming, such a hard time."

A NEWLY CAUTIOUS KRISTEN

In mid-October, Kristen was outside her house in shorts raking leaves. She looked completely at home in the outdoors. But something was wrong with this autumnal picture. She was wearing heavy rubber gloves and a face mask.

"I went out to get the mail last night," she said. "There was a brown parcel in there from somebody I never heard of in Eatontown, New Jersey. All our mail goes through Eatontown, and they found anthrax in that facility—yesterday."

Was it customary for this outdoorsy woman to be so cautious?

"Never. But I would never have thought my husband would have been killed in his office by a plane flying into his building. If I lived in Montana, I would feel differently. But they are definitely targeting New Jersey. They are all over New Jersey." Her fears sounded paranoid. Months later, a local FBI agent revealed that fifteen of the nineteen hijackers had been found to have resided in New Jersey for weeks, months, as long as a year before the attacks. Who knew?

The police officer who came to examine the unidentified parcel was so nervous he wouldn't go near it. He called the health department, and two men in hazmat suits showed up and bagged it in double plastic and took it away. Kristen apologized for their trouble. "I don't want them to think I'm some kind of psycho-fanatic. . . . But when you live with fear at your back door, twenty miles away from you, and you can look out from a hill and see the smoke . . ." The pall of that smoke would hang over Middletown for weeks, and worse was the smell. It penetrated to the most primitive base of the brain, never to be forgotten.

Kristen was creating a bunker in her basement.

A SCARIER HALLOWEEN

Time is my enemy," said Karen Cangialosi, the aerobics instructor with two young sons who lost her husband and the family's "head coach." "I am afraid of time. At first, my husband was just 'away.' Now it's more permanent, more painful."

Karen was on the floor of her sitting room in the Pond View section of Middletown. Her hands worked frantically on making posters for a fundraiser for the boys' traveling baseball team. Her face was drawn, her body shrunken by ten pounds; she couldn't hold up her jeans. This was normally a fit woman of forty who taught water aerobics to seniors. Sun streamed in on her dream house—"my center-hall Colonial with my 2.2 kids"—as she recalled what was supposed to have been the next phase of the Cangialosis' well-laid life plan:

"We were through the diapers and bottles and really enjoying the kids, they were little people. And Stephen was preparing for a possible career change. He'd had two job offers in Jersey without even trying." People in the financial industry were being laid off left and right. Not a few of the Cangialosis' friends were finding themselves abruptly unemployed with no backup plan. The Cangialosis weren't just talking about a change; they could almost taste it and had the foresight to plan for it. Stephen had been going to night school for two years to become a certified financial planner, because that would allow him to make his own hours and be home for the boys' baseball games in the event he was laid off. The Cangialosis were the fun parents of Pond View, the ones who were always out on weekends teaching the boys ice hockey or the girls pirouettes. "We were excited about his getting free of the daily commute to New York," recalled Karen, smiling, caught up in a moment of amnesia. "Once he started working in Jersey, it was going to be a totally different lifestyle."

The smile faded. She looked down and continued her work on the posters, her therapy, keeping busy. "Stephen organized the team fund-raiser, so now I'm going to organize it," she said bravely.

Her many friends and neighbors and relatives kept coming by and saying, "If there's anything I can do for you . . . ," virtually begging for some way they could feel helpful. It was a burden on Karen to think up jobs for all of them, but she was still operating in the heroic phase and thinking of everyone else first. Her girlfriends said over and over, "You're amazing—a pillar of strength."

Karen's eyes misted. She had heard this so often. Many of the widows and bereaved mothers were amazed to find what seemed like superhuman reserves of strength that got them through events where they were on public display. "It's game day, guys," another of the widows had told her teenage kids on the day of their father's memorial, "so step it up. Daddy would want you to be strong. We set the tone." Bleeding widows and mothers acting as the pillars, holding up everyone else.

But Karen Cangialosi had her moments of despair. And brand-new fears. She was worried about Halloween; she didn't want her young boys going from house to house alone, not in a climate of anthrax poisonings.

So, on Halloween, she accompanied her ten-year-old Jeffrey and seven-year-old Peter to a fenced-in Halloween party at a girlfriend's house, where the children streaked up and down the yard in their ghost and Frankenstein costumes while the parents huddled around a barbecue pit eating hot dogs. If this level of protectiveness became the new norm in our post–9/11 world, what effect would it have on growing children?

THE SURVIVORS' SONG

New Jersey had taken one quarter of all the lives lost in the Trade Center: 691 residents. The official count of the victims from Monmouth County stood at 138. The void was perhaps nowhere more evident than on the ferries from Middletown to Wall Street: all those empty seats; all those missing jokes; and in the temporary offices all over Midtown, all those traders' and brokers' desks occupied by strange new hires. The lost data, lost phone numbers, lost family pictures, lost motivation. This business used to be like a nonstop fraternity house. The party was over. Many survivors used the same phrase to describe their New Normal workday: "It sucks."

Bob Planer, one of a handful of survivors from his trading floor at Keefe, Bruyette and Woods, was back at work, but still deeply shaken six weeks after the attacks. He couldn't wait to get out of their temporary office in Midtown and back home to Rumson. Back to his house, his safety zone, which was hidden in a cul-de-sac beyond grandly spaced homes with broad-enough expanses between their great trees that the half-moon of mid-October and a sprinkling of stars were starkly visible. His home looked like an elaborate doll house. A wide rectangular Colonial with shuttered windows, the shades arranged by his wife so that a glow of warm light peeked through each one, just so. The front door stood open. Through the glass screen was the inviting center hall with a Chinese lamp and a broad staircase with family photos running up the wall.

The survivor was so eager to get home in time to take his twelve-year-old son, John, to football practice, he wouldn't stop to change out of his city costume—a deep blue shirt with white collar and a red tie. John had moved his bed into his parents' room, right up against their bed. He spent a lot of time sharpening long sticks, which he posted on either side of his pillow, crude bayonets to protect his parents against an invasion by Osama bin Laden, who had taken on the fantasy proportions of a monster in Saturday-morning cartoons.

Planer comes across as a straight-ahead guy with a full-frontal hand-shake, no frills, no feigning his feelings, which he was trying to keep con-tained but which leaked out from the place where he was still bleeding inside. His deep-set eyes showed dents of fatigue at the edges.

"I look older now," he acknowledged.

Paula Planer ran out of the kitchen chattering. She is a quintessential Irish lass, bubbly and inviting, with a big-toothed grin, square jaw, and snub nose, but these weeks had taken an obvious toll. Bob's wife was reed-thin and sputtered with nervous energy. Her auburn hair was yanked up off her neck into a skewed topknot. "When you don't have time to do anything with it, you just pin it up."

The kitchen was the center of action, as in most of these homes, while the living rooms usually looked as unused as parlors in Ireland. Paula Planer apologized for their "unfinished" den, though it looked like a page out of a decor magazine, with forest green walls, a Scotch-plaid carpet, oversized leather chairs, and a gas fireplace burning brightly.

Paula was in a panic over their lapsed efforts to complete college appli-cations for Cristy, their seventeen-year-old daughter, a lean blond champion runner in her last year of high school. A third child, a polite fifteen-year-old boy, Will, turned up later from lacrosse practice in his Christian Brothers Academy sweatshirt. He settled down in the kitchen with a math tutor.

Paula sat on the edge of the sofa, her elbows propped on her crossed knees and her forearms twisted around each other with her hands clinging to-gether. She was showing signs of referred trauma. Despite sitting close to the fire, just talking about that day made her shiver. "I got so cold that day, waiting to see if Bob would come home. That's what I think about with these girls who lost their husbands. Every day I cry for them. I keep wondering, are they cold all the time now?"

Bob admitted that he was irritable, wasn't sleeping, couldn't concentrate, and felt like he was on alert all the time—all reactions typical of acute stress response. He began talking angrily about a dispute with the coach of his son's Pop Warner team. "He's a big deal with the Alliance, and he wants you to know it—he doles out the money—it's an ego thing with him." After Bob got a few more beefs off his chest, his voice softened and he opened up. "Now it's beginning to really hit home. People are hurting, deep down inside. They're looking for real answers."

Bob described the memorial service his company had held at a church on Fifth Avenue. Two thousand people. A cocktail party and buffet dinner followed at the Palace Hotel. Paula noticed that only a few people from the company stayed to comfort the loved ones of the sixty-eight employees who had died. She surmised bitterly, "The men who were lost couldn't do anything for the company now, they're over."

The Planers stayed for hours, talking and hugging and sharing tears. Bob recounted awesome conversations with some of the wives of his colleagues—freshly widowed women who came up to him and said, "I'm so glad you're alive," and "It's not your time; it's going to be your time someday, but I'm really happy you survived." He choked up a little at recalling how unbelievable it was for these women to be so generous, how undeserving those remarks had made him feel.

But he was quick to protest, "I'm not one of those guys who feels guilty about this thing. I feel incredibly lucky that I was spared, that's about it. I don't feel guilty on this. At all."

Did he protest too much? What Bob didn't mention was the other spouses who came up to him at the memorial spewing accusations: "Why didn't you get my husband out?" Bob tried to explain he had gone outside hoping to help people. "You should have grabbed my husband and *made* him go with you!" Bob had pleaded, "I couldn't make anybody leave!" He ended up apologizing, "If I was a leader, I would have said 'Everybody outta here!' "

Paula had tried to comfort her husband on the way home. "You're not with either side—not with the mourners and not with the"—she lost her voice—"ones who won't come back. It puts you in a spot."

That spot is where people who survive mass violent death often remain, tormented by guilt, for many years. Some survivors of the Oklahoma City bombing are still struggling with this most pernicious of aftereffects—more than eight years later. Planer was almost certainly in denial about the depth of trauma he had experienced and the gremlin of guilt that was guiding many of his actions. He wouldn't dream of expecting sympathy or of seeking help. Like most survivors, he didn't feel "worthy" of it; after all, he was one of the lucky ones. His wife sized up the situation and threw him a lifeline—a way of reentering the trauma and changing the message.

"You were saved for a reason," Paula stated as a matter of fact. "Absolutely."

Bob nodded yes and no. "Possibility. I have two strikes against me now," he said, referring to his escape during the '93 bombing. "I feel like I'm tempting fate with the third one, going back to work. But I just feel I owe it to the company."

If he had indeed been spared in order to rise to a higher purpose, what might that be?

"I don't think it's going to be in this business," he reflected. "I've always felt I have to do some charity work in my life. Of all the good things that have happened to me in life, I feel I owe it to give it back, you know? I just don't know *when* I'm gonna do it and *how* I'm gonna do it. But I intend to do it, I've always intended to do it. That's why I never felt I was going to die in that elevator in '93. And that's probably a reason why I didn't die in the World Trade Center this time."

FORT WALL STREET

One month into the aftermath, the fires were still burning at Ground Zero. The first outpourings of hope and grief were still on display along the wall of Riverside Green Park in Red Bank. Already the handwritten notes and poems saying good-bye to husbands and wives and daddies were blurred by rain. The votive candles had melted. The mass cards were warped. The first fall leaves were scudding up against the floral wreaths and plush red hearts and teddy bears. But for the families, the pain was still fresh as the grass was still bright green in the park.

Widows and parents debated whether or not they wanted to see that violent burial ground called Ground Zero.

The news on the radio was dark. Mayor Giuliani declared that finding anyone still alive in the rubble would be "a miracle." The mayor was trying to let people down gently. He had been warned one week after the attacks by a federal emergency expert that the chances of anyone surviving the concussive force of 1,300 feet of concrete compressing down to 80 feet in a matter of minutes were virtually nonexistent. But no one wanted to deliver the message of hopelessness. There never would be an official declaration; each family and each rescue worker would come to terms with the terrible truth in his or her own time.

Downtown Manhattan was an armed camp. The first sound on approaching Wall Street was the deafening grind of rental power trucks massed around the perimeter of destruction to provide electricity for the massive dig-out. Broadway below the great financial houses looked like a snake pit, with a zillion cables running from the trucks across sidewalks and into the few buildings that were still functioning. Thick smoke billowed from underground, from the PATH subway station that had imploded and compacted into rubble from top to bottom, side to side, for a thousand feet. Huge waves of commuters coming off the Staten Island Ferry had to condense into a tangle of bodies, five abreast, two blocks long, and wait to descend into the only subway left operating on the downtown West Side.

Wall Street was only sparsely populated, even moments before the market opened. Brokers and traders walked to work in their traditional blue shirts, but now they wore running shoes. The Dollar Deli at the head of Wall Street stood empty. On its sooted window someone had written, "God bless America." A woman stopped to dip her finger in the soot on the windowsill and touched it to her tongue, reverently, a gesture of remembrance. On the newsstand, the tabloid *New York Post* screamed: SADDAM TERROR LINK.

Was this a propaganda effort by the U.S. government? Gulf War holdovers in the Bush administration would love a justification for attacking Iraq and gaining control of the second-largest ocean of oil in the world.

On a large police van was taped a badly mimeographed map of the whole financial district, with lines dividing it into seven zones of varying intensity of disaster. In the sixth zone of disaster, a couple of blocks from Wall Street, the sights were incongruous. Army tents in the pocket parks. U.S. infantrymen carrying rifles and National Guardsmen in their combat gear. The green-and-brown-blotched uniforms meant to camouflage soldiers in jungle warfare only served there, in the urban jungle, where everything was concrete gray, to make them stand out. A very young guardsman from a company in the northernmost corner of New York State who had never before set foot in Manhattan felt the incongruity: "If you told me a month ago that I'd be walking downtown Manhattan in combat gear, I'd have told you you're nuts."

From a block south of the devastation, it was possible to glimpse the steel skeleton of a building, maybe twenty stories of it. Three-pronged steel-faced shards stuck up out of the mountains of rubble. Still smoking. Red and burned. They looked like religious symbols from some alien faith. "What building is that?"

"That's the second Twin Tower, ma'am," said the nearest police officer. "What's left."

THE SHAKEN SURVIVORS OF KBW were holed up in their lawyer's office. The immediate goal was to find new permanent space. Bob Planer, being one of the six senior executives who had survived, was given a new title: New York City office manager. He was deputized to find the new space. He sought out each of the five members of the board of directors and laid out the new realities of their post–9/11 world.

"To tell you the truth—and this is something you should take back to your families—we were arrogant in thinking the World Trade Center wasn't going to be hit again," Planer told them. "Now everybody in the world including the president of the United States is saying the terrorists are going to do more. I believe they're going to hit Midtown. They're going to hit landmarks. Rockefeller Center. Right where you're thinking of relocating. I've already got two strikes against me. I'd like to lower my odds." And then, the kicker: "I think we should move the company to Boston."

While Planer was using avoidance—a typical trauma response—his boss, CEO John Duffy, was handling his trauma in a very different way. Duffy, too, was a survivor, although he had not been in the Towers on that fateful day. But his only son had been, and Christopher Duffy, only twenty-three, who had come to work for his dad's company, had perished. So had Duffy's co-CEO, Joe Berry. Thus John Duffy, having inherited command of a smashed workforce and a vanished place of work, glossed over his own inconsolable personal losses and relied on the old codes. What Paula Planer refers to as "the boy code." *Stiff upper lip, no overt emotions, put it behind us, charge ahead as if nothing has happened.*

A great round barrel of a man, John Duffy walked Planer back to his makeshift office, rocking stiffly from one leg to another, the walk of a man of far greater age than his forty-eight years. So great was his girth, his belt could not prevent his waistband from gapping. Perhaps all that flesh was the only cushion insulating him from intolerable emotional pain. As he sat down, his small features set in a flushed face dissolved into a hammock of chins. At the first mention of "survivors" he pulled his collar out from his neck.

Planer proposed the move to Boston. Duffy chuckled in disbelief. "We still have a hundred employees in New York. We can't let some MF terrorists dictate where we do business." He questioned whether Planer was thinking straight. Duffy took cover in the new mantra of predestination: "When your time's up, your time's up."

Subsequently, Bob Planer was not selected to be on the company board. He surmised that the partners had all decided the same thing: "I was being a chickenshit."

His wife attempted to rationalize the disappointment for him, but he was deeply hurt. "My motivation has taken quite a dive," he said after Thanksgiving. Bob continued to swear that he wouldn't let the company go down. He had been with KBW for twenty-four years. If he gave all his effort to re-building the company, he might feel a little better about being a survivor, but he would also have to postpone, again, finding a higher purpose. He did not want to die in the elevator of another arrogantly tall Manhattan office tower before he had done something more meaningful with his life. He was a fuse of conflicted emotions waiting to explode. Flying off the handle at little stuff. This legacy of sole survivorship was beginning to render him, to his children and his wife—even to himself—a stranger.

THE RABBI'S CALL TO CHANGE

As the holiday season approached, the rabbi of Rumson reminded his faithful of what we all said in the days immediately following 9/11: "My life will never be the same. Remember? We're going to change, we're going to be more connected, we're going to value the serious things, and many of us *have* changed."

But many others were glossing over.

In the Eastern European countries from which Rabbi Levin's forebears came, places like Vilna and Kovno, Jews were never allowed to own land. Levin grew up in a labor union household, a socialist household in Brooklyn, with a father who was vice president of the International Ladies' Garment Workers Union. For his father to move out of Brooklyn and to buy and own a house in New Jersey represented a supreme achievement. Thus was Rabbi Levin also torn by inner conflict. His inner struggle was between sacrificing for social justice and enjoying the good life in the rich little suburb of Rumson. This contradiction materialized in the car he drove—an old tank of a Lincoln Mercury—and the house he had bought two years before, which more than doubled in value and was now worth more than a million dollars.

The rabbi couldn't help thinking that September 11 was the Lord's message to those who had not made the commitment to building community, to getting to know one's neighbor, to the kindness and caring that sustains civilization. He saw his role as a rabbi "to reinvent civilization." He acknowledged, "It's a very countercultural job." Rabbi Levin began to warn his congregants about the beauty they were going to begin to discern in all the destruction. *Beauty?* He was prepared for the blind eye they would try to turn on it. Many people, including the president of the United States, were dismissing the whole event as "pure evil." One cannot learn from pure evil, except to be more afraid. But wasn't it possible, just possible, that in wondrous destruction there was a moral lesson?

In the Torah, he liked to remind his congregants, the ten plagues are not called plagues. They are called "signs and wonders." In the ongoing quest for revelation, one must ask, Why these plagues? What were they meant to accomplish? Then the rabbi would lay on the shocker.

"You know what one of the plagues was? *Anthrax.* There was bioterrorism even back then. What do you call it when the Nile River is turned to blood? I call it *bioterrorism.* What is bioterrorism? A transformation of the forces of nature to do damage in such an extraordinary way, it goes beyond the physical."

The question he wanted his congregants to ponder was this: *What is the moral message being sent through the medium of our enemies?*

Chapter Ten

————

PICKING UP STONES AT GROUND ZERO

No remains. That was the second robbery. Even the families who were trying to force out of their minds the fantasy that one day the missing one would walk through the door and shout, "I'm home—it was all a bad dream," even they could not believe what they could not see. So few of them had gotten back any remains of their loved ones—no word at all. They went ahead with memorials because they had to do something, but it was all fictional.

KEVIN AND THE NIGHT VISITS

Starting on the second night after the attacks, Kevin Casey went down to Ground Zero in search of some sign that his wife, Kathy, might still be found alive. She'd worked on the 104th floor of the South Tower for Sandler O'Neill & Partners as an equities trader. She always called him when she got to work and let the phone ring twice, to wake him up. He worked nights. And she had called on the morning of the eleventh, probably at 9:03, because he'd heard the two rings and woken up just as the second plane hit her tower. A beefy Irishman who coaches school and community sports, Kevin Casey had never been in a war, but the smoking ruins he saw the first night he went down to Ground Zero fairly hissed the words *no survivors.*

Kevin was not ready for such a total obliteration of hope. He needed an excuse to revisit the place again. And again.

As a manager with New York City Transit, Kevin supervised the reconstruction of subway tracks. It would be months at least before enough of the ruins were cleared that reconstruction of the subway tracks beneath the collapsed tunnels was an issue, but Kevin went back to work anyway. Too soon—within three weeks—and that became his excuse to go down to Ground Zero every night: to check out the future job site. "I didn't have to go down there," he admitted. "I was drawn back there. Especially late at night when things would get quiet. If it meant just crying or just talking, it was my way of communicating with her. I found myself for weeks crawling around that pile, looking for some sign she was still alive."

Kevin had worked nights for more than two decades. It showed. For a forty-two-year-old who coached all the ball sports, his hair was patchier and his gut paunchier than it should have been, but the body never does fully adjust to sleeping in daylight. Kevin had made every effort to compartmentalize his life. His wife worked days and got home from the city in time to take over with their only child so Kevin could leave for his night's work. He was in the habit of clocking a great deal of overtime on the weekends, so his interaction with their son, Matt, now fifteen, was mostly limited to coaching the boy's sports teams and being "the dean of discipline," as the adolescent boy called his dad in surly moods. The Caseys' marriage was a relay between Middletown and Manhattan, between the night-manager dad and the day-trader mom, and as far as Kevin knew, it worked. "I'd been in transit for twenty-three years," he said, "so I'm used to it. And that's the only thing I know."

Suddenly, he didn't know anything. Where to begin with his son, Matt?

Before Kathleen Casey was killed in the Trade Center, she and Matt had been exceptionally close. The boy had been in a nearly fatal car accident in his early years, and Kathy had overcompensated and waited on him hand and foot ever since. Now a fast-growing teenager, Matt was a fussy eater. His father knew nothing about cooking. He tried ordering out for their meals. Matt sat stony-faced, his eyes locked on the TV, refusing to eat. When Kevin forced the issue, the boy would balk. The two males butted heads.

"Mom would never yell at me," Matt brooded. "She typed my homework reports. *She* would get me whatever I wanted!"

Kevin knew the boy was hurting, but he was, too. So after coming home from his night's work and driving his son to school, Kevin would crawl back to bed. Sleep until after noon. "Just feeling sorry for myself." His sister flew in from Dallas, his brother drove down from Boston, his mother moved in from Brooklyn, and at the end of the day his guy friends would stop over to have a few beers. But Kevin had never opened up about his emotions. Even with his wife. Their marriage had been comfortably companionable, with very few problems. Frankly, he didn't know how to talk about the chaos of feelings inside.

"My sister would tell me, 'You have to go talk to somebody, you *have to*'—'Okay, okay!' " He smiled with forced tolerance. "My sister swears by any kind of mental therapy, anything that's politically correct." So off went Kevin Casey to see one of the therapists at Catholic Charities in Red Bank. It was late in the evening. The therapist had absorbed the sorrows of maybe a dozen of the bereaved or traumatized that day. Kevin sat with his back to the therapist. He began talking about how he was drawn to revisit the devastation at Ground Zero. Sometimes he imagined crawling underneath the debris and finding his wife and going to sleep beside her. Going to sleep would take away the pain.

No response from the therapist. Kevin turned around. She was crying. The *therapist* was crying! He forced a joke.

"Would you like to switch seats?"

PAT AND THE TOKEN CASKET

No condolence letter came from the company for which Pat Wotton's husband had worked, Fiduciary Trust. Not for almost a month, not until Pat's sister Brenda complained. When Pat or Kristen or other families went to one of the Fiduciary Web sites, looking for somewhere to post questions about their loved ones on the message board, they were confronted with a beautiful view of the Twin Towers and copy boasting of the company's prestigious address: *Our offices on the 90th–97th floors of Two World Trade Center . . . have breathtaking views.*

This message and picture would remain up until April 2002.

It sickened Mark Ebersole to see it. He was missing Rod Wotton terribly; the two had been good friends as well as coworkers at Fiduciary. Ebersole remembered clearly what he had seen on September 11. Ed McNally, another Middletown resident who was in charge of the technology group for which Rod and Mark worked, had ordered his staff to stay put after the plane hit the other tower. "Ed [McNally] was calling people together to delegate roles—who should report where and when—to do recovery in New Jersey," recalled Ebersole. Their boss was on the phone with Steve Tall, Fiduciary's chief technology officer, who happened to be out of the office that morning. Ebersole contended that McNally was kept on the phone for many minutes—from the time the first plane hit, when he and Rod ran toward

McNally's desk, at least until the time Mark left. Ebersole couldn't forget that terrible moment when he hesitated, torn between pulling Rod Wotton away from his boss's desk or racing for an open elevator himself. Those minutes were a matter of life—for those who escaped—and death, for those who stayed to help with "disaster recovery." Rod Wotton and Ed McNally were among the eighty-seven Fiduciary employees who were killed.

Five weeks after the attacks, Fiduciary held a service of remembrance at the Cathedral of St. John the Divine in Manhattan. Families were given a memorial book with profiles of the lost employees. Fiduciary's CEO, Anne Tatlock, gave a speech in which she instructed families who were still in shock, "It is essential to find a way to move forward."

Again, Mark Ebersole felt sick. "There was no mention at the service of the heroic efforts of their workers," he lamented. "These people died for the company, period."

Pat Wotton wasn't able to bring herself to attend Fiduciary's remembrance service. Steve Tall called Pat from his cell phone on his way to the service to see if she was coming. It was his first contact with Pat since 9/11. She told him of her last phone conversation with her husband, on the eleventh. "I heard from Rod they were running disaster recovery, and that's why he couldn't leave."

Tall claimed that wasn't possible, because it was against company policy. Thereafter, he responded to Pat's charge through the corporate-communications spokeswoman. He claimed that McNally had called him at 9:01 A.M. and reported only that a plane had hit the North Tower, flames were coming out, and people were leaving the office. Then suddenly, according to Tall, McNally had said, "Oh my God, something else has just happened, I've got to go!" and hung up at 9:03. That was when the wing of the second plane had sliced through their floor. "No one was asked to stay behind to back up systems" was Tall's official statement. "I kept strictly within our company policy in leading the disaster-recovery efforts . . . which is that everyone is to evacuate the building immediately."

Some days after the cathedral service, Pat held a private memorial for her husband combined with a baptism for their new baby. She hoped that combining the sorrowful ceremony with the celebratory one would restore some equilibrium to her dark mood. It didn't.

No remains. All she had to bury was love notes from their families and friends, tucked into a miniature box. She covered the humble token casket with flowers. In a fog after leaving the "grave site," Pat could hardly believe her eyes when Steve Tall showed up at the reception. The presence of the company representative stirred up the anguish over what she believed had been her husband's unnecessarily delayed evacuation. She could barely bring herself to speak to him.

In the weeks following, her big, bruised eyes overtook even more of her taut, girlish face. She could hardly bear to hold her new baby. The normal bonding between mother and child had been interrupted by the necessity of leaving her newborn in intensive care for three weeks. While others looked upon the chubby little facsimile of his father as a sort of resurrection, in Pat's depressed state the infant was an intruder. Rodney Patrick represented Life After Rod. She wanted to go backward in time.

FAMILY ASSISTANCE

Mayor Giuliani was quick to set up a Family Assistance Center at Pier 94 along the Hudson, where those impacted by 9/11 could seek out all available social services in one location. New Jersey families, however, were reluctant to make the long trip from their homes, across the Hudson into Manhattan, with its hangover of terror. When the governor of New Jersey saw the job that New York was doing, he directed that a similar "city" be set up for families of his state. The job went to a FEMA emergency manager. Bob Bellan had the look of a big, sad buffalo, but he also had a big heart, and he saw this job as the mission of his life.

A tin-can alley on the Jersey side of the river, across the Hudson from the Trade Center site, was laid with grass, and trailers were moved in to house a supermarket of disaster services—all in forty-eight hours. A grand old ferry terminal stood vacant nearby. With a hurried scrub-down and vats of paint, the terminal with its vaulted wooden ceiling was transformed into an airy dining room. Volunteers kept turning up from as far away as Alaska, Hawaii, Puerto Rico, and California. Bellan gained a consensus that their usual therapeutic strategies were probably of no use in this situation. "The call of this place is to provide family members a safe, warm atmosphere where we can guide them to the services they need," he told the volunteers. There was even a debate about whether or not to use the word "death" on the sign where one applied for a death certificate.

The New Jersey Family Assistance Center at Liberty State Park opened on September 19 and turned out to be mostly a marvel of sensitivity. From the moment families entered the reception tent, they were warmly greeted by a volunteer from the National Organization for Victim Assistance (NOVA), who would advocate for them throughout the day. What the state was offering in place of an unrecovered body was an urn full of dust from Ground Zero. This was presented in a ceremony in the terminal's waiting room, which became a serene chapel. To conduct the ceremony, the families could choose from a roster of clerics, including a Buddhist monk, a Muslim imam, and a Jewish rabbi. It culminated in the presentation of a tricornered military flag, just like those given to honor a fallen member of the armed services. The ceremony was surprisingly moving.

The ultimate experience offered to the families was a ferry crossing to visit Ground Zero. A mixed blessing, as most families saw it. They wrestled with themselves over whether they could bear witnessing the horror up close; many reserved a trip and then canceled. Bob Bellan counseled his volunteers on how to handle such a sensitive voyage: "We have to prepare those who want to go over to Ground Zero to face the realization that their loved ones are not coming back, and then work with them in a very emotional, compassionate, loving manner to get them prepared to go back home."

Pat Wotton wasn't at all sure she wanted an urn full of dust that mixed her husband's charred flesh with that of terrorists. But she forced herself to go to the Family Assistance Center in late October. Making the rounds of the disaster relief trailers, Pat happened to hit a couple of sticklers. A man from the New York Victims of Violent Crime refused to reimburse her for her husband's memorial service. On the receipts she had submitted, some were signed Wotton, her married name, and some Greene-Wotton, a hybrid of her maiden name and her husband's.

"I cannot have you make this difficult for me," Pat told the stickler politely. He wouldn't budge. "Sir, I filled out your papers, I submitted the receipts, please . . ." Pat, like most of the Middletown widows, was used to being on the giving end, raising money for good causes. It was humiliating to beg for $65 to cover flowers for the miniature box in which all she had to bury was love notes from family and friends.

Pat's older sister Brenda was running interference. She began at the Buddhists' table and found them a model of compassion, requiring only a marriage and a death certificate before they wrote out a check for $1,000. She found United Way much less concrete; they promised that local charities would get in touch at some future date. When Pat and Brenda sat down across from the Red Cross volunteer, it felt more like a welfare office than disaster relief.

"Whaddya got?" barked the woman volunteer, a former Catholic school principal.

Pat began pulling out her monthly bills.

"They're gonna tell you your gas bill, phone bill, your mortgage, was already paid in the check you got."

Pat explained that the first check had covered only one month's bills. "I understood that I was to calculate my monthly expenses and multiply by three. I thought that would be happening again for the next three months."

"You misunderstood," snapped the volunteer. "You're gonna get something more from the Red Cross in January or February. Say, a month or six weeks later, and you still have these other bills, you fill out another form. I helped a girl who asked for eighteen thousand dollars. I told her she probably wouldn't get it. She got four thousand." The volunteer asked if there were any child-care expenses. Pat said a physical therapist was coming to their home every day, to help her baby learn to breathe. Why was she paying so much? Pat said she had delivered the baby only five weeks earlier. For the first time, the Red Cross worker halted in her machine-gun bureaucratese and looked up.

"You delivered the second child after 9/11?"

"Yes."

"Okay, that's good."

Pat winced. It was not to expedite the volunteer's paperwork that Pat had waited until her husband's death to deliver their child. A month later, when Pat checked on the progress, it turned out the Red Cross volunteer had never filed the papers.

CROSSING OVER

Finally came the dreaded high point of the day: the ferry crossing to view Ground Zero. Thirty-five families had signed up for the trip on that October day. Some had dropped out. Not Pat; she was determined to go through with it. Her mother and sisters and a few friends had come with her for support. They and twenty-five other families were given white hard hats, respiratory masks, and plastic glasses. After a sober briefing in a chapel, everyone boarded buses. The family members were flanked by Red Cross disaster relief workers and NOVA "companions" and nuzzled by therapy dogs with thick coats ideal for petting.

Pat's sisters and friends leaned over their seats to keep up a lively banter with her. Pat's lips trembled as she fought with herself, trying to be brave but quite terrified at confronting the reality. After a brief bus ride, everyone was guided onto a chubby ferry boat. On dark days the ride across the Hudson could feel to families like crossing the river Styx. But that day was unseasonably hot and sunny—an eerie reminder of September 11. It was also windless, so there was no telltale smoke, no smell, no sign of destruction until the ferry drew alongside the huge glass cage of the Winter Garden with its webbed brow punched in.

"Oh my God," families gasped.

Giant-jawed excavators moved in the distance like exotic animals in a game park. Pat stepped off the ferry crying so hard, she didn't see the rut. She fell to her knees in the mud. Her companions gasped and grabbed for her, thinking she had collapsed. She was mortified: *Please, God, don't let me make a spectacle of myself.* She shook them off. Walking on, lips clenched against her fears, she sailed past the hazmat workers who held their helmets over their hearts. She didn't notice two giant men with their dreadlocks wrapped in American flag bandannas standing still as statues, but statues streaked with tears. Turning the corner onto West Street, she was scarcely aware of the phalanx of New York state troopers in black leather, all standing with hands behind their backs, and columns of firefighters and National Guardsmen who stood at attention, shoulder to shoulder, many of them crying. The trees were leafed with burned and blown papers. Pat passed the Memorial Wall with its vast inventory of teddy bears, still bearing up. A New Jersey state police officer announced, "We're going to be walking through some crazy areas, so I'm going to have to ask you to keep your hard hats on and stay very tightly packed together so we can keep track of you."

Approaching the perimeter of Ground Zero, the damaged outer buildings were demurely draped in black safety netting. Underfoot the unsteady planks of a catwalk led to a metal ramp. Finally, there was a set of short, steep steps leading to a platform. It was like ascending the guillotine. Still no wreckage could be seen—nothing but the excavators, which appeared more monstrously large and overpowering. Only upon reaching the top step did the reality suddenly strike each family member full in the face and gut—this was a giant amphitheater of death.

Pat let out a shriek of agony. It sent shudders through everybody else. She ran to the edge of the railing and screamed into the monstrous gouge of crushed concrete and still-cooking ruins. "Rod, Rod, come back! How could you leave me! Rod, come baaack."

In that instant, to the horror of all those watching, Pat Wotton seemed to regress twenty years.

Several EMS workers rushed to pull her back from the frail railing, fearing that she might break down completely and leap into the abyss. Pat sobbed hysterically. As her sisters saw her distress, they, too, began weeping prodigiously and took turns putting her head on their shoulders, repeating, "He's with you, he's in your heart, you'll always have him there." Pat pulled away and peered over at the specks of police and firefighters moving around like toy figures in the vast pit. She asked the NOVA companions to point out the South Tower, where Rod had worked. A single stump of concrete was left standing.

"That's all there is!" Pat cried out. Now a wave of rage came over her. Only later could she explain it. "I was thinking about the hard time the company is giving me. I thought, they must never have visited this site to see the devastation, and to realize he died working for the company."

KATHI THE FERRYWOMAN

To the usual trauma of terrorist acts, the World Trade Center atrocity added a special agony: This was a mute mass murder. Those of us far outside the buildings didn't hear the impact. We didn't smell it or taste it or even see a falling tower. One moment they were there, wounded, belching smoke and fire like the breath of great dinosaurs, and the next moment—to be precise, all of ten seconds later—the first one was down. Twenty-three minutes later, another shimmy of melting steel, and in less than a minute the North Tower, too, was gone. Vaporized into dust and ash.

Thus, disbelief hung on for many months. And that made the families' first visits to Ground Zero a second wave of the trauma. But it wasn't only the families and the survivors who were touched and traumatized. For many of the volunteer mental health professionals, the trauma became cumulative.

The logistics coordinator for the family visits to Ground Zero, Kathi Bedard called herself "a typical suburban Jersey rat." As a substance abuse counselor, she was not trained for the role she was given but considered it an honor. She was Charon, the ferrywoman, the leader in denim and hard hat who guided the Pat Wottons and other families across the river to the underworld of Ground Zero.

Kathi would never forget her first ferry trip as the families' chief companion. The pouring rain. The rocky river crossing. The faces frozen in anticipatory dread. Scrambling to get them umbrellas. The relentless rain. Stepping off the boat and hearing the whispers of "Oh my God" as family members glimpsed the shattered forehead of the Winter Garden. The shock of seeing the families' first sight of the pile, burned and broken, smoking, ribs sticking out of buildings. Kathi's eye began furiously twitching. She registered the professional's thought that everything she was seeing and smelling was burning itself into her brain. At that moment Bob Bellan came up behind her and whispered a truth:

"It never gets any easier."

But something else burned itself into her brain on that first day. As the families and Kathi's crew of volunteers all huddled on the small platform, the rain suddenly stopped. A feeble sun broke through the black-and-white scene. And over the smoking pit there appeared a partial rainbow. The world still had color.

Kathi was warned that repeating this exposure to trauma day after day would be dangerous to her health. The scars of secondary trauma can be severe on caregivers like herself, whose role is to absorb the anguish and anger that flails around wherever bereaved families gather. Indeed, by the third day Kathi began to notice in herself some of the most common symptoms of high anxiety—nosebleeds and short-term memory lapses. As time went on, she cried a lot and became less and less able to communicate with her husband when she got home.

"Seeing the relief on the faces of the families as we sat on the boat on the return trip—that's what kept me coming back," Kathi would say later. Many other volunteers could make the trip only once. "They knew this might break them, and they didn't try to be cowboys—I have a lot of respect for them."

She also found the strength to continue by banding together in a common mission with other volunteers. She made certain they gathered for a "debriefing" among themselves after every boat trip. The volunteers who stuck with her ferry crew she called her "Frequent Fliers." They began to call her "Captain Kathi."

"Kathi looked after *everyone*," marveled Richard Watkins, one of her Frequent Fliers. He watched her regularly leave the viewing platform to give flowers and hugs to the firemen and police at Ground Zero. "I saw these huge men crying in her arms," said Watkins. They were disturbed by watching family members break down when they saw the pile. Kathi would reassure them: "Coming here helps the families. On the trip back, they relax and you can tell by their faces that they feel a little relieved."

She could be tough, too. One day a tall New Jersey trooper climbed onto the platform and demanded of Watkins, "Who's in charge?" The volunteer walked him over to Captain Kathi. *"Her?"* Incredulous, the trooper confronted the little woman in denim and hard hat. "Are *you* in charge?" Kathi assured him she was. The trooper summarily ordered her to clear the families off the platform immediately; he was escorting the president of the Ukraine and the man had a tight schedule.

Kathi fixed the trooper with her game face: "You can tell the president of the Ukraine that he can kiss my American ass. The families aren't moving."

The look on the trooper's face kept the Frequent Fliers chuckling for days. But there were other days when they all felt the weight of sorrow and anger. Kathi looked for inspiration from one of the veterans who minister to people in trauma on a regular basis, Fred Trask, a Salvation Army "major" who accompanied her crew on the ferry trips. Major Trask kept talking about a passage from the Bible where God parted the river Jordan so Joshua could walk across it. One day, when Kathi was feeling especially vulnerable, she asked Major Trask to give a blessing to her and her crew. He recited the lines from Joshua:

> *The Lord said to Joshua,*
> *Take up twelve stones,*
> *Carry them over with you,*
> *And put them down at the place where you will stay tonight.*

> *In the future,*
> *When your children ask you,*
> *What do these stones mean?*
> *Tell them, these stones*
> *Are to be a memorial*
> *To the people forever.*

> *They took up twelve stones and they carried them over*
> *With them to the camp*
> *Where they put them down.*

Major Trask then told the ferry volunteers, "When we go across that river today, a lot of you are going to pick up stones, and they'll be heavy, they'll be dirty, they'll be ugly, they'll be stones of hate, and revenge, and fear. And you're going to have to learn to come back across the river and *put them down.*"

Kathi burst into tears. "Damn," she said, "it's nine-thirty in the morning and I'm already crying."

At Ground Zero, taking souvenirs was not permitted. The law enforcement people were very clear about that: "Make sure the families don't pick up stones or rocks." One day, a woman told her NOVA companion on the ferry trip over that her husband was supposed to come, too. They had lost their child. But he'd woken up that morning in physical pain—traumatic grief can do that—and he couldn't face the trip. "It would be really great if we could get him a rock."

So Kathi sneaked down into the rubble and got the woman a stone. She told the NOVA companion to ask the woman to shake Kathi's hand. As she did, Kathi passed her the stone. It was like a drug deal. The woman hugged Kathi and wouldn't let go. "You have no idea what this is going to mean to my husband," she said.

In the moment of that fervent hug Kathi realized that she would do anything for the families. "I remember thinking that I would commit felonies for them, walk on broken glass, carry them on my back—anything," she later wrote in her diary. "And even though I knew it was magical thinking, it kept me going—the hope that somehow I could make it better in the face of all of that devastation."

When Kathi did her debriefings with the families after their return from the site, she would make use of the metaphor: "Today we went over there and picked up stones. Tell me," she'd say, "what does your stone look like? What does it feel like? How heavy is your stone? What does that mean to you?"

Some people would say, "It's a big, ugly, heavy mother of a stone, and I can hardly carry it. But I'm keeping this baby." Others said, "Well, I found a gemstone, and I want to talk about the good things."

Kathi Bedard's philosophy was simple: "Let 'em cry, let 'em scream and yell—'I don't want your goddamn teddy bear!'—but watch their breathing, watch their knees." When people buckled, she and her team would carry them to and from the platform. Kathi performed her ferrywoman role every day, rain or shine, for fifty-six days in a row. The Pat Wottons never even knew her name.

LIEUTENANT KEEGAN AND THE GLASS HALF FULL

K athi was far from the only "ordinary" American who found extraordinary inner resources and performed calmly and compassionately in the aftermath of September 11. In fact, on that very day another astonishing event took place—off camera. Nearly one million people were evacuated from Lower Manhattan by water—not by official means or emergency pre-planning. They were rescued by a network of private and publicly owned watercraft that emerged to meet the emergency.

This mimicked the epic rescue of the British army at Dunkirk, but it was virtually ignored by the media. It didn't fit the visual of panic and disaster that is prized as made-for-TV imagery. In fact, people did not flee in panic. They behaved like the social animals that we are: sharing information, calling their loved ones on cell phones, engaging in collective decision making, forming hand-holding human chains, and helping one another to safety. The evacuation of the Towers was carried out in a calm and orderly manner—and 90 percent of the people in the Towers escaped. "The response to the September eleventh tragedy was so effective precisely because it was not centrally directed and controlled," observed Professor Kathleen Tierney, director of the Disaster Research Center at the University of Delaware. "Instead, it was flexible, adaptive, and focused on handling problems as they emerged."

Lieutenant Bill Keegan was one of those who took charge and handled problems as they emerged, beginning on the night of September 12, when he supervised his teams of volunteers to lay the groundwork—literally, a wooden board—to set up a command center. And like Kathi Bedard, Keegan would be tested again and again. He was so evidently a natural leader, his supervisor immediately designated him the night commander of Ground Zero. Officially, Keegan commanded only the Port Authority police, but the top brass of the New York firefighters and police rotated in and out, as did their men. Billy Keegan was at Ground Zero every night from five in the afternoon until five in the morning, for nine months. And his officers did not rotate. So as time went on, the chiefs of the other services always conferred with Keegan. He was another one of the "ordinary" Americans who was elevated to extraordinary behavior by confronting the life-and-death decisions in dealing with the destruction at Ground Zero.

There was the night that two of his brothers needed to be recovered. Their bodies were pinned near the core of heat beneath steel so unstable it looked like it was breathing. One team, led by Sergeant Kevin Devlin, tried to extricate the bodies, but the still-smoking metal was unbearably hot. They had to come out.

Keegan wrestled with himself: *Should I send in my men and risk more lives? Or, if I wait and the steel shifts, I risk losing the remains of my brothers. If I were in the families' shoes, what would I want done?*

Faced with an impossible choice, Keegan felt "zapped right out of my-self." His mind, maybe his soul—who knows?—left his body and flew up, then looked down upon Billy Keegan sitting on a stump of concrete, all alone, isolated, and the thought came: *Why was he being asked to make these impossible life-and-death calls?*

Keegan decided to send in another team. They brought out the first body. But only the legs of the second man were visible. A surgeon offered to sever the body. The Port Authority police chaplain, Father Dave Baratelli, saw Lieutenant Keegan agonizing.

"Father," Keegan appealed, "how can I give an order to cut my friend in half?" The priest said if he could bring out the man's head and heart and re-turn them to his family, that would be enough comfort. Keegan had to tell him, "That isn't the half we'd be getting."

Keegan remembers the blank stare that came over the priest. He put his arm around Keegan: "I can't help you, son. Whatever decision you make, God will support you."

Keegan sent his men in. Somehow, the torso deflated and the whole body slipped out. "I took that as a sign," Keegan recalled. "Some things are going to work out here."

Chapter Eleven

———

FALLING FROM GRACE

The wives whose husbands *did* come home became a thorn in the sides of those wives whose husbands did not. Immediately after the attacks, the names Planer and Bauer were all over Rumson as missing. Then Bob Planer came home and Dave Bauer did not. Paula Planer knew she had to get up the courage to go over and see Dave's wife, Ginny. "But I was a little frightened," Paula admitted. "Ginny was, well, in high school terms, the popular girl in town. The girl who could do all the sports, who was invited to every party, the girl who had everything. I was just the everyday girl."

GINNY THE BROKER

Ginny Bauer, a whip-slim tennis-playing mother of three adolescents, had grown up in Rumson when it was a small, ingrown town with many families like hers who had been there for generations. Ginny was known as "the popular girl." Ever since fourth grade, she'd had a crush on the biggest boy in class, Dave Bauer, who grew into a six-foot-four, 230-pound linebacker and played pro for the New York Giants. "But he wasn't jocky or mouthy," Ginny said, protesting the stereotype, "he was bright and a little shy." When Dave got a football scholarship to Villanova, Ginny entered a small Catholic girls' college, Rosemont, practically next door. Despite Ginny's protestations to the contrary—"I knew I didn't want to be just a housewife and stay home and take care of my children, I wanted to make a mark"—she married Dave Bauer at twenty-three. They had been life partners for thirty-five years. And theirs was a storybook suburban family life. It was close to a state of grace.

The day after the Cantor Fitzgerald family meeting, Ginny stood framed in the doorway of her Tudor-style mansionette, looking like a page out of *Town & Country* magazine. Appropriately perfect for a matron living on the river side of Rumson, her size-six figure was wrapped in python pants and a silk turtleneck. Her home was being repainted although it already looked meticulous. The first thing Ginny did was to bring out a photograph of Dave.

"Isn't he drop-dead gorgeous?" Her dark brown eyes flooded. "It was too perfect," she confessed, with the apologetic guilt of a Catholic schoolgirl. "I went to Mass every Sunday and I used to pray: *Thank you for Dave and these beautiful kids.* I used to be always afraid, well, not *always,* that something was going to happen, because it was *too* perfect."

She extolled the many talents of her husband. "He was an outstanding athlete. Any sport he played, he played unbelievably, he could beat the pros! And then he became a big success on Wall Street. He did very, very well."

As in any affluent suburb, the social hierarchy is largely established by the status of the husbands. The hard-charging men of Middletown had been climbing toward the crest of their careers in the great towers across the river, while their wives roved around town and over on Rumson Neck watching the "For Sale" signs with an eye toward "trading up."

That Dave Bauer had done very well was evident by Ginny's home and the photos of their family trips and many club activities. But Ginny needed to recite her husband's whole work history to underscore the elevation he had reached. After playing with Kansas City and the Giants, he had gone on to Merrill Lynch, then to Lehman Brothers as a managing director, then to Credit Suisse First Boston as the head of all global sales, and finally, at forty-five, he had been recruited by Cantor to become one of the top executives at its up-and-coming public company, eSpeed. He took a big cut in salary and a lot of stock options, believing it was worth it to get in on the ground floor of the electronic trading business. He had been there exactly one year.

In fact, it was Ginny herself who had set in motion the family's upwardly mobile trajectory. From an entry-level sales position at Merrill Lynch in Red Bank she had talked her way into becoming a broker. Heady stuff. At that time, the late seventies, females in the financial industry were as scarce as Mr. Moms. Ginny still downplayed it: "Selling stock was really easy at that time because rates were high and people trusted their brokers." Her confidence had swelled in her midtwenties. She didn't pretend to be a financial genius, but she didn't have to be; once clients met her, she involved them in a relationship. As she admitted, "I'm a good yapper. By the time I was twenty-six, I was making two hundred thousand a year as a broker for Merrill Lynch. It gives you a good sense of self-worth. I was able to buy us our first house, a four-bedroom in Little Silver."

But the role reversal didn't stick. Too revolutionary, perhaps. While her career was taking off, her new husband was floundering. His pro football career had not worked out. So, when he accompanied his wife as spouse on a sales trip to Puerto Rico, Ginny used her skills as a good yapper to persuade her boss to hire her husband. Dave Bauer drew on his personal charisma and natural salesmanship to become the successful broker in the family, and Ginny Bauer "retired" to tend the home fires.

Sitting demurely in the solarium of her home, she now referred to herself as "a little soapy housewife." That's what being robbed of a spouse by violent death can do to a woman.

Paula Planer had no concept of the pockets of vulnerability that Ginny Bauer might be hiding behind her apparent state of grace. When Paula drove over to Ginny's house on September 12, and circled round her cul-de-sac, and round and round, what she was fretting about was *How does the everyday girl just walk into the popular girl's house? Will she accept me?* Paula had baked chocolate chip cookies but she was so rattled, she had forgotten to put in the chips. She stopped the car and cried.

Ginny could not have been more gracious when she invited Paula inside. Paula sat with her for a couple of hours, not saying much, because they both knew that Dave Bauer was not just still missing. "Ginny, I've only felt I've known you for two hours," Paula said in her gentle, whispery voice. "That's not enough. I know it's not enough. But I do know just a little of what you're going through." Ginny was warm in her thanks. A week later, Paula found a special angel and candle and sent it to Ginny with a personal note. She never heard from Ginny. At a Halloween party a few weeks later, they ran into each other. Ginny looked at Paula, attached to her big, virile, live husband, said a quick hello, and left.

For the bereaved and the survivors of any traumatic disaster, it can take years before they are able to bridge the gulf between their experiences of the same event. The gulf is as big as it gets—the difference between death and life.

SECONDARY LOSSES

The widows' desperation, it now became clear, was not entirely about the loss of their steady cash flow. It was much deeper than that. It was about the loss of self.

If you aren't Ginny, wife of Dave; or Pat, wife of Rod; or Kristen, wife of Ron, then who are you? Along with the loss of identity comes a loss of status. Robert Bellah, the eminent sociologist, observed of Middletown after 9/11: "A bedroom community is no place for young bereaved women. They represent a destabilizing force. They need to become involved in something beyond their kids."

Ordinarily, Middletown is as status conscious as a teenager shopping for jeans. And Rumson, said one of its residents, "is a town made to sow insecurities." The hierarchy of prestige is determined, first, by location. "Girls who live on the river don't give the time of day to the girls like me, who live on the other side," said Paula Planer, who described the archetypal rich Rumson matron like this: "They speak in sweet little breathy voices and have sweet little snub noses and they can stick the dagger in so you don't even *feel* it until the next day."

Being a working mother is definitely not the approved path for women of means in Middletown, or Rumson, or Little Silver. The social pressure is to be a full-time mom and pick up the kids at school and bake homemade goodies for the school bake sales. "The girls" all drive the equivalent of small trucks and, in exchange for the chauffeuring of children and sick dogs and carting bulk household supplies, they often get to spend afternoons at one of the many informal beach clubs that line the shore. Evenings, they welcome the return of adult male company and look forward to feeling completed by a partner many referred to as "my balancing rod."

A curious artifact of Middletown life is the way these women in their thirties and forties and even early fifties still refer to themselves and their suburban peers as "girls." As if they are frozen at the stage of early marriage. In their minds, they are still twenty-eight. Within the confines of their realm, cattiness becomes an art form, only slightly more subtle than the competition of high school girls. "Let's say I'm invited to a party by one of the river girls—the hostess might walk right through me without even saying boo," Paula explained. "Then the next day, a girlfriend who wasn't invited will call me up and pump me: 'Who did you talk to?' When I tell her about being snubbed by the hostess, she'll say, 'Oh, she only likes to talk to *interesting* people.' That's how they do it! That goes straight to my insecurities, and she knows it. Oh, *I'm* not interesting. Just a housewife."

As long as times were generally good, these marginal differentiations were mostly masked. September 11 highlighted the divisions. The actual financial status of each bereaved family became a subject of open conjecture in the community. And the women whose husbands hadn't come home were exposed in a way they never could have anticipated. The newly bereaved half of a socially prominent couple is something of a misfit in the suburbs.

Suddenly, "the girls" had fallen from grace.

But the tragedy also had an important countervailing effect. People in this scattered suburb who might never have come closer than a parking space in a shopping center began to find common bonds. Even to cross the breach. Maybe you never went to the same party with a high-status Rumson girl, but now you shared something much more profound—the humanity stirred by September 11.

PICKING ONESELF UP

As the widows were sucked into the commercial vortex of the Christmas season, most of them focused their fears on their financial plight. Bills were piling up, Red Cross allotments were running out, United Way hadn't yet kicked in, and to get the necessary financial information out of the victims' employers or insurance companies required an exhausting expenditure of the survivors' time and energy. Some threw up their hands. Some had to swallow their pride and fall back on their parents. Some virtually begged. And some, like Ginny Bauer, dug in their heels: nobody was going to tell them to sell their homes or change their lifestyle to make up for the murder of their husbands. These were full-time moms who now had to be full-time dads as well.

A mass psychology seemed to be spreading among the bereaved women that tapped into universal bag lady fears.

Many outsiders asked the same question: *What were the widows of Middletown thinking? Did they have blinders on?* In this day and age, every woman knows her husband can say good-bye at any time. Divorce rates are as high as they have ever been, even for American Catholics. Books and articles have spelled out in real numbers how disastrously income plummets for a stay-at-home mom after divorce. One might assume that every woman in America today recognizes that at some point she might have to support herself.

Ginny Bauer is a template for so many of the widows who had worked in their twenties, usually on Wall Street or in related areas. That was how they'd met their big, handsome, hard-driving husbands. Most of the women were making pretty good money, some doing very well, and they had tasted the nectar of self-reliance. But despite mild feminist protestations about "just getting married," once they did tie the knot, a primal female gene rose to the surface and their outlook changed, radically. They moved to this outer suburb and somewhere along the way misplaced that independent identity in the gently supported hammock of a suburban stay-at-home wife's life. Soccer moms don't need to read *The New York Times* every day, or keep up with politics, or know the ups and downs of their family financial portfolio. The dimensions of their consciousness had shrunk, but not because these women weren't bright or capable; it was because they had slipped back into the old role divisions of the prefeminist nuclear family. So long as their marriages were solid and their husbands moving up on Wall Street, they liked being taken care of. They didn't notice the silent erosion of self-confidence that they could be just as effective outside the domestic realm.

For Ginny Bauer, the loss of self did not hit all at once on that demonic day. At first, she was quite hopeful that Cantor Fitzgerald would come through for its families. She had listened carefully to Howard Lutnick's pitch at his first meeting with the Cantor families of Middletown: He was holding out the promise that 25 percent of Cantor Fitzgerald's profits, which otherwise would be distributed to the company's partners, would be set aside to pay for ten years of health insurance for the victims' families, with any balance distributed equally among the families regardless of the victim's salary or title. But the only way to assure they would ever see that money was to help the company make money.

"I have a vested interest in this company," Ginny said, smiling, diplomatic. "Howard Lutnick did not kill my husband. I'm very cautious about maligning him. I may need him to put food in my kids' mouths. I don't think this is the time to be judgmental. But at the same time, I'm not going to let anybody take advantage of me." She stopped smiling. "I'm not as stupid as I look."

Did she think the government bore any responsibility? She began talking about the tax relief bill that would forgive the families their taxes for 2000 and 2001. The bill was being held up by conservative Republicans.

"If the federal government would pass that tax relief bill, it would be more helpful than anything Cantor Fitzgerald can do," Ginny said. "It could help the families immediately. And the federal government has the bigger obligation in terms of protecting us—for what they didn't do."

A suggestion was made by an outsider: "If you and the other widows of Middletown formed a lobbying group and went to Washington to see members of Congress, you could mobilize the media and have a tremendous impact. But the time to move is soon."

Ginny took in the idea. Within a month of losing her husband, she was back on her game. Actively coping. She started networking in October with friends of New Jersey senator Jon Corzine and was referred to his wife, Joanne. Not fifteen minutes passed after her first call to Joanne Corzine before Ginny picked up the phone in her kitchen.

"Ginny, this is Jon Corzine."

Ginny introduced herself as the wife of Dave Bauer, one of the many New Jersey women made widows by 9/11. "I need your help, Senator. I understand there's a bill before Congress proposing tax relief for the families." Corzine asked if she could meet him at the Molly Pitcher Inn in Red Bank before a Democratic party meeting. She not only met and convinced Corzine to help, she saw her state's other senator walking by and grabbed him. "Senator Torricelli, I need your help."

Once she had both senators and their staffs jumping through hoops for the families, Ginny cast about for anyone who could give her cause national exposure. "I need people in Iowa to understand why this bill is so important to the families," she said. But the media were consumed with the anthrax scare and terrorist alerts; tax legislation was a yawn. She remembered having played tennis with the wife of Geraldo Rivera before the couple had moved out of the area. Again, the wives cooked it up, and on November 13, when Ginny appeared on Geraldo's talk show, the popular host welcomed her with the warmth of a neighbor and gave her forty minutes on national TV to talk about her husband and the widows and the bill. That brought the rest of the media to her door.

Before Thanksgiving, Ginny went nowhere without her portable phone in the nook between her chin and shoulder, calling members of Congress to warn them that "we're active and organized and you've got to help us get this tax relief bill through Congress—before Christmas." By December 5, Ginny Bauer was ready to march on Washington. Politely.

THE WALKING WOUNDED GO TO WASHINGTON

Ginny did not like being a widow. She couldn't stand people feeling sorry for her. And she didn't accept help easily. But now that she had a cause, she was overflowing with energy—the adrenaline-fired, high-test type of energy—and moving, she felt, a hundred miles an hour. "I grabbed some of the local widows—most didn't even know what I was talking about, but they told me, 'Whatever you say, Ginny,' and we went as a group to talk about tax relief." Among the "girls" were Kristen Breitweiser, Patty Casazza, Sheila Martello, Lynn McCabe, Mary Beth Tucker, and others. They were joined by a crew from North Jersey, including the nation's new sweetheart, Lisa Beamer, wife of Todd Beamer, hero of the hijacked plane that had probably been diverted from the White House when he had said to fellow passengers, "Let's roll."

"It's amazing, but I was never nervous," Ginny realized as she dressed that morning in a strictly business herringbone suit. "I still think of myself as a girl from a small town who is relatively unsophisticated, but no one can trip you up if you are who you are. I'm not going down there pretending to be a lawyer or a tax specialist or an accountant. I'm just going to present myself as a woman whose husband was killed on our own soil and all he'd done was go to work that day. I feel one hundred percent confident."

By this time, Democrats and Republicans on Capitol Hill were sparring over who was first and best in responding to the plight of victims' families. The conservative Republican congressman Chris Smith had arranged a meeting with the Jersey delegation of House members. Democratic congressman Dick Gephardt sat with the widows on his couch and lent a sympathetic ear. Trent Lott, the Mississippi conservative and Republican Senate leader whose head seemed as big as his big hair, condescended to the widows. "He treated us like ditzy little lipstick housewives, coming into the big Texas Senate leader's office," groused Ginny. But the big fish was Dennis Hastert, Speaker of the House, a name new to most of the widows.

Ginny was in the lead, streaking across the Capitol's marble rotunda pitched forward on a thirty-degree angle like the hood ornament on a Jaguar. Right behind her was a long gray column of grim-faced widows, all headed for Hastert's well-hidden office. They were escorted like royalty into his bright yellow conference room. Beginning with Kristen, the widows told their emotional stories. They said their children didn't want them to leave to go to Washington, afraid that Mommy, like Daddy, wouldn't come back. They said they'd had no peace of mind to grieve. Couldn't the Speaker bring to the floor—before Christmas—the legislation that would forgive their taxes for two years?

Hastert listened impassively. The group got little but formalities: "Okay, well, we appreciate you coming down." Tough cookie, some decided, feeling it hadn't gone well. But Ginny Bauer lingered. Leaning straight into the Speaker's rugged face, she brought her old powers as a "good yapper" to bear on one of the most powerful elected officials in Washington:

"Mr. Speaker, I feel this is something our government can do to allow us to exhale—it would give the families a little breathing room until the insurance claims and estates can be settled and we see what's going to happen with the Victim Compensation Fund." What Ginny wanted to say was: *How can you object to a bill for women whose husbands were killed on American soil? I don't want to start pointing fingers, but all our systems failed on that day.* She didn't have to say it; Hastert was savvy enough to pick it up from the room's tone when all the widows had been there. As he ushered out Ginny Bauer, he told her, "We'll get this bill done for you."

Kristen and Patty got lost on the way to see Hillary Clinton. But they came out of that meeting with stars in their eyes. "God, is she *smart*," exclaimed Kristen. "She has this senator thing *down*." "Did you notice her suit—she matched her wallpaper!" said Patty. "She looks like a magazine layout." Kristen, whose mate had been a rabid Republican, quipped, "My husband would turn over, *if* he's in his grave."

That was probably the only moment of levity on the widows' maiden trip to Washington. Kristen and Sheila Martello stayed over to confront Kenneth Feinberg. The high-powered Washington attorney had been named by the Justice Department the "special master," imbued with Solomonic powers to determine compensation for the families of victims. But that night, paranoia ruled. The two moms wrote letters to their toddlers, because they didn't know if they would be coming back.

"Mommy went down to Washington to protect people. She didn't want anything to happen, but if you're reading this . . ." That kind of end-of-life letter. Kristen signed off with "I love you and I'll always love you. I'm with Daddy now."

But for all their inner fears, the effect of their maiden journey to Washington was powerful and potentiating for those widows who made it. They had gotten back up on the horse, and they hadn't fallen off again. Although they were scarcely aware of it, out of the void the silhouettes of a new identity were beginning to form.

GINNY BAUER'S OLDEST CHILD, David, named for his father and possessing the same quiet brand of strength, was only sixteen when he lost his dad. But Ginny knew he would feel the terrifying weight of responsibility to take on the mantle of man of the family. Right after his father's memorial service, she had told him, "Dave, you don't have to fill Daddy's shoes. You can grow into them eventually, but for now just stay in boarding school and be a good student and continue with your sports. We're going to be fine."

Fine? How could her children be sure? Since they had known her only as an at-home mom who made their lives run like clockwork, but who rarely engaged in public life beyond doing benefits, they were uncertain of how this "little soapy housewife," as she had seen herself, could make things fine in the absence of a father who was larger than life. Then they began to see their mom on television. They heard her on the portable phone talking to people with big titles in Washington, even as she was pouring the steaming pasta into the colander. This was a Ginny they didn't know. Sometimes, her rapid-fire rap scared the hell out of them. Mostly, they were surprised and impressed. The House finally followed the Senate and passed the tax relief bill in January. Ginny Bauer, once the popular girl, became a very popular woman around Rumson and Middletown. But the moment of sublime delight was yet to come. Ginny was invited to meet President Bush in the East Room for a photo op as he signed the bill. Her son David was a little shy at first, but when he stepped up to shake hands with Bush, Ginny had to smile. Her son was a half foot taller than the president of the United States.

Twanging the chords of Texas paternalism, Bush said to the sixteen-year-old, "Take care of your momma, son."

"I will, sir," David Bauer said, and added firmly, "But would you just get him? Get Osama."

President Bush looked the young man in the eyes and said, "We will."

Chapter Twelve

"AM . . . I . . . GOING . . . CRAZY?"

That was the terrifying question brought by some of the new widows and distraught parents to the first support groups in Middletown. Three months after the trauma, they found themselves still emotionally numb, often sleepless, melancholy, ill-tempered, anxious, jumpy, and constantly on alert. They floated through some days like zombies and other days bounced off the walls in hyperactivity. They repeatedly relived the experience, through dreams or nightmares, or in flashbacks as they woke up or after they had too much to drink. Anything that reminded them of that day—a smell, a sound, an uninvited rerun of the Towers falling when they flipped on the TV—could trigger the same emotional state and physical sensations they felt that day: sweating, chest pain, numbness, tingling, or global dread. Were they going crazy?

They weren't any crazier than many other Americans.

Several months after September 11, in a representative national sample of Americans surveyed by the University of California at Irvine, a majority of Americans from all over the country reported having the *very same reactions.* According to *The New England Journal of Medicine,* among the millions who lived in the New York or Washington, D.C., area, up to 90 percent registered acute stress reactions in the first three months, and of those, 20 to 30 percent were expected to develop chronic post-traumatic stress disorder. But even among Americans who were at some distance from the attacks and had lost no one close, *NEJM* estimated that 50 to 70 percent experienced acute stress reactions over the first three months. The UC-Irvine study found that stressful effects continued throughout the country among individuals not directly affected up to *six months* after. Sixty percent of them reported being scared that harm would come to their families in the future as a result of terrorism.

What made just as great and lingering an impact on so many people was watching the attacks live on TV—as 60 percent of Americans did—or seeing them replayed over and over in the following days. Given the saturation of our culture with disturbing news footage, this event, along with the assassination of President John F. Kennedy, was as close to a universal American experience of national trauma as any in our history.

Stress response is not the same as mental illness. Most Americans had a *normal* trauma response to a highly abnormal national trauma. For example, in the first few months many people engaged in what psychologists call avoidance behavior—staying away from tall buildings or postponing plans to fly, and trying to avoid triggers or TV replays that would cause them to think about or relive the attacks. For example, Bob Planer's proposal to his board that they move the company out of Manhattan, where he had twice narrowly escaped death by terrorism, was a natural avoidance response.

Most researchers didn't know what to make of the mental health emergency that was thrust upon them. They knew about post-traumatic stress disorder. PTSD is a pathological diagnosis clearly defined in the psychiatric literature. Criteria include direct exposure to one or more traumatic events that threaten death or serious injury to oneself or others, and stress symptoms severe enough after six months to impair one's ability to function.

"Let's wait before we start talking about PTSD," cautioned Rachel Yehuda, professor of psychiatry and director of the traumatic stress studies division at Mt. Sinai School of Medicine. "Trauma happens to all of us, but we are generally well equipped to deal with the aftermath." As one of the rare researchers who can claim to be an expert in the field of trauma studies, Dr. Yehuda emphasized that people are changed by trauma, but not all changes are bad. Those who are quick to pathologize trauma miss the life-defining growth that can be provoked in people by watershed events.

The most provocative conclusion in the UC-Irvine study was this: the way people handled the abnormal stresses of a traumatic event *in the first few weeks* had the greatest impact on how quickly they regained equilibrium or how severely they would suffer from long-term distress. And surprisingly, people who used good coping strategies soon after the attacks were consistently stronger and more effective in bouncing back regardless of their demographic status or whether they'd had previous trauma.

People who focused on a specific coping strategy were consistently better able to work through the stress and integrate the new realities. They concentrated their efforts on trying to do something to improve the situation, what psychologists call active coping. There were many ways that Americans tried to actively cope—giving blood, collecting money or supplies, reaching out to comfort those whose loved ones were missing, organizing grassroots volunteer efforts, writing poems or prose or music, helping children to make cards for rescue workers.

In fact, the study found that actively coping in the immediate aftermath of the attacks was the *only* strategy that appeared to be protective against ongoing distress, apart from acceptance—but typically, acceptance of the altered reality takes longer than six months. The positive effects of actively coping or accepting held true even after adjusting for all relevant demographics and for pre–September 11 mental and physical health status. Overall, women registered greater anxiety than men in the first weeks, but they also used better coping strategies than men.

WIDOWS' WAYS OF COPING

What is fascinating and useful is to match up the findings of this study against the real-life stories of the Middletown families. What allows some people to be resilient even in the face of severe trauma while others are not? The amazing thing is how well so many of those directly affected did cope—actively—even in the first months, without turning in droves to doctors or psychotropic drugs.

Kristen Breitweiser was one of the first widows to engage in active coping. She began as early as October to communicate with Washington power brokers on behalf of the families. When she read about the Department of Justice naming a "special master" who would in his singular wisdom decide what compensation to give the families, it set her blood to a low boil. Why should the families all just sit back and let the government decide what they deserved as compensation for having their lives smashed? Where had the government and all its agencies and armed forces been on September 11? Kristen couldn't get out of her mind the TV image of President Bush sitting in a Florida classroom, reading with second graders, *after* his chief of staff had whispered in his ear that a second plane had hit the Towers and the country was under attack. Her husband was in that second tower, maybe jumping, maybe waiting to be burned alive. Why wasn't the commander in chief on the phone with the air force making sure planes were scrambling to avert any further attacks?

So, on November 21, Kristen and a few other Monmouth County widows rallied the bereaved families of New Jersey to a meeting in the sterile lobby of an office building in Tinton Falls to hear about the compensation plan the federal government was preparing to offer. Wearing her husband's sport jacket, Kristen rose before an audience of more than a hundred poker-faced family members, many of whom had scarcely ventured out of their homes—their only "safe place"—until that night. "I just want you guys to know that we're all here together, and we need to fall in together and get our voices heard," she said. The Justice Department had set a deadline of five days hence for comments on their plan. Kristen urged the families to write their comments on forms being passed around. She promised that she and her core group of widows would spend the weekend in her kitchen consolidating their concerns in one document, which they would make certain was hand-delivered to Justice before the deadline.

"It is the families who have the power right now," she assured them. "The Justice Department, the president, the Congress, they're looking to us now, because we are the only ones in our shoes."

Ginny Bauer, the onetime broker, had rediscovered her gift as a natural "yapper" within one month of the attacks. By taking the lead in going to Washington to lay the groundwork for the widows' campaign on tax relief, and later giving press conferences and appearing on TV, Ginny was beginning to regain a sense of self that had dissipated from lack of necessity. In January, when the bill she had championed was signed by George Bush and she was kissed by the president on national TV, her children were stunned. It gave them confidence that their mother could hold things together even without their father.

Karen Cangialosi's way of actively coping was to assume her husband's mantle as the family's head coach. Only a few weeks after 9/11, she took on the fund-raiser for her son's traveling baseball team. She determined to learn the players and the terminology so she could talk boy-talk with her sons, not only about baseball, but about pro football as well. First, she had to find someone to teach her how to throw!

The number of prior traumatic events in one's life was not found by the UC-Irvine study to be associated with the severity of symptoms—with one exception: people who had suffered a traumatic event in the immediately previous year were likely to be already carrying an overall high distress level and, although it might sound odd, they would often express less concern than others about 9/11.

Sherry McHeffey, the silvery-blond grieving mother, for example, was already walking around with an open wound before the terrorist attack took down her only son. The trauma of being abandoned by her husband of thirty-two years had been the greatest shock of her life—and that had happened only nine months before September 11. She had come home from sitting with his dying mother to find her husband in a romantic phone conversation with another woman. He had left the next day.

"It hit me big time." Sherry grimaced with the still-fresh pain. "It's primal, isn't it—the fear of abandonment? His leaving left such a hole in my life, but my son Keith had tried his hardest to fill it." As she recalled that period, a smile came over her face. "Keith called me every day at work and stopped by at night, even if it was just to check the basement for rainwater. He and his two sisters and I were moving toward forming a new family. And then—"

When Sherry recovered her composure, she made an admission that startled even her. "My husband's leaving me was harder for me to handle than Keith's death. It was an absolute rejection, whereas I know Keith would never have left me."

Dr. Roxane Cohen Silver, a research psychologist with two decades of traumatic bereavement research behind her, was the one who launched the intelligent, longitudinal study at UC-Irvine—the only study of reactions to 9/11 that has pre–9/11 data and that is *ongoing.* Sherry McHeffey's response rang a bell with the psychologist from an earlier study she had done with senior citizens in which they were asked to cite the worst event of their long lives. Looking at the list of traumas generated by the participants—from having a spouse die in a car accident to being given a diagnosis of terminal cancer—the researchers themselves had argued over which was worst; it wasn't at all obvious. But a number of the senior citizens said it was having a spouse "desert" them. "That was how they phrased it, 'desert,' " says Dr. Silver, "and no matter what age they were when it happened, that was the worst event of their lives."

Despite her double traumas, Sherry McHeffey did not give up trying to cope. Shortly after holding a memorial for her son, she went back to work at the university where she had been a secretary for the past eight years. "I work with about eighteen other women," she says, "and they saved my life. I could come in and stare at my keyboard all day, they were that supportive." Just as important in her coping style was this attitude: "I try to look for the positive. It's almost as though my husband's leaving had a purpose to it—to bring us all closer as a family before Keith was taken."

Active coping also worked to counteract feelings of helplessness among

Middletowners who hadn't lost a family member. The town fathers and mothers who stepped up to the emergency from the very first day—people like Rabbi Levin and Reverend Musgrove, nurse Eileen Theall and Father Kevin Keelan, Police Chief Pollinger and County Prosecutor Honecker— these were the emergent leaders, people whose own distress was minimized by their concern about and competency in helping others.

Lieutenant Bill Keegan was an example of active coping under nearly impossible circumstances. When he was faced with the impossible choice between risking his men to retrieve the dead bodies of two of his fellow police officers and giving up on recovering them, Keegan felt "zapped right out of myself." This is a normal response to acute stress. Trauma experts call it dissociation. Typical symptoms are numbness, feeling dazed, and not feeling like yourself. It is particularly common among rescue workers and EMTs, who tend to ignore their stress because they *want* to be at the trauma scene and are focused on getting the job done. But Keegan returned to a focus on the reality and summarily made a decision. His decisiveness was rewarded with success, which gave him hope that something good would come out of his work at Ground Zero.

GIVING UP OR GETTING OUT

Certain weaker coping strategies, assessed shortly after the attacks by the UC-Irvine study, were the strongest predictors of later lingering problems. Least effective was disengaging from the situation. Not trying to do anything active, not seeking social support, checking out or turning off, was the strongest predictor of post-traumatic stress disorder in future. An "early giving up" response has also signaled severe negative consequences on physical health over time, among breast and prostate cancer patients and among gay men with HIV infection. It is particularly harmful in the face of any ongoing threat.

One Middletown widow kept inviting people over to talk, then canceling and apologizing, "I'm not doing well." Within the first few weeks, she took to her bed, sick, and waited for her son to come home from school and take care of her. She was apparently "giving up" on trying to cope, and assuming the identity of victim. Her son began having problems at school and withdrew from his friends.

Children's ways of coping follow closely the example set by the surviving parent. When the widow's son was injured in an accident, suddenly he became the designated "baby," and now his mother had to wait on him. The two traded this position back and forth for the next few months, in what seemed to be shaping up as a codependent coping style.

Pat Wotton sent out "take care of me" signals from the beginning. She had good reason, being pregnant when her husband was killed and delivering a baby with serious problems who was kept away from her during those first crucial weeks of mother-infant bonding. Pat refused antidepressant medication and became clinically depressed. She would "space out" for long periods. Her parents and older sister assumed the responsibility for taking care of her and her two children. As Pat became more and more dependent on others, she gave up trying to cope.

Mary Murphy, the former Cantor trader, was also pregnant when her husband disappeared from her life. She had two other young children at home and parents who lived in the Midwest. But her instinct was the opposite of passivity. She turned the darkness of emotion into motion. *Drive. I'll just get in the car with the kids and drive somewhere.* It didn't matter so much where, what mattered was being in motion. "I just wanted to get the hell away from the dark cloud over Middletown," she said.

So, six weeks after the attacks, Mary Murphy strapped her two-year-old son, Jimmy, and her four-year-old daughter, Morgan, into the back of the SUV, packed the CD player with children's songs, put a pillow behind her back as a counterweight to her five-months-pregnant belly, and swung out on the turnpike headed for Colorado, where her sister lived. She stopped off in Cincinnati to pick up her mother. From there, the two women traded off tending the children and commandeering the wheel. Right from the start, mother and daughter were empowering each other to keep moving forward.

Anna Egan also appeared to be "giving up" on trying to cope in the first few months. "Right now, my life is on hold," she said in December. She had relied heavily on her CEO husband to make most decisions beyond the care of their two boys. She had the constant stress of caring for a retarded teenage boy. But Anna had insisted that her other son, who had just departed for college on the West Coast, stick it out there. So here she was, alone in the half-empty trophy house in a town where she knew not a soul, and where a previous traumatic accident rendered her incapable of driving on busy highways. Waiting for her needy son to come home from high school.

Anna Egan kept reliving the nightmare of 9/11. "It's like watching a sci-fi movie. You're watching the replay of that plane coming in, and you want to hold out your hand and grab him out of the tower—but there's nothing you can do. You hold your breath and say, 'No, this is not happening, it's not possible,' and you hear him say in a rush, 'I love you, darling,' and the line drops—" Her sobs punctuated her continuing narration; she was stuck there. "I know there will never be anything found of Michael, because we were on the phone together that's part of the nightmare. I literally see him burning up. And I see him falling."

It was December, and Anna still could not escape that agonizing flashback. "I'm nervous. I'm scared something may happen again. Not for myself so much as for my sons. . . . I haven't gotten to the anger stage yet," she continued wistfully. "I'm still in too much pain." There was guilt, too. Because of the move to the trophy house, Matthew was severely regressing in school. "This was a kid who had been independent, running errands by himself and flying back and forth to Canada alone," she said. "And now the school here tells me he needs a chaperone to go to the bathroom and that he can't order his own food!"

But at this point, Anna did not have what it took to fight Matthew's battles. She had all she could do to attend memorials in New York City for her husband's employees. Every time she went in, she would have a panic attack: *I have to get back to Middletown in time for Matthew's homecoming from school!* After a while she stopped going to memorials. Stopped going anywhere. Stopped. Anna, too, sometimes wondered if she was going crazy.

FINDING A NEW "FAMILY"

The sheer scale of this event made a mockery of mental health disaster plans at the county, state, and even federal levels. The limitations of practitioners' experience with a mass murder of such magnitude quickly became apparent. There were actually therapists wandering into firehouses in New York and offering to write prescriptions for antianxiety drugs on the spot—probably as much to soothe their own anxieties—but they were mostly rebuffed.

Scarcely any Middletowners sought out psychosocial support in the first couple of months, much to the dismay of local mental health professionals, who felt powerless to help. Maureen Fitzsimmons did not let the initial disinterest stop her from offering support groups as early as October. The tall, straight-backed seasoned professional counselor was program director for Catholic Charities in Monmouth County, and United Way had awarded the contract to Catholic Charities to provide behavioral health services in the Middletown area. Fitzsimmons's idea was: Put out the word, and if they're ready, they'll come.

Five and a half weeks later, to her amazement, her conference rooms were filled with widows. "They were so traumatized, they were certainly nowhere near beginning the grieving process," acknowledged Fitzsimmons. But the word of mouth spread, and parents began to come, then adolescents. "There's something about three months that we have found in studying the grief process," said the counselor. "People tend to take a dive there, at ninety days. With all the confusion about whether victims were lost or gone, and the delayed onset of grief, I wondered if the same timetable would hold up. Well, let me tell you, week twelve arrived and our telephone began to ring off the hook."

Traumatic grief is very different from grief that is not accompanied by shock and trauma. What happens in trauma is chaos. People become disoriented. They have trouble finding a new path. They must find a new "family," because in many ways they are now misfits in their old family constellations or communities. The new family is not based on blood ties or defined by geography; it is an *intentional family* made up of people who understand what they are going through—either because they have been through it themselves, or because they are willing to walk the journey with the newly traumatized through the wilderness of grief, without judging them.

By December, there were ten in the widows' support group, another twelve in the parents' support group. Family members who found their way into support groups had a different profile from those who went to Washington to make their case. Some of the former were critical of the activists for being "so angry." Mostly, the widows in the support groups were reluctant to "waste time" focusing on themselves. They could give themselves permission to meet once a week. But grieving was a luxury for which they had little if any time. Who had time to grieve when there were endless forms to fill out, financial records to find, phone calls to make to lawyers and accountants and insurance agents and funds and government agencies, and frustrations to tame while sitting through endless computerized answer trees designed to make you lose patience and hang up? Who had time to grieve when there were parents who decamped in your home, and who needed hands-on assistance to operate your shower and oven and driving directions for every shopping trip? As necessary as was the help of parents, it was yet another frustration for the wives to be placed back in the child's role. Scar tissue covering the narcissistic wounds of childhood peeled off, and suddenly some mothers and daughters were snapping at each other as if they were locked back in the endless battle of adolescence.

Initially, the widows who sought out support groups had to overcome yet another assault to their personal identity. "I can't walk into a social agency, like some welfare case," as one said. "That's not who I am." These were women for the most part accustomed to selling raffle tickets or attending black-tie dinners to raise money to help *others*. They had never seen the inside of a charity office. Catholic Charities in Red Bank is in a historic house, its waiting room warm and plain and slightly shabby. It is a tribute to the staff that within a very short time, any embarrassment about being seen there evaporated. The support groups offered a new "family." This is a critical element in the comeback process.

"We have a group of girls, ten of us that lost their husbands," Mary Murphy observed in December. "It *is* helpful. . . . Some days you go and you cry the whole time. Some days you go and you get some good laughs. It's just comforting to be around people who are feeling pretty much exactly what you are." Everyone in the group was naturally a "sister," by virtue of sharing the same unique trauma and tragedy. No one would be judgmental. No one would dare spill a confidence. It was also a safe place to unload their anger. One facilitator opened a widows' support group by going around the circle to elicit Potato Head awards for the most insensitive things people had said to them:

"Everything happens for a purpose." (What is the purpose of mass murder—population control?)

"God doesn't give you more than you can handle." (So, God is a benign terrorist?)

"You've had the memorial, isn't it time to get on with it?" (Sorry, it took me a year to get over my dog dying.)

"You should try to find closure." (That word should be banned.)

"It's for the best." (I'd hate to think what the worst might be.)

Laughter broke the ice. Often, such remarks would be made by a mother or mother-in-law, or friends who were tongue-tied by the trauma themselves. Making fun of these well-meaning but hurtful remarks became a way of bonding within the group.

But support groups don't work for everybody.

One hazard of support groups is that they can reinforce the sense of victimization. People can lock themselves inside the group and away from the rest of the world, condemning everyone outside for being hopelessly unable to understand the misery shared by the members. But the "misery loves company" motif only serves to increase isolation and drive away other family members and friends who could extend one's support network.

Mary Murphy did not make that mistake. She attended a lecture series on bereavement given by a Red Bank teacher, Mary Logan, through the John

Day Funeral Homes. She learned a great deal about how to find some peace. "With a violent death, you have to concentrate on the fact that it happened, and not *how* it happened," Mary remarked. "I did that for a long time— imagining what happened to him. It's heartbreaking. It can really bring you down. And I don't want that to be my final image of him. So what I'm trying to do is concentrate on the fact that it happened. And accept that."

Some of the Middletown widows were adamant about *not* turning for support to a group "and sitting around crying," imagining the exercise to be wimpy and depressing. But that attitude did not prevent the more activist personalities from finding their own new families, too. Kristen Breitweiser's early activism, for example, introduced her to other actively coping widows in nearby towns. Gradually, as they worked together, and got to know one another's children, and e-mailed one another in the depths of despairing nights, they, too, began to form the bonds of a new family.

Fitzsimmons was receiving desperate calls from veteran funeral directors who pleaded they didn't know what to do. The New York medical examiner's office was calling to notify them about finding body parts; should they tell the families? suggest a burial? "We were all spinning," confessed Fitzsimmons, "but somehow, through it all, we seemed to be moving. If there was one central lesson that I learned, it's that there is no hierarchy in handling a traumatic event. We were all in this together, all facing this great unknown together, and we had to help each other to heal."

REACHING BEYOND THE WIDOWS

Dr. Mary Ann Cernak was as flustered as everyone else. She held the title of "disaster coordinator" for Monmouth County. New Jersey had taken roughly one quarter of the World Trade Center deaths, the greatest number in Monmouth County. FEMA (Federal Emergency Management Agency) was funding a mental health response county by county, but in order to qualify for a grant, Cernak had to identify the groups most at risk. She came up with six. The most obvious were people who had experienced the trauma directly, as escapees from the Towers or bereaved family members. The second group was rescue, recovery, and construction workers at the site. Third were mental health personnel, who would be exposed to secondary trauma. Then came the children and the elderly, and finally the eyewitness survivors.

"We are looking at thousands of people impacted, and we estimate that twenty-five percent of them will experience PTSD," Dr. Cernak predicted in December 2001. "We have a marathon to run, and very few experienced runners. Normally, we would look to New York for mental health personnel, but New York is tapped out."

Predictions of vast waves of psychopathology did not materialize, at least not at the three-month mark. "The people who called mental health professionals in the first weeks and months after 9/11 were actually the healthy ones," said Dr. Yehuda. "The people you worry about are those who are vulnerable but who aren't seeking treatment." Ordinarily, the process of working through a trauma takes from one to six months. It is believed that once post-traumatic stress reactions become chronic, the symptoms linger, on average, for up to seven years. With the unprecedented nature of 9/11, given all the unanswerable questions, missing bodies, and media saturation, clinicians tended to predict that post-traumatic stress responses could not be called pathological for at least nine months or maybe a year.

Prolonged stress does change the brain and alter the body's chemistry. Trauma experts argue over which methods of treatment are most effective in treating PTSD, but on one point most emphatically agree: the longer one waits to get help with chronic post-traumatic stress, the harder it is to get over it. Dr. Spencer Eth, professor and vice chairman of psychiatry at St. Vincent's Hospital, is still seeing survivors of the 1993 Trade Center bombing. "They didn't seek treatment or they didn't get good treatment at the time, and they didn't get better," he said. Some of these survivors and witnesses have gotten much worse in the aftermath of 9/11.

The old models weren't much help in predicting the longer-term outcome of different coping styles. The journey through traumatic grief is highly variable. People generally fall back on the coping mechanisms they have used in past times of crisis, which might be inadequate or even counterproductive under the extreme demands of catastrophe. The most active copers among the Middletown families in the first months feared they might crash later on, and their fears were not without foundation. Once hyperactivity wears a person out, the terrible feelings are still there, and there is no way around them except to go through them.

The rubber would not meet the road before the end of the first year.

PASSAGE TO THE NEW NORMAL

Without question, a trauma of this magnitude is a life-altering event for many people, and not just those directly impacted. As the deeper consequences of this national trauma began to unfold, people of all ages and in all parts of the country struggled with new fears and frustrations. We had left behind a world we knew and had been thrust headlong into a new world, without precedent or preparation. Somehow, we had to come to terms with the fact that we, too, live in a world of horror. Simultaneously, we needed to go on living with hope, freedom, and faith in the future. Those are two contradictory ideas. The struggle to compose that contradiction presented every one of us with an existential passage.

First, we had to rethink our views of self and others. Many people reported feeling a need to be close to those they cared about—their families and friends—or the need to "get back in touch" with important people in their lives—old classmates or colleagues or family members from whom they had become estranged. Relationships that were toxic or held together only by convenience or passivity needed reexamination in light of this crude reminder of our mortality. Fair-weather friends were exposed, while compassionate support poured in from surprising places. On an institutional level, churches and schools, law enforcement and health agencies, were put to the test. How well do our communities function under duress? Are we really our brother's keeper, after all? Were Americans likely to stigmatize all Arabs as suspected terrorists? Would the terrorists be successful in stirring up a new crusade of vengeance between Muslims and Christians?

Our concept of time was also shaken. Whether young, age-defying middle-aged, or healthy old, we had to give more thought to the possibility that our lives might suddenly go up in smoke. That forced a reassessment of our priorities. If you only had another year to live . . . fill in the blank.

Our perceptions of the ratio of safeness and danger in our daily lives were under constant assault, with warnings to "be vigilant" becoming normal background noise. A new government department was proposed to deal with "homeland security," even as our existing security agencies were forewarning that they could not be expected to stave off future terrorist attacks, which were deemed inevitable. In other words, no matter what our age, we were all called upon to accept a truth that most people never face until middle age: There is no one who will always be able to take care of us.

And finally, the brightness of our natural American optimism now had to incorporate the dark side. There was a price to be paid for being the sole superpower in a newly unipolar world. We would be hated by millions of people we didn't know and hadn't harmed.

These new truths would need to be gradually integrated into our worldview. This is what I mean by the national passage to the New Normal. Each of us, whatever our stage of development, had to work at adopting a post–9/11 psyche.

Chapter Thirteen

COMFORTING THE CHILDREN

Everyone's first concern was how to help the children of Middletown deal with death. Who knew what to do? There was a run at local bookstores on titles like *Guiding Your Child Through Grief,* and a new one by Harvard bereavement expert Phyllis Rolfe Silverman, *Never Too Young to Know.* "Contemporary child psychology largely ignores . . . death and grief, and their impact on childhood," writes Professor Silverman. But even these worthy books concentrate on familiar kinds of death. They don't discuss how children deal with mute mass murder. September 11 was a case study both unwelcome and uniquely valuable. It could teach us much about how children of different ages experience loss and how best to prolong healthy attachment to a deceased parent.

But for Middletown's parents and teachers, school principals and social welfare authorities, the need to know was now. They would have to fly by the seat of their pants.

TEACHERS AS HEROES

Karen Cangialosi, the aerobics instructor, spread out her paperwork on the steps of her children's school. It was only 2:20. Her sons, Jeffrey and Peter, wouldn't be coming out until three, but Karen had been arriving early every day because the principal let her use the Xerox machine. She was constantly copying death certificates.

"I just don't know how many more times I can fill out these forms," she said.

But almost from the first week, Karen had beavered away at the paperwork, whittling down the piles of forms and claims and stockpiling books on financial planning. Offers of professional accounting assistance had been extended by colleagues of her husband, but Karen politely declined. "I want to learn how to manage my family's financial affairs by myself," she would say, then demur, "My sons worry that I can't do it alone." Karen had cleared off her husband's desk and set up her own files. She had sought out a financial adviser to teach her how to manage a portfolio and invest for the future. And while she hardly found it pleasurable or distracting, after making dinner and settling her boys down to sleep, to sit down and focus on insurance claims and workers' comp and death certificates, unbeknownst to her, Karen was doing the best thing she could do to overcome trauma.

Actively coping.

From time to time, when she had to make a decision about where to invest, after "consulting" her husband—that is, drawing upon the conservative philosophy they shared—she knew what he would do. There would be a little buzz of anxiety plus exhilaration: "I did it!" But she hadn't had time to seek any emotional help or to expand her support network beyond her family.

Karen had taken her boys away to Vermont for the Thanksgiving holiday and they had loved playing in a tree house and biking the hills with their cousins. Karen had hated it. Every minute of it. Hated sleeping in a room alone.

Normally, in a community as heavily Catholic as Middletown, the primary burden of comforting the children would be borne by the Church fathers. But as Karen said, "It's so crazy around here, with so many people dead and so many families needing help, the priests are inundated." "You have good children," Reverend Monsignor Rebeck had told her. "They had a good father. You want them to be good men." To carry the burden of that charge, all alone, made her weak in the knees. Sitting on the steps of her son's school, she wept.

Then ten-year-old Jeffrey appeared at the door, chin up, chest out, proud of his role as hall monitor, who would hold open the door for the other children—a little man.

The one person Karen counted on more than any other to help share her new responsibilities was the school principal, Dr. Antonia Martinez. A dignified, diminutive woman of unusual sensitivity, Dr. Martinez had given twenty-five years of service in Middletown's schools. As the principal of Middletown Village Elementary School, one of twelve neighborhood elementaries in the district, the greatest crisis she had known was the teachers' strike of 1998. The schools had remained open, but the threat of children having to cross picket lines had kept teachers and parents tense.

MOVING TO MIDDLETOWN? THINK TWICE!

That was a billboard erected by the teachers' union during the '98 strike. "It was a very ugly experience," Dr. Martinez recalled. "But it pales in comparison to September eleventh. People look to the schools for guidance in difficult times."

At nine o'clock on that September 11, 2001, the children had been making announcements over the PA system, as usual, followed by the Pledge of Allegiance and the singing of a patriotic song. As soon as Dr. Martinez heard news of the second crash, what flashed through her mind was the many children whose parents worked in the Trade Center area, and the many teachers who were close to firemen and Port Authority police. She remembered that one of her young teachers had gone into New York that morning to shop for her wedding gown. The principal walked outside for a moment. She could smell the burning and see smoke.

After saying a prayer, she instructed herself, "Keep a cool head." Everybody who looked at her face would read from it, and how she behaved would cue them how they should behave. She snapped into action, making crucial decisions and communicating with her teachers by hand-delivered memos:

> *Dear Staff,*
>
> *Apparently the situation with the World Trade Center has escalated.*
>
> *I will try to keep you quickly informed of anything that affects us directly. For now, the most important thing we can do is to stay calm and to keep the children busy.*
>
> *The building is locked down. Please do not go outside today. Our advice to parents is that children are safe and calm with us, and that is where they should remain.*
>
> *Thank you for your cooperation. Pray.*
>
> *Antonia*

Elsewhere in the district, panic was spreading. Parents were pulling their children out of schools. Dr. Martinez met every parent who showed up at the Village School with reassurance and support. The children knew nothing, she told them. The school day would proceed as usual. She said she thought it was important that each family take time to compose its own way of explaining the tragedy of our nation to its children, once they got home. The parents trusted her, and they left their children with her. She set up an informal network of parent volunteers to give messages of reassurance by phone. When it came time for dismissal, she had her staff personally escort the children into their parents' safekeeping or onto the school buses, having forewarned the drivers to turn off their radios.

"We waited outside for our children, all of us with broken hearts and tears in our eyes," wrote one parent in a letter of praise for Dr. Martinez and her teachers. "When those children exited the building with smiles on their little faces, for one brief moment it made you forget."

Antonia Martinez was one of those creative and compassionate people who found extraordinary capacities of leadership when tested by that most tragic of days. She was not a professional therapist or guidance counselor; her academic training was in the sciences. But as Karen Cangialosi assessed from the start of the crisis, "Antonia just had it in her soul."

Her example inspired Karen, whose boys were the only ones in the school to lose a parent. "Karen was wonderful about sending the two boys to school right from the first day after the eleventh," Dr. Martinez was proud to say. "She made the decision that routine would be good for them." Karen loved all the teachers at the Village School and thought Antonia Martinez was the finest principal a parent could ask for. What better gift could anyone offer her boys in that time of chaos than routine?

On September 12, Antonia Martinez wrote out some guidelines for her staff and teachers:

> *Children will be anxious about your reaction. Keep the routine you've already established. A sense of order and continuity is important to reassure children.*
>
> *Be ready to discuss what happened. If you can guide the children to express what they know, give them facts, and validate their emotions, they will learn from you how to cope with disaster. Some thoughts: A bad thing happened. We don't know why it happened. The persons responsible are bullies. We are safe here. . . .*
> *Antonia*

On the thirteenth Dr. Martinez set up a penny collection for monies to be given to the Red Cross. By the next day, her children had collected $400, plus a load of socks and sweatpants for the volunteers. They were excited about being helpful, the best antidote to the sense of helplessness many were feeling vicariously from the adults at home. The principal's next immediate concern was that fear not turn into racial or ethnic scapegoating. There were four Muslim children in the school. She asked teachers to be careful not to characterize all Middle Eastern people as being like the terrorists. She suggested that if questions about Muslims came up, they use an existing program called "It's Okay to Be Different."

Antonia Martinez continued to write to her parents, finding it also therapeutic for her, personally. It was her way of actively coping, and her way of connecting with a new, extended family.

The toughest task for Antonia was to talk to Peter Cangialosi's second-grade class about the fact that his father had died. She knew that many of these youngsters had never dealt with the death of anyone they knew, but she wanted to use the tragedy, again, as a teaching opportunity. On the day Peter and his older brother, Jeffrey, were out of school to attend their dad's memorial, Antonia stood before the seven-year-olds. She began pedaling around the word "death." The teacher glared at her until she forced out the words:

"Peter's dad died. He's going to be sad. Let's talk about things you can do when you're a good friend and care about somebody and they're sad because they've had a loss." The children came up with suggestions: "You could cry with them." "You could keep on asking them to come out and play even if they don't feel like it." Antonia endorsed their ideas. The children made cards and pictures to express their friendship. Every day Antonia sent a package of good wishes home with the boys. The most important part of the exercise was to make it okay for the kids to talk about the new reality with the Cangialosi boys.

"I'm very big on family learning experiences," she said. "This is how you teach your children about loss and grief and worry and also how you provide security." She urged parents to maintain their routines. "You have to have meals. You have to take time to talk. You have to do your bedtime ritual, don't let that go."

With the first week behind them, Antonia Martinez was almost glowing. She told her teachers that by their composure and dedication, they had taught the most important lesson they would ever teach. She shared with them her own recommitment: "Teaching is the noble profession. This week was certainly a test of that. We, together, were the proof that it is true."

MARY THE MADONNA DEL PARTO

At the Academy Preschool, three little toddlers out of the school's eighty-eight families had daddies who worked at Cantor Fitzgerald. Director Norma Frushon knew that the four-year-olds would not understand when they heard the word "death." Five-year-olds begin to grasp it, and six-year-olds can take it in. "Hurt" and "bad" and "sad" are words that a four-year-old can understand, but it is inconceivable that someone he or she loves was here today and will be gone tomorrow, forever and ever. So each day he is gone, Daddy dies, over and over again.

"Four-year-olds have such a limited vocabulary, even though they are upset and grieving, they have a hard time expressing how they feel," says Norma Frushon. "So they usually express their hurt in aggressive physical ways. These children should be pushing their friends or crying with no explanation, that's the normal reaction we expect from children, acting out. But that's not what's happening. It surprises me very much. Maybe they still don't understand what happened. But the children are unusually quiet. Even somber." Perhaps reflecting the mood of the adults around them. Who *did* understand it?

One of those four-year-olds was Mary Murphy's daughter, Morgan. Another was Jacob Stahlman. The first week, Morgan and Jacob repeatedly told their teacher, "My daddy's not home yet," or asked, "When do you think my daddy will come home?" or said, "When my daddy comes home, we're going to go fishing." In circle time, one of their classmates popped out with the statement, "Some bad guys flew a plane into the big towers and killed lots of people." The teacher drew a breath and asked where he had gotten his information. "I saw it on the TV." The teacher verified his reality. "Yes, that's very true. Some bad men flew planes into the two World Trade Center towers. And a lot of people are hurt." Then they went on with their lesson.

By the end of the second week, Morgan showed some precocious comprehension. "My daddy, I'm not gonna see my daddy," she told her teacher. "He's not coming back." During circle time, little Jacob said, "My daddy was in the building and the plane crashed and he didn't see it. So he's up in heaven now." The other children were encouraged to share. One little girl said, "Well, my grandma's up in heaven, too. It's nice there." By a month after the attacks, Morgan and Jacob were routinely playing the tower game. Morgan would build a tower of Legos, and Jacob would drive a plane into it and knock it down. Jacob blurted out to another little girl, "My daddy's dead." The girl said simply, "Oh, I know."

Mary Murphy was grateful for all the efforts the school was making to normalize the abnormal. She had her hands full at home with her three-year-old son, Jimmy, who kept coming into the kitchen clutching his pillow and climbing into her lap to get some stroking. Mary tried to reconstruct the capable career woman she used to be.

She was the one who had worked at Cantor with her husband, Jimmy Murphy, and escaped with him from the '93 Trade Center bombing. "I was living my dream," Mary Murphy told a visitor six weeks after the death of her husband. "I had a wonderful marriage, healthy beautiful kids, a great house, great neighborhood, a lot of family and friends around. I was living exactly what I wanted."

The shirt she wore parted at the third button down. Mary folded her hands over the swelling there and shrugged at the absurdity of her situation. In four more months, her body would bring forth a new baby into the world. Her body was numb, the numb receptacle of a fatherless baby. Too late to say there's been a terrible mistake. Mary stared at the swell in her body with an expression of profound puzzlement. She looked like Piero della Francesca's *Madonna del parto* (pregnant Madonna).

Outside her kitchen window the pine trees stretched up to seventy-five or a hundred feet. Mary lived in one of the older developments. A man with a chain saw was trimming away at dead branches. "That's Anthony's gift," Mary said wistfully. Anthony Venditti, managing director of Nomura Securities, was one of the four men who had commuted together with Jimmy Murphy—and the only one who had lived through September 11. He had hired a landscaper, Mike Palmisano, to chop the wood and finish the job of fall cleanup that Jimmy Murphy would never complete.

Mary's daughter, Morgan, was already long and lean as a pretzel stick, even at the age of four. She reminded Mary so much of her husband. "They both have long curly eyelashes, that's a Murphy trait, big blue eyes, and these ridiculously long black eyelashes. . . ." Mary stopped and cried for a bit.

When Morgan came home from her half-day at preschool, she asked Mary, "Mommy, can't I stay at school all day? Why do I always have to go home?"

"You don't!" Mary laughed, delighted. School would serve as her co-parent.

TEENS AND THE MIDDLETOWN BUBBLE

The children who had the greatest problem expressing their fear and sadness were not the little ones, but the teenagers. At best, teenagers are not good at communicating about difficult issues. But around an event as daunting as death and destruction of such magnitude that even their parents couldn't explain it—that was deeply unsettling to Middletown's adolescents.

"We live in the Middletown Bubble" was the feeling of several students at Middletown South High School. They were aware of being insulated by affluence and the relative homogeneity of an outer suburb. "Most of the kids know nothing about what goes on outside the walls of our school, and they could care less," as one senior stated without censure.

In a town with no middle, people are defined by their divisions. And Middletown has always been divided. Most of the town's teenagers are split between the two public high schools, Middletown South and Middletown North, or between the brokers' kids and the townies. South's student body looks more like Beverly Hills High East: mostly fair-skinned blond girls injected into spandex jeans like confectioners' icing, and hipless boys struggling to appear cool as they slouch through the halls trying to keep up their baggy pants. Body art at South tends to be decorative rather than defiant: butterfly tattoos and belly rings for the girls, eyebrow rings for the boys. Students from blue-collar families attend South as well, but there is barely a whiff of poverty. Middletown North is much more rough-hewn, with middle- and working-class kids who are twice as likely to drop out as those at South. Both schools rank far above the state average on standardized student tests, and both schools send between 80 and 90 percent of their students to college in an average year, but Northies are twice as likely to settle for two-year or community colleges. Middletown South has everything going for it: a powerhouse football team, a virtually nonexistent dropout rate, and high-achieving students.

But for all their advantages, South's students had surged out of control. Over the previous sixteen years, they had helped to drive out five principals, whose visages were mounted in bronze in the entry hall, like trophies. Only two months before September 11, a tough new principal had been hired to restore leadership. Daniel Lane, now fifty-eight, had enjoyed far more prestigious positions, having been a professor of English and humanities at Fairleigh Dickinson University, but he had never been so excited about a new job. Where everyone else saw a history of horrible labor problems, Lane saw Middletown South as "a sleeping giant."

Daniel Lane is a bull-necked Irishman whose lopsided face is held together with mischief and bravado over the drag of deep sadness. On first meeting, one is struck by how much he looks and sounds like the actor-comedian Nathan Lane, who was at the time starring on Broadway in *The Producers*. Daniel Lane exudes the same zany energy. No accident. He is Nathan Lane's older brother.

Principal Lane believes in the resiliency of kids, pointing to his own life as testament. He grew up poor in a cold-water flat in Jersey City. The word "dysfunctional" is too mild to describe the pain of reversed roles in the Lane family. Their father was an alcoholic and their mother diagnosed as a manic-depressive who revolved in and out of institutions, never able to tell her children she loved them. As the oldest of three brothers, Dan Lane assumed the role of parent. He learned young and hard how to keep discipline in the midst of chaos.

"I was the surrogate dad for Nathan, I'd say, up until ten years ago," he said of his famous brother. "He had a couple of real down times in his career. One time I gave him a gym bag full of cash. He has repaid me handsomely over the years. We're very close."

As a school principal Lane uses his gravelly voice like a megaphone to project love—or fear. His first week in the school he told the kids, "I love you. I respect you. I care about you." He also communicated clearly that he was nobody to mess with: "I literally took back ownership of the building."

Lane stalks the halls between classes to make personal contact with the students. He is right in their faces—friendly, funny, hip, his blue eyes locking on to build emotional credibility. "No exaggeration, because I hate to embellish," he said with tongue in cheek, "out of the thirteen hundred kids who go here, I would say that I now know five hundred names." If he sees a student who looks especially freaky, he might break the ice with the praise "Hey, man, I love this outfit! Is somebody hassling you over this?" Once the boy relaxes, Lane might say, "All right, here's the deal. You don't have to remove your earrings or your lip rings. But drop some of the hardware on your belt." If a kid tries to con him with the "sir" act, Lane comes right back: "You're not going to con me, 'cause I'm the king of bullshit. If bullshit is measured in grains of sand, then I'm the Sahara Desert."

This father of five children, well seasoned in the ways kids have of manipulating their parents, believes that few parents today have control of their kids; the kids are controlling their parents. "The parents love their kids so much, they're afraid of losing their love. So the loss of love becomes the trump card the kids use against parents." He sees upwardly mobile suburban parents, driven to make up for what they themselves lacked as children, indulging their kids until they expect to be entertained 24/7: "I'm bored, Dad, take me to the mall. I'm bored, Mom, buy me that."

Dan Lane's tough-love approach quickly earned him the respect of students and cast him as an educator's hero. But it was the parents he aimed to please. Lane saw himself as president and CEO of what he likes to call the Middletown South Management Company. "Any place that has a budget of a hundred and six million dollars—that was our budget last year—is big business." And like most CEOs, he came into the job determined to clean house. He gave his assistant principals the game plan and told the teachers and staff that all their jobs were up for grabs. He fired three people in September. He told them, "I like you, but here's your evaluation. You're lazy, you're unprofessional, you're not part of my game plan, and you gotta find another job." When they whined about getting the union or their attorney on his back, Lane told them, "You can get a SWAT team of attorneys, but you're going. Why am I paying you seventy-five thousand dollars a year when I can pay somebody twenty thousand who will do a better job?"

This approach put Lane in the crosshairs of the teachers' union president, Diane Swain, an old-style labor leader with two decades of power behind her and a reputation for playing rough. In grievance hearings with Principal Lane, Diane Swain came on strong.

"Excuse me, Diane," Lane interrupted. "It doesn't have to be this way. Your sarcasm and your cynicism are most assuredly lost on someone of my stature."

Swain is a pear-shaped woman in her fifties, only a few years younger than Lane and quite sure of her own stature. As politically astute as she is socially inept, she has fought off factions who have tried to oust her and manages to command broad support among the district's teachers. When Lane laughed at her, his big, gregarious, cackling laugh, she was insulted. "Who do you think you are?"

"I'm just a simple man trying to do my job," he said, "but if you want to make this into some kind of a street fight, then you've come to the right store."

Swain closed her grievance book and stood. "Mr. Lane, you're the most obnoxious human being I've ever met." Later, she tried to get him fired, and failed.

To the beleaguered parents of Middletown's school district, however, it was thrilling to have a strong leader as principal. Many parents were willing to turn themselves inside out to help Lane succeed. "They treat me like I'm the mayor of the town," Lane says. "Such reverence, I've never experienced this before." He let out a loud whoop. "Wow! I waited my entire miserable life to find a job like this."

PRINCIPAL LANE KEEPS THE LID ON

The Middletown Bubble continued to insulate students at South on September 11—at least until lunchtime. Daniel Lane was walking the hallways when his secretary came running after him at about 9:15 A.M. His first thought was *My baby.* His oldest daughter was staying with his brother Nathan in Tribeca, much too close to the Trade Center for comfort. Of course, he couldn't reach her. Phones were down. Lane, the tough guy, cries at the drop of a hat. He ran through the office wailing, "Ohmigod, what am I going to do!"

He took his cue from his family history: In the face of chaos, keep the lid on at all costs. "Remain calm," he instructed his staff. "Don't give the kids a sense of crisis."

The next thing he remembers is a mother running into his office, screaming hysterically. It was Anna Egan, a woman he had met only days before, with her charming British husband, Michael—the trophy house couple. They had come in to ask the principal to look out for their son, Matthew, a Down's syndrome child of sixteen, who was attending a public school for the first time. Lane had assured them that the boy would be taught in special education settings with kids who had similar problems. The principal remembered how happy the couple had looked. Now Anna Egan was doubled over in anguish, unable to contact her husband, with no family nearby.

"I didn't really know this woman," says Lane. "I didn't know this man. I did not know this child. But they will be on my mind till the day I die. Their tragedy, to me, sums up the loss of life for my students, for Middletown, on a very primal level."

Lane withheld all information from students and teachers until 12:30 P.M. Finally, crooning as softly as he could, he announced over the public address system that there had been a crisis at the World Trade Center and both towers had fallen. "But no matter what happens, school is the safest place to be now. With me, in this building." He was proud that with 1,307 students, only thirty-two parents came to pick up their children before the end of the day.

But as students and teachers began to duck outside and listen to car radios, rumors began to circulate. In the cafeteria, kids sat staring at their food and whimpering, "What's gonna happen?" Suddenly a disembodied voice over the PA system would summon a student, and a child would run out, sobbing. Bridgette Parks, a swim team captain with a round face bland as a spring moon, sat mute. Since her parents' separation, Bridgette had grown very close to her father. The bad patch had begun after he lost his job. But his two years of joblessness had put him in close proximity to Bridgette, since he often did substitute teaching at nearby Middletown North and liked to pick her up after school. Her father had only started working at Cantor Fitzgerald the previous June, and he loved it.

"My father works in the World Trade Center," Bridgette blurted to her tablemates. She was only sixteen but somehow she knew, she just knew he was gone. Her tablemates froze. The Middletown Bubble was about to burst.

The toll would reach twelve at Middletown South; twelve students whose families were suddenly left with gaping holes. But it all happened so suddenly, so outrageously out of context, that most of the students said it felt as if they were watching a movie. "If you're from New Jersey, there's an automatic disconnect," said Elizabeth Howe, an exceptionally perceptive senior, "because you weren't *right there,* you didn't see it up close. But it loomed over us. For weeks. It was haunting to wake up in the morning and look out your window—maybe you'd forgotten for once—but you'd see that dark gray cloud over us, day after day. An ash cloud. It was just a constant reminder of all the troubles you had in the future. And the smell. You felt it in the pit of your stomach. It smelled like—like death."

After the first month, most of the kids appeared to shuck off their resolutions to be kinder and gentler. Their conversation reverted to the usual trivial concerns of high school—cliques, sports, cool shoes, hip-hop CDs, hair, zits, hunks, and chicks. A gulf opened up between Bridgette Parks and her friends. She had indeed lost her father. When Bridgette would refer to "my parents" in the plural, her friends might snicker nervously. She'd say, "But I can't just leave my father out." Her friends didn't seem to understand that Bridgette wanted to talk about it, needed to talk about it, and when she couldn't find anybody who wanted to talk about it, her misery turned into hostility.

Alex Kerr and her older sister, Kathryn, began to realize that they had something important to offer. They were students who had lost a sister in a fatal car crash exactly a year before. "After my sister was killed, my bubble popped," Kathryn recalled. "I tried to talk to my friends about it, but it was perceived as kind of a downer." Given their head start on dealing with a traumatic life accident, the Kerr girls understood the confused and frightened emotions that kept their classmates tongue-tied when it came to expressing themselves about the Trade Center attacks. "I think we can help make it okay to talk about all those feelings," Alex, fourteen years old and proud, said, straightening up to her full height. "I'm a pro at dealing with death."

Kathryn Kerr approached the student assistance counselor at South to suggest that they start a grief group. Terry Columbo, a cheerful woman with large, soft, raisin-brown eyes and a whispery voice, appreciated the suggestion. She put out feelers to the bereaved students. None responded. Some sent out an aura: *Don't come near me.* They were holding back the unruly emotions that could make their friends ostracize them. Even at home, they couldn't let it all out. Most were at pains to care for their surviving parent, whose grief took precedence over their own.

Gentle persistence finally paid off. The wounded teenagers of South found their way to Terry Columbo's cozy office, and just in time. The town was about to be rocked by another great trauma.

TEACHERS AS TALIBAN

E ven before September 11, Middletown was seen by some of its denizens to be a dysfunctional community. After September 11, Middletown became both more of a community and more dysfunctional.

In this antagonistic place, to which families often said they moved for the sake of their children, the public education scene was appalling. With roughly 1,000 teachers and 10,500 students, Middletown is the largest school district in Monmouth County. Middletown is also one of the seventy-five wealthiest townships in America. The median teacher's salary is $52,000, over the past seventeen years, and New Jersey often leads the nation in spending per pupil—almost $10,000 annually. Yet parents complain that taxes eat them alive and that for every dollar spent to educate students, teachers take 63 cents for salaries and benefits. And teachers complain that the parents are too preoccupied to show interest in the PTA. Coming out of the strike in '98, the teachers' union continued bitter divorce proceedings with the board of education while they worked without a contract for four years *after* striking. The bad blood had carried over.

"I'll tell you this," said Daniel Lane, "the leadership of the board and the leadership of the union—they *like* the pain. The egos and personalities are bent on mutual self-destruction."

It was rumored that after 9/11 board members referred to the teachers' union as the Taliban. "It's a secret cult, and the leadership is power-mad," declared one board member, hiding behind anonymity. Union members claimed the board was made up of a bunch of housewives who lacked political or administrative experience. Teachers complained the schools were falling apart. Bathrooms under delayed renovation had no doors. The superintendent, Jack DeTalvo, insulted them, saying there were lots of gas stations with bathrooms along Route 35 that they could use.

The longtime union leader, Diane Swain, had a strike vote in her pocket going into the 2001 school year. And she had intended to exercise it on September 12. After the events of 9/11, the union declared a moratorium out of respect for the dead. That respect lasted less than three months before the re-sumption of contentious behavior, for which Middletown would soon be-come nationally famous. Ostensibly, the issue was how much union members should contribute for their health insurance, but it was really an ugly game of brinkmanship. Each side was betting that the other wouldn't dare risk the revulsion of the community by bringing on a strike. On No-vember 29, all bets were off.

A TOWN THAT CAME TOGETHER IN GRIEF IS DIVIDED BY A STRIKE

Judge Clarkson Fisher threatened to send teachers to jail if they contin-ued to violate a state law forbidding public employees to strike. Diane Swain raised a fist and shouted triumphantly, "We're going to jail. Take us in!" Local TV cameras caught the retro image of sixties radicalism. Judge Fisher figured out a way to thwart Swain's tactics. He began arraigning her teachers alphabetically, denying Swain her moment of sacrificial glory.

The spectacle of 226 teachers being handcuffed and marched into the county jail less than a month before Christmas attracted national TV cover-age. Teachers waiting to be arraigned began wearing American flags wrapped around their heads, or hearts pinned to their shirts with the names of their incarcerated colleagues. Superintendent DeTalvo labeled the strike "a war." It was the largest jailing of teachers in New Jersey since a strike in Newark in the sixties. Some teachers spent five days in cells. Diane Swain predicted, "This will destroy the district. I declare it DOA."

All this took place in sixty-degree weather outside a courthouse in Free-hold decorated with Christmas lights and a Jesus and Mary tableau. A surreal spectacle. Sitting on the steps of the courthouse in a leather jacket and sneak-ers, waiting to be arraigned, was Steve Mermi, the school psychologist for Thompson Middle School. "This is a major stress on the kids and their fam-ilies, but I think this strike needs to happen," he suggested. "It's all about get-ting back to normal. This is part of everyday life. If the terrorists can disrupt that, then we've lost." Few others were as philosophical. A guidance coun-selor sitting next to him, who was afraid to give her name, opined about Sep-tember 11: "I was there for the kids that day. We kept them calm. We're commended for handling the WTC crisis and this is our thanks?"

Brianna Scatorchia, a fourteen-year-old girl from the same school, held up a sign saying "We Thought Kids Mattered." She was in mourning for the coach who had led her traveling girls' basketball team to countywide victories. When Paul Nimbley was killed in the Trade Center, Brianna quit the team. "I want to go back to school," she said. "We've been out for six days and it's getting out of hand. I'm sitting at home doing nothing. Teachers are as important in supporting me after this event as my parents." Meanwhile, younger children confined at home were saying things like "Mom is in the bedroom crying and my teacher's in jail and my daddy's never coming home."

Karen Joseph, a union spokeswoman, a heavyset woman wearing a blue union T-shirt, screamed, "It's a disgrace! I've never seen anything like this. They—the board—are vindictive. They hate the union. They are power-hungry egomaniacs!"

Inside the courtroom, a throng of fifty-plus teachers waited their turn to go before the judge. After the first four teachers were led away, Swain labeled them "our four martyrs." One of those "martyrs" was the physical education teacher at Daniel Lane's high school, Steve Antonucci. Two days before he was arraigned, Antonucci had coached South to the state championship. He was permitted to address the courtroom: "If that's the thanks I get from the board of education and the community, so be it," he said. He slipped off his wedding ring and handed it to his pregnant wife, kissed her, and was led away.

Judge Fisher announced that the answers of the defense were "visceral, not rational," and meted out his punishment without favoritism. He sent away the school nurse from Dr. Martinez's model Village School. Mrs. McGraw, nursing a migraine, voiced a bitter but common refrain: "I never want to work as a teacher in this area again." Sheriff William Oxley watched his own brother, John Oxley, a teacher and football coach for Middletown North, go off to jail. It hurt. As a former mayor of Middletown township, the sheriff could feel the disintegration of a community.

AFTERSHOCKS

Karen Cangialosi was trying hard to be fair. The teachers had a right to demand respect, she felt. "But for me personally, it was very hard," she said, "because my life now is about speaking to accountants, lawyers, insurance agents. The phone never stops ringing. And now I have to home-school my children."

For the grieving parents, already beleaguered by trying to make up for a lost partner, it was another trauma. Another rupture of security.

"It's going to take a long, long time for the parents to forget this one," surmised a mother as she dropped her child at the Village School. Moments later, Laurie Ruggeri delivered her son, a classmate of Peter Cangialosi. "My boy was scared when he saw his teacher on TV wearing handcuffs. I had to explain it very simply: 'Your teachers love you, your parents love you.' You've got to give them stability. Without that stability, after September eleventh . . ." Her voice trailed off. Many of the parents were concerned that the strike had eroded the children's view of their teachers. One ten-year-old asked, "Are my teachers jailbirds now?" A fourteen-year-old said, "I'll still respect them, but I don't think they acted very grown up."

The strike lasted seven working days. It ended at dawn on December 11, an hour before the judge was ready to fire all 226 teachers—one quarter of the union's membership. Principal Lane posted himself at the door of Middletown South to meet every one of his teachers as they entered the building. "Good morning, I'm so glad to see you, and welcome back," he greeted each one. And each one, in turn, said, "Good morning, Dan. Good to see you, too." Lane was stunned. The incarcerated teachers were incredibly quiet. "If anything, it was more low-key than a regular Monday." End of story, according to Lane.

It was wishful thinking. What appeared to be unusual calm, on the surface, only masked the virulent emotions underneath. Now it was the teachers who were trying to keep a lid on. Their true feelings spilled out at a public hearing on the teachers' strike held at Middletown South before a court-appointed mediator. The audience appeared to be composed half of teachers and half of balding men, many of whom identified themselves as conservatives. Typically, the men spoke about taxes, about being on pensions without raises, and about being unwilling to finance aid to urban or "so-called special needs districts." Their remarks produced loud applause.

Kathleen Sullivan, a broad-shouldered teacher in a sports jacket, was strident as she claimed the microphone. But when she came to her final point, the lack of respect, she was overcome with a coughing fit. "We have been referred to as the Taliban, shackled, thrown in jail—that doesn't go away. The board may have saved money. But they took our spirit. It's gone."

Kathleen Brazas, a senior English literature teacher who had taught *Les Misérables* to many of the parents in the audience, stepped to the microphone dressed elegantly all in black and proud to wear the silver jewelry she'd had to remove when she was jailed. That had been a personal humiliation to her on top of the fact that she had been widowed only three weeks before the strike.

"I was considering retiring, when my classroom was put in the gym with no heat," she told the mediator. "I went out and bought heaters, and VCRs and computers, you name it—anything for the kids. They are the reason I get up in the morning. The board is balancing the budget on the backs of the teachers, and there's no accountability!"

Her testimony drew thunderous applause. After three hours of emotional venting, the audience members left the hearing pretty much where they had started—antagonistic, divided. And the teachers still didn't have a contract. They would have to wait until fall of 2002.

A PAIR OF ANGELS outlined in white lights adorned Karen Cangialosi's dream house ten days before Christmas. She was proud of that accomplishment. She had already made up her Christmas cards and pasted on a photograph of Jeffrey and Peter, both smiling, with a hand-lettered message inside: *May Steve's smile, spirit and love live in us all. Let there be Peace on Earth.*

Karen herself was shrinking to a shadow of the well-muscled aerobics instructor she used to be. The plumbing was leaking; the garage door spring was busted. How was she going to get the car out? And here she was rushing to get to the Fifth Grade Fair and resume her duties as the Good Parent when the phone rang. Should she ignore it? Jeffrey's hair was still wet with comb marks; her ten-year-old was always ready before she was. He shifted from one foot to the other while Mom walked in circles with the portable phone to her ear. It was a friend urging her not to miss the next lecture in a bereavement series; it would last only seven weeks. Karen's frustration broke through.

"What happens after the seven weeks? Am I done? Am I cured? Is it finally going to be over, and maybe I can smile?"

The purpose of the Fifth Grade Fair was to raise money for the kids to have special activities. "Which they probably won't have anyway," Karen said dryly, "because after the strike, the teachers won't do any extra activities." That's the way it had been for several years after the '98 strike. Karen was ashamed of bringing a store-bought cake, but she was one of only a dozen dutiful class mothers who showed up.

A roly-poly mom announced, "I have a *good* story." She said her husband had done her the greatest favor. He had been laid off by Cantor Fitzgerald the previous summer, the same company for which Karen's husband had worked. "And the first thing he did was call me and say, 'But your kitchen will get done now!' " she squealed. "And thank God he was fired, because he worked on the 105th floor, and no one got out of there unless they had split-second timing." She bubbled on, apparently oblivious to Karen's feelings, boasting of how her husband had found a job locally and was now seeing much more of the kids—exactly what Stephen Cangialosi had been planning to do. Karen turned away. She didn't want to hear one more story about the lucky husband who had been on a golf outing that day or late to work because of a dentist appointment.

A few days later, Karen girded herself to have a conversation she knew would be extremely difficult. She had to tell Dr. Martinez, her boys' devoted school principal, that she was pulling her boys out of public school.

Antonia Martinez had all she could do to keep from weeping in front of Karen. She told her that as a principal, and a mother and grandmother, she cared deeply about Karen's beautiful family. She said all the teachers talked about Jeffrey and Peter—"those two wonderful boys." And she felt that the school had done everything possible to protect the boys and to make their sorrowful passage from a full family to a half-staffed one as smooth as could be hoped for.

Karen agreed wholeheartedly. She hated to leave, she said, but the strike had robbed the public schools of a sense of structure and security. "I know that's something I can't control," she said, "but after what happened to my husband, I need to have some sense of control." A group of traders and brokers who had worked with her husband had held a fund-raiser in his honor and given her a gift check. "I can't think of a better thing to spend the money on than an investment in my children's education," she said. She had enrolled the boys in a fine local private school. "At least there," she told Dr. Martinez, "I'll know my children will be in school every day."

For Antonia Martinez, after seeing some of her teachers go to jail, it was another defeat. She struggled not to take it personally. She understood, she said, that the disruption in the boys' daily routine caused by the strike was the worst thing that could have happened to their fragile sense of security. And she couldn't guarantee that there wouldn't be more turmoil. "But we will be very sorry to see the boys make a change," she said. And then, succumbing to the personal, "I hope you will let me stay in touch."

A month later, Dr. Martinez was still shaken. So much so, she could not speak without weeping. "To be perfectly honest, I'm not able to discuss this, because it's too raw," she said. "Everyone involved is experiencing the ravages of the strike. It's made me reevaluate what I'm doing with my life. This might be my last year at this job."

The behavior on all sides seemed to be pushing the edges of extremity. No wonder. The people of Middletown were stretched beyond their limits. It felt as though nobody had regained equilibrium. People's usual coping and defense mechanisms were exhausted by the ongoing burdens of fear, sorrow, anger, disrupted routine, and the constant harangue from federal officials to be "on alert" for the certainty of further acts of terrorism.

Middletown just needed to catch a break.

Chapter Fourteen

CHRISTMAS FAVOR

COLLAPSE OF THE ALLIANCE

Christmas was coming on, with its burden of undone guilt. The prospect of buying a tree, dragging out ornaments, and spending on gifts while their financial standing was so precarious left most of the families limp at best. Or paralyzed. Support groups offered by the county's hospitals were going begging. It was all just too much effort.

And then, even the Alliance of Neighbors let them down. This was the grassroots group formed by a few prominent Rumson men to help the families. Jim Wassal, one of its founders, was proud to say he had "jumped right in, thinking that giving out money would be great." He had persuaded a couple of trained crisis counselors to give one training session to his few volunteers. He soon learned, when handing out money, that "it's very hard to be fair." Before Thanksgiving, the competing interests and egos among chiefs of the Alliance had become so intense that its next benefit concert was canceled. Rick Korn resigned. By December, Ed McKenna, the mayor of Red Bank and a board member of the Alliance, admitted, "We were overtaxed, with too few volunteers." They were "reorganizing." Some $300,000 to $400,000 of contributions would sit in the bank until the following summer, awaiting the creation of a proper board and a clear mission. The Alliance wasn't returning the families' phone calls or urgent e-mails.

One night, an energetic entrepreneur by the name of Allyson Gilbert stopped for dinner at Danny's Steak House. Allyson is a brown-eyed woman whose arms always seem to be outstretched—doing things, directing things, giving herself to the moment. She asked the owner, Danny Murphy, who was one of the board members, whatever had become of the Alliance. "We expected you guys to raise the money, and our little group of women would coattail on you to offer some services," she said. Families were complaining that all lines of communication to the Alliance had gone silent. Danny explained in shorthand: "We ran out of volunteers and spirit."

Some suspected, however, that Wassal also had a hidden agenda. He was the retail director of Cushman and Wakefield, an international company that represents retailers who want to expand into new commercial developments. Wassal had his eye on the coastal barrier off Middletown, Sandy Hook, as an ideal scenic location for retail development. There was a slight problem. Sandy Hook is a national park. It would require a massive public relations effort to get the town behind commercializing one of the last three open beaches on the Jersey shore. Wassal was relatively new in town. Few people really knew him. As the face of the Alliance of Neighbors, he would be introduced to the townspeople under the most favorable of circumstances.

Judith Stanley was suspicious. She was passionately anti-sprawl and a power broker in town. An unusual mixture of grande dame and Steinem-vintage feminist (they were at Smith College together), Judith Stanley had been at the helm of the town's planning board for a quarter century. Together with her third husband, Judge Stanley, she occupied one of the most beautifully preserved Georgian homes on the Navesink River Road, with a lawn that sloped down to the water. If one wanted to make changes in Middletown, one did not want to get on the wrong side of Mrs. Stanley.

"I always find that when a developer is trying to do something, he tries to put on a good face," she said when Jim Wassal's name surfaced in December "like Venus out of the sea" in connection with a massive development project he wanted to place on Sandy Hook. Unbeknownst to the locals, he had formed Sandy Hook Partners in 1999 and interested the local National Park Service representative in his plan to save the historic buildings on the Hook. Mrs. Stanley was incensed. "Ecologically and environmentally, the Hook is unique. I just don't believe in commercialization for 'preservation.' " Wassal's plan was to put retailers in half of the ninety-six buildings, with all the attendant commercial traffic. Stanley couldn't get a copy of the lease agreement between Wassal and the government, so she couldn't get a valid environmental or traffic study done. But nobody held off Judith Stanley for long.

THE FAVOR NETWORK

With the self-appointed saviors among the men gone to ground, it fell to the women to figure out how to help the grieving families. Before she left Danny's Steak House, Allyson Gilbert table-hopped, promoting the goal of her little group. "I know you two have a house in Long Beach Island," she tested out a couple she knew. "Maybe you could offer your house to a family for a weekend, or a week—for those who don't want to take a plane?" They were more than happy.

The "little group" Allyson referred to was a grassroots network that had seeded itself the Saturday after 9/11 with a car wash by the Boy Scouts outside the Dunkin' Donuts. Janet Dluhi, a vivacious mom with china skin and dark hair, couldn't believe the way people threw money at her kids to benefit the families—not just twenties, but hundred-dollar bills—a total of $4,600 in five hours. The next day Janet began running her mouth as fast as her feet on the treadmill at the WOW gym. "If we could raise all that money for the families in five hours, just think what we could do if we put some real effort into it!"

Allyson Gilbert was on the next machine. She hadn't been sleeping since September 11, and she didn't know why. Her own little trauma on that day was something she had numbed herself against recalling. The fleeing out of Midtown, on foot, with no information. The growl of fighter planes above. The misinformation—"five more terrorist planes up there are headed for New York." The jolt of energy that had flown her feet all the way to the Hudson. Glimpsing the blue river and believing she could swim it; yes, if she could just get back to Jersey, she'd be safe! No way. She was locked down in Manhattan, away from her husband and children, overnight. But Allyson was one of the lucky souls who made it home. And somehow she felt compelled to make up for it.

Allyson would not make a conscious connection between her personal experience and her immediate response to Janet Dluhi's idea—not for a full year. All she knew was, she was hurting for all the families in town. She didn't know a thing about organizing a volunteer campaign. But her business was management consulting. She switched straight into action mode.

An idea was hatched for a grassroots support network to reach out to the wounded families. The women's initial goals were far more modest than those of the Alliance—to raise $1,000 for each family—and their approach would be far more hands-on. Janet Dluhi and Allyson Gilbert were moms themselves, with full-time jobs and young children at home and undone laundry and husbands waiting for dinner to be put on, but they knew only too well what they would miss if their husbands were suddenly gone, and it wasn't just love and money. They'd miss help with shopping, meals, accounting, baby-sitting, buying the kids toys for Christmas.

"Let's call it FAVOR—Friends Assisting Victims of Terror."

"But 'terror' doesn't begin with *r.*"

"So, we'll make it Friends Assisting Victims of terro*R.*"

Allyson approached it first like a communications campaign she might mount for IBM—but the FAVOR campaign would be for building community. They had to create a network of people who wanted to help. No sooner did they establish a board of five working mothers than word of mouth attracted thirty volunteers (ultimately eighty). Allyson sought out her friend Laura Wilton, an attorney who owned a small business in Red Bank. Like Allyson, Laura had never been involved in any sort of not-for-profit organization and didn't fully comprehend what they could do for a community. But one thing she did know: small-business folks can't write a very big check, but they can give gift certificates or merchandise or services. The women got out the Yellow Pages and split up into teams to canvass retailers along Route 35, to contact the plumbers and lawn service people, the painters and chimney sweeps.

How to match up the goods with the families? They printed up applications asking the makeup of each family and what they most needed—but how to handle the logistics? They knew the families were being inundated with mail and were afraid to open it, given the anthrax threat. The volunteers would have to show up in person, but first, they would need sponsorship by pillars of the community. They made honorary members of a popular state senator, Joseph Kyrillos, Jr., and school superintendent Jack DeTalvo. Then they called on the chief of police.

John Pollinger was just as hungry to find a way to help as were Janet and Allyson. "I'm a classic rescuer," he says. "I have to fix it." The Chief had suffered from a sense of helplessness before—"it happens when a passenger is trapped in a car and dying and you can't cut him out in time"—but that was nothing compared with the helplessness he had felt on 9/11. Chief Pollinger did more than give the FAVOR ladies his blessing. He told them he was divorced. "I happen to know a lot about what women running households without husbands need—I know because my ex is always calling me up!"

What about lawn mowing, snow removal, gutter cleaning? he suggested. Allyson and Janet agreed to find volunteers to offer those services and many more. The Chief offered to send one of his detectives around with the FAVOR ladies, and he knew exactly which one. Detective Joe Capriotti knew many of the victims, and he had already volunteered to be the thankless cop who knocked on doors and gave people news they would not be able to comprehend—that remains of their loved one had been found. "No one in our history has been put in a situation where he had to notify this many families in this short a period of time," Pollinger said. He dabbed at his eyes.

Tall, soft-spoken Detective Capriotti would knock on the door, show his badge, and assure the family, "No bad news. We just wanted to check on you." Then he'd introduce the FAVOR volunteers. "They're going to help you guys. Here's the application."

"All these women were isolated," observed volunteer Adele Friesen-hahn. "They were so happy to open the door in the middle of the day and find somebody there who cares." FAVOR's visits began to create a sense of belonging. The volunteers, too, were deeply affected by the rawness of the problems they learned about when they knocked on the doors.

Thirty-two families completed their applications. Adele created spreadsheets with the demographics: fifty-seven children, including one not yet born. Twenty-nine of the children were under the age of ten. The FAVOR founders decided they would make two distributions—one before Christmas and a second in March. To their amazement, after being in business only eight weeks, they had raised nearly $100,000. But money would not be their focus. It would be about maintaining normalcy, especially for the children. Keep the Friday-night pizzas. Keep the dance class and the karate class. Help the families to minimize the otherwise drastic changes to their lifestyle.

So highly charged were Allyson and Janet, they'd each wake up in the middle of the night with another idea and start furiously e-mailing. One night they noticed the times on their e-mails—they were both up at 2 A.M.

They started with baskets. Hand-delivered. A handsome Thanksgiving basket filled by St. Leo's Catholic Church. It was received not as charity, but as neighborliness. People began calling FAVOR asking to donate: free art therapy; six months of free chiropractic care; a year's free tuition to a private preschool; the WOW gym wanted to give guest memberships. When the first big snowfall blanketed driveways, a FAVOR volunteer went around and plowed every family's driveway before 9 A.M. Widows looked out their windows that morning and some wept. Instead of waking up to say, "Oh no, I can't get the damn car out because my husband isn't here to do the snow shoveling," they felt cared for by someone who knew what they needed even before they themselves did.

A week before Christmas, thirty noisy women squatted hip to hip on the floor of Allyson Gilbert's pocket basement to create Christmas baskets. One wall was piled to the ceiling with donated toys. Each volunteer was assigned a family as her ongoing responsibility. "You need to build your own basket based on your family's needs," Allyson explained. "That will give you a smidgeon of what they are going through." Then an auction was conducted with each volunteer bidding for "my family."

"Who wants this monster bottle of wine?" Allyson started off.

"Give it to a woman with young children!"

"I got two free months of yoga!" Janet called out.

"I need that skateboard for the boy in my family!"

"Who wants a take-apart truck, or a Magna Doodle?"

"I don't have enough for Mr. Beatty's basket."

When it came to Mary Murphy's basket, the volunteers grew weepy. She was the mother of the one child yet to be born. Tenderly, the women lined her basket with a complete layette and a receiving blanket. The rest of the baskets were filled with everything from videos to toasters, and fluted with free passes to ball games and movies and pizza parlors. By midnight, Allyson's garage was covered with thirty-four bulging adult gift baskets and thirty-four monster bags of toys. The finishing touch was a $1,000 check for each family, on top of goods and services probably worth $5,000 per basket. But more important, the women had come out of their separate enclaves in Middletown to volunteer and most hadn't even known one another. After an evening of sharing laughter and empathy for strangers who needed help, the core network was laced together. Excitement was high as the volunteers powered off in their SUVs imagining the happy faces behind the doors that would open for them the next morning.

THE FIRST STOP WAS at the home of a woman whose husband had worked on a high floor of the South Tower. She was tall and gaunt but, for a bereaved mother of three very young children, she acted strangely upbeat. "Oh yeah, come on upstairs," she chattered. "You can put the bags in my mother's room. I lost my mother along with my husband. Oh no, I'm fine now. I talk about it all the time. I'll need therapy down the line, but I'm fine now!"

She showed the volunteers the photomontage of her husband in a scrub suit, holding each of their three newborns, then on a hobby horse in the yard with the children all over him—three days before September 11. Then she showed the photomontage of her mother, a typically warm Italian grandmother cradling the babes in her bosom. It was all the volunteers could do to hold back their tears.

The gaunt mother of three had a two-year-old daughter. The child pulled out the wedding video and asked Mommy to put it on so she could watch it for the hundredth time. When it came to the part where her mother was dancing in her beautiful white gown with her handsome father in his tuxedo, the toddler buried her face in the cushions and started to sob.

When Pat Wotton admitted the cheery volunteers, she was so depressed she showed no emotion. She hadn't bought a tree. Her attitude seemed to be "Don't push Christmas on me. If and when I'm ready, I'll do Christmas." Most of the families made excruciatingly brave attempts to reward the FAVOR ladies with cheerful smiles. They fumbled for the words to express their thanks, but in that obligatory social way of people with something else, something far more crucial, on their minds. It was the same scene in each home: a little child, or two or three, wrapping himself around Mommy's legs like a scared puppy, a halfhearted attempt at Christmas decorations, and on the dining room table piles of documents, stacks of condolence cards, a hill of unmailed thank-you cards, a mug of cold coffee, maybe an ashtray with the evidence of a reactivated addiction. One widower, Kevin Laverty, and his twenty-one-year-old daughter, Deena, were too embarrassed to invite volunteers in. They had both taken to sleeping in the living room until afternoon.

So this was where the widows were at the three-month mark. Still in shock. Unfocused. Preoccupied. Locking the keys in the car, forgetting to pay bills, forgetting best friends' names, forgetting everything but September 11 because for most, it was still September 12. One widowed mom drove her child to school in her nightgown and walked like that right into the classroom without noticing.

After Christmas, the two founders of FAVOR, Allyson Gilbert and Janet Dluhi, got together and laughed. Not one person approached by FAVOR to donate had dared to turn them down. "All of a sudden, Middletown feels like a small town," Janet said, beaming. "I would never have expected this town to come together—it's never happened before." Her son Jason, a sixth-grade classmate of Jeffrey Cangialosi, spoke up.

"Nine-eleven never happened before."

ANOTHER "ANGEL" HAD COME forward, offering to draw portraits of victims free of charge for any family wanting one. Nancy Gawron, an artist with forty years' experience in portraiture, was grateful that she and her loved ones had escaped the personal horror. Her husband and son both worked in Midtown Manhattan and had returned safely. One of the first Middletown widows to take her up on her offer asked that Nancy insert her husband's likeness in a family portrait that included the baby born a few days after his death. When the widow picked up the drawing, she dissolved into sobs, murmuring, "Now I know what we would have looked like."

Gawron became dedicated to her work and committed to sketching all three thousand victims if she was asked. At the rate of one portrait a day, she figured it would take her ten years. But already, by the first Christmas, she found the work was changing her life. "It's a privilege to be part of the healing process," she said.

Janice Tietjen, for instance, the mother of PAPD officer Kenny Tietjen, was thrilled that the artist was able to capture the twinkle in her son's eyes. The first thing any visitor to Janice's home is shown is Kenny's portrait, proudly hung just inside the front door. The artist, too, was a spiritual person. Nancy Gawron summons her subject before she begins to sketch, and she believes the victims themselves help her to capture not only their likenesses but their personalities and their souls. As Christmas approached, and her offer became more widely known, Nancy heard from families across the country. After she mailed out a portrait to a man who had lost his twenty-year-old son, the father called her up. "When I opened the box," he told her, "it was like my son said, 'Hi, I'm home!' "

LIEUTENANT KEEGAN—FATHERING THE GROUND ZERO FAMILY

The Port Authority Police Department (PAPD) had lost thirty-seven of its own. It was the largest loss of police officers in a single day in the history of America. While New York's police and firefighters dominated the news, a band of grief-stricken survivors from the PAPD who had asked to be assigned to Ground Zero quietly pursued their mission of bringing out the remains of the lost. Every night they were on the pile; rain, sleet, fair, or fog, they were there combing through the dead, looking for anything they could find to give back to the families.

Christmas Eve was no different. Except that the Port Authority Police chaplain Father Dave Baratelli conducted a midnight Mass right there at Ground Zero. Families of the deceased were invited into the rescue team's humble trailer. Laurie Tietjen Quinn was relieved; her mother had been inconsolable that day. All the Tietjen family could think about was how Kenny had loved driving around town on Christmas Day to drop off the bicycles he always bought for needy kids. "We couldn't have been at a better place that night," said Laurie. "The Port Authority officers have become my new brothers." Mike Ashton, Kenny's partner, also showed up, admitting that it was the first time he'd attended a Christmas Mass in fourteen years. Father Dave declared he would hear a "mass confession." Otherwise, he quipped, "I could be here all night!"

Always there with the men on the pile was Lieutenant Bill Keegan. Once designated the night commander for Port Authority at Ground Zero, this unassuming Irishman carried on his shoulders a great weight: not only of the souls of thirty-seven friends and comrades, but of the physical and psychological well-being of his team of sixty men. Most were in their twenties or early thirties, some only a year out of the police academy, some pulled from the emergency services unit because they were trained to cut bodies out of car wrecks. For some it was a very personal mission, searching for a lost brother or son. Others were retirees, men in their fifties and sixties who had pleaded to join the team. Before Christmas, by process of elimination, the men themselves had handpicked the men they wanted to work with, and had evolved into a permanent team. And unlike any of the other uniformed services, members of the Port Authority recovery team would not be rotated. They were committed to working on that pile twelve hours a day, seven days a week, for as long as it took—an extraordinary experiment in the human capacity to endure unceasing exposure to traumatic stress.

"To be able to do this day in, day out, takes a mental toughness," said Keegan. "Not to have contact with the outside world or much contact with our families. You're here for twelve hours. It takes you an hour to get home. You sit around for an hour or so, go to sleep, get up, eat, and go back to the pit."

Down in that pit, one lost the city for the site. Above, New York went on working as before in all its brassy brilliance, but down below there was only the grinding of heavy machinery under the sulfurous white of stadium lights. The pounding of the wrecking ball was like a deathly heartbeat. A smell might waft over the ashes. The smell of death. The men would grow excited. A call would sputter over Lieutenant Keegan's radio: "Think we got some legs." That would be a good night. A bad night was when even the cadaver dogs slept.

Port Authority offered the men "debriefing" by professional police psychologists, but very few accepted help, fearing that it would count against them in future assignments. So the PAPD cops hiked up their overalls and sucked up their feelings until Ground Zero became their home and their work became an obsession. Some volunteers, like Rudy Fernandez, a huge oak of a man in rough overalls who despite his junior rank was chosen to run the temporary morgue, felt honored. "There is nowhere I would rather be, and I'll carry this the rest of my life," he told me. Rank soon dissolved as the men ate, joked, wept, and risked injury together. "You won't find a tighter bunch of guys," said Fernandez. "We're not going to have the kind of problems that you'll see in the New York City cops and firefighters who've been rotated in and out," he proudly predicted. "With the caliber of men that we have down here—handpicked for being strong-minded, mentally and physically—we're going to be better off in the long run."

But Bill Keegan knew his men were merely human, and hurting; trauma would take its toll. Hundreds of self-proclaimed "mental health people" had descended on the site, but Keegan shooed them off. He was particularly amused by an evangelical preacher who announced his presence with a booming Texas drawl: "Hiyah, boys, jus' get down on yo knees and 'cept the Lord and it's all gonna be fahn." Keegan had to tell the pushy preacher that his "boys" from Queens had trouble understanding Texan.

Keegan reached out to a police widow who would understand his men. Donna Lamonaco had lost her husband, Phillip, a New Jersey state trooper, twenty years before when he was shot by a domestic terrorist bomber. In those days before grief counselors, the traumatized widow was treated like a mental case. "I'm not nuts. I'm in pain!" she wanted to shout at the psychiatrists. Since then, having recovered the hard way, Lamonaco has devoted her life to taking other police survivors under her wing and serving as national president and president of the New Jersey chapter of COPS (Concerns of Police Survivors).

"We recognized in Donna's eyes that she'd dealt with immense loss," said Keegan. "That allowed her to connect with us." So every Friday night, at Keegan's invitation, Donna would poof her blond hair, paint on the eyeliner, don work pants and boots, and pile her twenty-one-year-old daughter and another police survivor into her Jeep to make the rounds of the forgotten survivors among Port Authority cops. It became her unpaid mission. She drove from the PATH trains to the tunnels to the bus terminal, bucking up cops who resented *not* being selected to work the recovery site. She would arrive at Ground Zero after midnight and hang tight until after sunrise, making a point to seek out and touch every one of the men.

For the first weeks the men's faces were stony, their eyes bloodshot, and they moved like robots. "I'm just here to be with you," Lamonaco told them. "You don't have to talk. And I'm not taking names." Gradually they gave up their first names.

"Tony? Fred? Paulie?" Donna would tease. "You guys must know that under this hard hat I'm a dumb blonde 'cause you're only giving me easy names." Once she began to get bear hugs, she used those hugs as diagnostic tools. Was the man tense or shaking? If so, he got a neck massage. Was he a boy in a man's body? Donna brought the men games and toys and got them to stop, in the middle of raking through grit, and play punch ball. "We gave them twenty minutes of laugh therapy," she said.

Slowly, the men came to see Lamonaco as their night angel. They saved up their feelings to spill on her. A man who couldn't sleep described the nightmarish sound of falling bodies as they hit concrete—the sound of watermelons bursting—how to make it stop? Donna said that, in his shoes, she would see the falling body sprout the wings of an angel just before it touched ground, and she would replace that other sound with the sound of angels' wings. The next time she saw that officer, he shouted over the machinery to her, "You! I'm sleeping! It's cuz of you!"

And so the FAVOR ladies who came together hip to hip in a suburban basement, and the recovery workers who came together shoulder to shoulder seven stories down in the underworld of the pit—each, in their own way, forged the bonds of a new family and found dignity in doing the work of angels.

Chapter Fifteen

MUSLIMS IN MIDDLETOWN

THE GABR FAMILY

Just off the Garden State Parkway exit to Middletown sits a modest white house on a bare hill rutted by car tracks. It has the look of a dwelling in a developing country. No sign signifies ownership, and thousands of local residents drive past the house every day without any idea that it is a place of worship for the Muslims of Middletown.

On the Friday afternoon following September 11, a large crowd gathered there for Jomah, or prayers. The house is a temporary *masjid* (Arabic for "mosque") opened only five years ago as the Arab Muslim population of Middletown exploded in tandem with the growth of information technology and the demand by AT&T and Lucent for technical professionals. Unbeknownst to many residents, about two hundred Muslim families now live in town, another two hundred next door in Holmdel. A much larger, more elaborate *masjid* is under construction next to the modest white house.

Hondas, Toyotas, and the occasional Lexus SUV converged from every direction until the hill was covered with more than 150 cars. The crowd swelled with every age group from toddlers to teenagers to graybeards. But only men, some looking majestic in long, flowing traditional Muslim dress, most in business clothes. The men embraced one another intimately, talking and smiling. Given the confines of the temporary *masjid*—the size of a one-room schoolhouse—the women have been told to stay at home to make room for the men. The only females were a few teenage daughters, their heads covered with white shawls, but like most first-generation hyphenated Americans, they were costumed in contemporary hip: jeans and leather jackets.

Everyone seemed to belong. It was a parallel universe, held together by religious beliefs and strictly observant practices. Until this week, it had flourished as almost a closed society. No more.

Unnoticed were two unmarked cars manned by detectives. Chief Pollinger had sent them. He was not about to tolerate another incident like the beating of a hardworking Indian gas station attendant by some wacko on a motorcycle who claimed he was expressing his "patriotism." Pollinger had driven over to the mosque on the very day of the tragedy and spoken to one of the founders, Mohammed Mosaad. "I didn't want any idiots thinking we were going to allow punch-outs of Arab people, any more than when Tim McVeigh blew up the Federal Building in Oklahoma City. We didn't go around beating up white people." Mr. Mosaad, an engineer who is a vice president at Prudential Financial, was surprised and relieved.

"But when the people of Middletown heard what happened, they went out of their way to be nice to us," said Mr. Mosaad, who was later invited by Chief Pollinger to speak at the town's memorial service. "Middletown is a very polite society."

It may be a superficially polite society, but it is an almost exclusively white society. The Ku Klux Klan used to operate next door in Red Bank. Chief Pollinger's instinct to keep a more protective eye on the Arab community was keen. After September 11, the once quiet, inbred Muslim society of Middletown experienced an abrupt visibility. The Gabrs, a Muslim-American family who had lived comfortably in Middletown for ten years, saw their identity in the community change overnight.

"We have so few minorities in Middletown, all you have to do is look around and see that you are different," says Mary Lynn Christopher, the guidance counselor at Middletown North, where four of the Gabrs' five children have attended public high school. "We're mainly white, Republican, and conservative. That's what is so interesting about Mrs. Gabr—the fact that she has raised five children here and chooses to live in this town, which is not that open-minded."

Eklas Gabr, the mother, a warm, nurturing woman who is Palestinian by birth, left Jerusalem for the United States at the age of fifteen. Her father had lost his business in 1967 because of the Six-Day War, when Egypt and Jordan had attacked Israel and lost. "My father wanted to go as far away as he could to start his life again," she said. Her husband, Abdel, too, had fled the Middle East because of oppression and lack of opportunity. An Egyptian, he had been president of his medical school class during an uprising when medical students had been hauled off to jail. After finishing his degree he had sat home, waiting for work like so many young men in Egypt, humiliated by receiving his food from the government dole. When the Gabrs met in Connecticut, where both were studying and working, they were already sufficiently liberated that Abdel dared to break up an arranged marriage to marry the lovely Eklas.

Abdel Gabr is a doctor, a rheumatologist. He treats clinic patients at the four hospitals operated in the county by Meridian Health Systems, while continuing to study for the foreign doctors' exam that will allow him to open his own practice. The family moved to Middletown because they heard the schools were better, and the Gabrs are fervent supporters of public schooling. Mr. Gabr believes in exposing his children to many different views, because if they learn only one view, that is not going to help them learn how to think. The observant parents also send their children to a *madrasah,* where they learn the Arabic language and have Islamic religious studies.

The Gabr home in Middletown sits on a typical middle-class block where suburban children play in the street until well after dark. Their backyard holds the ubiquitous barbecue. A broad front porch leads into a small living room, conservatively decorated in Middle Eastern style (every room has a wall placard with a gold-lettered prayer or the ninety-nine names of Allah). The furnishings are tasteful but budget, just as the cars outside are old and worn. The Gabrs' investment is not in possessions but in their children. On top of the TV are displayed the high school graduation pictures of three attractive children: daughter Randa, an honor student who is now at Rutgers University; Caleb, who attends Montclair State College; and Wallid, a tall, handsome football star known as "Mr. Personality," who was set to graduate from Middletown North in 2002.

"They all know me because I got a weird name," says Ehab Gabr, sixteen, the youngest of the Gabrs' three sons, fated to follow his two high-achieving brothers through the same public schools. Ehab does not put much effort into distinguishing himself as a student. He is always outside working on used cars that he buys and sells to generate his own spending money. Wallid's and Ehab's heroes are rappers like Jay-Z and the Notorious B.I.G. The youngest of the family is Aya, a spirited girl of ten, the only Muslim in her elementary school. Her social life is largely confined to the kids she meets at the mosque. Aya accepts that she must remain a virgin until she marries. Her father would not object to her marrying a non-Muslim, as long as he's not an Indian.

The kitchen has the feel of a *Brady Bunch* rerun. It holds a square wooden table around which the Gabrs gather every night as a family. The men come home and retire to pray. Mrs. Gabr comes home from her half-day teaching at KinderCare and prepares an elaborate four-course meal. When she feels comfortable, she removes her *hajib,* revealing a head of startlingly red hair. Frequent references are made to clippings of Wallid's football triumphs, which dot the refrigerator door.

"This is a family that may be Muslim and may be Arab but they are really into doing things that American parents do for their kids," observed Ms. Christopher, the children's guidance counselor, who has known Mrs. Gabr for seven years. "She has wanted the American dream for her kids—to go to high school, to do well, and get into a good college and study what they choose and to be successful in life. She has provided them with every opportunity that she could possibly do."

But that day in September altered the Gabrs' existence in ways they would never have imagined.

"HOW'S YOUR UNCLE OSAMA?"

When news of the attack hit Middletown North High School, Ehab Gabr was sitting with the sophomores in a U.S. history class. His teacher, Mr. Fleiger, was lecturing on the railroad era; they wouldn't get to the building of the World Trade Center until the end of the year. Suddenly another teacher burst into the classroom screaming that a plane had hit the World Trade Center. Flustered, she admitted she didn't know what to do. She got a radio for the room and the students listened, mute, miserable, disbelieving—it was too real to be true.

Ehab's first thought was *I guarantee they're going to say it's Arabs. No matter what movie I watch where a plane gets hijacked, it's always an Egyptian or a Palestinian saying, "Kill these people, they hate us."* As the sixteen-year-old son of an Egyptian-born father and Palestinian-born mother, Ehab immediately shifted into self-protective mode. He asked his teacher if he could use his phone. "For what?" the teacher demanded. "It's an emergency!" Ehab pleaded. He contacted his brother Wallid, the popular football star of the senior class. "Meet me in the hall—we got to talk!"

They called their mother at the school where she teaches. "Mom, did you hear what happened?"

"Yes, stay where you are!" Mrs. Gabr ordered.

Young Ehab was already covering his fear with defiance: "Mom, listen. God willing, if anyone says anything bad I'm going to punch them." Mrs. Gabr gave the boys no rope: "Stay out of trouble. If they dismiss you, make sure that you go straight home. You call me when you get home, *and don't go out.*"

That night as the Gabrs gathered around the kitchen table for a serious strategy session, the redheaded mother served a most appropriate dish: "upside-down" she calls it. A traditional Palestinian stew combining chicken, eggplant, tomato, and brown rice, it is baked and then flipped over. Their safe, traditional parallel universe, too, had been upended.

"We didn't believe that Muslim people did it," says Dr. Gabr. "We think that people are hiring terrorists and framing the Muslims. Before September eleventh, there was a very good relationship between American and Arab countries. I feel somebody wanted to make this relationship stop working. A lot of people hate us."

In the days and weeks following the attacks, the Gabrs became progressively more upset and conflicted. In the mornings they would get their news from *Good Morning America* and at night they would flip on the satellite and pull down the news from Al-Jazeera, the CNN of the Arab world. The coverage clashed. While American TV constantly reran footage of Palestinians celebrating, Arab TV focused on condolences sent to American victims and reports of Arab government reactions that—with the exception of Iraq—condemned the attacks.

"I began to feel the news in America was filtered," says Abdel, the father. "It might have been Osama bin Laden, but if so, somebody hired him."

The atmosphere around the family members turned increasingly suspicious. "It was difficult in the beginning—everybody looks at you like every Muslim is the same," says Mrs. Gabr. She had a fright in the checkout line at Kmart. A man looked at her *hajib,* the traditional head covering, and sneered, "Why don't you go back to your country?" Mrs. Gabr gave him a critical look. "I have more things to say," the man snarled. Mrs. Gabr spoke to him like a teacher to kindergartners: "It's better if you don't say anything else." But she was afraid to leave the store. She asked for the manager. The woman manager was sympathetic and said, "I'm going to stand by you to make sure he doesn't bother you." After more incidents of this kind, some Muslim women began asking their husbands if they could stop wearing their *hajibs* in public.

The Gabr family were well known and liked in their neighborhood, except for one family on the other side of the street. When a basketball tossed by a kid from that family rolled into the Gabrs' driveway, Ehab threw it back. The neighbor's kid, he says, called him "a fucking terrorist"! As the weeks went on, Ehab absorbed more blindly racist taunts from teenagers: "How's your uncle Osama?" The slurs made him angry but all the more determined to defend his religion, equally blindly. "I don't think they've even proved that it was Arab terrorists," he would say, repeating the mythology promoted on Arab TV that Americans themselves had been responsible for the World Trade Center attack. "I heard that twenty-nine hundred Jews took off work that day," said Ehab. "I'm not saying it was Jews, I'm just saying it's weird that they point the finger at us."

Eklas noticed, "All of a sudden people are afraid to talk to me. Why? I'm human, I have feelings, and I lost people in the Trade Center, too." Relatives of her sister-in-law, a Moroccan couple from Casablanca who worked as computer consultants on the ninety-sixth floor, died on September 11. Her sister-in-law was forced to send the couple's two young children back to Casablanca because she could not handle the responsibility and cost of raising them. Eklas reflected, "We all came to this country from somewhere else—if it's not us, it's our parents, or our grandparents. We didn't come to hurt or bother anybody. We're here just to go on with our lives."

Some Muslim residents of Middletown pulled their children out of public school. One of them was Dr. Wael el Koly, an Egyptian resident of Holmdel who was an assistant professor of medicine at Yale. The school bus stops right in front of his family's house, but he and his wife chose instead to drive their two young daughters four hours a day to and from an Islamic day school in New Brunswick. Unbeknownst to most people, New Jersey has seventy-two Islamic centers, sixteen of which operate private religious schools.

The most humiliating encounter befell Abdel Gabr. The director at Riverview Hospital, where Dr. Gabr works, asked him if he believed in suicide bombing. He tried to take it not as an insult, but as an opportunity to educate. He went back to the Koran to clarify for himself exactly what "jihad" meant and the teachings on violence. Still, whenever he saw the Towers fall again on TV, Abdel suffered from flashbacks. Months later he said, "We have not recovered."

HEAR NO EVIL . . .

On December 13, the night before the final day of Ramadan, the holiest month in the Islamic calendar, the White House released a videotape showing a jubilant Osama bin Laden laughing and boasting about the "martyrdom operation" that had killed more than three thousand people on September 11. It was a shocker. Suspense about the CIA-seized tape had built up for a week, while independent interpreters verified it as authentic. Once released, it played over and over on American TV. Bin Laden recounted listening with others to the radio when the news came across that a plane had hit the World Trade Center. "They were overjoyed when the first plane hit the building, so I said to them: 'Be patient.'" He gestured with his spidery fingers how the second tower had gone down. He said he had calculated which floors would be hit, and the number of casualties, counting on fire from the gas in the plane to melt the steel structure of the buildings. As a Saudi sheik showered him with kisses and praise from religious figures in Saudi Arabia, that country was linked definitively for the first time to the al Qaeda terror network. Egypt was also exposed. Bin Laden was flanked on the tape by his top deputy, Ayman al-Zawahiri, a former leader of the Egyptian Islamic Jihad, and applauded Mohammed Atta, from the Egyptian al Qaeda family, as the leader of the attacks.

But the talk among men at that Friday's prayer service in the little white house in Middletown was not about bin Laden. These were the most faithful of men of the *masjid,* most of whom had spent many hours in the spartan mosque during the holy month of Ramadan. It was carpeted in fake green grass and warmed by a small space heater. The imam had already done his recitation at the larger 1 P.M. prayer service. His deputy, gowned in a long white shirt, led the chanting. The men arranged themselves in one line, bent from the waist, knelt, kissed the floor, and touched their foreheads to the floor five times, chanting quietly. They repeated their prostrations for fifteen minutes. Then a plastic tablecloth was spread on the floor and they passed around a delicious drink called *hoondrook,* a shake of milk, honey, and banana, along with souvlaki and goat cheese. In the middle of this rather sparse ethnic refreshment, one of the men walked in with three boxes of Italian pizza. Everyone's eyes lit up.

The men mumbled their wishes for understanding. Ramadan is normally a period of personal soul-searching. It had special meaning for them this year, they said. "We take this time to make supplication to the Almighty to understand our point of view, to help us bridge the differences. Why are we blamed?" Another man suggested, "I think that the media is looking for some reason, and they focus on the Muslims in the United States." A third man was even more defensive: "Yes, this is what they did on September eleventh, but you have to ask why. What is the cause? Why should people hate so much?"

What followed was a recitation of grievances that Muslims have against

America for using a double standard in dealing with their people. Chief among them is the American government's support for the Israeli occupation of Palestinian territory. They questioned the American insistence on enforcement of economic sanctions against Iraq while the UN resolution ordering Israel to return the Golan Heights to Syria went unheeded and Israel unpunished. "And the Israelis aren't Arabs!" one man erupted. "They're not even Middle Easterners! Middle Easterners look like this." He pointed to his skin, which was the color of dark caramel. "They're all Europeans, from Russia!"

The dialogue grew more and more ethnically confused. Another man protested the American invasion of Afghanistan. "They say the hijackers were fifteen Saudis and four Egyptians, so why didn't we bomb Saudi Arabia and Egypt? Afghans are good Muslims and they're not Arabs anyway, so why are we bombing them?"

Mohammed Mosaad, the articulate engineer who had lived in Middletown since 1984 and was one of the volunteers who had started the *masjid* there, spoke at the Middletown memorial service for the victims of 9/11. "I swear to you, it was breaking my heart," he recalled. "Because I'm a father, I know what you feel about your children even when they don't come back home from work on time."

Since Mr. Mosaad was the director of children's religious studies at the Middletown *masjid,* he was a good source to ask about the claim by some Islamic scholars that jihad—holy war—is an obligation. Did he believe that?

"We are not allowed to kill innocent children and women and elderly," he replied heatedly. "To kill innocent people that have nothing to do with anything, or to destroy homes, is against Islam. But jihad, meaning to resist people who attack you, yes, you can defend yourself or defend weak people through jihad. Let me tell you, what happened in Israel to those Palestinians, because it's their land, they're defending their homes—that's considered jihad."

Mr. Mosaad claimed not to have seen the bin Laden videotape. Asked if there was still widespread disbelief among the local Muslim community that bin Laden had been responsible for the attacks, he said, "I tell you, for them, there is not enough evidence." What would convince them? Real evidence, he insisted. He had a satellite dish and watched Al-Jazeera regularly. He was asked if he wasn't interested in watching the bin Laden tape in Arabic, to decide its veracity for himself.

"It's not like we talk about the attack all the time and try to analyze," he said impatiently. "I have no idea who al Qaeda is and what their goal is," Mr.

Mosaad added, dismissing the subject. "I don't relate to those people. It doesn't matter who did it. A terrorist is a terrorist."

All the rest of the men begged off when asked what they thought of the bin Laden tape. They hadn't seen it, didn't know about it, didn't care. Most likely, they didn't want to watch the Osama video because they didn't want to have to defend or reject fellow Arab Muslims. Hear no evil, see no evil, speak no evil, seemed to be the mass psychology promoted by the *masjid* of Middletown.

CHIEF POLLINGER EMPATHIZED WITH the conflicted feelings of local Muslims who might have thought of bin Laden as an underground folk hero. "Now you have their 'hero' suddenly claiming something that goes against Muslim faith." But Mr. Mosaad had assured the Chief that even if Osama was found to be responsible for the attacking planes, and somehow that act resulted in world peace, it still would not be condoned by those true to the Muslim faith.

Later that same month Mr. Mosaad took his family on their pilgrimage to Saudi Arabia. Strangely enough, it was in that country, on Al-Jazeera, in Arabic, that he saw another videotape of Osama bin Laden. This time, he couldn't help seeing the evildoer for who he was. "I saw him praising the people who did the attack on America," said Mr. Mosaad. "His left arm was not moving. It looked like it was injured. It was really clear to me that it's him. I was surprised for him to admit and even take credit for it. I'm not afraid to say it after that: Osama bin Laden doesn't represent the majority of Muslims."

Chapter Sixteen

ANGER RISING

EAT, DRINK, AND BE MERRY . . .

The New Year brought relief for many people who had suspended their usual level of getting and spending out of respect for the dead. Seldom faced with a more resounding example that life is short, many slaked their anxieties by adopting the philosophy of "eat, drink, and be merry, for tomorrow . . ." The founder of *Cigar Aficionado* magazine, Marvin Shanken, for instance, used to smoke the rarest of his stogies—Dom Perignon cigars made in Cuba—only on special occasions, like an anniversary or when he made a big killing in the market. Now, he said, he smoked one whenever he felt like it.

Immediately after September 11, manufacturers and dealers of luxury items were being skunked, given the combination of fear, recession, and the reluctance of the rich to spend in the face of national suffering. "They were struggling with guilt," said Judy Milne, a Manhattan antiques dealer. "They felt it wasn't the time to indulge themselves." But in January 2002, pent-up demand was released with a vengeance. The Stella Antiques Show, which opened in New York on January 17, set an attendance record. "It was like chickens picking up corn," gloated Steven Moore, of Moore and Moore Antiques. The show's success signaled that it was now okay to resume redecorating your dining room.

Buyers didn't wait for the annual New York National Boat Show to open its doors. A securities broker in New York wrote out a $1 million check over lunch in a private Wall Street dining room as the down payment on the yacht of his dreams—a 106-foot-long fiberglass pleasure boat. "You sit back and say, 'Realistically, how long am I going to live?' " explained Alan Fields. And he wasn't the exception. The New York National Boat Show has been a bellwether of consumer mood for nearly a century. In 2002, it racked up the best sales record in thirty-four years.

It wasn't only the superrich buying. A fireman came down to the boat show on his break, one of a record number of firefighters flush with overtime pay who were now only too eager to take early retirement. Another strong undercurrent at the show was the escape fantasy. A boat was seen as a family redoubt—a way out if New York was attacked again. Darren Matthews, vice president of a boat dealership who lives on Long Island, figured that the only evacuation route would be by water. "Loading your family on a yacht and sailing into the wild blue yonder is everyone's fantasy." A luxury boating magazine promoted the line, "What could be more secure than your own floating island?" The illusion of self-sufficiency had resurfaced with a big price tag.

The disparity: although for many Americans the chaos of the previous fall had begun to be pacified by distance and routine, for those robbed of loved ones, the New Year brought no sense of regeneration. On the contrary, as the anesthesia of shock wore off, the reminders of reality stung.

You wake up and the indentation worn into the bed beside you is not warm. He is dead. You put on coffee and warm the milk because that's how he likes it. Oh, he's dead. The clock shows 5:30 A.M. Why are you up? The guys he commutes with will be at the door at six. Oh no. He's dead. They're dead, too. All except one. You flip on the outside light anyway. Going through the motions. Numb. Back to bed. It's okay, he'll call at 6:40 to wake you to get the kids up for school. Oh no, he's still dead. Thousands of such fits and starts—hundreds of thousands maybe, who knows?—before the reality seeps into the bones and the heartache assumes constancy.

Then begins the next phase of traumatic grieving: anger.

Much of the country began moving into anger and vengeance mode, led by President Bush as he sounded off with angry battle cries the day after the attacks: "We're going to find those evildoers, those barbaric people who attacked our country. . . ." "We will smoke them out of their holes. We'll get them running and we'll bring them to justice." In an offstage conversation with Vice President Dick Cheney, as reported by Bob Woodward, Bush was livid. "We're going to find out who did this, and we're going to kick their asses."

A fascinating finding about how different parts of the country responded to the terrorist attacks was made by Michael Johll, Ph.D. In an attitudinal study of stress and coping reactions done a month after the attacks of September 11, the closer the respondents were to the East Coast, the *less* pronounced was the lust for revenge. The unique finding was that the *least* vengeful were New Yorkers. "Where the rest of the country wants payback and retribution," concluded Dr. Johll, "those directly in the epicenter of the attack show more compassion."

ANNA AWAKENS

Anna Egan had been in isolation and depression in December, feeling "abandoned" in the trophy house her husband had bought shortly before he died. Some leapt to the conclusion that she would be among the slowest to recover. The opposite would turn out to be true. Conservation of one's energies—physical, emotional, spiritual—is the most urgent task of trauma survival. Having shut down for the first several months after her loss, Anna woke up in January.

"Right after Christmas I told myself, okay, I need to get down to business," she said. "I got on a roll." She began investigating how to become an American citizen. Although she was Sicilian by birth and Canadian by citizenship, she decided she was going to spend the rest of her life in the United States. Just making that one decision helped to counter the sense of floating.

People in traumatic grief sometimes describe their thinking process as being like an overcrowded train switching stations. They keep jumping from one track of thought to another. One track is: *I don't think I can stand this pain. I'm totally helpless. I don't see how I can survive this.* Another track is: *Dammit, how could this have happened? Whose fault is it? I'm mad as hell!*

Anna was a prime example. Even though she was still feeling her loss as physical pain and was scarcely able to eat, the anger began working on her. "Logic says there's an explosion, fire, it happens all the time, you evacuate immediately." Her voice condensed to a hiss. "Why? So many doors [the Towers had 828 emergency exit doors], so many stairs, especially after the '93 bombing, why didn't they know?" Her son Matthew, whose room was festooned with medals from his enthusiastic participation in the Special Olympics, had taught Anna a lot about dealing with life when life deals you a rotten hand. "How he lives with his disability has taught me to be a fighter and to look at reality," Anna reminded herself. She corrected her posture and, standing knife-straight, described her new reality:

"The facts are, I moved to Middletown, lost my son to college, and my husband was brutally murdered. Dammit, I feel like shit! I lost everything. It's normal! I'm mad as hell, and I'd be worried if I wasn't angry." She softened a little. "The days that I think I feel good, I need to stay with that."

Doug Manning, a former minister and nationally known facilitator of grief groups, described it viscerally: "Anger is when you hit rock bottom and the emotion comes back up. Anger's very healthy, because that's when you start moving up from denial or despair."

Anger is also a very effective way of keeping oneself shielded from more painful emotions. It was anger that fired many of the widows into action. Anna began moving the pieces of her shattered life around: putting the family house in England up for sale, selling her husband's car, and considering moving out of Middletown. She knew nobody and she didn't drive. "I've got to get out!" she declared.

It's too neat to call anger just a phase. And grieving is anything but neat. Anger does not dissipate if one sits there and swallows it. Grieving experts, like Manning, caution, "It's not enough just to be angry. Your anger needs a focus."

But that's another problem peculiar to the 9/11 survivors: Who or what to be angry at? It's one thing more that suicidal terrorists rob from their victims. Who can focus anger on a bunch of dead terrorists whose names one can hardly pronounce? How satisfying is it to train one's anger on hazy TV images of a gaunt Islamic caveman with wormy lips and dead eyes who parades around with long robes and a rifle?

MR. LAVERTY'S FURY

More typically, the anger finds a personal channel. Kevin Laverty, who was waiting for his wife to retire to move to a condo in St. Petersburg, was totally at sea when she never returned. Anna Laverty, a legal secretary at Fiduciary, had run the whole ship. Kevin had been a tax assessor at US Trust Company, but he hadn't been able to return to work since losing his wife. One hundred and twenty days since Anna's death and Kevin had scarcely been outside of the modest home in Middletown he now shared with his twenty-one-year-old daughter, Deena.

"I hate the place now," he said. "Empty, hollow." He had been sleeping until two or three in the afternoon on the couch in the family room with the drone of the TV his only companion. "I'm not going in the bedroom. It smells like Anna." He was bedeviled by dreams of himself in the Trade Center, pulling his wife out of the rubble and scolding her, "I told you to leave the building!"

In January he accepted an invitation to lunch. There was quite a pause before he opened his front door. Kevin's hair, full and black in recent pictures, had retreated deeply on both sides of his high forehead and turned gray, but it was combed and he was neatly dressed. In the background, his petite daughter was still in her pajamas. Deena Laverty had been attending a trade school to gain a medical technician's degree. She was working in a doctor's office when she learned of her mother's death, the mother who had taken care of cooking, cleaning, bill-paying, everything. After that, whenever Deena had to draw blood from patients, she thought of her mother and spaced out. It was too dangerous. She had quit the job and school.

"Could we go somewhere else?" Kevin Laverty asked shyly. "My daughter just got up and the house isn't picked up yet." He led the way to his four-door Plymouth, hesitated, and asked nervously how far a drive it was to the restaurant. Not very far, about five or ten minutes. Once behind the wheel, he asked for directions. "It's on the other side of the bridge in Red Bank." The car screeched to a stop. "Oh, I don't know if I can go that far," he said. "I don't trust myself driving. My nerves are shot." He accelerated again and plowed over the median on Highway 35. His hands trembled. He had to be helped to steer. Chagrined, he confessed, "This is the farthest I've been away from home since September eleventh."

Settling down at a bar before noon, Kevin ordered a beer. "That's my pill right there, Coors Light." He painted a picture of Anna, the love of his life. "She was petite and absolutely gorgeous. She weighed about ninety-eight pounds. Love at first sight. Oh Lordy, I can't explain it. She just had a radiance. . . . All I knew was that was a woman I wanted to be with the rest of my life." Then his hurt and fear and frustration broke loose.

"Angry at her! One hundred percent. Because she didn't do what she should have done. I told her, 'Get the hell out of there, now!' She was the fire warden on the seventy-eighth floor, with a flashlight, taking people down the stairs. But her boss forgot her pocketbook. I know it for a fact. Anna was so kindhearted to people, I just know she waited for her boss. She should have left. She should have known that after '93. So, sure, I'm one hundred percent angry at her. She left me and her daughter!"

Doug Manning, the grief expert, said, "It is not unusual for a widow or widower to be angry at the dead spouse for dying—*'Why did you leave me like this?'* That's an okay place to point your anger. Some get mad at God—

that's okay, too. He's big enough to take it. The one place you don't want to direct your anger is at yourself. You can tell because you obsess about the 'if only's.' " He talked about Jacqueline Kennedy Onassis. "As long as she lived, she obsessed over the 'if only's'—'If only I hadn't let him go to Dallas. If only I had just moved to the side.' That was her anger turning inside. I'm amazed at how often it happens."

LISA'S ANGER

Lisa Luckett did not have her first dream about the tragedy until January 2002. A building was collapsing, not the Trade Center, but some sort of collegiate building that somebody blocked her from seeing.

"Psychologically, I was blocked," she recognized, but only months later. "Totally shut down. The anger I felt helped me with the shock. I couldn't find Teddy. I couldn't find the love. I knew in my heart he was the love of my life but I couldn't . . ." She wept. "I couldn't feel anything except being left holding the bag."

Lisa had been left with three young children at a point in life, in her early forties, when a natural tropism for a former businesswoman is to turn toward the lights of the big city and the resumption of a career. Of course, the loss of a spouse puts such plans on hold. It was very disturbing to Lisa to feel anger at her husband in the first few months after his death. Logically, she knew that very often people get angry at those they love and lose in order to make the separation easier. But her husband was murdered; how could she blame him? The way Lisa got around it was by engaging in frenzied activity and lashing out at those closest to her. Not at friends, because she desperately needed her friends now, but at family, because family had to love you no matter what.

"First I was angry at Teddy, because he died with unfinished business. After I got through with Teddy, then it was his family. Then it was my family: 'Why don't you know how to help me!' "

Then, an epiphany: "Your anger doesn't necessarily come out at the terrorists, it comes out at whatever was a problem for you before." Then she realized, "How can they all be wrong? I can either change the way I think or I can be miserable."

Despite all of Lisa's admirable efforts at moving on, she was still caught up in the anger phase. So was just about everybody else. Kristen's outlet—battling over the inequities of the fund—did not appeal to Lisa. "It's a no-win conversation," she felt. "If you get less money than you think you deserve, you'll feel bad. If you get more, you'll feel guilty."

Despite the diagnosis of agitated depression, Lisa had resisted medication, arguing, "I need to be strong enough to handle this myself." Once persuaded to take a short course of antidepressants—as one would take antibiotics for an infection—Lisa found it smoothed out the swells and troughs of her emotions and allowed her the clarity to appreciate something surprising: She was learning so much, so fast, about herself.

KRISTEN TAKES ON THE SPECIAL MASTER

For some, like Kristen Breitweiser, with her naturally combative personality and law school background, the anger can blood the eyes and dull the heart's ache almost from the start, and keep the raw, intense grief at bay for a very long time, even years. Kristen was a fighter. She would claim that she'd rather curl up on her couch with her two-year-old and grieve, but in truth she felt a whole lot better in battle mode.

Kristen found her first target in the official empowered by Congress to administer the Victim Compensation Fund. This blunt instrument was hastily tacked onto a bill designed to bail out the airlines before they could be eaten alive by lawsuits over 9/11. Swept up in the emotional aftermath of the attacks, members of Congress were as eager to do something to help as everyone else. What they didn't want to do was get into specifics of putting a value on human life, so they earmarked $6 billion for the human bailout and left the details to a man as blunt as his instrument and his title.

"Special master," the Republicans called the role, and with it came the powers of Solomon to put a dollar value on pain and suffering and to designate an individual dollar value for each and every victim's family. Most people would cringe at such a challenge. Kenneth Feinberg seized on it. A prosecutor by personality and background, who served in the U.S. Attorney's office under Rudy Giuliani, he went to Washington in the mid-seventies as Senator Ted Kennedy's chief of staff. Feinberg is a unique blend of dedicated public servant and almost comically arrogant smartboy. "I'm the final word, that's right," he declared. He and his wife were deeply involved in Jewish philanthropies, and he had earned enough in private law practice to be able to take the special master post pro bono. He was cute about the two reasons he was selected by the Justice Department to take on the lightning-rod role of special master.

"You gotta be tough. You can't be afraid to confront people and tell them what to think," he said. "The other reason I got this, frankly, if you're cynical enough, [Attorney General] Ashcroft said, 'Let's put Feinberg in, that's Kennedy's guy, we're certainly not going to hear from the liberal Democrats out there that his decisions are unfair.' Talk about a buffer!"

The basic gist of the fund was that "victims" would have 120 days to file their claim and present their evidence and walk away with a check. The catch was, by opting to go into the fund they forfeited all possibility of suing any concerned party, and they had to make that choice without knowing what amount their settlement would be. One widow told *The New York Times,* "It's like playing 'Let's Make a Deal.' We don't get to know what's behind Door 3." Once the special master decreed the worth of their loved one's death and subtracted all the "set-asides"—meaning life insurance, death benefits, and pension funds—there was no appeal. Feinberg's pitch when he tried to sell this idea to the families was a rapid-fire monologue: "File your claim, we'll process your claim, in 120 days here's your check. End of story. As opposed to, 'Let's litigate for seven years. Let's explain why your husband or your wife died a horrible death on the 103rd floor. Let's litigate again and again why they didn't know the plane was going to hit the World Trade Center. And let's look at damages again. Versus: Here's the money, good-bye!"

Kristen was not alone among families who bristled at what they saw as the bum's rush. Beyond their financial needs to compensate for a breadwinner's lifetime, they had an emotional need to prolong the process. Kristen had addressed the first meeting of the New Jersey families back in November, urging them to stand together and send in their comments on the fund before final guidelines were set in stone. "Some people need the money now," she acknowledged. "Other people are in a better situation, they don't need the money right away. We should be given the choice of saying, 'I want the 120-day expedited version. Or, I think I need a little more time and I expect my circumstances to be heard.' For some people, like myself, I want to sit there and say what a wonderful person my husband was and what my daughter's life is going to be like without him. I want to do that. It will be part of my healing process."

The very concept of a special master was infuriating to many of the families. Kristen's first face-to-face exposure to Kenneth Feinberg brought her blood back up to a boil. "Bombastic" doesn't do him justice. Feinberg is a tall streak of a man who zooms in and out of his offices in Washington and New York, drops down into a chair, plants one foot up on the conference table, and barks in his heavy Boston accent, "Hey, how're you doin'? Let's talk! Let's do some business!"

Kristen picked up right away that this lawyer, expert in working wrongful-death cases, was not used to dealing with victims. He was used to dealing with other attorneys, where it's all-out combat in the courtroom and then the lawyers go out and have a drink together. Kristen had her new role cut out for her. She had to play hardball. She had first requested a face-to-face meeting with the special master in December to tell him that the families believed his rulings were too abrupt and arbitrary to apply to everyone.

"You're going to tell me my two-year-old daughter's pain and suffering for not having her daddy for the rest of her life is worth *fifty thousand?*"

"Yayus," he replied. "You got it, fifty thousand."

"I don't want it. This is not about me. It's an insult to the children."

"Did you know that in certain states, children cannot recover anything for pain and suffering?"

"That's egregious," countered Kristen. "You don't even have to put a number on pain and suffering. You can calculate therapy costs. Having to carry the baggage of this for the rest of their lives, these kids are going to need therapy for a long time." Kristen raised another sore point among the families—the "collateral offsets" deduction, by which those dead taxpayers who had been the most responsible about providing generous insurance benefits for their families would be the most penalized by the fund's "set-asides." And those surviving parents with the youngest children would lose all Social Security benefits that would have been held for them.

"The collateral offsets—life insurance and pensions and death benefits—I have no control over that!" Feinberg exclaimed. "That's in the congressional statute. And there's not much I can do with Social Security. We *may* be able to do something on workers' compensation."

"My daughter, Caroline, is two years old," Kristen explained. "If her father had remained alive until she reached the age of eighteen, her Social Security account would have amounted to $139,000. You're saying that has to be deducted from her $50,000 pain and suffering award. She'll net out at less than zero! How would you like to try to explain to a child that their pain and suffering is worth less than zero?"

"Those are the rules set up by Congress. There's no flexibility in the rules."

"There's always flexibility."

This was a wrongful-death action, Kristen argued. And the government was taking away the families' rights to sue for wrongful death.

"Let's say your husband was killed by a drug dealer and his car was totaled," Feinberg proposed. "That's a wrongful death if I ever heard one. Are you going to get money from the government? No."

She argued that the fund would be setting a dangerous precedent.

Exactly, Feinberg turned her argument around. "What about Oklahoma City? The embassy bombings in Africa? The first World Trade Center bombing? Lockerbie? Those folks didn't even *ask* for awards from the government."

Kristen became more and more lawyerly, charging that the fund was in effect tort reform. "This fund will set a precedent for what it will cost the government or any manufacturer to pay off for children killed by their carelessness. If it's only going to cost them $50,000, do the math. What's the motivation for them to clean up their act?"

Feinberg became implacably polite. "Come back and chat with me again. Maybe we can help get you a better grounding."

They shook hands and Kristen left. It was only their opening argument.

OVER THE NEXT six months Kristen would turn herself into the chief thorn in the side of the special master. At most of the meetings Feinberg held with families anywhere in the metropolitan area, Kristen and her crew of four angry moms from New Jersey were there, sitting in back.

"Here's the Gang of Five!" Feinberg would point them out.

At a particularly hot-and-heavy meeting in northern Jersey, Congressman Rush Holt rose to introduce the special master but first tried to earn some political points of his own. He was shouted down. "We don't want to hear from you! Siddown! We want to hear Feinberg!" Holt finally caved. "All right, let's forget it. Now, Mr. Feinberg . . ."

The chance to turn around a hostile crowd appeals like red meat to Ken Feinberg. He started out in courtly fashion. "I am now going to talk, and my talk is going to be characterized by the following: A, a healthy dose of compassion. B, a healthy dose of empathy. C, a healthy dose of flexibility. D, resolve to do the best job I can. And finally, a healthy dose of candor. No bullshit—here it is."

That did not calm the crowd. You could feel the hostility. But Feinberg began shouting and barking and waving his arms, rocking on his heels with his sober blue tie wagging from side to side across his starched white shirt. After an hour and a half of listening to the special master ask—and then answer—his own questions, the families were bristling to get to the microphones themselves. Feinberg kept pontificating. Kristen and her Gang of Five began interrupting. He saw they were "galvanized" and invited their questions, which were pointed. About the "set-asides" and whether or not there was a cap. After an hour and a half of verbal jousting, Feinberg called time-out for a press conference but promised he would get back with the same families for another meeting. The widows left angry.

"He's a good orator," said Kristen with new respect. "Now I see how naive I was when I started this. Let's call me 'Clueless in October.' No idea of what I'd have to confront, or that it would become all-consuming."

Feinberg, too, knew it was going to be an ongoing and emotional argument. There would be many more meetings with the families, and in-his-face meetings with Kristen. "I sense that it is part of the grieving process for these victims' families. They are utterly determined to give more value for the memory of the person lost. It's a psychological quest to value the dead." But his early estimates of success in signing up families for the fund were greatly inflated. "I think a lot of these claimant families are going to just come right in and get right out: 'Here's our papers, cut us a check and leave us alone.' " I asked him about all the families who didn't like the way this game was set up and were vowing to sit back and wait to see what the early awards looked like. "You vastly overestimate the calculating design of these claimant families," he said. But sit back and wait was exactly what most of them did.

Kristen turned to a lawyer who was a family friend and one she knew Feinberg would respect: Vincent Fitzpatrick, who had represented Blue Cross/Blue Shield in its successful lawsuit against the tobacco industry. He agreed to help her pro bono. Kristen called Feinberg constantly and continued to show up at his meetings. But Feinberg knew how to play hardball, too. When he met with a reporter at the end of January, he was smug as he handed her a copy of a news clipping.

"Take a look. Front page of today's *Washington Post.* Check the headline."

SEPTEMBER 11 GREED

"Steve Push [a widowed spokesperson for Families of September 11, Inc.] says I'm responsible for this backlash." Feinberg did sound overly eager to pass on the characterization. "If victims are going to claim they want more money, then the natural reaction of some is to write back and say, 'You're being greedy.' " Feinberg was defensive. "What I don't get is these same five or six women that I see over and over again who claim to represent the four thousand, if they really speak for them," he complained in January.

Feinberg was asked if he slept well at night.

"No. What goes through my mind is how to maximize the awards and how to administer the program fairly. Since these people can't realistically litigate in court, all the pressure's on my shoulders." Most of the venting, he said, rolled off his back. But once in a while, a comment would stick. The worst yet was the widower who looked at him with venom and said, "I hope it happens to you."

Kristen was sandbagged by a right-wing radio talk show out of San Diego while being interviewed about the fund. A caller who had lost her husband in a tragic accident lashed out at Kristen: "I've got three words for you—get a job." Kristen heard the bitterness in the woman's voice. "I refuse to turn into that person," she vowed. She would force herself to smile and take long walks and play with her child. But the surfer girl who had referred to herself as "Clueless in October" was being clued in fast as to how the game is played. "We're up against people who know a lot more about how Washington works than we do," Kristen acknowledged. "I think the spin came from the White House—spin this to make the wives look greedy—so we'll be spending all our time hovering in the corner, worried that everyone thinks we're grasping, instead of pointing out that the fund is unfair. And you know what? It's working."

In future months, Kristen became indelible in Feinberg's mind. "Kristen is a spitfire," he later said. "I see lots of angry families. But she's an angry *lawyer.*" Coming from Attorney Feinberg, this was a high honor for a girl with a degree from Seton Hall and three days of actual law practice. Her nemesis came to respect and even enjoy her; she was a worthy opponent.

There was some blow-back of anger in the community toward certain of the widows who were quite obviously well off. Sheila Martello, for instance, had made herself publicly prominent by joining with Kristen and Ginny Bauer in their successful media campaign and legislative lobbying effort to win the two-year income-tax exemption for the victims' families. Sheila and her husband, Jimmy, a hefty Jersey guy who had gone from varsity linebacker at Rutgers to successful trader at Cantor Fitzgerald, had been very recent relocatees to Rumson. Only a few weeks before 9/11, Sheila's husband had bought her a six-million-dollar home in the exclusive enclave. He was forty-one when he was murdered. Sheila expected to collect from the federal government's fund the equivalent of her husband's peak income until he would have reached sixty-five—somewhere in the neighborhood of $25 million. Despite the fact that she had two young sons, she was not automatically a sympathetic figure in the eyes of most middle-class Middletowners.

"Most of these women were not to the manor born," observed Maureen Fitzsimmons, the social worker who supervised the Catholic Charities support groups. "They were fortunate enough to marry these very ambitious young men whose success on Wall Street catapulted their families into a very high living standard. Some of the women developed a sense of entitlement that has stayed with them after 9/11."

TERRY TURNS HER BACK ON ANGER

This was not the case with Terry Fiorelli. Her family was solid working-class stock and proud of it. Her father had been an electrical engineer all his life and, although retired, liked nothing better than to strip down to his undershirt—he still had the body of Zorba the Greek—and Sheetrock an addition on his daughter's house. Terry's husband, Stephen Fiorelli, was an engineer who managed tunnel projects for the Port Authority. Terry had met Steve at the Port Authority headquarters when they both worked in the Trade Center. She was a green-eyed girl, generous to a fault, always giving out gifts and satisfied to be a secretary and supportive to her boss.

But Terry was no shrinking violet. She was tall and muscular and, at least in the summer of 2001, she was still fractionally taller than her twelve-year-old son and able to jump for a rim shot he couldn't block. Terry coached basketball at her son's parochial school in Red Bank. Sports was where she really lived.

It was her son who expressed the anger in their family. "I'm ninety percent mad at bin Laden and I'm ten percent mad at Daddy for not getting out in the beginning. Didn't he think about us?"

Terry went over and over the brief communication from her husband that morning. Steve had called her from the sixty-fifth floor of the North Tower. "What are you still doing there?" she cried. The fire department told them to stay, he said. Steve Fiorelli had trained in fire safety, and he knew from being in the previous bombing that smoke could be more lethal than fire. As an engineer with the agency that had built those towers, he also had complete faith that they would never fall. So her husband and fifteen others remained in the Port Authority office, wetting their clothing and stuffing it under the doorways. What happened next she had learned from one of the two survivors. When they opened a door and checked the hallway, it was clear of smoke and lights were still on. Steve Fiorelli and another Middletown resident, Patrick Hoey, a civil engineer for the Port Authority, made a decision to shepherd the group down the stairs. The two men were last in line so they could encourage the women to keep going. The group proceeded at a calm pace until they reached the twenty-second floor. Everything began violently shaking. The survivor dove into a corner and blacked out. When he came to, all he saw was blue sky and a tangle of steel beams. He was lying on top of fifteen feet of rubble, buried in which were Terry's husband and Patrick Hoey, along with twelve others.

Terry tried to explain it again and again to her son and her eleven-year-old daughter. "You have to remember, Daddy was a manager. A leader. He was doing what he thought was the right thing to do. Helping his people to escape. He was just at the end of the line. . . ."

She told herself after the first months, "I can't dwell on anger. That doesn't do anybody any good. You have to redirect it to something positive." She vowed, "Okay, I'm redirecting it into raising my kids. My house. The bills. Whatever I have to do. Getting ready to go back to work."

WHO'S THE VICTIM?

Bereavement groups began popping up with "forgotten" in the title: The Forgotten Parents, The Forgotten Fiancées. Some were not facilitated by a professional. Karen Dalla Valle helped to start a group dedicated to the proposition that the fiancées were the forgotten victims, relegated to insignificance and financial limbo. Karen had lived for three years with Kenny Tietjen. She, like Kenny, was a police officer with a divorce behind her. She had an adolescent son from the previous marriage, whom Kenny loved and who idolized Kenny. The couple had bought a house together but hadn't married.

Soon after Kenny's memorial service, Karen lashed out at his partner, Officer Mike Ashton. "You're no friend of Kenny's!" Mike, who was already beginning to slide into despair and semi-isolation as he wrestled with the guilt of having survived his partner, was so upset he had to stop talking to Karen. He refused even to speak her name. Karen accused Kenny's other friends of ignoring her and lavishing their attention on Kenny's family.

Karen had hired a lawyer weeks after the death and was pursuing a claim for the money from Kenny's estate. Kenny's sister Laurie and his father made several trips to the New Jersey Family Assistance Center to satisfy themselves that Karen's mortgage and bills were being paid by the various charities. When the fiancée's attacks continued, further upsetting Kenny's parents, Laurie grew frustrated. "She's just not thinking straight," she said. "I know a lot of fiancées have been left out in the cold, but she's not one of them. Of those monies that have come in, my parents wanted to turn over the majority to her. I hope that one day she realizes how lucky she is. She wants to be treated as if she was Kenny's wife, and unfortunately, she wasn't."

The situation was aggravated by the rumor that his parents had rushed out and bought a Mercedes. Laurie laughed at the implication. Her parents still lived in the pocket-sized ranch house in the blue-collar Belford section where they planned to die. "We grew up in this tiny little house—all three kids and my parents in a five-room house—and now we joke about it: How did we fit so many people and great big Kenny in that little house?" Laurie said. The Tietjens were known for being among the most charitable families in Belford. Every Christmas the family collected clothes, food, and toys to distribute to the needy of their community. Kenny's job had always been to buy bicycles for as many kids as he could afford from his own savings.

The Tietjens continued to make overtures to Karen. They wanted to reach out to her son, even though he was not Kenny's child. Those overtures, too, were blocked. Although the situation caused them anguish, they acknowledged, they tried not to discuss their problems with Karen outside the family.

Admirably, the Tietjens did not see themselves as victims. "We see ourselves as proud parents of a wonderful young man," said Janice, Kenny's mother. "A lot of people talk about wrongful-death suits," said Laurie. "There's no wrongful death here. My brother wasn't supposed to be at the Trade Center that day. He was there because he wanted to be. And if we were standing right next to him, we couldn't have begged him to change his mind. It's tragic, we cry every single day, but . . ." Kenny's mother finished the thought: "That's what he wanted to do."

"That's what he wanted to do," Laurie repeated.

Kenny's mother said, "That's who he is."

The family continued to be haunted by the expectation that any day his body might be found.

Chapter Seventeen
———

FEELING THE HOLE

FINDING KENNY

White nights. Already the Port Authority recovery team had spent 153 white nights digging in the groin of downtown New York under the livid glare of stadium lights, and for weeks they had come up with nothing resembling human remains. But one night in mid-March, Rudy Fernandez had a feeling they were going to find Kenny.

"Kenny's recovery was special," said Rudy, standing over the hole where the South Tower once stood. "I mean, they're all special, but his was special insofar as I got to know the family. It became like a personal mission of mine to deliver Kenny to his family."

Rudy Fernandez, the great oak of a young Port Authority police officer who had been assigned to temporary morgue duty, had befriended Kenny's younger sister Cindy before September 11, but he hadn't made the connection until he gave Laurie Tietjen a tour of Ground Zero. *Tietjen:* Now it clicked! That was the name of one of the bravest young Port Authority officers buried under the pile. But Rudy and his brethren had to wait while a bridge was constructed over the remains of the South Tower to allow heavy trucks entry into the site before they could begin to dig into that particular mountain of debris. Once they began to demolish that pile, they found some equipment at what had probably been the promenade level. A rescue must have been in progress.

"That led us to believe that we would recover Kenny," said Rudy, "and we were very excited, very, very excited." On the night of March 13, they kept digging. No telling what time it was; the nights were as white at 1 A.M.

as they were at 7 A.M. No one watched the clock down there; every minute, no matter how monotonous, held a possibility. "It was a very dangerous recovery," said Rudy soberly.

The next morning, Laurie was on her way to the Port Authority Technical Center in Jersey City on a happy mission. She was excited to meet with Inspector Chris Trucillo and Chief Joe Morris to give them more details about contributions offered by her company. When the inspector called her cell phone from the road and told her the meeting was off, she knew.

"You found my brother, didn't you?"

The inspector went silent. Laurie could hear him choking back sobs. Sounding as calm as you please, but in shock, Laurie asked the inspector, "Where are you? I'll come to meet you." She began to drive. Her cell rang again. It was the chief of police from New Jersey Transit calling to ask, "How're you doin'?" All at once, it hit her. Her fire wall cracked. The pent-up emotions she had held back for five months came flooding out and she was crying hysterically behind the wheel, driving aimlessly, until she found herself in Newark and hopelessly lost. When she spotted a police car parked in a gas station, presumably monitoring traffic, she pulled in. Still weeping hysterically, she tried to get the cop's attention. "Please! I need directions!" No response. She leaned on her horn. The cop still wouldn't look in her direction. Furious, she got out of her car and ran over to the police car and banged on the window. No reaction. She looked again. It was a dummy. Dressed in a cop's uniform, sitting in the car.

"Goddamn it, Kenny, I'll kill ya!"

It was like one of her brother's practical jokes. If only. If only it were just another of Kenny's practical jokes.

IT WAS WEEKS BEFORE Laurie could talk about the recovery. "I had a picture in my mind of what happened on the eleventh, that it was very sudden and peaceful, and that's what I could live with," she said. "When Kenny was recovered, that picture changed dramatically. The brutality of what happened there really came to life." Rudy Fernandez declined to be specific with her about what they found: "There's going to be some things here that I'm never going to talk about, I'll take with me to the grave."

Officer Tommy Johnson, Kenny's best friend, had refused to leave Ground Zero until he found Kenny. He slept for the first two weeks in the kennel with the rescue dogs. He was summoned in March when the recovery finally took place.

"One of the things that helped is that they found Kenny surrounded by EMS equipment," Laurie learned from Rudy and Tommy. "They also found evidence that there was another person there with him. So they have clues that he was helping somebody at that time. And that helped me, because he died doing exactly what he was born to do."

Kenny's mother, Janice, a religious woman, prepared herself mentally by saying, "It's in God's hands, whatever happens. We have no control over it." It was weeks later that the recovery team found Kenny's gun and part of his holster, flung far from where they had picked up bits that could have been from his body. They kept these grisly details from Kenny's father, but he was puzzled when he visited the Port Authority trailer at Ground Zero and studied the blackboard where the names of the thirty-seven dead officers were chalked. "Why isn't there a star next to Kenny's name?" he asked. A star indicated the recovery of enough of a body to be identified. An officer gently explained, "Well, they have to wait for DNA on Kenny for identification."

The Tietjen family had a few visits with a psychologist. They asked for help in curing the canker caused by the complaints of Kenny's fiancée. The doctor told them to give up trying to assuage her. They needed to draw boundaries to protect themselves. "The psychologist explained that she had adopted the role of victim," Janice related. "That's it in a nutshell."

More important, the therapist helped them with accepting the truths of Kenny's last moments. "Part of my heart has died to lose a child," said Janice. "I'll never be the same. But I feel very close to Kenny, so I know he's at peace. He lived his life so actively and so fully, and he made so many friends, he just could not cram enough in. I think God allowed that because he was going to have a short life."

PAT AND THE SECOND DEATH

How death invades your life, again and again. The doorbell. The detective with the doleful face. Fear like a penknife scoring the heart. Not wanting to hear about the irrefutable remains. Not wanting any more information, not even commiseration.

It must be a mistake, it's someone else, another woman's husband.

Out of the thirty-two missing on the list of Middletown detective sergeant Joseph Capriotti, the remains of only ten had been identified as late as February 2002. He did not look forward to reporting any more positive identifications. He lamented, "When they begin to accept it and decide how they're going to carry on with the rest of their lives, it bothers me to walk in and give them the news and watch people's lives collapse around them." It was like reporting a second death.

Pat Wotton opened the door to Capriotti the week before Valentine's Day. "No!" she cried. "It can't be." Dorothea, her two-year-old, was screaming from the bathroom. It was a nightly scene now. Dorothea would refuse to take a bath. She wanted Daddy to give her the bath; that was their nightly ritual, Daddy bathing her with his big, strong hands and carrying her to bed and snuggling alongside to read her *Goodnight, Moon.* Ever since September, when her life had been turned upside down, Dorothea had been terrified of taking a bath. Pat had tried everything she could think of, changing her bath toys, buying new shampoos, inviting a friend over to take a bath with her, but the scenes were only growing more horrible. Just try to lower the child into the tub and Dorothea would scream—not a spoiled scream, but a terrified scream.

She was screaming now. Pat panicked and then blanked out.

The detective and a social worker, together with Marian Fitzgerald, the spiritual director of Pat's widows' support group at Holy Cross in Rumson, sat with Pat for three hours while she slipped in and out of accepting the finality of their news. She didn't wish to hear what part of Rod's body had been found. For the memorial service in October she had been numb. Now she would have to plan a funeral. Shortly thereafter, the baby had to be hospitalized for respiratory problems. Pat stayed with the baby and organized the funeral from the hospital.

In her despair, she couldn't even remember back to the person she had been before she met her husband: the career woman who entertained herself and supported herself. "I don't know her," she said. "And I don't know who I am now. I'm a shell."

Days after Pat laid her husband's remains to rest, she opened an anonymous letter attacking her as a greedy person. A copy of her husband's obituary was clipped to blowups of fake $1,000 bills.

ANNA AND THE MIDDLETOWN BUBBLE

I'm thinking of buying a house and moving back to Connecticut," Anna Egan announced in early March.

Sitting in her nearly empty trophy house, the hole Anna Egan was in felt more like a bubble. "Everybody in Middletown has been too nice, which is wonderful, but it's not normal," she said. "It's like living in a bubble. Everybody wants to protect you. I'd like to start in a new town where people don't say, 'You know, she's the lady who lost her husband and sister-in-law in the Trade Center.' "

Anna felt her life was still on hold, but just thinking about moving brought some color into her otherwise colorless world. She had never wanted to leave Greenwich, and now, of course, she wouldn't be able to afford to move back to such a pricey community. But maybe that was for the best. She'd look for a house near enough so she could see selected friends, but not so close that the old Greenwich friends would see the hole where Michael used to be the dominant figure in their family.

Her older son, Jon, was thrilled to hear she might put the trophy house on the market. He called her constantly from college on the West Coast to say, "We're a team now, Mom." He wanted her to e-mail the specs on any house she saw. They would make the decision together. He would always ask about his younger brother, Matthew: "How's my boy?" Jon had every hope of stepping into his father's shoes.

Anna did not have the burden of some of the other Middletown widows, who were at pains to maintain the image of the perfect upper-middle-class suburban wife. She had no problem acknowledging "I'm a little insecure about being on my own. I've always had a partner in life. I'm sure I'll make mistakes. But I'm just going to have to cross those bridges on my own. That is reality."

KRISTEN IN WITHDRAWAL

Once Kenneth Feinberg decreed in March his final rule for the September 11 Victim Compensation Fund, and sent out his thirty-page commentary, Kristen the spitfire lost her worthy opponent. She had worn out most of the widows who were her lieutenants in the fund fight. Friends were urging her to give it up and get on with her life. It had been so much easier when she was in full battle mode, the portable phone wedged into her shoulder day and night. She wouldn't hit the pillow until 3 A.M. and she'd be up at 5. Suddenly deprived of a target, she was left for six weeks staggering around in what she jokingly referred to as Ken Feinberg withdrawal.

"I had a huge breakdown," she said. She immediately deflected this uncharacteristic confession by describing how her car had broken down on Route 35, and how it had happened just as her daughter, Caroline, was having an acute allergic reaction. Kristen described running the child's stroller down a four-lane highway to get to a pharmacy, and that night having to take Caroline to a hospital. It was a lot easier to talk about the problem with her car and Caroline's allergies than it was to address her own deep emotions.

"Now, every once in a while, in the back of my brain, it just seeps in that I'm totally alone," she said, barely audibly. "He's not coming back. And it's terrible."

LISA AS INSPIRATION

I'm fine. I don't cry," Lisa Luckett repeated like a mantra. "And I don't want to waste my time sitting around with a bunch of weepy women in a support group. I want to be *helpful.*" And she was. Even as she directed her energies outward and kept busy helping everyone else, from time to time Lisa would say, parenthetically, "I'll probably crash sometime down the road, but right now I have important things I want to get done."

Other widows saw her, variously, as an inspiration—the perfect widow—or a daunting model. "How can she do all these things?" they would marvel. "She's just so together."

Lisa escaped Middletown, in February, to Mexico. It was her first vacation without Teddy. She was accompanied by her parents and her children and fully expected it would be a relief to get a break. Instead, grief finally tore the first hole through her resistance. She felt the hole, the hole where Teddy would have been. They had planned this trip together. "It was bittersweet," she said. "Now vacations always will be."

In late March, on the ferry ride from New York to Middletown, the sky oozed pellets of thick rain. The bay heaved and spat against giving in to what the calendar designated as the first day of spring. Lisa's home was a warm refuge. She microwaved instant coffee and kept up her usual cheerful banter. What was different this time, at the six-month mark, was that Lisa could cry. Every time she talked about "the hole," her lips turned down and her throat closed up. She would dart out of the room and come back blowing her nose, saying, "I really apologize for all this congestion."

Through her tears, though, Lisa was adamant. "I am not going to let our kids have unhappy lives because they lost their daddy. I cannot let it do that. "We'll take him with us in our hearts, always, but we're going to go forward."

She was becoming relentless in going out and about with her children. "This is us, this is our family," she was telling herself and the world. But her old friends saw the hole. She could read it in their faces. "It's very glaring to them that Teddy is missing. The first time, it's probably a slap to people looking at us. It may create discomfort, but we all have to be uncomfortable. It's not going to go away." What buoyed her spirits were the new people in her life. Like the nanny she had hired and called Mrs. Doubtfire. And the therapist she had taken on after interviewing many others.

"Why are you interviewing me?" the psychiatrist had asked.

Lisa shot back, "Let's just say I've had a lot of bad dentists."

These new people who came into her life after her husband's death perceived her differently. So did the people from her life before Teddy, the college classmates with whom she had reconnected. "They don't see the hole. They see me as having a future."

She laughed. "Which is an interesting concept, having a future."

She had plunged into working with Rick Korn on a series of creative projects. Her enthusiasm was infectious. They staged a neighborhood concert with several nationally known artists, including Phoebe Snow, meant to showcase the healing power of music, and they filmed it. The goal was to have a documentary ready for a network to air on the anniversary of 9/11, tracing the journey of healing. One day in March, Korn was on his way into New York to pitch the treatment when Lisa reached him on his cell:

"We can't do this," she told him. "It's too soon."

Chapter Eighteen

THE GRIEVING SPIRAL

G rieving is not linear. Grieving is a spiral. The mind takes in only what it can handle. A person may seem to be moving on, until a memory or a sensory detail invades or further trauma piles on; then the person loops back and down into the vacancy of despair, and another thrust forward is needed to complete the loop and move forward again. For the families of 9/11, the constant reminders in the news and the confused accounts of what allowed those towers to vaporize—all the why's—kept them tumbling, spinning, hurtling round and round in the messy spiral of grief. They no sooner took a few steps forward than they lost their footing, again. And being kept off balance made it almost impossible to begin the passage to recovery.

September 11 was not the first time Americans were intimately devastated by an act of terrorism. The families and survivors of the Oklahoma City bombing have been on their journey of recovery since April 19, 1995, when a domestic terrorist blew up the Alfred P. Murrah Federal Building. The figure of 168 people killed does not begin to tell the story. More than two hundred children lost a parent, seven thousand people lost their workplace and beloved colleagues, twelve thousand volunteers and rescue workers were exposed to the horrors of the site, and over one third of the population of the city knew someone who was killed or injured. The invisible psychological wounds and secondary trauma persist to this day.

Man-made disasters are more stressful than natural ones. Usually, relatives and local grassroots groups make the first efforts to care for victims' families and survivors, well before officialdom moves. A new community of the dead gives rise to a magnified mirror image—a much larger community of caregivers who are willing to share the trauma. As the psychoanalyst Erik Erikson conceived of it, this enlarged community of "spiritual kinship" functions as a "source of commonality in the same way that common languages and common cultural backgrounds can." Such communities sprang up immediately after the 9/11 attacks in many places: at Ground Zero; at the family assistance centers at Pier 94 and in New Jersey's Liberty State Park; among the Pentagon family; in Shanksville, Pennsylvania; and in all the Middletowns of America. This spontaneous outpouring of love and caring and commemorative efforts is the part of the story we like to focus on—the progressive narrative.

Eventually, however, officialdom does recognize its own shortcomings. Around the six-month mark, New Jersey's professional caregivers began to reach out to their Oklahoma City counterparts. A nonprofit group in Princeton sponsored a two-day seminar for the counselors and facilitators working with 9/11 families and victims, many of whom were struggling to develop expertise in this new field of traumatic grief therapy.

"I don't think there is such a thing as grief therapy or grief counseling" was the startling opening by Doug Manning, a grief facilitator from Oklahoma City. "I think that the only effective effort is through 'companioning.' People in grief usually need someone to walk with them."

Manning, who describes himself as "a recovering Baptist minister," became interested in grief intervention when a church member who had lost a child came to him back in the mid-seventies, hysterically sobbing. Everyone was trying to calm her down. She snapped back, "Don't take my grief away from me!" His ineffectuality led him to read the fewer than half-dozen books on grieving then available. Manning tried putting together grief groups and recognized that the standard mental health model was insulting to those in grief. "They're not mentally ill, they're having a normal reaction to terrible loss," he concluded. In 1982, he resigned from the church and began writing books and training grief facilitators and giving seminars. The candor of his talk in New Jersey gained him respect from many of the clinicians: "Every one of us who has written in terms of stages of grief stole from Elisabeth Kübler-Ross," the M.D. and psychiatrist who wrote the groundbreaking 1969 book *On Death and Dying.* "But I don't like the concept of stages— they're too clear-cut. There's a different way to talk about it. Grief is like peeling onions. It comes off a little at a time, layer by layer. Nobody has an onion like anybody else's onion. Your layers will come off at your own pace."

The grim truth we should have absorbed from Oklahoma City is that terrorist-caused psychological trauma is *cumulative.* And "getting even" doesn't fix it. Manning made a profound plea to the clinicians: "In the New York–New Jersey area, you have to learn how to get past the anger at a horrible event. In Oklahoma City, at least we had a villain to catch. We thought when they caught McVeigh, that would help. It didn't. Then they tried him. We thought that would help. It didn't. Then we fried him. And a lot of us watched him fry—we were certain *that* would help. It didn't."

Three years after the bombing in the heartland, many survivors were just entering the bleakest period of grief. In fact, the need for help in containing the psychological fallout and behavioral problems began *increasing* after three years—among many survivors, family members, and ever greater numbers of rescue workers and their family members who had initially been the most resistant to help. It was no coincidence that this bleak period began right around the time that Timothy McVeigh received the death sentence. Now the universal target of rage for the survivors and families had been neutralized, and they were left to wander in their own private hells. The healthiest person among the bereaved of Oklahoma City, as Manning sees it, was the man who declared he would not attend the McVeigh trial or his execution. Why not? Manning asked him. "Because Timothy McVeigh has already taken every moment of my life he's going to get," the man said. "I'm going to live every second of life I have left."

Manning says in the last stage of peeling the onion, you turn a corner and decide to get well. The pain will still be there, but it will be a dull ache.

OKLAHOMA CITY, APRIL 19, 2002

It has never yet rained on Oklahoma City's Remembrance Day, April 19. On that day in 2002, seven years after the terrorist event, the April air was warm and soft. Everyone gathered under the Survivor Tree, a mighty American elm that stood close to the building and had appeared to be totally destroyed. This was the same kind of tree coveted by the pioneers because of its superior strength; they used it to make the centerboards for their covered wagons. The Survivor Tree with its twin trunks forming a V for victory had completely revived, and that April it was just leafing out.

On a promontory beneath it were gathered a few hundred people, some smiling and hugging members of their "spiritual family," some appearing as grief-stricken as they had been on the original April 19, holding flowers to their chest or pictures or teddy bears. All looked across the reflecting pool toward the sacred ground—another grassy knoll that will live in infamy in

America's history, this one covered with 168 empty chairs. The chairs sat stoically in rows on the footprint of the Federal Building, their backs of bronze and their seats made of glass cubes etched with the names of each of those killed. This outdoor room is bracketed on either end with massive free-standing walls of stone known as the "gates of time." Huge numbers are carved in their surface; 9:01 at one end and 9:03 on the other; two minutes within which time stopped, not only for the dead but for some of the survivors and the families, who now stood expectantly looking for some sign, some salve, something else to happen.

The dread moment. The two minutes of silence. A lone guitar and the tremolo of a black woman's voice piercing the air of this once-segregated state with the unshaken faith of "Amazing Grace."

It was at this point, every year, that Priscilla Salyers felt the sinking again. Priscilla is a survivor who had worked in the Federal Building. It was something like the feeling she had when she fell through five floors, thinking she was having a heart attack or a seizure, but then came the calm, the quiet, the painlessness. Would it have been better to lie there and forget about fighting for life, let her soul drift up, never to know the silent agonies of the survivor? She walked over to embrace another survivor.

"We need each other," Priscilla whispered. She is a small, softly contoured woman with fine brown hair who might have gone through life working for Uncle Sam and knitting and believing in the simple verities. She is different now. She needs to stay in touch with other survivors. "We all know each other; maybe not by name, but by now we're all family. We have become an extension of those who died."

SURVIVING SURVIVAL

The families are important, but my heart goes out to the survivors of September eleventh, because I can tell you, the survivors also go through hell," Priscilla confessed in a private moment. "The attitude is 'You lived, you're lucky.' Hearing that from everyone, including your own family, you become silenced. You don't dare speak up and say, 'I'm hurting, I'm in depression, I lost my good friend or I lost my staff, I didn't deserve to be saved'—those things don't count because you didn't lose your life."

She was asked to tell her story. She retold it as vividly seven years later as if she were living it all over again.

"Three of us were in the office that morning. I was the only one who survived. I was talking to Paul—my dearest friend—we sat side by side for years. I saw more of Paul than my own husband. I was sitting at my desk when Paul came up and asked me a question as we heard the bomb go off. I can still see his face and the look in his eyes. I knew that he had heard it but there wasn't even enough time to think, 'What was that?'

"I can remember a whirlwind going around in my head. Thinking, 'Am I having a heart attack?' I put my hand on my chest and thought, 'Well, I'm not in pain.' Then I felt like I was having a seizure. I'd lost control of my body. I kept trying to fight against it. That was me falling through from the fifth floor—the floors all pancaked—and I fell down to the bottom. I didn't even know that I was falling.

"When I landed—of course, I didn't know I landed—all of a sudden everything just became very quiet. It was dark. I couldn't see anything. I heard nothing. 'Okay, okay, I'm not having the seizure anymore, I'll try to sit up.' I couldn't move at all, except my left arm. As I got a little more oriented, I realized there was stuff on top of me. We have little cubbies that hang over your head, and I just thought that they had fallen on top of me. And Paul was going to come and get the cubbies off of me and, you know, we'd laugh about it.

"I thought I was still sitting at my desk on the fifth floor.

"I heard a woman's voice near me say, 'This is the child-care center. We have a lot of children.' And I was thinking, weird. The child-care center is on the second floor and we're on the fifth. I heard a man's voice respond, 'We know, we're trying to get you out.' Then it went dead silent again.

"It was real hard for me to breathe. I was telling myself to calm down. After a while, I heard another man say, 'We've got a live one.' I felt his hand touch mine. He asked me my name. Then he said, 'Do you know why you're down here?'

" 'Down here? What are you talking about?' "

PRISCILLA SALYERS probably could not have come closer to death. Her family was elated that she'd made it out alive and expected that when she came home from the hospital, everything would go back to normal—better than normal, because she would be happy, too. They were baffled when she became moody, then detached and withdrawn, and finally, they feared she was becoming suicidal.

"I felt survivor's guilt very bad, and I did have suicidal thoughts," she admitted. "I would remember how it was when I was lying down there in the rubble . . . it was so peaceful. And I didn't have any pain. I knew that if I had died, it would have been like going to sleep. And it would have been easier than what I had to face."

Priscilla had been a passionate knitter. She always had her knitting with her. She would knit on her lunch hour, knit waiting for the bus, even sometimes knit in a boring movie. Before the bombing she was working on a Christmas sweater. "The FBI agents found my yarn, scattered all over. They gathered up what they could and returned it to me, but I couldn't knit anymore. I met a woman at the Nichols trial who'd lost her baby. She used to sew, but after the bombing, she couldn't sew anymore. Then there was a man who used to do woodwork. He'd lost his grandson, the one he used to make wooden toys for. He couldn't do woodwork anymore. Well, at the trial, when I heard these things, I got mad. I said, 'They killed 168 people, but they're not going to get me.' "

On the seventh Remembrance Day, Priscilla showed some of the "family" the sweater she had knitted for one of her coworkers, another survivor, a young marine who was still fighting traumatic reactions.

"When did you go back to knitting?" a colleague asked her. "Right after the Nichols trial," she said. "I call it the Victory Sweater. The chaplain takes it with him when he speaks to survivor groups. He tells them, 'She knit her life back together.' "

With the benefit of seven years of hindsight, Priscilla Salyers can now see how long it took to peel her onion. "It took me a little over a year just to work through the survivor guilt. It took probably another three years to feel I wanted to grab back onto life, not just exist."

The long, heated fights over what the Oklahoma City memorial should look like provided one of the most effective mechanisms of healing. For a while, different divisions of "the trauma club" fought one another. Some of the mourning family members took out their fury on survivors, arguing that they shouldn't have equal say. But the pain and anger became converted, with time, into a harder compound fused with passion. It resulted in a place where the significance of all their losses could be marked, and named, and visited in private or in shared gatherings of commemoration—like the one on this anniversary.

Following the ceremony under the Survivor Tree, the mourners descended steps to the grassy knoll and walked among the chairs, which are arranged row by row according to the floor on which those who died once worked. People stopped by a special chair and made a private ceremony, then fanned out to greet one another. This gathering of the survivor network is the most powerful and comforting aspect of what otherwise would just be a mournful remembrance. People don't have to speak. They don't have to say any special comforting words. Their hugs and shared tears say it all. They don't do small talk. But they can do jokes. And they can definitely do "How's that grandchild?," speaking about what's still living and growing.

Vicki Hamm, another survivor, paused at the top of the steps. This was the spot on which she was able to lay down the heaviest of the stones she had carried from that day in 1995. A woman of generous heart and body, Vicki was one of the many office mothers of the Murrah Building. Over the eighteen years she worked there, she made a point of recognizing all the faces, even if she didn't know all the names. She saw people get married, went to their baby showers and their children's graduations. "What happened is, they became your family," she said. "You didn't realize it until it was taken away."

On the morning of April 19, 1995, Vicki had called in sick. Eight people in her office died that day. For the next five years Vicki lashed herself with thoughts like " 'It shouldn't have happened without me there.' I don't mean I wished that I had died in the bombing. I'm not saying things would have been different. But that's where I was supposed to be that day, no matter what."

Vicki's outlook began to change only on April 19, 2000, when the memorial was dedicated. "At one in the morning I walked down these steps for the first time and past the reflecting pool and onto the grass where the chairs were. I felt this peacefulness come over me that I hadn't felt since the bombing. I felt the life in the glowing chairs and I could smell the grass. It was such a wonderful feeling. It was as if I had been wearing this heavy, heavy overcoat and carrying all my feelings in it—the anger, the hate, the frustration, despair. I had been carrying it for five years and it kept getting heavier and heavier. That day, I was able to take that overcoat off and leave it there. I felt so much lighter. I felt free. And I was ready to live again."

The next step on her journey of healing was a transitional phase that many survivors of trauma find helpful—becoming what I call a "survivor guide" who educates others. When Vicki volunteered to be a guide at the memorial, she felt "I was back where I belong." She would work at her full-time day job, and then rush to the memorial and work another few hours. She couldn't wait to tell the story to visitors; in fact, she sometimes had to hold herself back and let the poor, innocent visitors at least walk into the museum first. "I'm telling the stories of the lives that were in that building," she said, her eyes gleaming. "It's not my story. I let the visitors know that I'm blessed to be here and if things had been different, that chair in the fourth row would have my name on it. And the people those chairs represent would be up here, telling these stories."

But this transitional phase, too, can have a downside. Vicki, like some of the other survivors who eagerly volunteered as guides in the memorial's first year, was still running on adrenaline and driving herself faster and faster—mainly to avoid confronting painful feelings. The accumulation of stress, exacerbated by fatigue and frayed relations with their own families, who felt neglected, took a heavy toll on the survivor guides.

One of the most common complaints one hears from families of survivors is this: "I'm living with a stranger."

That was the angry reaction of the families of both Priscilla Salyers and Vicki Hamm. Why were they working fifteen or twenty hours a day? Why didn't they talk about what they were doing? Vicki tried to brush off her family's concerns by saying, " 'I'm moving around. I'm fine.' But they wanted to see that everything was back to normal. But it was not normal. It's still not normal. And it never will be normal again. They want the old Vicki back and she's not coming back."

Vicki Hamm didn't know she was suffering from survivor guilt until she was persuaded to see a psychologist. "It crept up. I was keeping so busy with my full-time job and doing guide work at the memorial, I'd drop off to sleep in the car. Or cry in the car on the way to work. I wouldn't cry at home, thinking I was protecting my family. I began having thoughts of killing myself. I don't think I was processing the grief. I just wanted to escape the pain. Through the help of a therapist, I learned that there's no way to get to the other side without going through the pain. After the first year of volunteering, I had to slow down."

Vicki and Priscilla were both able to pull their families back together, once they accepted the fact that their husbands and children could not be expected to be much help with the psychic burdens they still carry. Those burdens they take back to the memorial. "The heavy overcoat sometimes comes back, but I have a place to put it down—and what a perfect place," Vicki said. "That's what memorials give survivors. I think about the families from New York, how important it would be to have a memorial. Because they have to have someplace where they can lay down the heavy overcoat."

VICARIOUS VICTIMIZATION

The mental health professionals who worked with the survivors and families and rescue workers of the Oklahoma City tragedy were part of an unprecedented effort by the federal government to reach out to the devastated community and offer mental health support. It was called Project Heartland. Volunteers went door to door to tell residents they were offering workshops, one-on-one counseling, and educational meetings. So deep and prolonged were the community's psychological needs, Project Heartland had to be extended several times and lasted for five years. Even today, a hot line remains and some of the original volunteers still privately counsel people suffering from post-traumatic stress disorder.

But the toll this effort took on the mental health caregivers was severe. Stark conclusions were drawn in the Justice Department's final report, dated October 2000. The report, "Responding to Terrorism Victims—Oklahoma City and Beyond," was meant to be a warning.

> *Caregiving professionals and victim advocates, while skilled in dealing with victims' severe emotional distress, were not prepared for the scope and intensity of the traumatic reactions experienced in the weeks, months, and years after the bombing. Significant levels of secondary traumatic stress were experienced by a wide range of professionals and were exacerbated in many cases by the cumulative effect of exposure to other traumatic events.*

All six of the clinicians who stayed with Project Heartland through the five years developed serious physical illnesses, along with many of the other sixty employees who worked closely with families and survivors. "Most of these illnesses are going to be with us until the day we die," said Gwen Allen, who was assigned to be director of the mental health project. "And most of them—the autoimmune disorders, the heart attacks, the depression—can be tied back to the work that we were doing. The combination of constant stress from listening to the horror stories, never feeling we could do enough, not taking care of ourselves, giving everything we had to the work, and going home to collapse but finding it hard to sleep—it resulted in another class of victims."

Gwen Allen developed MS. When she was first diagnosed, her employer, the state Department of Mental Health, denied any connection to her work with bombing victims. She is no longer working and lives on Social Security.

Linda Wagner, a clinical social worker, had a heart attack while in session with a client. She underwent a triple bypass and is no longer employed. She lives on Social Security disability.

LuAnn Smith, also a social worker, developed superventricular tachycardia. Surgical interventions were unsuccessful. It wasn't until her heart leapt into arrhythmia during the anniversary remembrance six years later that LuAnn realized her physical problems were related to the bombing. She didn't bother to pursue workers' compensation after seeing how the Mental Health Department administrators had dealt with her director. She now provides mental health services to an Indian tribe and loves her work.

Kent Matthews, who worked with the most severely affected group and the most resistant to treatment—the first responders—developed a neurological disorder that threw off his equilibrium. For a while he couldn't drive and walked with such poor balance, he had to hold on to a wall. Under treatment for Ramsey Hunt syndrome, he is doing better and continues to offer counseling to "his" first responders.

Cheryl Hanlon, an office manager, became ill with both diabetes and lupus. Jim Norman, a social worker, needed extensive dental work from grinding his teeth and was troubled by intestinal problems.

None of these caregivers was given workers' compensation for his or her physical health problems. The federal government's Victim Compensation Fund, set up for the 9/11 people, was not approved by Congress to include the families, survivors, first responders, or mental health caregivers of the Oklahoma City bombing.

The lessons for mental health professionals and the recovery workers at Ground Zero were clear. When constant stress persists for much longer than a month, the normally protective rush of stress hormones is disrupted and, over time, can run amok. After twenty years of resistance by many in medicine, there is now widespread acknowledgment that chronic stress can invite illness and even serious disease. It does so when it derails the finely tuned feedback between mind and body and weakens the immune system. Dr. Bruce McKuen, director of the neuroendocrinology laboratory at Rockefeller University, has shown that when our systems are not given a chance to rest and replenish the brain's chemical equilibrium, we can damage our brains, shrink our memories, damage our hearts, and invite depression, stroke, diabetes, and rheumatoid arthritis, and accelerate our aging.

It's not just the stressors themselves that do it; reminders of past trauma make the heart beat faster and blood pressure soar and stress hormones flood the body and interfere with digestion and sleep. Then there are the by-products of this state of mind: the tendency to self-medicate by eating fatty foods, smoking, overindulging in alcohol, skimping on sleep, and driving oneself to the point of withdrawing from soothing social contacts and inviting family backlash.

The dirtiest word to the families and survivors struggling through the passage out of traumatic grief is "closure." It isn't a clinical term. Closure is a feel-good notion that comes out of the self-help movement. Doug Manning, the Oklahoma City grief facilitator, believes the rush to closure is wishful thinking that things will return to normal, an attempt to anesthetize ourselves to what has been incontrovertibly changed. "When we urge others to seek closure or 'get over it,' it comes from our own very human need," he suggests. "We try to shut people down because we don't want to face death."

Chapter Nineteen

———

STIRRINGS OF NEW LIFE

Y*ou can't die with the dead.*

That looked to be the way Kevin Casey was leaning. After the weeks of crawling around the smoking pile and looking for some sign that his wife, Kathy, was still alive, he had become somnambulant. Oh, he still showed up at work and came home to sit across from his son, pushing takeout food around the plate and trying to make conversation, but he moved like the walking dead. Maureen Fitzsimmons, the supervising Mother Hubbard of the Catholic Charities support groups, was not going to let Kevin Casey slip through the cracks. She reached out to tell him about a new group that was starting for adolescents. Would he like to bring his son? He agreed to try it.

KEVIN AND TERRY

That Tuesday night in late October 2001, the atmosphere inside the Catholic Charities house was more like a funeral home than a social agency. Four or five stony-faced, suddenly single parents sat as widely scattered as possible around the waiting room. Kevin hung by the door. With his baseball cap on backward and two days' growth of beard, he clearly was not looking to make small talk. He intended merely to drop off his son, find out what time the child would be finished, go home and brood, and come back.

A green-eyed woman sitting on the bench said hello. Her face was open and engaging. She introduced herself, Terry Fiorelli. She had brought her son, too. They began talking about their spouses, identifying them first by the floor they had worked on in the Towers. In no time, they were reminiscing about their missing mates—in the present tense. Kevin kept standing. Close to the door. But he found the green-eyed woman surprisingly warm and easy to talk to; he almost got comfortable.

As the weeks went on, Kevin started shaving before he showed up on his son's meeting nights. He took off the baseball cap and revealed his receding hairline. He found himself looking forward to seeing the green-eyed woman there, and talking. Amazing, what they had in common. Terry Fiorelli, like Kevin Casey, was tall and lean and very athletic. She, too, coached recreational sports. He could tell that she was a remarkable mother, the kind of person who took care of everyone else before she thought of herself. He saw it at the session where Terry brought her eleven-year-old daughter, Chrissy. "Terry was sitting on the bench and Chrissy laid her head on her mother's shoulder. Just so natural and comforting, it was beautiful to see their bond." Kevin got up the nerve to ask Terry for her number—just in case he had some information to pass on. Terry tore off a scrap of paper and carefully printed her name, her children's names, and her home number. He never called.

Over the Thanksgiving weekend, Kevin hit the wall. Not only was it his own birthday, it was his wedding anniversary, the anniversary of his father's death, and the kind of damnable family holiday that can rip your heart out if your family has a hole in it. He had taken his son up to his brother's house in Boston. He couldn't bear to stay and drove home alone, in a funk.

"I remember reaching in my pocket and finding a lumped-up piece of paper—Terry's number. I called her up and we talked. And we talked. Until my portable phone died. I just sat there in awe. I thought, 'What a wonderful person this is.' I called her back on another phone and we went on talking for hours. She was better than any therapist. And she didn't cry!"

"You can't die with the dead," Terry was telling him. She knew he was in a bad way. "You're still living, and you have to think of what Kathy would want for you. She wouldn't want you to stay in bed all day. Remember, you have a son." They talked about their faith; both were Catholics. They talked about their marriages; both had had loving marriages. They talked about the folly of thinking there is always time.

"My husband liked to work weekends on the house," Terry confided, "and my thing, I always wanted us to spend a weekend together at a bed-and-breakfast. I never made the reservations. The kids got older and it would have been easier to leave them. But I never made the reservations. You take for granted they're always going to be there. We never spent that weekend alone."

They cried together about having made the same mistake.

At the next session, Terry was not sitting on the bench when Kevin walked in. He found out she was sick. He was deeply disappointed. It occurred to him that she was the first real true friend he had ever made. At the next session, Terry arrived dressed in a silk overblouse and something leopardy—Kevin couldn't recall the particulars of her costume, but the overall impression was *Whoa!* "She's naturally beautiful, no matter what she wears, but this was the first time I was aware of the physical attraction."

Over the Christmas holidays, Kevin and Terry went to the circus with their kids. Kevin took along a camera; one of his regrets was not having taken many pictures of his wife and himself. In January, when he got around to developing the roll, he called Terry. "You won't believe this. The first five frames are pictures of Kathy and me on Cape Cod from a summer ago. The sixth frame is of you and me. What do you think it means?"

They both had to struggle with guilt. Terry questioned herself: *How can I have feelings for this man and still miss my husband so much?* Her answer came when Kevin first kissed her. She closed her eyes and for once did not think of her husband. She and Kevin were in the land of the living, and it felt so very good to feel the rumble of life again. She came to the conclusion that she couldn't give up having a relationship in her life. *My husband is not coming back,* she told herself. *And I'm not a teenager.*

"Kathy and Steve [her husband] may have something to do with us getting together," Terry told Kevin. "And I think God had some say in this, too."

On a gentle evening in April, when Maureen Fitzsimmons was leaving the Catholic Charities house, the supervisor passed through the waiting room and said good night to the parents of the teen group. She made an effort to contain her smile. Kevin Casey and Terry Fiorelli were sitting on the bench side by side, their hands touching.

AMANDA AND THE PHANTOM BROTHER

Sherry McHeffey was distraught about her youngest daughter. "My daughter was clearly depressed. She spent three solid weeks on the couch after September eleventh, crying. I kept calling her from work, but she wouldn't pick up. She couldn't move."

It was alarming, but not altogether surprising. Amanda McHeffey was only halfway out of the cocoon of girlhood, having graduated from college the previous May with no idea on earth what she wanted to do. And given an economy pitched toward recession, her résumés were a one-way ticket to nowhere. So it was back to the old summer waitressing job and sliding by in a day-to-day sort of existence, living at home and waiting, like so many of her friends, for grown-up life to start. Oh yes, and her father had walked out that year, leaving her mother after thirty-two years for the arms of another woman. Amanda had turned for comfort to her older brother, Keith McHeffey, a thirty-one-year-old equities trader for Cantor Fitzgerald.

"Keith came in like the new dad in the family," her mother liked to say.

Amanda had watched the televised horror show on September 11 with her mother and her older sister, Leigh. Why Amanda lay on the couch day after day for weeks afterward, unable to move, she couldn't begin to explain until months later. "A lot had to do with my father having left. And then one day a plane flies into a building and my brother is gone, too?" She shakes her blond ponytail. "It's unreal. The two came back-to-back." Amanda had not yet begun to absorb the first trauma. The second one paralyzed her.

"Why don't one of you have a baby?" her mother would say to the two girls. "Just to make things better."

It was said kiddingly but seriously, says Amanda.

Then who should appear on a dreary day in October but a likeness of her lost brother: a young man of the same age with the same strong jawline, similarly broad-chested and blond and given to flushing bright red across the bridge of the nose after too much beer. Gregg Kennedy had been one of Keith McHeffey's best friends. Gregg, too, had been laid low by the loss of Keith and, like Amanda, he had stopped going to work.

Unbeknownst to Amanda, her worried mother had e-mailed Gregg a couple of times and told him Amanda wasn't handling this well. Sherry had asked if he would stop by and try to cheer up her daughter. Now picture Amanda, a golden-haired child-woman laid out barefoot on the couch, her blue eyes pinked with pain, her thick black lashes dewy with teardrops, her future a blank wall. It was a natural setup for a fairy-tale romance.

Gregg sat by her on the couch and reminded her of the day, September 13, when they all had gone into the city together with Keith's other friends to search every hospital and temporary morgue. He told Amanda he had seen something in her that day he had never before seen in a girl. "Something clicked," he told her.

Five months later Gregg would commit to taking Amanda as his wife. How this all happened so fast is open to various interpretations. Amanda herself gropes for a coherent story line: "Gregg came over one day in October, just to talk to me. I didn't really think anything of it. It was just Gregg. I'd seen him a million times, because he was one of Keith's best friends."

Gregg waited a few more weeks before approaching Amanda's mother to ask if she would mind if he went out with her daughter. He expected her to be shocked, or miffed; after all, it was an unwritten rule that older boys didn't fool with their buddies' little sisters.

"I think it's a great idea," Amanda's mother said. She gave him her big dimply smile. "In fact, Gregg, you can marry her."

So one day in early November, Gregg pulled Amanda aside and told her straight out: "That day we went into the city, I fell in love with you." Amanda was stunned. "I thought Gregg was cute, but I'd never thought of him in that way," she admitted. Marriage was the farthest thing from her mind. Gregg was eleven years older and had his own house and the ideal bachelor life, which earlier had led him to boast that he'd probably never get married, or maybe, eventually, down the road, he'd settle.

"We kept it secret," Amanda said of their courtship. "We didn't think Keith's friends would think it was right. They knew I wasn't in the right state of mind." She hastily amended that idea: "But I felt like I was fine."

That first Christmas without Keith, the three females of the McHeffey family had no tree, no stockings, no church service, not even a sprig of holly. Amanda's mother cringed whenever she heard the screen door bang. That was the sound her son had made when he came by every day to check up on her, the sound that had brought her back to life after her husband had left. And now, such a sad, shrunken little family. Half joking, Amanda's mother said she might think about getting a dog.

After Christmas, Gregg took Amanda away to California with him. He was going to look at graduate schools in Los Angeles, and the two needed an excuse to be alone together. Amanda returned glowing. Some weeks later, when the pair announced their engagement, the ripples of shock touched just about everyone they knew.

"My friends are in disbelief—it's too weird!" she said. "When I told them I was engaged, they said, 'Whoa, you're the first!' " Most of her girl-friends had never even met Gregg. Amanda was twenty-two. She sounded as surprised as anyone.

"Was Amanda looking to get married?" her mother's friends asked. "No, it just happened," her mother would say contentedly. She might add, with a delighted little giggle, "In my dark, dreary world, I almost think Keith put them together."

Amanda's older sister, Leigh, was more practical in her approval: "Any kind of hole has to be filled in somehow. It's definitely a blessing, because Amanda was really depressed, not that she didn't like him—"

Amanda's mother might interrupt and supply the Sleeping Beauty story: "I had even gotten her on Zoloft because I was very worried about her. But Gregg brought her out of it." Sometimes, telling this story, Amanda's mother would slip and use the name of her son, Keith, in place of "Gregg."

Gregg's own mother raised the big question: Could the two be supplementing their loss of Keith with their emotional attachment to each other?

"I don't think so," Amanda's mother dismissed the idea. "This is a good match. Good for both of them."

The wedding was held in May. Out of town. Across the country in Los Angeles, at the Bel Air Hotel. "We had only thirteen people so we could do everything top drawer," said Amanda's mother, pulling out the wedding album, which recorded the brilliant sunshine of southern California and the romantic pond with the gazebo and swans where a Catholic priest who was a friend of the family conducted the out-of-church ceremony. Afterward, posing for the wedding pictures, Amanda looked every inch the fairy-tale bride with her golden hair swept up and her soft shoulders exposed by a strapless white organza gown. But there was something slightly off about the pictures. Amanda looked self-conscious.

"I look so fat," she explained. "I had to ask the tailor to let out the seams three times on both sides." She didn't tell her friends that she was four months pregnant.

Her mother picked up the narrative and supplied the happy ending. "Our family was on a downward slide. Now we have a son-in-law, and"—her eyes shone—"a new baby coming. It's like we turned a corner."

ANNA AND HER ENGLISH COTTAGE

Anna Egan was certain the little English cottage in Connecticut was too small. When she first saw it, in March, she told the realtor she would need more space. It took some time to adjust her inner eye to frame the actual dimensions of her new family: now that her oldest son was away at college and her husband was never coming home, it would be just her and Matthew, her sixteen-year-old son. Weeks later, the realtor suggested a revisit; the price had just been lowered. Seeing the house again was, for Anna, as if she had clicked down from "f-stop 4" to "f-stop 16."

"Why did I think this was too small?" Anna exclaimed. "It's just right!"

So it was that on a lovely spring day in early May, Anna Egan was meandering about in her yard with her second cup of coffee, taking a few moments away from the thank-you notes and the endless paperwork concerning her husband's estate, to think about the new life to come. She was day-dreaming about the English cottage in Connecticut. It evoked exactly the opposite images of Michael's trophy house, with its glass walls and grand staircase and cold modernity, a house in which she felt a prisoner. When Anna thought of the cottage on which she had just closed, she thought *cozy, informal, a couch in the kitchen, firelight in the dining room, maybe an old-fashioned four-poster for the bedroom, yes, and an English garden. Oh, lots of roses, a trellis covered with roses, and a path and a bench with a dedication to Michael, where I could sit and read a book . . .*

The cottage had almost no windows in front. The windows in back looked out on woods. This was a shelter. Just what she longed for now. Easier to take care of; less expensive. But most of all, it was exhilarating to take title in her own name. *My little house.* And in another two weeks she would have a brand-new identity to go with it. On May 20, Anna Egan would become an American citizen. She was curious: What would she be like as a fifty-year-old single American woman?

"I need to rediscover myself."

Anna looked so much fresher. The circles under her eyes were far less dark and deep. She was thinner than ever, her tiny arms hanging like poles from a sleeveless spring blouse, although she had stopped chain-smoking. She carried an unlit cigarette, twirling it in her fingers, but she didn't smoke it. Anna was busy building a whole new life structure in her mind, a structure realistically suited to a life without a husband, but not a life where she would always be known as a widow of 9/11. Michael's insurance had left her financially secure, so long as she was careful. Had he lived, his high-six-figure income would have provided a different sort of lifestyle. She hadn't bothered to follow up with the Red Cross after it lost her file. And once the "set-asides" were deducted, she wouldn't get enough from the Victim Compensation Fund to make it worth the hassle.

"You kind of lose your self-esteem," she said. "I felt better when I decided, okay, we're not going to ask for help. We're going to do it on our own." She planned to work part-time; full-time work was out of the question with her son's special needs. She would volunteer again with the Special Olympics. And she planned in the following year to take a trip on her own, back to Sicily, to reconnect with her roots. Even as Anna chattered gaily about the cottage to which she would move in the summer, she wanted to show off the trunk of mementos that she was preparing for her son Jon.

She knelt on the floor of Michael's office in the Middletown house and cataloged each of her husband's childhood toys and historical artifacts from his hometown of Hull, England. It seemed fitting to pack up these memories and pass them on to Jon, in preparation for her next step as a widowed American woman. Before closing the trunk, Anna wrote a card expressing her feelings for her son and laid it on top.

There, she had gotten through an hour and a half of talking about her husband and she hadn't cried once.

"I'm starting to see a little light at the end of the tunnel."

VACATION FAVORS

I've got to escape!"

That desire became dominant for many grieving Middletown families as spring vacation crept up. Loneliness was gnawing now. The children would be home from school. The widows had exhausted the video rentals. Middletown had no singles bars, and even if it had, imagine the talk around town if one of the widows so much as had a drink with another man in public.

The FAVOR women's network once again anticipated their needs. Allyson Gilbert and Janet Dluhi and their ninety volunteers had ranged beyond their original intention of visiting the families monthly with a basket of goodies and favors. FAVOR had found church women willing to cook and deliver meals. They contacted sister Middletowns around the country—all eighteen of them—and were disarmed when the smallest of them, Middletown, Virginia, population 1,200, sent its mayor and police chief to New Jersey to deliver in person a collection of $10,000. In all, FAVOR raised more than $200,000 in cash and an additional $500,000 in goods and services. But the biggest favor they could do for families who had been in deep mourning for over six months was to offer them a vacation—a ticket to escape. Diversions would contribute to their healing process.

The volunteers consulted travel guides and wrote to just about every family resort from the Catskills to Florida. They asked friends to offer up their getaway houses. By the time they were finished, the FAVOR ladies collected sixty-four vacations. At the spring planning meeting around Allyson's dining room table, the chore was to custom-tailor the vacation offerings. Allyson brought out her enormous flow charts showing each family's profile. But by now, the volunteers knew their families' idiosyncrasies.

"Okay, we have six long ski weekends at Stratton Mountain over

Easter," Allyson began the bidding. "Two trips to Washington, D.C., and a time-share in the Catskills or an overnight in the Poconos for families who won't fly."

"My widower in the wheelchair wants to go to Atlantic City, the Taj Mahal."

"Maybe we can buy him a weekend."

"Here's a one-nighter in Harley, Pennsylvania, a hole in the wall!"

"Forget about it. We have ten free weeklong vacations donated at an exclusive Caribbean resort, Punta Cana Resort & Club in the Dominican Republic."

"Ooh, isn't that where the Clintons like to stay?"

At first, the widows were excited by the offers. Then, second thoughts. What fun would a vacation be when they'd be up all night, alone, watching TV in a hotel room with the kids asleep next door? Gene McCabe, who had lost his brother, Michael J. McCabe, in the Trade Center, took on the task of creating an appealing weekend vacation package. Soliciting donations from hundreds of local businesses, McCabe created a long weekend holiday in Newport, Rhode Island, complete with hotel, meals, museums, tours, and other entertainment. After offering it to all thirty-two Middletown families, he was disconsolate when not a single one signed up, at least not until June. But those families who eventually did muster the motivation to try taking a trip that first spring were almost universally delighted.

One of those was Karen Cangialosi, the aerobics instructor with two young sons.

"I wanted the boys to be able to go skiing," she said when she accepted the trip to Stratton Mountain. "That's what Steve and I had promised them for this year, and I don't want their lives to be deprived because they lost their father." No sooner had Karen set her mind to making the four-day trip, driving ten-year-old Jeffrey and seven-year-old Peter without a copilot, than panic began to set in. Their old '95 Mercury station wagon had a cracked headlight. She hadn't been able to sell the car for sentimental reasons: it had belonged to her husband. When she took it in to be fixed, the mechanic noticed that her inspection was overdue.

"Oh," she said, "it was due to be inspected last September."

The day before the trip she raced to the Motor Vehicles Bureau to get a new registration. Setting her apprehensions aside, she drove to Vermont through snow and ice with her two little sons in their Princeton haircuts reading the map and calling out navigational signs. It gave her a sense of raw physical power. They had no sooner checked in to the ski lodge than Karen attempted to make a fire—a chore that had traditionally belonged to her husband. The family was just settling down with hot chocolates when the screech of a smoke alarm broke through. The boys had never heard this sound before, and given their state of hypervigilance, they looked scared. Karen consciously projected calm. She asked the boys to put on their boots and step outside. She opened the windows and climbed up and removed the battery in the alarm. With newly practiced aplomb, she invited the boys back inside.

The surprise for her was that bedding down alone was not as bad as it had been back on the Thanksgiving trip with her in-laws, when she had been the only one without a partner. "I remembered going to bed that night and turning to talk to Steve, and he wasn't there. This time, I was alone with the boys. No phone, no paperwork, they got to come first." The family skied and laughed and forgot their troubles for hours at a time.

"I knew once I got back home, I would feel better about having gone," Karen said. "And once I got back, I did feel better." That was in March. By May, Karen had concrete evidence that she could pull off both the mothering and fathering roles. Jeffrey wrote a letter to Karen for Mother's Day. He recounted all their funny little adventures, and how he never knew Mom could do so many things—Mom was Superwoman!

"When I read Jeffrey's letter, I saw that he now believed exactly what I want my boys to believe," Karen said. "They are going to be okay. Mom can handle it."

THE MADONNA DEL PARTO GIVES BIRTH

I'm Mary's mother—oh, and a new grandmother!" said the attractive middle-aged woman who opened Mary Murphy's door on a bleak February morning, where the only spot of color among the naked trees was the pink balloons bobbling off the lamppost to announce the arrival of a baby girl. "The first question she asked as the baby was coming out was 'Does it have all its parts?' "

The newborn weighed a little less than Mary's two previous babies, but she was robust at seven pounds, nine ounces. She had come through incubation in the womb of a joyless mother in perfect order and with a placid disposition. And Mary's milk came in. Mary entered the kitchen with the tiny, bright-eyed baby peeking over her shoulder. "She's as laid-back as her father," Mary said, smiling broadly. She had fallen in love with the baby.

Finger of Doom

Aerial view on 9/11 of smoke from the Twin Towers
reaching due south to blanket Middletown.

Liam Gumly, MODIS Atmosphere Group, University of Wisconsin—Madison

September 11 widow Kristen Breitweiser with her daughter, Caroline: "Where is the book for a thirty-year-old woman with a two-and-a-half-year-old child whose husband was killed by terrorists and who watched it on TV?" *Photo © Harry Benson*

Ron Breitweiser. *Courtesy of Kristen Breitweiser*

Anna Egan in her husband's "trophy house" with son Matthew: "The facts are, I moved to Middletown, lost my son to college, and my husband was brutally murdered."
Photo © Harry Benson

Anna in her English cottage with sons Matthew and Jon: "I'm rediscovering Anna, and it's like, oh my God, I survived!" *Courtesy of Anna Egan*

Michael Egan.
Courtesy of Anna Egan

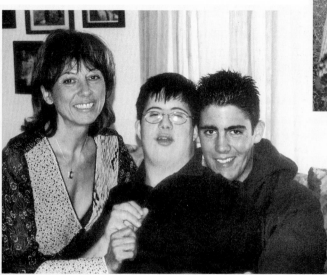

In June 2002, Pat holds a photo
of her husband, Ron, in his
black-draped garden, where
she created a memorial to him.
Photo © Harry Benson

Pat with her post–9/11
baby, Rodney Patrick.
Pat was determined to
create new family
rituals. *Gail Sheehy*

Mary Murphy, Post–9/11 Mom

Mary marks the first anniversary of 9/11 at her husband's beach with her children, Jimmy, Morgan, and her post–9/11 baby, Meredith.

Photo © David Schofield

Mary works on a portrait of her husband, Jimmy: "I'll never forget his eyes."

Gail Sheehy

Officer Kenny Tietjen

Portrait of Kenny by Middletown
artist Nancy Gawron.

Officer Tietjen's Family

Laurie Tietjen, Kenny's sister,
wearing his police badge,
March 2003.
Courtesy of Laurie Tietjen

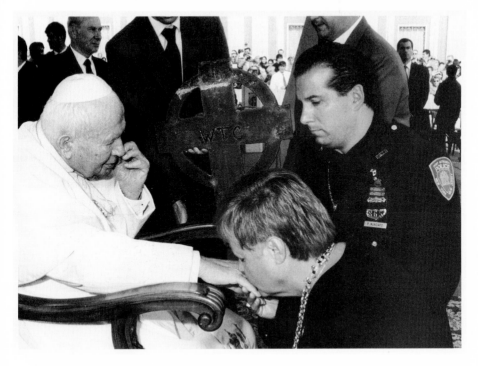

Janice Tietjen, Kenny's mother, presents to
the pope a steel cross forged from the ruins of the
World Trade Center. *Vatican photo*

The Survivor and His Wife

Bob Planer with his wife, Paula: "We got through it with faith, family, and belief in each other." *Photo © Joyce Ravid*

The Widower and the Widow

Kevin Casey wanted to go to sleep at Ground Zero
beside his dead wife, until he met 9/11 widow
Terry Fiorelli, who told him, "You can't die with
the dead." *Gail Sheehy*

The Ground Zero Family

Lieutenant Bill Keegan, night commander of Ground Zero, who led a team of Port Authority police in the recovery effort, with Donna Lamonaco, a police widow his men came to trust.
Peter Turnley/Corbis Sygma

The FAVOR Family

Two of the founders of the grassroots volunteer network FAVOR, Allyson Gilbert (center) and Janet Dluhi (right), filling Christmas baskets for Middletown's 9/11 families with volunteer Heidi O'Neil, December 2001. *Gail Sheehy*

The Chief and the Educators

Police Chief John Pollinger: "I don't have problems, only distractions." *Gail Sheehy*

Antonia Martinez, principal of Middletown Village School: "This is how you teach your children about loss and grief."
Photo © Joyce Ravid

Daniel Lane, principal of Middletown South High School: "I don't know how to deal with my grief." *Gail Sheehy*

Clergy of Rumso

Rabbi Harry Levin
(right) found partn
in "soul work" in
Episcopal minister
Ophelia Laughlin a
Presbyterian minis
John Monroe.
Photo © Joyce Ravid

**Muslims of
Middletown**

The Gabr family.
Right to left:
Dr. Abdel Gabr,
a rheumatologist;
Ehab, a car nut;
Wallid,
"Mr. Personality":
Aya, the only Muslim
in her elementary
school; and mother
Eklas, a teacher.
Gail Sheehy

The McHeffeys

Keith McHeffey (left), a thirty-one-year-old 9/11 victim, with best friend Gregg Kennedy in 1999.
Courtesy of Sherry McHeffey

Sherry McHeffey (right), Keith's mother, told her lost son's best friend, "Gregg, you can marry her." Sherry is shown here at the wedding of her daughter, Amanda (left), to Gregg Kennedy.
Photo © Eric Brooks

Karen Cangialosi

Karen, a 9/11 widow, checks out her new hairstyle on the morning of the first anniversary of the September 11 attacks. *Gail Sheehy*

Karen with her husband, Stephen, 2000. *Courtesy of Karen Cangialosi*

Ginny Bauer and Son

Ginny with her husband, Dave, Paris, 1998.
Courtesy of Susan Bethke

"Take care of your momma, son," President Bush told Ginny Bauer's son David. "I will, sir," David Bauer said. "But would you just get him? Get Osama."
White House photo

Just Four Moms from New Jersey

Ready to roll from Middletown to D.C. for another "widows' walkabout" around Capitol Hill to fight for an independent investigation. Left to right: Lorie van Auken, Kristen Breitweiser, Mindy Kleinberg, and Patty Casazza. *Photo © Joyce Ravid*

It's Never Over

Lorie van Auken listens to survivors testifying at the first public hearing of the 9/11 commission. *Ruby Washington/ The New York Times*

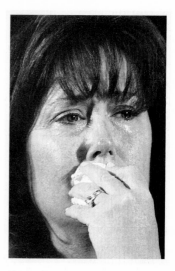

Patty Casazza reacts to testimony at the first public hearing of the 9/11 commission she helped to spearhead. *Ruby Washington/ The New York Times*

Middletown Connects with Oklahoma City

Three wise men from the East. Left to right: Imam Abdur Rahim Mohammad, Rabbi Harry Levin, and Father Jerome Nolan.
Gail Sheehy

Rabbi Harry Levin leads community guardians from Middletown in a healing chant under the Survivor Tree at the Oklahoma City National Memorial. *Gail Sheehy*

The healing connection in action: Middletown and Oklahoma City caregivers share strategies and hope.
Gail Sheehy

Jimmy, her three-year-old son, bent over the newborn and gently rubbed her face with his own sacred blankey. "Baby like me," he announced proudly. Like other young children in the homes of the widows, Jimmy was subdued. He didn't run around yelping and bouncing off the walls; he mostly played quietly and came over frequently to lay his head on his mother's knees or crawl up in her lap for a reassuring hug.

The delivery had gone like lightning, so fast, in fact, that Mary's father had stepped out of the delivery room for a moment and missed it. Her mother had been there and her sister and her mother-in-law, all in the room to welcome this sacred resurrection of the spirit of Jimmy Murphy.

Mary said she was just glad the birthing was over. "It was like going to the grocery store, just another thing on my list of things to do." But she was concerned that she hadn't felt the same about this pregnancy. "Usually you make a connection when you're pregnant," she had told a friend. "I haven't felt that. I still feel like I'm watching a movie, this couldn't possibly be my life. I'm just going through the motions and doing what I'm supposed to do."

Three months after her baby's birth, the widespread sanctification of those lost on 9/11 was beginning to get Mary Murphy down. How could she talk to a saint? And it pained her not to have Jimmy there in the flesh to share the magical moments when baby Meredith gave her first smile or uttered her first gurgle of pleasure.

"For a long time, he was just gone," she said. "I couldn't find him. I couldn't make that connection. I'm completely outnumbered by his family, and of course to them he's a saint. You couldn't say anything about him. I knew he had faults. Not many. We had a good marriage and a lot of fun."

Mary had investigated art therapy. Friends of Amanda, a private foundation, had funded the idea of a pair of clinical psychologists to offer free art therapy for the young children of 9/11 in the Middletown area. Amanda's Easel, they called it. Mary was told this kind of intervention is particularly well suited to young children, who don't have the verbal skills to express unfamiliar feelings and fears. She thought it sounded like a good idea for her four-year-old daughter, Morgan.

"Trauma memories are not necessarily stored in the verbal parts of your brain," explained Laura Greenstone, one of the therapists. "Trauma fragments them. If you don't address the trauma element, it can lead to a pathological grief process. That's why art therapy is so valuable, because it helps the children organize their memories in another way, without having to talk about it." Once Mary enrolled her daughter in the preschoolers' art therapy group, the director encouraged Mary to join the mothers' group. The first thing they asked her to do was to draw "your safe place." That brought Mary a flood of tears. She couldn't draw, she said, and she couldn't talk about it.

She tried other ways of communicating with her husband. One day in the car, impulsively, she grabbed a gas receipt and wrote to him: "Give me a sign." But no sign appeared. By April, the isolation of being back in the kitten box with a new baby had begun to get to her. She did not truly feel a stirring of new life until she went away. She couldn't have gotten much farther away from the car-choked parkways of New Jersey than the Outer Banks of North Carolina. With a girlfriend she took a house for two weeks and they spelled each other watching their collection of six kids. Mary began running. She was able to run in the fine white sand for a whole hour and maybe catch a glimpse of wild horses and let her mind run free.

"It felt great. Away is good," she discovered. "Away is very good."

She began to sense her husband's presence for the first time. "I tried to speak to him like I normally would. Nothing artificial." The amazing thing was, once she got beyond the images of halos and saintly glows, she was able to see her husband as an imperfect human, "and now it's more like I'm having a conversation with him." The great surprise was that their relationship was changing. "Now I'm the boss," she said, laughing. "I feel like I'm giving orders. 'Tell me this. Am I doing the right thing? You've got to help me.' " She had the sense that her husband was watching her. "I think," she said, "that Jimmy would be proud of me."

Once back in Middletown and the muddle of daily chores, Mary would roll her eyes like this was weird and crazy. "Sometimes I think, 'Is this what my life is, talking to my dead husband?' " But Mary had made one of the most important strides in the journey of grieving. The people who are the most important to us, if they are taken from us by death, are still among the most important people, and they always will be. Our relationship with them doesn't end. The healthiest approach is to allow the relationship to change and be transformed, just as it would in life. By talking to Jimmy, Mary had stumbled onto a simple, profound truth, just as the playwright Robert Sherwood had after the death of his wife:

Death is the end of a life, it is not the end of a relationship.

Chapter Twenty

PASSING THE TORCH

Despite her brief "breakdown," Kristen's fire had not ebbed. If anything, her fury was increasing in ferocity. But now her target was not merely the special master. Now she had in her sights the entire United States government and then some. One day in April she went on a rant:

"How could there be such a colossal, systemic, utter failure that morning? Between the FAA, the NSA [National Security Agency], the CIA, the Secret Service, the FBI? I don't understand it. There is no possible way that four planes could be simultaneously hijacked above the United States and no one know how to stop them until they hit the buildings."

While she spoke, her daughter, Caroline, fell down and began wailing, the phone rang, the dog dragged in roadkill—the usual chaos of domestic life—but Kristen the lapsed lawyer did not miss a beat in rehearsing her summation before punching out an op-ed piece on her computer. As early as the previous October, Kristen had begun to clip news items and buy all the books on 9/11, trying to connect the dots about what was known before the attacks and how, on the day of the attacks, the government had performed so abysmally in its most fundamental duty—to protect and defend its citizens. She picked up her rant:

"All planes were supposed to be grounded [after the attacks on the WTC]. So you've got two planes left up in the air that aren't accounted for, and you're telling me the FAA has no idea where they're going and that one is allowed to crash into the Pentagon? I don't understand why normal American citizens don't find this, like, mildly disturbing. We spend billions of dollars on national defense for intelligence. You think I was a thorn with Ken Feinberg? Like, I haven't even begun."

Although Kristen was a fountain of information, she knew that neither the American public nor the media were putting the pieces together. That was why she felt so strongly about the need for an independent investigation. "They had Moussaoui in custody. [On August 16, 2001, the FBI and the Immigration and Naturalization Service had detained Zacarias Moussaoui, who was enrolled in a Minneapolis flight school, because they suspected he was involved in a hijacking plot. But no one at the FBI had connected the Moussaoui investigation with the heightened terrorist-threat warnings by the intelligence agencies in the summer of 2001.] Before 9/11 and the Patriot Act, you couldn't just hold someone in custody without probable cause. They had the warnings from the FBI agents about the flight schools. Plus there were orders on Wall Street to short American Airlines and United Airlines. Where was our government? Did they know this was going to happen? What were our husbands—collateral damage? The widows just want the underlying story. We want to know *why*."

Kristen couldn't carry on this crusade alone. She needed allies. She had burned out all except one of her Gang of Five in the largely unsuccessful fight for fairness in the Victim Compensation Fund. Patty Casazza, a widowed mom from neighboring Colts Neck with a young son, was still a willing soldier. Kristen had no political clout, no cohorts, only a crusade that she could not accomplish by herself: to unearth the truth behind the colossal systemic failures that had allowed terrorists to use live Americans as cannon fodder to kill other Americans, before it happened again. To Kristen, with only thirty years on this earth, September 11 was a first. What she didn't know was that she was part of an expanding community of wronged widows that went back at least twelve years. Those who would emerge to help her came from a widows' group formed many months before in northern New Jersey.

THE PAN AM 103 CONNECTION

Cathy Tedeschi is a thirteen-year veteran survivor of terrorism who lives in Princeton, New Jersey. Her husband, Bill Daniels, was killed in the Pan Am 103 terrorist bombing over Lockerbie, Scotland, in which 188 Americans were blown apart in midair at the behest of Libyan leader Moammar Khadafi. At the time Cathy's three children were two, seven, and ten.

Having moved straight from the nest of her parents to marry Bill Daniels after finishing college, Cathy was all about family. There was only one way she could survive without a husband, she thought: leave New Jersey and go back to her parents in Oklahoma.

"But I promised a friend here in Princeton that I wouldn't do anything until the first year was up," she said. "By then, I couldn't leave the other Pan Am 103 families. I had gotten so close to a bunch of them."

Cathy is in her midforties, with curtains of strawberry blond hair that swing on either side of her broad, rosy face. The only telling physical sign of her passage through grief is her eyes; they are tugged down at the corners. But she smiles a great deal, a full and toothy smile that dimples her cheeks and makes one forget her tragedy. Cathy gained considerable grit by sticking it out in New Jersey.

Knowing how vital networks of women can be in offering families of trauma some guidelines on where their passage might take them, Cathy Tedeschi made it her business to seek out the widows of 9/11 in northern New Jersey. Surfing the Net, she found the state police Web site, which listed the victims and the towns in which they lived. She scrolled through looking for anybody who lived between Somerville and Trenton and up to New Brunswick and Princeton. She made cold calls.

"Hello, my name is Cathy Tedeschi. I lost my husband on Pan Am 103, the Lockerbie bombing. Have I gotten the wrong number? Did you lose somebody on September eleventh?"

Stunned silence. Tentatively, a wife or mother would start talking. And once started, she couldn't stop. The first links were forged. From there, Cathy gave an interview and picture to the local newspaper expressing her wish to reach out to the people of 9/11 and share her experience. The sincerity in her smile inspired Ruth Goldston, a certified group psychotherapist with a Ph.D. from Rutgers, who had been struggling without success to help another widow with traditional one-on-one counseling. Tedeschi and Goldston teamed up and e-mailed an invitation to thirty bereaved wives and mothers to come to a first gathering.

"It was October tenth," Goldston recalled almost giddily. "I give us credit—that was mighty early! And the amazing thing—they all came." It was the same lesson learned by Catholic Charities when it offered the first support group in Middletown in October, and when FAVOR started ringing doorbells in November: put on the light and people who need light will come. "Even more stunning," said Goldston, "they all kept coming."

All the freshly made widows started out with the same conviction: "You can't possibly understand what I'm going through." Cathy was right there to affirm the others' experiences as normal and predictable. "You feel like it's all a blur, sure, my whole first year was a blur," she told them. Six and a half years after losing her husband, she had remarried. Some of the widows in the group were comforted by Cathy's personal testimony. But there were a few others who also concerned themselves with the larger question: How could this have happened? Who was responsible? What kind of advocacy role could they play for the families who felt as ignored as they did?

Uniquely, the Princeton support group also had a male member: Bob Monetti, another thirteen-year veteran survivor of terrorist murder and president of Families of Pan Am 103. He had lost his son, Rick. Monetti is a big, gruff man, and at the April 2002 meeting of the Princeton widows' group, he injected a testosterone-fueled fighting spirit.

"You can't sit back and let the government treat you like shit," he challenged them. "Dammit, if it were me, I'd be out in Lafayette Park carrying a picket sign." Well-mannered widows like Mindy Kleinberg and Lorie van Auken shrank back. Monetti's own wife gave him a kick under the table. But on the drive home to East Brunswick, Mindy and Lorie reconsidered and realized that Monetti was right.

Once, Mindy and Lorie had thought themselves exempt from politics, by virtue of the constant emergency of motherhood. They had a bond beyond widowhood: both were mothers of preadolescents. It was a bond as strong as that between sufferers of migraines. But that wasn't all they shared: they had both grown up as "borough girls," Mindy born in Queens and Lorie in Brooklyn, and so both had dormant street tough beneath all their suburban-matron polish.

Their first brush with political activism had come a few months before, when they were asked to attend a hearing before the New Jersey state legislature. Families were challenging the state law prohibiting financial claims for pain and suffering by relatives of victims of violent crime. The two northern Jersey widows had been corralled by Patty Casazza, the nurse from the Middletown area who had been one of Kristen's original Gang of Five. It was only in the car on their maiden trip to Trenton that Patty broke it to the two political neophytes that they would be expected to testify.

"We have to speak?!" Mindy nearly drove off the road.

The three widows heard stories that day that had nothing to do with September 11, but they were able to empathize with people pleading for their government to understand the devastation of violent crime on those left behind. Their hearts broke listening to a mother whose child had been rendered brain-dead by a violent crime, and whose mental anguish made it difficult for her to hold a job; she was told she couldn't collect any insurance for her pain and suffering.

"It was early for us to be introduced to the Big Picture," said Mindy.

"It was like Eve biting the apple," said Lorie.

So in April, on the drive home, Mindy and Lorie replayed Monetti's words: *You can't let the government treat you like shit.* That very night they called up Patty Casazza. "We have to have a rally in Washington."

"Oh God," Patty groaned. "That is huge, and it's going to be painful."

Mindy used her most unctuously girlish voice: "I promise, Patty, this is the last thing we'll ask you to do."

Patty recognized her own ploy. "You lie a lot."

They'd have to e-mail Kristen Breitweiser, Patty said. If Kristen was up for it, Patty would go along. Mindy hesitated. She wasn't Internet-worthy, she admitted. But Lorie was. In fact, Lorie had in her basement what looked like a NASA command module; her husband had been an amateur designer and Nethead who had configured his computers to browse information sources around the world. Lorie e-mailed Kristen: *We're going to rally in Washington. Are you with us?*

Kristen shot back two words. *Let's rally!*

Thus did a new Gang of Four bond around a bigger and better cause. They pledged to try to pull off a rally on Capitol Hill in June to demand a full, independent investigation of the failures of 9/11.

KRISTEN AND "THE GIRLS"

Okay, there's the House and the Senate—which one has the most members?"

Lorie laughed at herself. "I must have slept through that civics class." Mindy hadn't read *The New York Times* since she stopped commuting to Manhattan to work as a CPA and let her husband, Alan, take over the family support. The political education of Mindy and Lorie was in the hands of Patty Casazza, and Patty wasn't exactly a Beltway insider. Seven years old when her father abandoned her and her mother and four siblings in a St. Louis motel, Patty had hoisted herself out of poverty. As the wife of John Casazza, a Wall Street trader, she had an eleven-year-old son and a house in the hills of Colts Neck. An introspective woman, she had a sympathetic face with plump cheeks and a snub nose. To look at her, one would not be surprised to learn that she was studying for a degree in nursing. Patty could at least coach "the girls" on how to find congressional Web sites and rehearse them on the names of their own political representatives. That was, on days when Patty could talk, and there were days when the ache of loss was so crippling she could not even speak. She experimented with medications; it was a roller coaster.

"I don't know where I'd be without these women," Patty said. "It's a connection like no other. When I'm in the pits, I can call them. They are my lifeline."

It was the same story for Mindy. She needed "the girls" in her support group for an identity check. Before September 11, Mindy would have been described as a stand-in for Samantha on *Sex and the City.* Her lush body had reached the peak of mammalian sexuality. On the brink of forty with a sleepy voice and a tumble of honey-blond hair playing around her animated face, she could still pass for a girl. But these days she felt more like one of the Golden Girls—a baggy-eyed, one-woman situation comedy. Every night, she and her three children would roam their house, trying one bed after another, until maybe the four-year-old would finally pass out, while her seven- and eleven-year-olds were still fitful. One day in the window of a furniture store Mindy spotted a monstrosity of a bed, a jokey display item. It looked like it would sleep four. Mindy bought it out of the window.

Unlike Mindy, Lorie measured her progress in recovery by how many aisles she could get through in the supermarket before her eye fell on one of her husband's favorite items and she dissolved in tears. Forty-six when her husband, Kenneth van Auken, a bond trader at Cantor Fitzgerald, was murdered, Lorie had acquired a fierceness in her demeanor. Her posture was knife-straight, her beautiful face as sharply chiseled as an arrowhead. Her dark brown eyes had a reddish glint and burned with a fervor that was further emphasized by dark, thick brows. Black hair hung straight to her shoulders. The only vulnerable spot was a dimple in her chin.

Lorie worried more about her son than her daughter, because being a girl her daughter could write songs about her father and throw darts at the face of Osama bin Laden and stay up all night talking and crying with Mom about missing her dad. But Lorie's son, like Mindy's son, wouldn't or couldn't talk about it. The fourteen-year-old boy had been in a science classroom on September 11.

"They neglected to turn off the TV, so he watched his father die on TV at school," Lorie said bitterly. "I found out later he broke down hysterically crying and they put him in a room with counselors. That will be with him for the rest of his life." The boy could not forgive himself; he had heard his father getting ready for work that morning, but he'd been too sleepy to get up and go downstairs and say good-bye to him. Ever since, he would wake Lorie up every morning to say "I love you," adding nervously, "I'll see you later." More recently, his mute grief had begun to congeal into a hard fury. He spiked his hair and started spewing angry slogans. Lorie had called Mindy to ask if she was having problems with her kids.

"Are you kidding?" Mindy commiserated. "My four-year-old had a meltdown in the store the other day. Crying, crying, crying, and saying, 'Everybody's died 'cept me.' Ever since his father disappeared, he can't get this picture out of his head." Alan David Kleinberg, only thirty-nine, had loved skating with his three children. The night before his death, he had been at a township council meeting in East Brunswick, advocating for a community skate park that his children would enjoy.

But the worst was yet to come when, shortly thereafter, Mindy's husband's remains were found. That ripped away the emotional guardrail of denial for her eleven-year-old son. "I hope we're not raising the first generation of American terrorists," Lorie said jokingly. But neither mother thought it was funny.

As May came on and the June 11 rally date became real, Lorie retreated into the computer room in her basement. She was the network's designated researcher. Kristen had told her to leave aside the shocking failures of the security agencies to connect the dots in the months before September 11. Concentrate on the failures of every organization to connect the dots once the attacks began. Focus on the time line. Who knew what, when did they know it, and what did they do about it?

Once Lorie began surfing the Web, she couldn't stop. She found a video of President Bush's reaction on the morning of the eleventh. According to the official time line provided by his press secretary, the president arrived at an elementary school in Sarasota, Florida, at 9 A.M. and was told in the hallway of the school that a plane had crashed into New York's World Trade Center. This was fourteen minutes *after* the first attack. The president went into a private room and spoke by phone with his national security adviser, Condoleezza Rice, and glanced at a TV in the room. "That's some bad pilot," the president said. Bush then proceeded to a classroom, where he drew up a little stool to listen to second graders read. At 9:04 A.M., his chief of staff, Andrew Card, whispered in his ear that a second plane had struck the Towers. "We are under attack," Card informed the president.

"Bush's sunny countenance went grim," described the White House account. "After Card's whisper, Bush looked distracted and somber but continued to listen to the second graders read and soon was smiling again. He joked that they read so well, they must be sixth graders."

Lorie checked the Web site of the Federal Aviation Administration. The

FAA and the Secret Service, which had an open phone connection, both knew at 8:20 A.M. that two planes had been hijacked in the New York area and their transponders turned off. How could they have thought it was an accident when the first plane slammed into the first tower twenty-six minutes later? How could the president have dismissed this after 9 A.M. as merely an accident by a "bad pilot"? And how, after he had been specifically told by Card "We are under attack," could the commander in chief continue sitting with second graders and making a joke?

Lorie ran the video over and over. "I couldn't stop watching the president sitting there, listening to second graders, while my husband was burning in a building."

The White House account said Bush "huddled with advisers" and made his way to the school's media center for what was to be an education speech. It wasn't until 9:30 A.M. that the president appeared on TV. In oddly informal language, he delivered the news of "an apparent terrorist attack on our country." *Apparent?*

Mindy pieced together the actions of Secretary of Defense Donald Rumsfeld. He had been in his Washington office, engaged in his "usual intelligence briefing." After being informed of the two attacks on the Trade Center, he proceeded with his briefing until the third hijacked plane struck the Pentagon. Mindy relayed the information to Kristen:

"Can you believe this? Two planes hitting the Twin Towers in New York City did not rise to the level of Rumsfeld's leaving his office and going to the war room to check out just what the hell went wrong." Mindy sounded scared. "This is my president. This is my secretary of defense. You mean to tell me Rumsfeld had to get up from his desk and look out his window at the burning Pentagon before he knew anything was wrong? How can that be?"

"It can't be," said Kristen ominously. Their network being a continuous loop, Kristen immediately passed on the news to Lorie, who became even more agitated.

Lorie checked out NORAD, whose specific mission includes response to any form of an air attack on America. It was created to provide a defense of critical command-and-control targets. At 8:40 A.M. on 9/11, the FAA notified NORAD that flight #11 had been hijacked. Three minutes later the FAA notified NORAD that flight #175 also had been hijacked. By 9:02 A.M., both planes had crashed into the World Trade Center, but there had been no action by NORAD. Both agencies also knew there were two other hijacked planes in the air that had been violently diverted from their flight pattern. All other air traffic had been ordered grounded. NORAD operates out of Andrews Air Force Base, which is within sight of the Pentagon. Why didn't NORAD scramble planes in time to intercept the two other hijacked jetliners headed for command-and-control centers in Washington?

Where was the leadership? Lorie wanted to know. She called Kristen in a lather.

Kristen further fueled Lorie's anxieties. "It didn't have to be an aggressive attack," she said. "There's a whole protocol for graduated responses against an aberrant plane. I have a clip about Payne Stewart's runaway plane, the golfer who almost crashed into downtown Dallas." When an air traffic controller lost radar contact with the crew a half hour after the plane left Orlando, Florida, for Dallas, the golfer's Learjet was picked up by the Federal Aviation Administration. The FAA summoned air force fighter jets. As the plane porpoised across the country, it was pursued by F-15s and then F-16s all the way to South Dakota, with the military pilots making every effort to contact it until, out of fuel, it fell into a field.

Lorie went back to her computer searches. It was 9:39 when the third plane hit the Pentagon. That was fifty-eight minutes after the initial warning of a hijacking by the FAA to NORAD. She called Kristen back to report this troubling time line. "And the acting head of the Joint Chiefs of Staff, General Meyers, was in a meeting about confirmation hearings for the next day. He said in his testimony that it wasn't until the Pentagon was hit that they made the decision to shoot down planes."

(According to Bob Woodward's book *Bush at War,* it wasn't until close to 10 A.M. that Vice President Cheney called Bush to urge him to authorize U.S. military aircraft to shoot down any additional commercial airliners that were controlled by hijackers. The vice president had to explain that a hijacked airliner was a weapon. Even if the airliner was full of civilians, Cheney insisted, giving American fighter pilots the authority to fire on it was the only practical answer. "You bet," said the president.)

"I can't look at these time lines anymore," Lorie confessed to Kristen. "When you pull it apart, it just doesn't reconcile with the official story line." Lorie said she had to get off the phone, just talking about it was making her too upset. But she couldn't stop herself from researching further. She hunched down in her husband's swivel chair and began to tremble, thinking, *There's no way this could be. Somebody is not telling us the whole story.*

When her mother called her upstairs for meals, she ignored her. Didn't go upstairs to bed. Sat frozen before the computer screen. The longer she sat there, the more she researched, the more unnerved she became. Until she had to lie down on the floor. "I didn't feel safe in my own home," she said. "It got that bad."

Before dawn, Lorie called Kristen. "They're coming," she hissed. "I know they're coming to get me." She said she had called a neighbor to come over and stay with her until her parents could get there.

Kristen got Lorie's mother on the phone. "How long has Lorie been down in the computer room?" she asked. Lorie's mother said she hadn't been able to drag her out for three days and nights. "Get her off the computer and out of the basement," Kristen urged. "Right now. She's making herself crazy."

Much later, Lorie began to understand the pernicious combination of personal trauma and loss, and learning more than you really want to know about what looked to be a public cover-up. "You've isolated yourself from your family and your friends, because you can't talk to anybody about this stuff—it's too upsetting."

On May 16—three weeks before their rally—the four moms no longer had to beg for press coverage of their cause. That morning, *The New York Times* carried a shocking headline:

BUSH WAS WARNED BIN LADEN WANTED TO HIJACK PLANES

Kristen had heard the revelation the night before on the *CBS Evening News* and immediately phoned Mindy and Lorie: "He knew! Bush knew!" The White House had confirmed that the CIA had warned the president in early August 2001, during his daily morning briefing, that bin Laden planned to hijack planes to attack the United States. The CIA had been listening intently to foreign transmissions over the July Fourth holiday and, according to an investigator, had heard "a lot of static in the system suggesting something was coming." But the FBI had done nothing to investigate Middle Eastern men enrolled in American flight schools, despite the fact that an FBI supervisor in Minneapolis had sent a memo to headquarters warning that bin Laden and his followers might be using the schools to train for terror operations. The supervisor had told investigators that he was trying to get people at FBI headquarters "spun up" because he wanted to make sure that Moussaoui did not take control of a plane and fly it into the World Trade Center.

So they weren't just a bunch of silly, paranoid women. And it wasn't such a mystery anymore why the White House had shown no interest in the joint inquiry of House and Senate investigating intelligence failures on 9/11, and why the CIA and the FBI were holding back on congressional requests for documents. This was a White House that had put out the coordinated message through National Security Adviser Condoleezza Rice and others that no official had had any idea that airplanes could be used as weapons.

Kristen couldn't sleep that night for the excitement. Suddenly "the girls" were firing off e-mails to their network of families and fielding press calls asking for their reaction. "Our reaction is to rally—June eleventh—on Capitol Hill," Kristen told them all. Still sleepless and in her pajamas the next morning, Kristen was punching out an op-ed piece with one hand while the other hand fingered her cell phone like a musical instrument. An AP reporter kept pressing Kristen: Just what is the name of your organization? They didn't want a name, Kristen said; this wasn't going to be their life's work. The AP reporter said if she was going to send out a story on the wires, she needed the name of the group putting on the rally on Capitol Hill.

"Just four moms from New Jersey," Kristen said.

BUILDING A NETWORK OF NETWARRIORS

The embarrassing revelation about what Bush knew and when he knew it appeared to be scaring off some of those on Capitol Hill whom the widows were counting on to come out in support of their rally. It was set to take place on June 11. "The girls," as they refer to themselves, had sent over a thousand e-mails and followed up with phone calls to members of Congress. They were counting particularly on the two standard-bearers of the bill that would create an independent investigatory commission, Senators Joseph Lieberman and John McCain. But a couple of days before the rally, Senator McCain sent word he couldn't attend the rally. Scheduling conflict. They desperately needed some Republicans. It would be bad enough if none of the congressional heavyweights showed up, but what if they gave a rally and none of the families came? Everybody was moaning about baby-sitter problems, not wanting to fly, the expense of spending a night in Washington—these were, after all, mostly young mothers who lived in New Jersey and New York.

So Kristen rounded up "the girls" to go to Washington the day before and get some name officials on board. They stopped at Home Depot to buy wood to make signs. The wood came only in long flats. Not to be deterred, they knelt down and hand-sawed the flats. Then they had to drop off their children with Mindy's mother. Caroline clung to Kristen; she had been bed-hopping every night. Lorie's thirteen-year-old daughter pleaded, "Don't get hurt, Mom." Mindy's eleven-year-old son said plaintively, "I'll miss you when you're in heaven."

But once they set off in Kristen's SUV for the four-hour drive to the Capitol, jokes and teasing relieved the tension. They compared notes on the oppressive sanctification of all the victims, including their all-too-human husbands. Was a saint someone who never has to take out the garbage? "There's nothing left in our lives, but we can make each other laugh," said Kristen.

It wasn't until they pulled into a Capitol parking lot that the girls went about changing into attire for the business at hand. They wriggled and giggled. "Check out Mindy's four-inch wedgies—I thought we were going to be comfortable."

"Mindy goes to bed in her four-inch wedgies," Lorie teased. "And wait till you see how she carries her pocketbook—over her wrist like the Queen Mother."

Kristen wore one of her husband's sport jackets as a statement, with khakis and après-ski clogs. Patty was the most sedate of the four. She had brought a silk scarf for Kristen and tried to teach her how to drape it properly. Kristen fought with the thing as if it were a live animal. "It might start as a scarf, but by the end of the day it's going to be a boa constrictor."

They teased Patty about wearing a twin sweater set—very *Town & Country*. "Patty *accessorizes*," said Kristen derisively. "She knows how to drape that cardigan over her shoulders so it never slips off."

Being built a little lower to the ground than the others, Patty changed from pants into a long skirt and high heels. She would be sorry later.

"Okay, are we ready to do a widows' walkabout?" Kristen said. "Good, you're laughing." But the others still looked hesitant. "I always chakra up before I do public things, get centered, get in the zone. I learned it in law school." She showed them how.

Patty was their Storyteller. She was the softer one who wore her emotions on the outside, so she carried their "show-and-tell"—a bulging album with candid photographs of the dead in vivid living color, kissing their brides, cavorting with their children, stretching out tan and sexy at the beach. Patty could narrate some of their stories and humanize the losses. "Patty is able to articulate her emotions," Kristen said appreciatively.

Kristen was their Hammer. "I'm back to the wall: 'I'm pissed, and here's what we want done about it.' We're a fierce team."

Half the names on the roster of legislators they needed to visit were at best vaguely familiar to them: Robert Torricelli and Jon Corzine, the two Democratic New Jersey senators; Lieberman and McCain, the two sponsors of the Senate bill; and on the House side, Democratic congressman Tim Roemer, sponsor of the House version of the McCain-Lieberman bill. Roemer actually met with them in person.

"Look, we see you as working for us," Kristen told him. "You're *our* prosecutor. No reason why we shouldn't get the answers."

When the Indiana congressman seemed taken aback by the young woman's aggressive approach, she admitted, "We want elected officials to think we know how the game works." He chuckled. Then he responded in just as businesslike a manner. By the time the meeting was over, Kristen turned girlish and told him, "I love you. You're my kind of guy."

But it was the women they attracted to their network who would make all the difference. They had made a die-hard supporter of Mary Noonan, the top aide to Congressman Chris Smith, a conservative Republican from New Jersey who had chaired hearings on the bombing of the U.S.S. *Cole*. Noonan broke the news to them that although Smith was sympathetic to their cause, he would decline to speak at their rally the next day. Like the rest of the Republicans, Noonan said, her boss saw the McCain-Lieberman measure as "a Democrat bill." Kristen pounced. "Mary, c'mon, you're telling us he's such a great speaker—we'll get him to speak! Just get us in to see him." And by the end of the congressman's meeting with "the girls," he agreed to make an appearance at their rally, although he gave no promise of his support.

Noonan then passed the torch to Eleanor Hill. Kristen at that point had no idea of the value of this contact: "She's somebody important on the intelligence committee's staff." Eleanor Hill was only a few days into her new job as chief of staff to the House-Senate Joint Inquiry on Intelligence, but she was the real thing.

Hill had been chief counsel and staff director for Senator Sam Nunn, who chaired the largest investigative subcommittee in the Senate. She had basically run the subcommittee for fourteen years and spearheaded all kinds of investigations between 1980 and 1995. After serving as President Clinton's inspector general at the Department of Defense for four years, she had moved a block from the White House into the luxurious offices of a white-shoe southern law firm, King & Spalding. Yet after three years in the private sector, she was itching to get back into government service. Her interest was piqued when the Senate and House intelligence committees decided to do something unprecedented. They would join together in a single effort to look at the performance of the intelligence services around 9/11. And they would hire their own staff. Eleanor Hill had given up her cushy wood-paneled office for a low-ceilinged, windowless basement cave where she nonetheless felt right at home. She had started work only a few days before the widows' arrival in Washington. One of her first calls was from Mary Noonan. The chairmen of the committee were not available; would Miss Hill meet with the four moms from New Jersey?

Eleanor Hill received them in a congressional hearing room. A tall, slender, erect woman with copper hair, intense green eyes, and delicately chiseled features, she was conservatively dressed in black pants and a black turtleneck and vest with tiny diamond-stud earrings. Her demeanor was calm and reasonable. But from her facial and body language, the widows could tell that she was ready to listen to them.

"The distinct message I got was they felt no one in the government was really listening to the families," said Hill. "They had been through trauma and it didn't seem to be getting any better. They were trying to go beyond their own personal situation and do something to prevent this from happening again."

The widows talked about their children. Patty showed the photo album. The more Eleanor Hill heard, the more she empathized. "I did relate to them as a mother, because I could imagine what they're dealing with, with their children."

What was flashing through the investigator's mind was her own personal trauma on September 11. She had been working at the law office, which was only half a block from the White House. When the Pentagon was hit, her building was evacuated. The street was full of thousands of panicky people being herded away from the White House by swarms of police and Secret Service agents. Why? Hill learned that the FAA had grounded planes. But why are *we* being evacuated? Hill asked an agent. "They told us that there was a fourth plane in the air and they didn't know where it was going, but they thought it was coming here. I remember thinking to myself, 'We're under siege.' "

They were hustled into a park. The stunning beauty of the day made it all the more surreal. Hill stood among her friends and coworkers, searching the sky, and thinking, *Where's the plane? Is there a plane that's going to shoot out of the sky at us?* "It was a horrible experience."

She had an eight-year-old son in Catholic school. She couldn't get her car out of the building; it was locked down. D.C. was a traffic zoo anyway. Cars were at a standstill. Car doors were open and radios on, with people huddled around trying to hear what was happening. It reminded Hill of those end-of-the-world movies from the fifties. She and her colleagues began walking, walked all the way from Pennsylvania Avenue over the Key Bridge. From the bridge they could see the Pentagon billowing smoke and helicopters circling over the top; the Pentagon, where she had worked until three years before. Just then, she heard F-16 fighter jets grinding overhead. They kept walking, into the town of Arlington, Virginia. Hours passed before she was able to reach her husband on the cell phone and tell him where to find her.

"Obviously, my experience pales by comparison with what people like Kristen and Patty and all the other families have gone through," Hill said later. "But it was trauma all day. It certainly changed me. I felt personally that we were under siege. It was a clear and present danger."

She kept thinking, *How could a country like ours, which is such an advanced superpower, be cowed by someone from the caves of Afghanistan?* "To me it was just amazing, frightening."

And that day wasn't the end of the trauma. Her office was evacuated several times in the weeks following, when there were further threats to the White House. And at night, her family went to sleep hearing the sound of military planes overhead. Her eight-year-old son would waken and come into her room to ask, "Is that the mastermind?" "No, it's not a mastermind," she would tell him. "Those are our planes." But she worried terribly what it would do to the mind of a child to think of Osama bin Laden as mastermind of the world.

It was because of these experiences that the seasoned investigator agreed to become the interlocutor for four moms from New Jersey. Hill knew full well that 9/11 was not just an intelligence failure; it was an organizational failure. She agreed with them that it was a systemic failure. "All our very advanced systems of defense and intelligence didn't cut it." But she was up-front with the widows: the mandate of her committee was limited to intelligence information. The widows had a whole host of other questions involving many other agencies and all the way up to the country's leaders.

"The questions you want answered from people like Rumsfeld and the Joint Chiefs and the president and his key advisers have to do with how our country responded on that day," she told them. "That is not our focus, we're not talking policy failures." Well, then, when the committee held public hearings, could they be heard? the widows asked.

Hill agreed to take their request back to the chairmen. She would become their network's link to the all-channel political network of the joint inquiry—which uniquely combined members of both House and Senate, and among them outspoken critics from both the Republican and Democratic parties.

But even when the day brought so much good, the widows always faced the night with fears for their children. When one of the four moms called home, the news was that her child had had a panic attack at school.

RALLY ROUND THE GIRLS, BOYS!

The rally day was a stinker of a hot one. The speakers' platform was set up beyond the Senate Swamp in an unshaded spot. Even before the speeches were scheduled to begin, at high noon, the hundred or so widows and orphaned parents and assorted other grievers and shakers who had traveled to D.C. began sticking to their seats. Many wore pictures of their loved ones on plastic laminates hung around their necks. The leaders of several other family groups passed out leaflets. Ginny Bauer stood on the sidelines, elegant as always in a black T-shirt and white pants, swooning from the heat. "I'm just here to be supportive. Kristen and the other girls supported me on the tax fight. But why did I wear black!"

At ten minutes past noon, the chairs on the platform saved for members of Congress were noticeably empty. Notwithstanding, Kristen stepped smartly to the microphone. She had tied back her long, flyaway hair and worn a string of pearls under her T-shirt as a concession to Capitol Hill formality, but she minced no words:

"My name is Kristen Breitweiser. My husband, Ron, was on the ninety-fourth floor of Tower Two and was killed on September eleventh. The victims of September eleventh were Republicans, Democrats, independents; and some who died were too young to even vote. Our call for an independent investigation has nothing to do with politics. It cuts across all party lines. It has everything to do with seeking out the answers that we so rightfully deserve. . . . This Sunday is Father's Day. My three-year-old daughter's most enduring memory of her father will be placing flowers on his empty grave. She is not alone in her sorrow. More than ten thousand children lost a parent on September eleventh. We need an investigation so that not one more child has to grow up knowing that her mother or father's death could have and should have been prevented."

She thanked Senators Lieberman and McCain and Congressman Roemer "and the many other elected officials who have supported us," adding hopefully, "many of whom are joining us today." But when Kristen introduced her friend Mindy and turned to sit down, she noticed that the officials' chairs were still empty.

"My name is Mindy Kleinberg," began the young woman in the red T-shirt and blue pants and wedgies, who looked like she belonged with her three children at the beach on a hot June day, but who, again, surprised the crowd with her specificity. "This has happened before, twenty-one times since 1980." She ticked off a few of the previous terrorist events involving Americans: Pan Am 103; the '93 World Trade Center bombing; the Khobar Towers; Oklahoma City; the two American embassies in Africa. "It pains me that I did nothing to help the victims' families of those events to make change. Now, my conscience will not permit me to rest, us to rest. How many more lives must be lost before we as a nation recognize the need for change? We need to investigate not only the FBI and CIA, but all the agencies: the Federal Aviation Administration, the Immigration and Naturalization Service, the National Security Agency, the Port Authority, the public corpora-

tion that owns the World Trade Center property and all the buildings on it."
A wave of applause built as she named the expanded menu of culprits the
crowd held responsible.

By now, word had spread on the Hill that the rally was surprisingly well
attended. More important, the media were there. Politicians didn't want to be
left out. Before long, the chairs on the platform were filled and an impressive
lineup of senators and congressmen began gathering to wait their turn to
speak. Senator Bob Torricelli, wearing some of the expensive Italian haber-
dashery paid for by an Asian influence peddler that would later result in censure by his Senate colleagues and a decision to drop out of politics, was the
most outspoken. He told the crowd, "Members of Congress have flailed from
denial to rage, trying to grasp the magnitude of the loss. The government of
the United States—in ways we still don't understand—let our people down.
The institutions—the FBI and CIA and FAA—are still defending themselves, rather than concerning themselves with the larger national problem.
Each of these institutions has a constituency in the Congress, protecting
them. And we have to break through it." Then the clincher: "There *will* be a
national commission." Over the applause, Torricelli added realistic quali-
fiers: "It may be next month, next year, ten years, but we want—"

Shouts of "NOW!" drowned out his last words.

Connecticut's Senator Lieberman was next. His best-received line was
"Some say further terrorist attacks are inevitable—I don't accept that." He
closed by endorsing the families' wish to be heard before the existing Joint
Inquiry on Intelligence:

"The walls of opposition will crumble at the power of your testimony."

Senator Corzine followed, a gray beard creating a soft hammock under
his creased and reddened face. He brought a more thoughtful, Socratic tone
to the increasingly florid rhetoric. Then came Hillary Clinton, whose oddly
formal remarks were less well received than the passionate, air-pumping
criticisms of her fellow New York senator, Chuck Schumer, who referred to
testimony from the FBI he had heard after 9/11 as a member of the Judiciary
Committee. "I couldn't believe the FBI has more primitive computers than
the $1,400 model I bought for my fourteen-year-old daughter. Does anyone
think that if those hearings hadn't been public, the FBI would have moved as
fast to correct it? So we will never, never, never . . ." and so on.

Kristen announced they were waiting on Congressman Chris Shays and
House Majority Leader Dick Gephardt. While they were waiting, she said,
she wanted to introduce a special person, Bob Monetti. "Our love and grati-
tude must extend to the Monettis, who lost their son on Pan Am 103, and
who inspired us to do this rally."

The big-shouldered man stepped to the mike. Monetti spared no feelings of the assembled congressional royalty. "So far, you, Washington, have not treated these people very well." (Applause.) "You have retroactively abrogated their legal rights." (More applause.) "You've created a heartless Special Master program [more applause], and you've portrayed them as being greedy. And still they're here, looking to you for answers." Monetti fired off a few questions of his own, most memorably the question of why it was that civilians using cell phones had been able to absorb, synthesize, and transmit to their loved ones critical information that might have saved their lives, while no federal official could? "Why, hours after the first hijacked plane crashed into the World Trade Center, was it up to Todd Beamer and other brave passengers to keep Flight 93 from crashing into this building behind us?" The bereaved cheered. Some of the members of Congress looked uncomfortable.

Monetti went on to draw a parallel with the fight that the Pan Am families had put up and the long fight ahead of the 9/11 families. "Now my son, Rick, is dead. He was murdered by Moammar Khadafi, and neither the U.S. government nor Pan Am did anything to prevent it. I know these things because there was a Bush presidential commission which investigated the events, and because there was a civil suit against Pan Am which further explained what happened. Now our government is telling us that these people who lost their lives on September 11 can't have an independent commission to tell them what happened."

Dripping by now with passion and perspiration, Monetti punched out the last of his remarks with the resounding "pings" of an old-fashioned cash register. "Two hundred and seventy people were murdered on Pan Am Flight 103, leaving about nine hundred immediate relatives, and you've seen what we've done in the past thirteen years by staring in Washington's face. The September eleventh disaster cost almost three thousand lives. So they probably left about ten thousand family members. How long can you stonewall ten thousand pissed-off people?"

The crowd leapt to its feet and roared. It was a therapeutic moment for all those widowed, and the orphaned parents and relations, who had made the effort to get to Washington, many to attend the first political rally of their lives. But for Kristen and her cohorts, the best was yet to come. When Congressman Chris Smith took his turn, he announced that he was ready to join Congressman Roemer as the Republican cosponsor of the House bill calling for an independent commission.

The rally had exceeded all their expectations. Having drawn out so many big guns on the Hill, the widows were suddenly on the radar. The media, which usually fold up their tripods and put away their tape recorders after the high-ranking members have given their sound bites, stayed for almost the whole two hours. Senator Lieberman remarked, "It's very powerful that the families came down here. And this was their idea." But to Kristen, this was no time to let up. While everyone else was ducking off to find a cold drink, the four moms from New Jersey decided to skip lunch.

"C'mon," said Kristen, "we'll do another widow walkabout."

They would track down Senator McCain. He had already been briefed by his staffer that the rally had been a great success. The senator himself invited them into his office. Patty Casazza bantered with him about the Yankees playing against his Arizona team, the Diamondbacks. She showed him the album of the families' pictures. He commented on Lorie's son's spiked hair. Then he offered them more than his unqualified support for their cause; he began that day mentoring them in how to play the Washington game.

"You guys are going to have a tough fight. You'll have to be strong and come down here again and again. Every bureaucracy in this town is scared to death of an independent investigatory commission. We haven't got the votes. The only way we'll get there is to round up more Republicans."

Kristen said, "Just give us the list, Senator, we'll go after them."

The four women came out of that meeting with spirits sky-high. "Up to then we'd had to fight and scrape and do everything ourselves," said Kristen. She sighed a little wistfully. "You have to understand, we don't have male figures in our lives anymore. It's so nice to have a man like McCain, who everybody knows, who feels like he's in control, supporting us! You look at this man, he's a POW, and you're awestruck. He's a great model."

By the end of the day they didn't know the difference between exhilaration and exhaustion. The four regrouped in a parking lot and dissolved on the hot seats of Kristen's SUV. Balancing Styrofoam containers on their laps, they poked at the tasteless takeout food and grew quiet. It was what often happened after all the razzle-dazzle of public protest; they would each retreat into a private chamber of longing for the men whose lifeless images they wore on tags around their necks. Even Kristen caved in. *Am I just in deep denial?* she wondered. It had been like that when she lost her mother to cancer; it took a long time to accept the finality. Silently, she rehearsed her new reality again: *I'm a mom with a daughter and a dog. Family of three. This is it. I have to make this a life as best I can.*

Patty Casazza was in the backseat rubbing out of her feet the soreness of two days of pounding the marble corridors of Congress in high heels. She was thinking of her dead husband. Her soft voice floated a wish that might have been in the minds of all four moms from New Jersey.

"Okay, we did the rally, now can they come home?"

Chapter Twenty-one

——

THE TOLL

I'm living in a different way," said Kevin Keelan, the popular young priest at Holy Cross. "My expectations have changed. I don't want us to go back to business as usual."

By July, nine months into the passage to the New Normal, startling changes in behavior began to widen the gulf between those directly touched by the losses of September 11 and much of the general population. Resistance to thinking about something as painful as 9/11 was in full force among those who didn't have daily reminders. For Middletowners, all they had to do was drive over the Sea Bright Bridge and look north: typically, if they had a clear view across the bay to the sun glinting off the Towers, they knew it would be a good beach day—but now that axis of their world was missing.

"Those at the epicenter have had their lives changed forever," observed Father Kevin. "I see them reflecting on a deeper level. You don't have superficial conversations with these people anymore." A ripple of this new consciousness spread out from those most directly affected to the extended family of friends and neighbors who responded to them and the mental health counselors and volunteers and support group people who were regularly there for them. Their lives, too, were often transformed. As the ripples spread out farther, people who shared churches or community activities with the families of victims felt varying degrees of the change. Gradually, the background tone of living was changing for many people in the many suburban "Middletowns" around New York that had taken hits. Manhattan itself had a whole different, more humane feeling.

The young priest had hoped that Americans across the board would wake up to the fragility of life and see more clearly the importance of love and faith. But by summer, his expectations were diminished. "I'm afraid, as I travel around the country, it's back to business as usual."

California was notably removed. A psychologist who has practiced for thirty years in Berkeley recounted her professional experience on September 11. She was in her office in the morning until late afternoon and saw a half-dozen patients. "It wasn't until I got home that night that I knew something had happened in the outside world," she said, adding with a knowing smile, "To neurotics it's all about them."

Father Kevin was particularly worried about evacuees who had escaped the Towers in time but had seen things no person should ever see. Plus, they bore all the guilt of surviving. "But these people stepped back, they deferred to the families who had suffered direct losses," he observed. "I don't think that any of them got the counseling they may have needed, and I think they will suffer for that."

VICARIOUS TRAUMA

Merely lifting the large goblet of Burgundy to her lips made Paula Planer wince. The slightest shift in posture could thrum the strings of pain emanating from her ruptured disk. She sat over her untouched lunch in the Oyster Point Hotel restaurant, scarcely aware of the spectacular view of early summer greening the banks of the Navesink River. Paula was nervous, jumpy, fidgeting with her fork; her monologue came out in short bursts.

"Bob is on sensory overload," she said, speaking of her husband, one of the few survivors of his trading floor. "His consciousness and his spirit aren't here anymore. I'm making every decision. I don't even tell him about it. He won't remember anyway. So my body snapped. But I can't baby myself. I just eat to survive. I have to stop and make myself eat. Or I'll just keep going. And I have to stay healthy. Because I have to take over for Bob."

Paula had just come from the physical therapist who had been working on her ruptured disk. Some days she's fine, she said; other days, she's in excruciating pain, especially just after she has had therapy and she dashes to the mall and runs home to prune shrubs and then can't sleep all night for the pain. Paula was still on full alert. Ever since that fateful day, she would rise at 6:45 and tell the kids to put on CNN Headline News. It wasn't until she had watched ten minutes into Regis's 9 A.M. show without news interruptions that she could take her shower and start the day, satisfied that her husband had made it through another morning without being killed by terrorists.

The crisply pressed man's shirt she wore served like a wind-puffed sail to hide the rigidity of her spine and shallowness of her body. She picked at her food as she spoke. Her voice was toneless, less than a whisper. It had been like that since the event, as if she was afraid to hear what she might say. But once the conversation turned to September 11 and she began recalling the smoke, the frantic phone calls, the coldness that had come over her, Paula's demeanor completely changed. Her eyes sank back into her face, she began shaking, her skin drained of color. She dropped her fork. Her voice was barely audible when she said, "I feel all the same feelings I felt that day—that cold, empty feeling, that total helplessness. If I talk about it, it all comes back, and the whole emotional register that goes with it."

Paula's sensory flashback suggested a classic case of vicarious traumatization. With the best intentions, she had taken on the role of her husband's therapist, pledged to carry his fears for him, and it was literally making her sick. Bob, too, was suffering from a whole assortment of mysterious symptoms, yet doctors could find nothing wrong with him—physically. It had started with distortions in his sense of time.

"I feel like September eleventh was a decade ago," he admitted one day while he and Paula tried to relax on their sun porch. "I remember everything about that day in minute detail, but ever since then I have no sense of time. For example, I recently went to the doctor about these pains in my chest. I told the nurse, 'I'm sorry, I know I was just here in February.' She looked at me funny. She said, 'No, that was February a year ago.' The big dividing line for me is 9/11. Ever since then, my mind has been fried."

"He doesn't remember a thing I tell him," Paula chimed in. Their dialogue, almost daily, went like this:

BOB: You never told me that.
PAULA: But I did tell you. I told you four times. You don't hear me!
BOB: Whatever you decide is fine.
PAULA: But I had to order the door from Kmart yesterday, and you never said which one you liked.
BOB: Whatever you want. I don't want to be bothered.

Paula said, "Sometimes, it's like talking to a ghost."

Bob had begun with January of the New Year to throw his efforts into rebuilding the company. "This will be my therapy," he insisted. Since he was the executive who had been with KBW the longest—his entire working life, in fact—he was made responsible for much of the firm's accelerated hiring program. Some days he appreciated the giddy energy of the aggressive young new hires he had brought into the trading room. And other days he would resent the hell out of the new hires for their insouciance; to them, 9/11 was just a news story. He and the other veterans of the two bombings could hardly remember the old days when they used to shoot paper airplanes across the floor and split at four in the afternoon to get back to Jersey in time for a swim. He groped to explain the change: "It's almost like we're not supposed to be happy now. Or we've seen too much."

At the same time, his good works as one of the company's "shepherds," who volunteered to look out for families of the company's sixty-eight victims, were winding down. "Except for those close to me, they're starting to shut us out now," he lamented, even those he had cultivated with phone calls and personal visits in the first months after the tragedy. "They don't call back. Maybe because I survived and their husbands or wives didn't. And when they hear my voice, they reassociate with KBW, and it brings out the pain again. They want to move on."

The Planers had hoped that if they took a nice long vacation in the Caribbean, Bob would snap out of it. "It was our first vacation since 9/11," Bob said. "We slept for a week. I came back totally exhausted." And the heaviness in his chest felt heavier than ever. An EKG registered nothing.

All four of the Planers' children, following their parents' lead, remained hypervigilant. Their oldest daughter, Kerry, a junior at a faraway college, had always been the most independent, but being distanced from her family on the day her father was missing had deeply affected her. She had come home for the summer and "zipped herself to our sides," according to Paula. She wouldn't let her father out of her sight. Their twelve-year-old son, John, still played the role of Warrior, sharpening his sticks and sleeping with them beside him to protect his parents in the night. Will, their sixteen-year-old, took on the role of Reporter and read and watched everything he could find about new terrorist warnings to keep his parents fully briefed. Cristy, their track-star daughter who was preparing to start college, was the Writer, able to express her feelings and fears only by composing long, affectionate notes to her father.

"After 9/11 we learned about our children in ways we probably wouldn't have seen for ten or twenty years from now," says Paula. "We saw their souls."

Bob couldn't wait to get back from vacation to watch TV for any documentaries about the Trade Center. "When I see it on TV, I'm drawn to it. I want to know more about it. I guess I'm looking for answers."

"You think about it every day," Paula said to Bob.

"No."

"Yes, you do. *I* think about it every day," she said.

As if there were no clear membrane dividing yes and no in his mind anymore, Bob repeated almost robotically, "Paula and I think about it every day."

"He has nightmares," Paula added. "It's catching up."

Nine months after the events of 9/11, Bob and Paula Planer were worse off than some of the widows. The cruel irony of it was, Bob Planer had not been one of those stuck in the Towers on September 11. But he was stuck there now.

IN SEARCH OF SPIRITUAL MOORINGS

Some of the widows and widowers who had accepted church teachings rather passively were thrown into a crisis of belief. "Where was God?" was an existential question that everyone, including the pastors and priests and rabbis, wrestled to answer. Some widows couldn't rest for worrying "Where is he now? Between heaven and earth and hell?" Some looked for relief by watching John Edwards's TV show where he claims to speak to the dead for members of his audience. When they found out the waiting list to be in his studio audience was over a year long, they hoped for "a visit" from the loved one who had disappeared from their lives without a trace.

Paula and Bob Planer began shopping for a new faith home. Their favorite priest was Father Kevin Keelan. He had reached them and many others in sermons that wrestled with the lessons of 9/11. But by summer, the word got around that Father Kevin was leaving Holy Cross. The Planers were invited to a farewell ceremony for him in July, which turned out to be a lavish lawn party in Rumson where the priest conducted a sober Mass under a large white tent followed by a barbecue buffet.

Father Kevin sat apart from the post-Mass festivities and described a tragic vision.

"Evil is infiltrating the Catholic Church," he said. "I'm looking at the sex scandal as the World Trade Center tragedy for the Church. I don't believe in coincidence. September eleventh happened and everybody looks to the Church for faith, hope, and love, for meaning, for answers. But the very place they're looking to for consolation is being attacked by another face of evil. People get shaken up. They turn towards the darkness. They lose their hope, or they lose their faith. Evil grows in all that doubt and fear."

He offered a personal confession. "There was sex abuse in my family. So it's real for me. That is an insidious evil that is passed on from generation to generation to generation—talk about original sin! It's passed down in the darkness. It breeds in the darkness—the family secret. If the Catholic Church keeps it as a family secret, it's going to continue to breed and spread."

His response was both passionate and public: "I say bring it out into the light! Shout it from the rooftops! That's the only way it's ever going to stop. The only way healing is going to take place."

Father Kevin was being transferred by the Church to a parish in rural South Jersey. It meant leaving behind the support group he had started for widows and in which he had participated as their spiritual leader. Why would the Church move him at such a sensitive time? His reply was empty of passion.

"The Church is a corporation like any other."

FIRST SMILE FOR THE TIETJENS

Laurie Tietjen was the self-appointed Strong One for her family, always first to absorb any grim new details of her brother Kenny's death as he'd fought the fires at Ground Zero. She had initially sought strength in her religion.

"This tragedy hasn't tested my faith in God, but it's made me look down on the Catholic Church," she acknowledged by summer, as if giving personal voice to Father Kevin's fears. She had never forgotten how Father John Dobrowsky at St. Mary's had ignored her family's need and the needs of other families for guidance and consolation in the aftermath of 9/11 and had sought media attention instead. In his TV and newspaper interviews the priest often talked in an avuncular way about Kenny Tietjen, as if they had had a close relationship. This was not only untrue—Kenny belonged to another church—it rankled Laurie that the priest would use her brother's death for his own glory. Such animosity was widespread in his congregation, to the point where a Web site designed by another group of parishioners became an outlet to "flame" the priest with scorching criticism and unsubstantiated charges.

By June, the bishop of the Trenton diocese relieved Father Dobrowsky of his position at St. Mary's. Laurie read the statement released by the bishop's office that seemed to attribute Father John's difficulties to the stress he had endured because of his involvement with the families of 9/11. Furious, she called the bishop's office to question this characterization, "knowing that the priest never even called us or other family members." A diocesan official told her to hold her fire until the bishop himself came to St. Mary's to meet with the parishioners. But at the meeting, the bishop chastised Father John's flock—particularly those who had designed the Web site—for having "driven out" the priest with their angry complaints.

Laurie Tietjen and other attendees were disgusted. How could anybody blame the congregants for begging to be consoled and feeling further abandoned when they couldn't get a response? But she wasn't going to let a personal grievance rob her of her religious life. "My faith in God is separate," she came to understand, "because the Catholic Church is full of people, and sometimes people make mistakes."

The Tietjen family had tried to focus right from the start of their grieving on what they had left, rather than on what they had lost. They had an alternative extended family to that of their church—the Port Authority officers who had loved Kenny and embraced his family. Laurie found herself with three or four surrogate brothers—great, hulking young cops who routinely came by and hugged her and her family and accompanied them to every ceremony, who could talk nonstop about how much her brother had meant to them. "Our family never got to the anger phase," Laurie said proudly, "because right from the beginning it was absorbed and neutralized by all the love and friendship we were offered by the extended Port Authority family."

For the first six months the Tietjens had resisted seeking therapeutic counseling, but when the family finally did agree to see a local psychologist recommended by the parish nurse, it made a world of difference. They were encouraged in their instincts to look hard at their life choices and reevaluate what was truly important. Laurie agreed to join in, but only on one condition. "I don't want you bringing my marriage into this," she told her family. She was adamant about it. Although her parents loved her husband, they did not think it was a good match.

One day, out of the blue, the therapist turned to Laurie and said, "I'm just going to ask you a question. What's the deal with your husband?"

Laurie almost fell off the couch. "Why do you ask?"

"You talk about the people who are supporting you. And you haven't once mentioned your husband."

The therapist had pricked the boil. Laurie's feelings spilled out. She had married young, and although she thought her husband was a good person, there was a great deal missing in their marriage. She had told him before September 11 that she was unhappy. But the idea of divorce had always overwhelmed her with fear, guilt, remorse; she'd put it out of her mind.

The eschatological shock of seeing her brother's life go up in smoke, when he was only thirty-one, had completely changed her concept of time, and "time left to live." Kenny had packed so much into his few decades—he'd traveled, he'd seen adventure and risked his life and raised hell on his dirt bike, and laughed a great whoop of a laugh—and what had she done? She hadn't traveled, hadn't even taken a vacation in five years; she and her husband just worked all the time. They had no children. And now, without Kenny to make her laugh, she scarcely smiled anymore.

Not long after the therapy session in May, Laurie said, "there was a day when I knew it was over. My parents were going down to Ground Zero for the first time, and they wanted me to go because they were nervous. I told my husband, 'I really need you to be there with me, because I need to be strong for my mom and I'm going to be a mess.' He told me he couldn't go. For me, that was the minute that I said, I'm done."

As summer came on, Laurie had more than a few epiphanies:

Life is too short to "make do."

If a traumatic event doesn't cripple you, it can make you a lot stronger.

Divorce wouldn't kill her. Her brother's death was so brutal and graphic, and the recovery so prolonged, she couldn't imagine going through a crisis any worse. "So September eleventh didn't cause the divorce," she realized, "but it gave me the courage to do it."

The divorce was quick and amicable; since they had no children, they just divided their few possessions. And Laurie was amenable to letting her husband remain in the house, where he had his own business. Then she settled down to deal with this new passage.

"For a couple of weeks over the summer, I couldn't hardly get out of bed in the morning. I was so tired all the time. I was probably depressed."

Even though this ending was what she wanted, it opened another big hole in her life. But Laurie's epiphany was borne out. She emerged from depression by early September and was almost immediately swept up in a dream come true for her family: They had been chosen by the Port Authority to take a cross from Ground Zero and visit the pope!

When Kenny's mother, Janice, heard that the Tietjens would be representing all the Port Authority mourners, she rushed out to buy a hundred sets of rosary beads to be blessed by the pope and brought back to share with the other families. She was ecstatic but nervous merely thinking about being in the pope's presence among the crowd of ten thousand in St. Peter's Square. Her entrance was grand enough, led by two giant police officers. Then she was separated from the delegation and escorted to the stage by a Port Authority police officer, Paul Nunziato—she would be sitting within a stone's throw of the pope! The Holy Father stepped out of his popemobile without assistance, took his chair, and spoke greetings in six languages, the last one being English.

"We have representatives from the Port Authority of New York and New Jersey here, bringing a relic from the World Trade Center." The crowd was applauding, Janice was weeping with joy; then all at once she was being propelled toward the feet of the pope—she'd had no idea she would be touching him! Her head swam and her knees buckled. Officer Nunziato labored to hold her up while she tried desperately to remember the prayer she had prepared—"Jesus, please heal our pope"—when suddenly she was on her knees and looking into the pope's face and singing out, *"Jesus!"*

The pope smiled and gently patted her head and touched her face. He said slowly, "Please tell the families that our prayers are with them all." He squeezed her hand. Janice was immediately calmed. Then the pope bent over Officer Nunziato and said a prayer "for all the police officers who suffered so much in this time." Finally, Janice held up her bounty of rosary beads and the pope blessed all one hundred.

On the Tietjens' return, they had so many stories to tell, so much laughter. Laurie said, "It's wonderful to see my mother smiling again—not just smiling—beaming."

TRAUMA OVERLOAD

There were many others in town who hadn't faced a direct loss, but who were suffering from the pileup of traumas great and small that had been visited upon Middletown.

"It's been a terrible year," said Terry Columbo, the student assistance counselor at Middletown South. "We have an epidemic number of teachers with physical fallout from all that's happened—the teachers' strike on top of September eleventh. We have teachers with high blood pressure, depression, hospitalization. Students are angry at the teachers, parents are angry at the teachers, there has been no closure."

The one bright spot was the grief group in which the half-dozen students who had lost a parent could meet privately in Mrs. Columbo's office and talk about their deepest feelings of loss—with a raw candor they found their friends unable to accept. Bridgette Parks, the swim team captain who had lost her father, found acceptance in the group for her changing perspective. "Like, my main worry isn't about what to wear for homecoming or what I'm going to do this weekend," she said. "I think I've positively changed, because I used to worry about the stupidest things. Now I put much more energy into school and my family." Her sense of time had also changed. "I'm more hurried. I just don't sit on the rocks anymore, I like to get everything done." Approaching her senior year, Bridgette was seriously preparing college applications.

Antonia Martinez, the principal who had performed so valiantly in guiding the parents and children of the Village Elementary School through trauma, also felt the toll taken by the year. In addition to losing the Cangialosi boys, she had watched her teachers go to jail. Just thinking about it months later still brought her to tears. She had seriously considered retiring. She had the years, she had the age, everything. But when she tried to imagine a different future, she couldn't see herself in any place more meaningful than at the very desk she occupied at the Village School. She stayed on, more dedicated than ever.

Even Ken Feinberg, the special master granted the Solomonic role of deciding how to compensate the families of 9/11, was having trouble absorbing all the chaotic emotions that survivors brought to their meetings with him. He had to ask a Washington psychologist, Jeanne Marks, to accompany him to meetings and help him sort out his emotions afterward. By summer, the rawness of shock had worn off. Families had either come together with a united strategy, or fissures that were there before had become painful splits and family members were fighting among themselves about whether to file a claim and take whatever money they got, or wait and see, or hold out to sue and satisfy their anger. The families' questions were becoming more informed and sharp, often delivered drained of emotion but with a personal barb.

"The problem, Mr. Feinberg, is if I accept your invitation to come in and sit down with you in a closed room with no jury to argue my case, I have no idea what your decision will be," one silver-haired widower said at a New Jersey meeting in June. "Why is so much in the rules left to your discretion?" demanded a younger man. "Why should we trust you?"

Feinberg would counter in his big, bombastic voice, "These awards are going to be posted. You can see how fair the first ones are before you come in." He grimaced, Scrooge-like. "There's no fairness in this life. But there *is* fairness in this fund! If I can't convince the people in this room—"

"Mr. Feinberg," he was interrupted by a third man, "if you had lost your wife and your brother, and you were standing in my shoes, what question would you ask of me?"

"That's exactly the right question!" the special master shouted, as if to stall for time to compose an answer. He then addressed himself: " 'Mr. Feinberg, show me! Yeah, very nice, very glib, now show me!' You've articulated it perfectly, now I have to prove to you . . .''

And so it went for several hours. Just as Feinberg was preparing to close the contentious question period, who should dash in but his old nemesis Kristen Breitweiser. She had sped in her SUV all the way from Shelter Island with her daughter in the backseat to catch up with the special master. She whispered in his ear. He smiled. After the meeting Feinberg claimed that he was becoming callused from all the stories he had heard—"Rolls off my back."

His private psychologist, who was waiting to debrief him on the plane ride back to Washington, would hear a different story. Jeanne Marks encouraged him to unload the remarks that had been most hurtful, so she could put them in context. She told him in the car how beneficial the meetings were. "Seeing you in person makes an enormous difference. When people see you on television or read about you, sometimes you come across as arrogant or somewhat insensitive." He admitted that at every meeting, he still heard things that he'd never thought of or that hadn't been raised before. "It's mind-boggling."

Marks sympathized: "I think it's a much bigger and more daunting feat than anybody anticipated." Feinberg was having some trouble sleeping. He had found he couldn't take more than two meetings a day, preferably one. He was human, after all.

THE ALL-AMERICAN MUSLIM IS ACCUSED OF TERRORISM

The New Normal presented Americans with another vexing question: How tolerant should we be? How do we separate Islamic extremists from the good Muslims who live among us? Would Middletown Americans find it easy to stigmatize Arabs living among them as suspected terrorists?

The father of the Muslim family that had lived in Middletown for ten years, Dr. Abdel Gabr, had worked as a rheumatologist at several area hospitals. Yet colleagues would now say to him, "I can't believe you're Muslim, because you don't look like a terrorist." An official at the hospital where he had served the longest asked him straight out, "Do you believe in suicide bombing?"

It seems that humans are tribal by instinct and form groups that regard the Other with cruel and even murderous chauvinism. Since humans are not born with tolerance, it must be taught, or imposed. The radical sixties set Americans on a path of codifying tolerance in our laws to restrain ourselves from practicing racial segregation, anti-Semitism, anti-Catholicism, and the stigmatization of women and homosexuals. We have come to venerate tolerance today as another pillar of the American way. "It's All Right to Be Different" programs in Middletown elementary schools were an example. But at Middletown North High School, where racial tensions normally ran high, the Gabr boys became an easy target.

On a warm spring Friday in the feverish school week before final exams and the senior prom, Wallid and Ehab Gabr were hanging out in the student parking lot of Middletown North High School. As students streamed out of the sprawling brick building, the parking lot took on a social life of its own. Once out from under the watchful eyes of teachers and hall monitors, feuds and flirtations inevitably flared.

Wallid was sitting on the hood of his used Audi. He and Ehab were "kicking it," as they like to say, passing jokes among friends. Ehab, a heavy-set boy of sixteen with sharp blue eyes and sand-colored skin, plays the perfect foil to his older brother Wallid, the tall, handsome, theatrical football star. Wallid doesn't always act like the serious honor student he is, but his dynamic personality and trendy hip-hop clothes make it clear why he was voted senior council leader, "best dressed," and "most school spirit." The brothers are each other's protector and comrade. They pray together at the mosque on Fridays and go bowling with shared sets of friends on Saturday nights along Route 35.

In a fit of spring exuberance, Wallid, always happy to draw attention to himself, jumped up on the hood of a friend's car. He was up there peacocking when his least favorite classmate, a heavy-set blonde with a cop's walk, strutted by. The two classmates had had a cantankerous relationship since eighth grade.

"I hope you fall off," she taunted as she walked by. "I hope you die."

This girl was not an honor student nor a class star. She was an average student with a few friends, but whenever she passed the football star in the hall, she knew just what to say to knock him down. Wallid always thought that racism was behind her attitude. "She was like, 'Who are you? You ain't nobody.'" Neither Wallid nor his classmate had made any effort to work things out, so the tension had mounted.

In the parking lot Wallid cursed her out. He turned his back on her and got into his car to go home. While he and Ehab were waiting in the long line of cars to leave the parking lot, the girl drove past and leaned out her window.

"You're garbage!" she shouted. "Go back to your country!"

"I *will* go back to my country," he shouted back. "And I'll bring a fucking gun!"

Wallid got out of his car and walked toward her. He formed his hand into the shape of a gun and pointed his finger in the air. Amanda turned her car around and headed straight for the principal's office.

Dr. Abdel Gabr was on his way home from Friday prayers at the Middletown mosque when he received the call from an assistant principal telling him that his son had just made a "terrorist threat" to another student. Wallid wasn't surprised when his cell phone rang and it was his father. "Where are you?" Dr. Gabr asked. "Meet me in the principal's office."

"Oh boy," Wallid said to Ehab. "Oh, this is it." He turned the car around. A Middletown police officer was waiting for the boy and his father at the principal's office.

The officer told Dr. Gabr that he was going to have to arrest his son. Ever since the high school shootings in Columbine, Colorado, the school districts of New Jersey had followed a "zero tolerance" policy. Any threat that involved words such as "kill" or "gun" by one student to another required that disciplinary action must be taken. Wallid's words to the girl fell within that policy, but the call to the police took it a step further. The officer explained that he had to make the arrest because of the high-alert atmosphere in the town and the country. After the school officials explained that Wallid's record was otherwise clean and they had a good relationship with the Gabr family, the police officer decided not to arrest Wallid. Instead, he filed a report to the state supreme court. The Gabrs went home distraught, not knowing whether Wallid would be allowed to graduate.

Over the weekend, the family canceled all their social plans and found themselves soul-searching. Wallid knew he had made his family look terrible. He went round and round with the "if only's."

"I could have said, 'This is my country—I was born here,' " he chastised himself. "I don't use guns. I hurt my religion because of what I said." He reminded himself of a basic tenet of his faith: "If someone says something hateful to you, then you should be a better man or woman and walk away."

On Monday morning Eklas Gabr accompanied her son to a meeting with the head of student guidance and a number of assistant principals. A school psychiatrist was also present. Mrs. Gabr felt humiliated and in disbelief that her superstar son had caused such unrest in the school. In an instant she saw her identity change from "Mrs. Gabr with the four children"—the kind Arab woman who would frequently stop by the school office with a bag full of Egyptian treats—to the mother of a delinquent. Since September 11, she had been uncomfortable coming into the school in her veil and had stopped making her frequent visits. Now, almost nine months later, she had found the courage to show her face again, and all she could do was cry.

"I'm sorry he said it, I was expecting better of him," she told the school administrators. "I'm not on his side, but speaking for him as a gentleman, he's not going to let any woman or anyone put him down, especially in front of his friends."

It was not his mother's input that influenced the administrators. It was the action Wallid had taken when he had first been summoned to return to the school. Administrators had put him and his accuser in separate rooms to write statements about the run-in. Their accounts had very nearly matched.

"I showed them I was an even better man," said Wallid. "I didn't have to lie."

LIEUTENANT KEEGAN IN THE FINAL DAYS

Apprehension ran high among the men of Keegan's Ground Zero team starting in May, as they thought about being separated and sent back to their old jobs of directing traffic or patrolling a bridge or tunnel. How would they cope with the dullness of everyday life? Most fearsome of all, how would they get along without one another?

Port Authority made it mandatory that the men who had worked recovery for sixty days or more attend a two-day retreat in a hotel room, conducted by PAPD medical division police psychologists and motivational speakers. But the men, if they were absolutely honest, and opened up to the wrong person, knew it could result in their forfeiting their gun and being put on medical leave. So Keegan's men sucked up their feelings and hung tight with one another. They had become a family.

Something unexpected had happened to these men down in the pit. Most were young and religious about working out; they were bulked up and pretty narcissistic about their physical prowess. But most were strangers to the range of emotions they would feel, dealing with the Dantesque levels of hell they were seeing every day. They had to read one another, comfort one another, spell one another, force some laughs, and accept tearful outbursts. At first, when the police widow Donna Lamonaco began doling out her medicine—big bear hugs—Lieutenant Keegan had reeled backward. Almost tripped over himself. Police lieutenants didn't hug on the job! "But it felt good," he had to admit. He began looking forward to her hugs. Then the men began hugging each other. Great, long, cheek-to-check, back-patting hugs. It felt good. They were family now. Keegan's men became used to wearing their feelings on the outside of their skins. And they weren't ashamed of it.

"It's my understanding that a lot of the trauma won't hit for months to come," Lieutenant Keegan anticipated in May. "It's going to take us a while to break down the defenses that have enabled us to work here." Keegan got an inkling of that painful process when he took his first days off in May to speak to a victims' group. His boss insisted he go.

"I'd never had time to catalog the emotions," Keegan reflected, much less time for the familiar emollients of family; he hadn't spent more than an hour a day with his wife and less with his three children. "When you have to go through those feelings," he said, "that's the time that you start to fall apart."

He asked Donna Lamonaco if she could help him write his speech. "What am I going to say to a bunch of victims?"

"You're one, too," Donna said.

"Me? C'mon, my job is to soothe victims."

"Uh-huh, and what do you tell them?"

"I tell them that violent things can just happen to you, and they happen quickly. You need to know it wasn't your fault," said Keegan.

Donna nodded and waited for a smile to indicate that the lieutenant had crossed an unthinkable bridge for a cop. He began to recognize himself and his men as, yes, secondary victims.

Gradually Keegan's anger was transmuted into resolve. And his resolve into hope. He said, "I never would have put it together unless I had to think about being victimized. And then, once you have gone through the victim stage, you can come out on the other end, a survivor."

Some of his men were young and stoic. Crew members like Rudy Fernandez, who had been chosen to run the temporary morgue, felt honored to be a part of it. "There is nowhere I would rather have been. I'll carry this the rest of my life," he said. Fernandez was certain they would be better off than the police and firefighters who had been rotated in and out. Keegan wasn't so sure.

He was aware of the lessons of Oklahoma City. He knew that the reactions to that terrorist bombing by many of the police and firefighters who worked at the Murrah Federal Building site—isolation from friends and family, divorces, alcoholism, gambling, suicides—had only begun showing up eighteen months *after* the event.

"At Ground Zero, we became so totally involved with the recovery work, we lost almost all social contact with the rest of the world," he said. "At home, any family problems had to be tabled." In their last weeks, raking mere powder, their minds had time to drift. The frustration level rose dangerously. Keegan knew he had to start talking to his men about how to reenter the world. He could not allow any of them to drift away into isolation. He knew enough about psychology to know that traumatic grief is cumulative.

After looking into various therapeutic approaches, he won the commitment of the chief of psychiatry at St. Vincent's Hospital, who offered to send a team of social workers trained in trauma response to meet regularly with his men for a minimum of one year. It would be funded by New York City's Project Liberty program for mental health services, but it would operate under the radar, although with the tacit permission of the Port Authority. The men would learn that there is a reason they won't remember what their wives told them five minutes before: memory lapses are common signs of post-traumatic stress disorder. If they snapped at their families or forgot to pay their bills, that, too, could be related to their traumatic experience. The men would be taught how to spot the signs of suicidal behavior in one another. They would remain a family.

LISA AT GROUND ZERO

Lisa Luckett, who had been reluctant to visit Ground Zero, was invited down by Lieutenant Keegan on the last night before the recovery effort ended, May 29, 2002. She stood to one side while Bill Keegan addressed his men at their last roll call. Lisa's husband, Teddy, was not one of those whose remains had been found. The PAPD men had not been able to find a third of the officers they had lost. They, too, were faced with the finality of a funeral pyre that was now merely a finely raked construction pit. Lisa stood awestruck. As she listened to the men's commander address them for the last time, she realized what these men had sacrificed on behalf of families like hers.

Lieutenant Keegan described how they would stand at attention the next morning, during the walkout ceremony, as a flag-draped stretcher was carried out of Ground Zero symbolizing the unrecovered. At the mention of the unrecovered, a shudder of emotion spread through his men. Virtually all of them carried the burden of believing they had not done enough.

Keegan saluted them for putting their hearts into that hole. But he had to tell them, "Our work is not quite done. Once we leave here, *we're* going to experience the pain that others have felt since September eleventh."

Suddenly, the widow felt herself standing outside the fishbowl. People were always lavishing attention on the families of 9/11, but what about the mental health of these men? They hadn't had any recognition to speak of, no therapy, not even relaxation time with their families. They'd had to push the sludge of painful emotions down in order to do a dirty but honorable job. Their journey of recovery was only now about to begin.

Lisa asked to speak to them. Her voice trembled. "I'm so honored to be here. I know what you've given up. I'll tell all the widows what bravery I've seen tonight." Tears overtook her. The men in their overalls shuffled and pulled their noses.

Keegan spoke for them all. "We did not achieve our goal." His chin quivered. "But we did not fail." The men didn't try to hide their tears. "Now that we're finally removed from doing the job that we had been sent to do, we now can look at the families and look them in the eye"—his lower lip curled up and his voice broke—"and tell them, 'We did the best that we can possibly do.' "

He spoke from the heart about the living legacy he wanted to see come out of all that destruction. He said, "So much brotherhood and sisterhood— we'll probably never experience it again in our lives. The dichotomy of such evil and then such goodness—we have seen it in almost everything that happened down there in the pit. Now the huge devastation is gone. And now there's just emptiness. It's almost like what's been happening to us. That mountain of anger and hate we took into ourselves, we were filled with it— with rage and sorrow and the sense of helplessness. At some point we emptied. Just like we emptied this pit. Now we can start to build. But what are we going to build? Hate? Revenge? Alcoholism? Addiction? Family breakdown?

"No." Keegan's voice condensed down to a beam with the power of steel. "Somehow," he vowed, "out of all this, *goodness has to win.*"

Chapter Twenty-two

FRAGILE PROGRESS

By August, some victims' families had healed their surface wounds and the long bright lazy days worked their soporific effect. But anticipation of the first anniversary of 9/11 hung over the summer like a gathering storm cloud.

Most of the widows were weary of standing on a pedestal as icons of pity through whom others could exorcise their own grief. Hung with the label "widows of 9/11," they couldn't seem to get out from behind it. Their public persona stood in the way of their personal grieving. They were expected to appear at all kinds of memorials and remembrance services. One week it would be their husband's high school class, the next it was his bowling team or church group or his fraternity brothers who wanted to honor him. Every day leading up to the eleventh, another invitation would arrive.

"I don't think we've even started to grieve yet," Karen Cangialosi, the aerobics instructor, acknowledged. "We've been so inundated with paperwork and public appearances and trying to settle our children down—when do you have time for yourself? You can't be at every memorial and ceremony. People mean well, but it's emotionally draining."

There was no escaping the media buildup. Every time a TV promo of the anniversary coverage would flash onto home screens, unsuspecting viewers would see the planes hitting the Towers again. One family member said, "I don't see hijackers attacking America, I see my mother being murdered again. It's one more piece in our lives that we've lost control over."

Children were particularly vulnerable. Allyson Gilbert, one of the founders of FAVOR, was watching a TV show with her son, a fifth grader, shortly before the anniversary. Talking heads were debating whether or not Osama bin Laden was alive and whether or not he could mount another terror attack. "Mom, you know what I'm afraid of?" her son whispered. "I'm afraid Osama is going to come here to the house and kill you."

Allyson was shocked. She had no idea the little boy was harboring such fears. But he was hardly alone among the children of Middletown, as the next week's events would reveal. It was not surprising that children would personalize the assault to their sense of security, particularly when they could put a face to those fears—a face that looked like the evil sorcerer Saruman in the *Lord of the Rings* movies. Osama/Saruman took on the proportions of an omnipotent monster who could appear and disappear at will. To Allyson's boy, as to any ten-year-old, his mom and dad were the most powerful figures in the world. Moreover, his mother was out in public as the spokesperson for FAVOR. And she was pure good. Osama was pure evil. Why wouldn't Osama know how important his mother was and want to get rid of her?

"Osama doesn't want to kill someone like me," Allyson tried to reassure her son. "He wants to be able to kill freedom and liberty for us. So he would want to attack something the United States has."

"Like the Empire State Building?"

"Yes, that would be something he might want to attack," Allyson said.

"Well, we should just wipe them away, with an atomic bomb."

That outburst shocked Allyson even more. She had no idea her little boy knew about atomic weapons. "It was a reminder that we live in a different world since 9/11," she said, and when her son left for school, she wept as if at a funeral—a funeral for the America her son would never know.

Bruce Springsteen, who lives on the Rumson Neck, faced similar problems at home. The hardest thing about 9/11 for him personally was trying to explain it to his three children, ages twelve, ten, and eight. "I think it's become placed in their lives in the same way that the nuclear bomb was when I was a kid," he told *Time*. "It's the really dark, scary thing, and they're not sure where it can touch them. Can it touch them at school? Can it touch them in the house? Does it have limits?"

Carol Veizer, a Middletown-area psychotherapist who specializes in trauma therapy, confirmed the concerns of parents like Gilbert and Springsteen. With the approach of the anniversary, Veizer's nonprofit mental health center in Red Bank was receiving more worried calls than ever from parents of children upset by the Trade Center attacks—many of them children who had not lost anyone personally.

"To the little children, Osama is the archetypal monster," said Veizer, director of the New Jersey Center for the Healing Arts. "Some of my little children at the center said, 'Osama does evil magic.' One seven-year-old who was not directly affected by the attacks is now obsessed with drawing tombstones with Osama's name on them. The fact that Osama is elusive, never caught, adds to the fantasy component."

Veizer points out that this event has not only changed our world externally, she sees strong evidence that it has changed the inner landscape of our children's world. Six- and seven-year-olds dream about planes flying into buildings, and it comes out in their art therapy. A six-year-old who engaged in repetitively building and toppling two tall towers would stop and stare, in between, at the fallen blocks. When a therapist asked why, the child said, "I want to see if they are going to stand up again and fall down again." Veizer explains, "To some children who saw the attacks replayed on TV, it felt to them like the Towers crashed over and over again, and still do."

In anticipation of his mother going away on a business trip, a ten-year-old boy was brought to the center because of night terrors. Normally very social, the child had become more withdrawn from his friends and clingier with his mother as her departure drew closer. He was finally able to express his fear: "They never found Osama. He made those planes fly into the World Trade Center. How do I know that when you go up in the sky, he's not going to reach out and grab you?"

The fact that children are talking in these metaphoric ways shows that the event is deeply imprinted in their psyches, says Veizer. She admits that therapists do not even have diagnoses in their manual that fit the problems they are encountering. She makes an ominous prediction: "We are going to see a PTSD generation growing up here."

MARY MURPHY THE POST–9/11 MOM

Mary Murphy was ready to complete the drawings for her "trauma narrative." This was the exercise offered to the mothers' group by Amanda's Easel, the free art therapy program for Middletown's Twin Towers families. Mary's five-year-old daughter, Morgan, and fifteen other young children were finding it a helpful outlet to express their more riotous emotions without need of words. Drawing pictures of her father had opened Morgan to connecting with her father in other ways. She told her mother, "I want to make a list of things I did with Daddy," and asked Mary to help her with the letters for "bike" and "swim" and "lobster." On the drive home from the art therapy sessions, Morgan liked to make up songs about her father. Then she would say her prayers for the whole family and end with "God bless America, Amen."

The first drawing the therapists asked the mothers to make was of their "safe place." Mary Murphy sketched a bed with her husband's ghostly body beside hers, his arm over her like a guardian angel's. She promptly dissolved in tears. It took coaxing to get her to attempt the next drawing. Cindi Westendorf, the clinical psychologist who had started Amanda's Easel to work with abused children, explained that the idea was to do a sequence of drawings, each one representing another phase of the trauma response. She emphasized that the response is normal and instinctual: "It's not a sign of weakness, it's your mind's best defense." Confronted with an event that threatens our own life or that of a loved one, the mind-body response produces sensations such as shaking, sweating, coldness, numbness, paralysis, blanking out, feeling outside one's own body. "If you slam on the brakes of your car as you see a head-on collision about to happen, you might cascade through all the phases of the trauma response in a matter of seconds," she explained. The longer the time spent in trauma, the more intense are those memories.

"This whole year has postponed the response," observed Laura Greenstone, the program's licensed art therapist. "Some of the mothers have been frozen in the trauma response, and that postpones grieving." Research has found that trauma memories are not stored in the same region of the brain that other memories are, and unless they are retrieved and the fragments put back into context, they can be triggered by any similar sight, smell, sound, or situation, even when there is no actual danger. Eventually, this can lead to post-traumatic stress disorder. Psychological numbing may block the emotional memory, so most people can't find the words to describe what they are feeling. Art therapy helps the recall because it is multisensory.

Mary was pregnant and withdrawn when she started the drawings, in January 2002. In terms of the severity of her traumatic agitation, the therapists estimated she fell about midrange. It took Mary eight months to complete the series. She was eager to hear the therapists talk her through them, to help her create a narrative with beginning, middle, and end.

In Mary's first drawing, she was in her SUV with a cell phone to her ear listening to her father giving her the first news of the attacks. "This is the startle phase," the therapist explained, "where you react with disbelief." Mary was pleased to note that her heart no longer leapt against her chest the

MY SAFE PLACE: "This was the place where I felt peace and comfort and how much I was loved." *Courtesy of Mary Murphy*

THWARTED INTENTION: "I stood in my kitchen glued to the TV." *Courtesy of Mary Murphy*

ALTERED STATE OF CONSCIOUSNESS: "I felt as if I was watching a movie of someone else's life." *Courtesy of Mary Murphy*

THE AFTER PICTURE: "Mom, Mom, pack it up!" "It was incredibly liberating just to pack up and go." *Courtesy of Mary Murphy*

way it used to do. In the next picture Mary had drawn herself in her kitchen staring at the TV screen with "WTC" written all over it. Her arms were outstretched, as if to pull her husband out of the building, but they were pinned behind the countertop. This is called the "thwarted intuition phase," when one becomes frozen. "How are you doing with that body sensation?" the therapist asked.

"I still feel paralyzed when I open his closet," Mary said. She hadn't been able to move her husband's clothes—that was true for most of the widows at that point. "This shows me where I'm still stuck." Another drawing showed Mary and her two little children sitting before a movie screen, watching themselves weeping. This represented the "altered state of consciousness" phase, or an "out of body" sensation, when the shock is so overwhelming it feels like it must be happening to somebody else.

"It doesn't feel like that anymore," Mary commented quietly. "I know it's my life now."

The bodily response phase was depicted in a drawing where Mary had a blue face and transparent body outlined in black. "I remember how I was feeling," Mary said, "the coldness, the numbness, the emptiness. I've moved past that. I'm sad. But I'm not back there anymore." In the next picture Mary sat limp, head in hands, while family members reached out to help her. "That's the automatic obedience phase," the therapist translated, "when you feel like a robot." Mary smiled; she was anything but a robot these days. Working out at the gym had brought her postpartum body back into shape, and just the week before, she had put on a bikini again.

A drawing in which Mary was doing household chores, taking a shower, and taking a walk was interpreted as the "self-repair phase." For the final picture she had been instructed to draw a "return to normalcy." This one was in color. It showed Mary's three children sitting in her SUV, with Morgan beckoning excitedly out the window, as Mary came out of the house with a shoulder bag—ready for a road trip.

"Mom, Mom, pack it up!" might have been the caption. This was how Mary's children had come to feel about the spontaneous road trips she invented to escape whenever the walls of grief began to close in. The first trip had been the cross-country drive to Colorado she had undertaken only six weeks after the attacks. As described earlier, Mary was being inundated with mail and phone calls from well-meaning friends asking, "How can we help you?"

"Nobody can help you," she knew but dared not say. "I had to get away, and start to figure out what my life was now."

Most people would think that driving halfway across the country five months pregnant and with two little kids just after your life has been turned upside down would be more chaos than anyone could bear. Mary Murphy found it just the opposite. In the midst of struggling desperately to get hold of a life that had spun completely out of her hands, a road trip was a way of restoring one small zone of control. When to go, where to turn, when to stop, where to sleep—all the decisions belonged to the widow Murphy and her kids. To keep the children entertained, she had rigged up a portable TV in the back of the SUV and popped *The Wizard of Oz* into the VCR. For her own companionship, she stacked the CD player with her husband's favorite mellow music. Then she lit out for Colorado, stopping only overnight in Ohio to pick up her mother.

Even before she married, Mary had always loved road trips. Having busted out of the prison of victimhood so early, Mary had proven to herself that even without a husband, even with little kids, even pregnant, she could still have a life and give her children joy. "No trip ever felt so freeing as that drive to Colorado," she said. "The children knew a bad thing had happened, but it was incredibly liberating just to pick up and go."

Since then, her children had come to share her spirit of adventure. All she had to say was "Want to go on a road trip?" and they would be in the car shouting, "When are we going, Mom!" After the first hour on the road they would begin nudging, "Are we still in New Jersey?" Morgan could tick off half a dozen states she had visited. Only six weeks after the baby, Meredith, was born, Mary had strapped her in a baby seat and driven the whole family up to Killington, Vermont, so the kids could enjoy the snow.

"We only stopped once, so I could breast-feed while the kids made pit stops."

Her relationship with her departed husband was becoming more natural and supportive. "I think he likes talking to me," she said. "When I'm really ticked off at the kids, I'll take a step back and say to myself, if he were here he wouldn't be so tough on them—and then I'll think, *But he is here.* I don't need to scream. He keeps me in check somehow."

She still didn't have a mental image of where he was at rest. She tried to picture him sitting around with the forty-some other men of the Cantor mortgage group with whom she had worked for ten years and for whom she still had no room to grieve. "Sometimes, I can see them sitting around heaven and laughing."

It had helped that Mary and other widows from her Middletown support group were invited by Lieutenant Keegan for a private tour of Ground Zero by his Port Authority team. The women brought flowers and candles and felt the awesome serenity of that pit. Keegan walked them around the footprints of the two towers and helped each of them to locate an approximate spot where their loved one had last known life. He was able to tell those whose husbands had been on the uppermost floors, "They rode the Towers down," and others that the smoke or the implosive force of so many floors collapsing so fast had most likely made the end swift. Each widow found her sacrosanct patch of dust and crouched to pray or meditate or try to commune with a restless soul.

Despite these positive efforts to move on, Mary Murphy was dreading the first anniversary of 9/11. "There's so much focus on this anniversary—I feel like I'm being pressured to fall apart on that day. It drives me insane." Everyone had ideas for how she should spend the day. She wasn't buying anybody else's advice. She would wait until the night before, when she would sense what and where was the right place for her and the children to be. Mary had worked through the trauma. Now she knew she could trust herself to make her own decisions about how to grieve.

PAT THE ABSENT MOM

Pat Wotton's almost-three-year-old daughter, Dorothea, was hitting, shoving, even choking her baby brother. Born after 9/11, the baby, Rodney, was only eight months old and still gasping and wheezing to pump enough breath out of his underdeveloped lungs. When Pat was home to hear the shrieking of her son under attack, she would pull Dorothea off and scold her. The little girl would only shriek the louder in her frustration.

"I want the baby to go away so Daddy'll come home and we'll be happy again!"

But Pat was seldom at home to see the dangerous behavior. Her children were being watched by a series of aides provided by a home health care agency. Her parents, who had all but given up their lives in Florida to stay with Pat, were at the end of their rope. Things were spinning out of control.

Play therapy may have saved the life of Pat Wotton's post–9/11 baby.

Pat had found the one therapist in town who agreed to treat Dorothea. Chris Bellissimo, a dedicated young play therapist, was working with a number of the preschool children who had lost a parent in the Trade Center. "There's no question in my mind that children of three to five are capable of expressing grief and mourning and anger," he told worried parents like Pat.

"They haven't yet developed the ability to articulate their thoughts and feelings verbally, but they have an enormous capacity for self-expression through their play."

"But how is playing with my child going to help?" parents asked.

Bellissimo would show them the play therapy room. It was small and round and scrupulously structured, with puppets in one cabinet and stuffed animals in graduated sizes in another, cutout figures to represent adults and children, and a sand tray, an easel, hats of every variety for role-playing, and a puppet tent that a child's imagination could turn into a rocket ship, a store, a safe place, anything. The idea is to provide an environment that is consistent and predictable, so when children return after a week, everything they played with will be in exactly the same place and they can pick up the story where they left off.

"A child who is experiencing PTSD will reenact—and reexperience—the traumatic event through their play," he explained. "Their play is deliberate and repetitive, it doesn't change at all." In that case, as a play therapist, he would listen empathically and offer words that might give the child some insight into what he or she was trying to express through play. "Here, I may be able to help them gain a sense of understanding of their experiences and become more familiar with their emotions, so they become less frightened." Gradually, the child may begin to alter the ending of the traumatic event, providing a conclusion to the story that reflects the child's wish. For example, children who witness domestic violence might use a medical kit to "treat" the abused parent, or adopt the role of the abuser and reenact the beating of his mother, then take the mother's part and fight back. This reconstructive play, Bellissimo suggests, "can alter a child's perspective from one of passivity and helplessness to a mind-set of action, control, empowerment."

With a child as young as Dorothea was at the time her father disappeared—only two—the therapist first had to assess her ability to engage in symbolic play. Dorothea demonstrated her ability by picking out dolls or animals or cutouts that consistently represented her parents and her baby brother; she was developmentally ready to tell her story.

One day in August, Pat received an urgent call from Bellissimo, reporting that Dorothea was expressing destructive anger at her mother and her baby brother. He urged Pat to observe their next session. On a TV monitor in the waiting room, Pat was able to watch Dorothea act out her confusion over the arrival of the baby coinciding with the mysterious disappearance of her beloved father. Rational explanations had no effect on the child. As Bellissimo explained to Pat, it isn't until the age of seven or eight that a child is developmentally ready to accept the finality of death. The child's wish for her father's return probably explained, too, her hysterical refusal to allow anyone else to replace him in giving her a bath. Dorothea desperately needed more of her mother.

Pat was shaken out of preoccupation with her own loss. She began to see that behind her frantic activity—rushing from one support group to another—was a longing to escape the reality of her new life. She was running away from her children.

"I saw the damage I could be doing by not bonding enough with my children," she said. "I didn't want to risk losing them." She invoked the parental aspect of her dead husband: "Rod would have been so upset with me." This encounter prompted Pat to take the first concrete step to change her way of coping. She couldn't allow herself the luxury of wallowing in depression or seeking escape. Acknowledging that she needed to take care of her children *emotionally,* she committed to spending more time at home with them.

KAREN HEADS OFF A CRASH

Over the summer, Karen Cangialosi had gained back some of the twenty pounds she had lost. She was back again at the Y with her seniors teaching her water aerobics class and working three days a week as a dental assistant. She had been playing lots of ball with her boys and taking over the yardwork once done by her husband. A neighborhood dad was coaching her on the blunter points of football so she could talk plays with her sons. Karen said with considerable pride, "We're getting used to the New Normal."

But she, too, felt the same kind of social pressures described by Mary Murphy. "Like I'm supposed to have the perfect family and be the perfect widow who's moving on—I feel that constantly." Karen realized it was just another form of the competitive pressures of suburban life. She wasn't going to let other people's expectations throw her off track. On at least one point she had total clarity:

"The only way you can be perfect is in the eyes of someone who loves you."

But a week before the anniversary, she felt the anxiety mounting like some invisible nerve agent sucking up the hard-won equilibrium in her household. She had kept the TV off for a full year, but she couldn't hide her sons from reality forever. Together, they watched a couple of the magazine shows about 9/11; Karen herself was featured in one. It set them all on edge. The boys had trouble sleeping again. Karen dropped ten pounds and once again had to hike up her size-four jeans. Her hips were gone. Dressing to go to work at the gym, Karen surveyed herself in the mirror. "I couldn't stand the way I looked. Sad face. Stick body." She felt like she had turned off the womanly part of herself.

The day before the anniversary, Karen picked up the phone to call the new spa in town, the Atlantic Club. She asked for the beauty salon, then hung up before they answered. Fought with herself. Was she being frivolous? Thinking about her hair instead of concentrating on grieving for her dead husband? At nine the next morning, Karen sat down nervously in a stylist's chair and allowed herself to be draped for a haircut. A half hour later, she was given a hand mirror. Her sad face split open in a grin.

"I can't believe—I look like a woman again! It's coming back."

THE NOTHING MAN

I am the nothing man.

That was the refrain from the newly released Springsteen album, *The Rising,* that rang over and over again in the ears of Bob Planer. The song is heavy with guilt and self-deprecation; not the story of a hero or a victim, but perhaps that of a cop who didn't die, or a regular guy like Bob Planer who got away without a scratch.

Drawing on the experiences of people like those in this book, Bruce Springsteen had found all the creative authority he needed to turn America's nightmare into art. Living in Rumson, he absorbed the angst of families as they awoke to the "Empty Sky," barely able to breathe, and within days after the Towers collapsed he was writing songs. Turning reporter, he called up some families and heard their homely, heart-wrenching descriptions of what loss feels like when a loved one disappears in a plume of ash. He put flesh on the intensity of their losses in song: *But you're missing.* When the album debuted at number one in eleven countries, many of Springsteen's neighbors in Middletown found some comfort in the fact that their homegrown bard was telling their story to the world in a muscular Jersey idiom.

"His CD haunts me," Paula Planer said. "His songs go over and over in my dreams, especially 'Lonesome Day.' " It was the week before the anniversary. Bob Planer, who had been feeling better over the summer, admitted the heaviness had returned in his chest. "The gray cloud is coming back."

Paula saw the melancholy settling on her husband again. "I call him one of the gray people. They feel nothing. They're gray."

Bob repeated the lyrics buzzing in his ear: "I'm a nothing man."

PATHFINDERS OF THE SPIRIT

Not even the local spiritual leaders had been able to cope with the past year on their own. Some of those who had tried had fallen short and lost some credibility with their flock. But others had been challenged by September 11 to reach out for their clerical colleagues across the usual boundaries of religion and denomination, looking for support and strategies.

Rabbi Levin and the pastor of the First Presbyterian Church of Rumson, John Monroe, might have seemed an unlikely team. They both had sons who played saxophone in the same middle school, and the two fathers had shared some chuckles when they met at school concerts. But while Levin's father was a Brooklyn union organizer who had been on freedom marches in the South with Martin Luther King, Monroe was a southerner who now presided over a very proper Presbyterian church in a town dominated by rich Republicans. It was on the night of the first September 11 that they had come to appreciate each other's depth. Both had been summoned to the Tower Hill Church, where they faced a packed sanctuary of terrified people and had to do soul work on the spot.

In the weeks that followed 9/11, Pastor Monroe couldn't help thinking as he looked out from his lectern on Sunday mornings, "We were dead men walking. This struck people at the core. It blew away our sense of security and our identity. I think we stayed in depression, my sense is, for six months."

An element of trauma hung over his parishioners even after that. About two dozen members of Monroe's church were survivors of the Towers or had watched the horror up close and run for their lives. Some had adopted the defensive view "All right—I dodged that bullet, don't invite conversation with me," but others were open to spiritual reflection and looking for some path to renewal. The pastor and the rabbi found that other members of the clergy felt the same sense of inadequacy in overcoming the depressed state of their flocks.

How were the spiritual leaders to point the way to renewal when they felt so alone themselves? They would have to drop their defenses and own up to their own sense of vulnerability. The clerics began to meet in small groups, and before long they were telling one another intimate stories about their own lives. Rabbi Levin welcomed Father Jerome Nolan, the Catholic priest whose small church sat directly across the street from the rabbi's synagogue. The middle-aged priest was surprised and delighted. "I love coming over here," Nolan said. "It takes me back to my boyhood in Brooklyn." He told a story that revealed a shared appreciation of humanity far stronger than the divisions of religious dogma. Nolan had been raised in a Jewish neighborhood, and when his father died, it was the Jewish women in his apartment house who knew how to respond to death and take care of his family. "And when I decided to become a priest, it was the Jewish people who supported me more than our own," he told the rabbi. "Because to them, family is all-important, and to sacrifice having a family in order to serve God is deserving of the highest respect."

Another member of their informal meeting group was Reverend Ophelia Laughlin. As the first ordained woman priest in the Episcopal church in Rumson, she was battling fear of the new. What's more, she was a single parent. "We felt a very definite intentionality in strengthening the bonds between our faiths and between our denominations," she said. On a more personal note, she acknowledged, "We needed help from each other."

Levin boiled it down still further. "We also have to give each other practical strength. I was in Ophelia's office one day talking about my own situation, and she said, 'Anytime you want to hurl yourself down on my couch, just know this is your spiritual home.' " Ophelia had told Levin she felt the Christian church did not pay enough attention to Hebrew Scripture. The rabbi had invited her to join his Torah study group, and she had spent much time over the past year in the synagogue.

Having walked through unfamiliar doors with his colleagues in the faith business and forged new and deep personal connections, Rabbi Levin wanted to expand the embrace. How to bring their congregants with them? How to use the dreaded anniversary to inspire people to higher ethical standards of behavior and greater efforts at neighborliness?

What happened on September 7, 2002, was emblematic of the sea change.

TEKIYAH! TEKIYAH! TEKIYAH!

As the harsh, penetrating voice of the shofar horn sounded, the tightly packed crowd in Rabbi Levin's synagogue froze. It was the sound always heard on Rosh Hashanah, but nothing else about the Rosh Hashanah service at Congregation B'nai Israel on September 7, 2002, was familiar to Rabbi Levin's flock.

"The shofar for thousands of years has been a powerful force in calling us back to the truths of our identities as Jews," Rabbi Levin intoned from the raised sanctuary called the bimah. "We come together today to show that our commitment not to stand passive while our neighbors suffer is a true and enduring commitment."

The atmosphere in the temple was electric. The rabbi knew well that Rosh Hashanah is one of the most intense and particularly Jewish religious observance of the year. He was aware that it is virtually unheard of to bring non-Jews into the synagogue on Rosh Hashanah. But in anticipation of the anniversary of 9/11, he believed the shock would be justified. The idea had come about in a beautiful, creative way, he said. The rabbi had been looking for a way to honor the man who traditionally blew the shofar, David Rosensweig, who was president of the New York City firefighters dispatchers unit. Most of the congregants had no idea that Rosensweig had worked at Ground Zero from day one and had helped console people at 150 funerals of the victims over the past year. Rabbi Levin intended to use Rosensweig to represent the best of the Jewish soul to many invited guests who weren't Jewish. And while he was at it, to do a little outreach! The crowd that Saturday morning was standing room only.

Rabbi Levin looked out upon rows of conservative Jewish men draped in prayer shawls and women in long skirts, but sprinkled among them were men in police uniforms, men in white Roman Catholic collars, men and women in the suits of civil servants, a woman in a white Episcopalian collar, and a Presbyterian minister in a gray suit whose only distinguishing feature was a nose so long and narrow he could have been looking down from a spire of the Church of England. This was Rabbi Levin's new best friend, Pastor John Monroe.

Rabbi Levin was in his element. His voice projected from his full chest with the sweet power of a cello. He explained the sound of the shofar, improvising with a metaphor as effortlessly as a jazz musician.

"In Jewish tradition, it is said that *tekiyah,* that sustained note, is our illusion that the world never changes. The next group of sounds is short, *truah, shvareem, truah,* all disrupted, pointed sounds, to show that the wholeness has been broken. This is the voice of wailing and mourning when that solid structure comes down. The sound of shofar shatters doors that were never opened before. And then you'll hear the return to *tekiyah.* That sound inspires those who have the courage to realize that, despite the burdens, despite the anguish of this shattering experience, we have no choice but to unite to other people."

Rosensweig's blowing of the shofar did seem to shatter doors. The final note of *tekiyah* was sustained to an almost unbearable tremble. In the silence that followed, Rabbi Levin seized the moment to honor many non-Jewish members of the community in order to deepen their connections. He asked Police Chief Edward Rumolo of Rumson to stand up. He told the story of how the chief had reacted the previous spring when the rabbi had reported that hate literature was turning up on people's lawns. "I told the chief that it's recent in our thinking to turn to the police to care for us. In the past, many Jews had seen police as out to do them damage or oppress them. But the chief responded with such rapidity and such desire to see justice done, I had to tell him how profound a shift that was, especially to some of our people who have experienced the Holocaust."

The superintendent of schools was asked to stand to be honored for having created a diversity training program in the schools. The rabbi called upon the local mayors to stand. He spoke to each of them as to a friend, recalling the experiences that connected them. He praised Bob Honecker as "the best prosecutor there is anywhere," and described how Honecker had handled the perpetrators of the hate crimes. When the two young men had heard that they were going to jail, they had protested that they were only first offenders, it would be setting a historic precedent. "Bob didn't back away. Both offenders did two days in jail. I love you, Bob." He saluted as a neighbor the Catholic priest from across the street. "Father Nolan is here today. Father, when we saw the funeral cars pulling up in front of your church day after day, and the mourners stepping out, our hearts broke."

It came time to say the mourner's kaddish, the prayer for all the dead. Traditionally, the rabbi would read it, but seconds before the time came, a truly door-shattering idea occurred to him. He called up to the bimah a man named Rich Katz, vice principal of the Rumson–Fair Haven Regional High School. He then said, "I'd like to call up a gentleman by the name of Dr. Don Warner, a major leader in education. Dr. Warner is president of the board of trustees of Brookdale Community College and interim pastor of the Mount Pisgah Baptist Church in Asbury Park." As the black man climbed the steps and took his place on the bimah, a few gasps could be heard from the congregants. *Black man on the bimah!* Rabbi Levin spoke to their shock: "If you look at photographs of the people who picked through the rubble of Ground Zero, you will see people working together who under other circumstances would never even talk to each other. Here they were, cooperating intimately to be of service to others. We have to sustain that level of ethical service." He turned to acknowledge Katz and Warner: "Jew and non-Jew, white and black, on the bimah together."

Spontaneously, the Jewish man and the black man put their arms around each other's waists and each read his part of the prayer. Some people began crying. The rabbi was not surprised to note that others, "the people who came with negativism about race, were shaking with fury."

But over the course of two hours, Rabbi Levin managed to resurrect the spirit of oneness and tender neighborliness that had made people feel better about themselves in the candlelight vigils of the year before. When the service was over, Jews and non-Jews clasped hands warmly and exchanged introductions and greetings. As Chief Rumolo led his police officers to the door, a spontaneous reception line formed. They were elders of the temple, all in prayer shawls, many speaking with Eastern European accents. As they reached out to hug the chief and his men, Rumolo realized that some of them had been through the Holocaust. Once he and his men were outside in the parking lot, they couldn't keep from weeping.

Of all the bonds that were forged in that extraordinary service, none pleased Rabbi Levin more than seeing the effect it had on the police. "The police take all kinds of garbage," he said. "Here, they saw that they were honored men. And that's the ongoing inspiration."

BOOK TWO

———

THE REST OF THE STORY

There is a land of the living and a land of the dead and the bridge is love, the only survival, the only meaning.

—Thornton Wilder,
The Bridge of San Luis Rey

Chapter Twenty-three

THE ANNIVERSARY CLOUD

A year had passed. As the long day of anniversary ceremonies for the 3,025 victims of 9/11 began, a tense world held its breath. In Washington, live heat-seeking antiaircraft missiles were deployed around the capital. In the middle of lunch at the Oyster Point Hotel, Monmouth County Prosecutor Bob Honecker pulled out his pager and learned that New York and New Jersey had been bumped up to Code Orange, the second-highest state of alert. Intelligence data warned of possible suicide bombings, or worse. Honecker canceled plans to take his kids in to Shea Stadium for the ballgame that night.

What could he tell his children?

Every war needs a rationale that can be shaped into a coherent story; how else to recruit the people to support the sacrifices of blood and treasure that will inevitably be required? In the first months after September 11, the Bush administration had a solid rationale for taking revenge on Afghanistan for harboring the Taliban and al Qaeda. The story line was the hunt for bin Laden. "Those who make war against the United States have chosen their own destruction—we will smoke them out of their holes," the president vowed. "We'll get them running and we'll bring them to justice."

In the first few months of the war on terrorism, Osama and his terrorists were indisputably on the run, but where had they run? The staggering airpower of the world's superpower had scattered them to sixty different countries. The outcome was "like smashing quicksilver with a hammer," in the colorful description of John Arquilla, author and professor of defense analysis at the Naval Postgraduate School in Monterey. A strategic analyst for

RAND, Arquilla had a valuable insight into the real nature of America's "war on terrorism." It was the first major confrontation between a bureaucratic state and a virtually leaderless network. How to make war on a network of terrorists that uses the Internet and Web sites to rally its stateless, messianic army was a brand-new challenge for the cumbersome American bureaucracy.

In modern warfare there are always two major battles: the Battle of the Field and, no less important, the propaganda war, or the Battle of the Story. As early as December 2001, the Bush administration began shifting the Battle of the Story from the hunt for Osama to the unfinished decapitation of Saddam's Iraq. "It was easier for America to make war on a state—for example, Iraq—then on a terrorist network, because that's what we know how to do" was Arquilla's analysis.

The president wanted to introduce this new story in his State of the Union address in January 2002. Bush's chief speechwriter gave a simple, fateful directive to wordsmith David Frum: "I was to provide a justification for a war," the speechwriter recounted in his book *The Right Man: The Surprise Presidency of George W. Bush.* "Bush needed something to assert, something that made clear that September 11 and Saddam Hussein were linked after all and that for the safety of the world, Saddam Hussein must be defeated rather than deterred." The absence of any evidence to connect Saddam to September 11 at that time did not dampen Bush's enthusiasm for this story. Frum came up with the rationale that substituted three "terror states" for the elusive terror organization. He sent the infamous memo suggesting that Iraq, Iran, and North Korea be linked together as an "axis of hatred" against the United States, dangerous regimes that couldn't be allowed to obtain weapons of mass destruction and against which the United States must reserve the right to strike first to protect itself and the world. A simple substitution of the theological language preferred by Bush, and the "axis of evil" became the boogeyman to replace communism.

In a world-shaking but underreported speech before the military cadets at West Point in June 2002, President Bush began laying out the predicate for abandoning the Cold War doctrine of containment and replacing it with his own doctrine of preventive war. It was only in retrospect that Americans began to realize that this declaration was aimed at preparing the country for a preemptive attack on Iraq.

Meanwhile, al Qaeda was pumping out a simple, absolutist narrative line as old as the Crusades: "holy war" by Islam against the "infidels" of America and their allies in Israel and the West. Throughout the summer, the administration appeared to be in disarray about its next moves in the war on terror, but the tight team of advisers who cocooned the president was hard at work on a strategy to sell their new policy: war on Iraq. Andrew Card, the White House chief of staff in charge of coordinating the strategy, said, "From a marketing point of view, you don't introduce new products in August." As if to divert Americans' attention from the threat of al Qaeda and its mastermind, who was nowhere to be found, the face of the elusive Osama would be morphed into that of Saddam Hussein. The White House intended to tell "a compelling story," according to the communications director, Dan Bartlett. The "rollout" of the administration's new story was timed for the September 11 anniversary.

Yet America's leaders had not yet come up with a coherent narrative to help its citizens live in the reality of the New Normal. Or to cope with its fears of terrorism. Nowhere was this absence more noticeable than among the adolescents of Middletown, who had just been coming to political consciousness when their fundamental assumptions about America's story had been shaken.

HIGH SCHOOL STUDENTS AWAKE

On the morning of the first anniversary of September 11, students filed into Middletown South High School with some trepidation. For the whole previous year the school had been shuttered away from acknowledging the tragedy or addressing it in classes. Shortly before reopening in the fall, however, the school had sent a note to parents acknowledging that "many of the children in Middletown have not had the opportunity to speak about their fears related to 9/11 . . . or wondering if their parents would be the ones that didn't come home that evening. Those children who lost parents on 9/11 feel somewhat isolated knowing that other children feel uncomfortable to discuss the deaths of their loved ones."

Middletown FAVOR had done yet another favor for the town. It was Allyson Gilbert who had a brainstorm for how to start a dialogue about the teenagers' fears. Allyson had seen a dramatic performance about 9/11 created by a drama therapy troupe from New York called ENACT. Professional actors, drawing on interviews with students who had lived through September 11 up close, in a high school near the Trade Center, spoke to the fear and helplessness that so many had felt on that day. Allyson had arranged for funding from United Way to bring the show to Middletown's high schools for the anniversary. It was an interactive way for the students to begin constructing a story about what had happened and how to think about it. Professional grief counselors from a New Jersey group called Adventures in Teaching had volunteered to be available to meet with students after the shows.

On the anniversary day, Daniel Lane, the principal of Middletown South, was not his usual ebullient self, not standing at the door to welcome his teachers and banter with students. He was in his office, pulling at his black knit tie to loosen the collar on his black checked shirt and trying to think of what to say. At 8:30 he made the morning announcement:

"People, we have a moment of silence at 8:46 in memory of the heroes who perished in 9/11. I want you to know that today is a difficult day for all people in America. But since it is a historical day, I'm hopeful that we as a school can pull together as people, as a family, and as professionals, to make today a positive day for all those individuals who lost people in 9/11."

When he finished, he wiped tears from his eyes. "I love being here at school, but I have five children, two of them still at home, and I feel a little bit squeamish about not being with them to say, 'Hey, how you doing today?' " For Dan Lane, the anniversary of 9/11 was a reminder of the personal chaos of his boyhood home life. Quietly he confessed, "I don't know how to deal with my grief."

The seniors were first to see the performance by ENACT. They were riveted. Afterward, the troupe's director, Diana Feldman, had to work hard at encouraging students to stand up and speak. No one raised a hand. Finally, a pretty blond-haired girl in a row of identically pretty blond-haired girls rose. Her voice was barely audible: "To wake up today and remember where you were a year ago, the whole experience comes back. It's too overwhelming. It's like being beat over your head." Now a skinny Boogie Boarder stood and complained, "We're inundated with 9/11 memorials. It doesn't really do anything for me. Can't we just shut up and get on with it?" Diana Feldman looked pleased. It was when kids got angry that she could break through their resistance. She urged the seniors to voice their anger. "Just yell out the words."

"Violated"; "pissed off"; "angry and helpless at the same time"; "angry at so many ignorant people out there trying to downplay what happened."

More and more students opened up. One young man spoke of his confusion and hurt. "Our government represented that we're kind of invincible. Then how could something like this possibly happen?" Other students wrestled with the shock of learning how much hate there was for America out there in the world. Feldman was satisfied that the students who spoke up were handling their emotions quite well. It was the many students who sat silent and sullen that worried her. Most of them were boys. One tall, well-muscled student leader in a bright red T-shirt and modest Mohawk got up to speak but sat down again and leaned over, elbows on his knees, and dug his thumbs into his eyes. Other boys in the audience sat with their arms wrapped tightly around their chests. It was apparent that many strong feelings were still locked inside.

When the junior class watched the show, predictably, the students squirmed and giggled and manifested discomfort with emotional content they didn't know how to handle. The sophomores were similarly cowed when asked to give feedback in front of their peers. Finally, Alex Kerr, the girl who had lost her sister in a car accident, raised her hand. "I don't think people understand what they lost. Like, everyone says, 'Forget it and move on.' They don't have an understanding of death."

After the performances, Elizabeth Howe, an articulate senior, touched the roots of the anger expressed by so many of her classmates: "First, you're angry at your parents. As children you go to your parents for protection. And I have great parents. There was always the feeling that whenever there was something wrong, if you went to your parents and they weren't scared, then you'd be okay. September 11 was the first time I saw my parents cry." Elizabeth didn't dare express the anger many of her classmates felt at school officials for keeping them in the dark that day, or their anger at teachers who didn't know how to console them, or their anger at the government for being unable to protect them. But the grief counselors heard plenty of such sentiments. The students felt all the adults had failed them on that day. "You're not just angry at one person, you're angry at everybody," Elizabeth said. But after seeing the show, she said she felt compassion for her parents and her teachers. And for fellow students whose feelings remained as tangled and private as hers. Outside, looking up at the American flag whipping in a stiff breeze, she came up with a metaphor:

"Every time I think about it, I cry. But then I block it. The blocking goes by the name *Under Construction*. A year later, it's still there—the hole. People ask me, 'Why don't you get over it?' I say, 'We're under construction. The people.'"

MIDDLETOWN, AMERICA, REMEMBERS

At last, the town had pulled itself together to create a community memorial. Funds had been donated to build a Middletown Memorial Gardens. The groundbreaking became the centerpiece for a remembrance ceremony on the night before the anniversary. The gardens were intended to be a "beautiful, tranquil place where friends and neighbors can reflect upon the effect the loss has had upon our community." The dubious location was next to the train station, hardly a tranquil oasis, especially since it was from the very same station that most of the dozens who died had departed on the morning of September 11, 2001.

The stubbled grass field beside the busy commuter train station was set up with two hundred folding chairs, not nearly enough to hold the streams of mothers, fathers, sisters, brothers, grandparents, children, and infants in strollers who turned out to share that solemn night. The field swelled with nearly a thousand standees. Two fire companies had pitched their ladder trucks to form a broken arch, between which hung a giant American flag. The sky above was a mellow golden pink. The bandstand was chockablock with row after row of speakers. What started out as a local affair had mushroomed once the mayor began inviting state officials. "We couldn't beat them off," commented the police chief dryly. Behind the bunting sat virtually the whole political establishment of the state of New Jersey.

It was a night the politicians would search for the words to give meaning to the story of Middletown's tragedy.

Spotted through the audience were some—not all, by any means—of the families of those being remembered. Kristen Breitweiser was absent; she had no interest in either religious or political events to commemorate her husband's murder, she said. Lisa Luckett was also absent.

But for those present in the field that night, a sense of community solidarity was palpable. Mayor Rick Parkinson opened the ceremonies with a moment of silence for the coworkers, volunteer firemen, fathers and mothers, sons and daughters, husbands and wives of Middletown's lost friends and neighbors. Like most politicians and clerics who officiated at the many services that day, he neglected to mention the sisters and brothers. Laurie Tietjen, Kenny's sister, sat lifeless as a statue. "These days are especially hard," she said, and her feelings were not unusual. Over the course of the year it had been the sisters and brothers who bucked up their families and contained their own feelings. On this anniversary, notably, it was the siblings who were often doubled over in inconsolable sorrow.

The mayor acknowledged the tireless work of FAVOR and its founders. Allyson Gilbert and Janet Dluhi stood and were warmly applauded. Allyson put on a game smile, but inside she was thinking, *I didn't lose anybody personally, so why aren't I getting over it? How am I going to move on? Maybe I can move on, but I can't forget.*

Senator Jon Corzine set a theme that was repeated throughout the evening. "Ground Zero may be in New York, but there's an emotional ground zero here for the 691 families in New Jersey and the 138 in Monmouth

County." Congressman Rush Holt reminded the crowd, "Middletown has more people who died than any other place." As if to emphasize the reminder, trains stuttered over the tracks behind the speechifying. Families grew restless and resentful at politicians pontificating on the back of their tragedy. Yet it was the former governor of New Jersey, Christine Todd Whitman, who best captured the private emotions yearning for some larger, meaningful context.

"September eleventh, 2001, a day that will define this new century in a way we couldn't possibly have imagined on September tenth," she began. "Here in Middletown, September eleventh has a meaning all its own. It was a day that ordinary people left their homes for their regular jobs from the station right next door, followed by the night as their cars sat unclaimed in the parking lot, giving new testimony to the magnitude of the loss of this community. September eleventh tore families apart and shattered dreams. It produced the raw ache of personal loss and the empty feeling of helplessness. September eleventh didn't happen to someone else, someplace else. It happened to us. It happened here."

The starless sky turned a blackened blue as she spoke. An occasional jetliner soared soundlessly overhead. Governor Whitman worked at coming up with a narrative to help the citizens live in the reality of the New Normal.

"The days and weeks and months that have followed September eleventh have told a story about us as a nation and a people; about sharing tragedy, about us grieving together, about us united in our resolve to go forward.

"If we have learned nothing else, we have learned that grieving is personal and that healing takes time and will only occur at its own pace. And we cannot judge how that is for others. . . . Middletown has shown us in a million different ways, from providing everything from casseroles to counseling, how to come together to support your neighbors. You have provided an example of pride for the rest of America and an example of defiance to the terrorists who launched their attack on that day. . . . America isn't about our buildings. America is about our people. And nowhere in America has that strength been shining more brightly than here in Middletown, America."

MORGAN'S RAINBOW WORLD

Mary Murphy had been uncertain about where and how to spend the anniversary day. At the end of the train station ceremony, she said, "Now I know. I'm going to take the children down to the beach tomorrow to watch the sun come up."

The beach was windy. Mary sat in the sand cuddling her baby girl while Morgan and little Jimmy leaned against their mother and they all looked out at the soft, blank horizon and waited for the ball of gold to rise and gladden them. Mary felt vacant, exhausted. She still had one more ceremony to go. Spring Lake was honoring her husband, whose family lived there, and four others. "All right, this is the last public thing I'm going to do," she said.

At the dedication of the little garden across from the beach, Mary could hardly be seen. She was surrounded by a stand of Jimmy Murphy's seven brothers, tall as pine trees. She couldn't stop herself from thinking, *If Jimmy was one of his brothers, he would be here now, holding me.* But no one among the other mourning families was holding one another; they weren't even touching, just standing stiffly, each in his or her own private hell. It struck Mary that this is what grief looks like when it is blocked. It could consume you. This is what she used to look like, unable to break through her Scandinavian reserve. She could not allow that to happen. She had three children to raise. She vowed then and there: *My grief has to change. I have to get through it.*

She reached out to her husband's mother and father and the three hugged one another and wept for a full ten minutes. The waves of sadness calmed.

For Morgan Murphy, now five, the year ahead was full of firsts. The high-spirited child had started kindergarten at the Middletown Village School. She had moved on from Jacob, the fatherless child who had been her partner in spontaneous play therapy, and had a new "boyfriend" whom she liked to chase and kiss. This day, too, would mark another first.

"We thought you and your mom could work together on an art project," Laura Greenstone said in welcoming them to Amanda's Easel. Morgan hesitated; she was used to working only with other children. But once she was settled beside her mother, Morgan looked eager to plunge into this new exercise. The art therapist gave the child a huge white sphere of poster board.

"What could that be, Morgan, a big circle like that?"

"Earth," Morgan said.

"Good. You and your mom can work together to make a world. Any kind of world you want. Real or imaginary." The therapist spread out colored markers, stickers, bright-colored paper, and glue for cutouts. "What do you think you need in your world, Morgan?"

"Green and blue."

The therapist expected the child to draw grass and sky, but Morgan ignored those normal dimensions and put in no grounding at all. Instead, she drew ocean waves. Then a small bright sun, followed by a heavy dark blue cloud. "What else would be good to have in your world?" the therapist coaxed. Morgan considered. Suddenly animated, she reached for a handful of multicolored markers and created a brilliant pinwheel.

"Fireworks!" she announced.

That was so like Morgan, her mother thought, to want excitement and spontaneity in her world. Morgan continued to draw inanimate objects, a shell, a starfish, no people. The therapist asked her mother what she wanted in her world.

"I'd like love in my world," Mary Murphy said. "I need people."

Once her mother began working on cutout figures, Morgan started on a separate sheet of paper drawing people to populate her world—her mother, her baby sister, her brother, her favorite cousin, herself—but there was no daddy. They were a half hour into the session and Morgan hadn't mentioned her father.

"Who's that?" Morgan pointed to one of her mother's cutouts.

"That's Daddy."

"Weird."

"Why is he weird?"

"It looks like he has a beard."

Mary said, "Well, I'm drawing him in the early morning, before he shaves."

"He's weird," Morgan repeated. There was something jarring to her about adding her father to their world. And so began a negotiation between the mother and daughter about how Daddy should be remembered. Morgan argued that he had too much hair. "Is he naked?" "No, he's wearing a brown suit." "Weird." "You can change it if you like," her mother suggested. Morgan remembered a pair of yellow pants that her father particularly liked. She recolored his pants yellow. They discussed where to place the cutouts of family members. Mary said she was going to put Daddy first, then she would be next to him, holding his hand.

"But you're not holding his hand!" Morgan insisted, clinging to her new reality.

"I want to hold his hand," Mary insisted, claiming her ongoing attachment.

"Okay, can I be holding your hand?"

The therapist interpreted this whole interaction as therapeutic. Morgan and her mother were collaborating on their memory of Jimmy Murphy. Morgan was struggling to accept that her father wouldn't be with them again in the real world, while her mother was showing that he could still be with them in memory. They could have an ongoing relationship with him.

Morgan placed the family high up in their world, above the ocean. Finally, at some distance, the child drew a small rectangular object, the smallest object in the whole mural. "House," she pronounced. She colored in a tiny red square in the center. Mary said, "Oh, yes, we have a red door."

"It's not a door," Morgan corrected her. "It's a window."

So it was a house, but it wasn't accessible. Laura Greenstone interpreted that Morgan saw no real shelter for her family in this world. All the elements—ocean, sun, fireworks, clouds—were widely separated. The therapist asked the child what she would like to name her world. Morgan gave it considerable thought.

"Rainbow World."

RAINBOW WORLD: Art therapy drawing by Morgan Murphy, age five.
Note family at top, dark cloud at bottom, and shark at extreme left.
Courtesy of Mary Murphy

Morgan lettered in the cheerful title. Now the therapist held up the big white sphere and asked the five-year-old if her world had everything it needed. Morgan studied it from afar. "Oh, I forgot something." She took out the red and yellow markers and drew a slithery little monster, sneaking in from the edge of her Rainbow World, underwater. "What's that?" her mother asked.

"A shark." Morgan drew black teeth and red blood dripping from them. She sat back, satisfied. "I'm thinking ahead."

So, at the age of five, Morgan Murphy was already able to construct a profound story of how the world works: even when you expect the best—rainbows—you always have to be on the lookout for the monster in the wings who can do you harm.

"Is your world finished now?" the therapist asked.

Morgan wanted to add one more thing. She drew a little pink head with a funny face. "My baby sister. Being born." That made her world right again.

The most important thing about this mother-daughter art adventure, the therapist said, was that Mary and Morgan were creating their new world together. This paralleled what Mary had been doing by jumping in the car and taking road trips with her children. She had been giving Morgan the cue, since six weeks after the tragedy, that you didn't have to stay sad all the time, you could change your reality. Every time she and Morgan planned another trip—and they had several in mind for the next year—they were collaborating on experiences that would bring new colors into their world.

After class, Morgan climbed into the backseat of their giant new SUV and opened her window wide. Mary pressed the control to close it. Morgan protested; she wanted to control her own atmospherics. She won a concession that she could have it halfway down. Morgan leaned back and draped her legs over the open window. A broad smile came across her face as a gust of wind whipped up her long hair. She sang the latest patriotic song she had learned at school: "You're a Grand Old Flag."

Mary said she'd forgotten about a school vacation week coming up. "Do you want to go somewhere?" she asked Morgan. "Yes!" "Maybe we could drive down to Cape May," Mary suggested. "Will we still be in New Jersey?" Morgan wanted to know. "Yes, but at the very tippy tip."

"Okay—traveling is fun!"

Mary looked pleased. "I do think traveling is tremendous fun for the children. It lifts the sadness away—for a little while. I think they feel it just like I do." Mary had developed a new philosophy. "In most of your life, in anyone's life, you don't have control. Things happen. When you have the opportunity to plan something out and have control, it feels good."

The SUV was their own little world.

"That's right." Mary laughed. "I want to live in Morgan's Rainbow World. Because it's good."

Chapter Twenty-four

JUST FOUR MOMS FROM NEW JERSEY

I can't talk. I have three weeks. I'm speaking for all the families of the three thousand victims." Kristen was in full monastic retreat. In the weeks leading up to September 18, she didn't answer the phone, didn't go out, seldom even changed her clothes. The FAVOR volunteer who dropped off the monthly basket had to leave it in Kristen's driveway. The former surfer girl was planted night and day at her dining room table, poring over binders bulging with the news clips she had collected since 9/11 and preparing for the command performance of her life.

Middletown widow Kristen Breitweiser and Washington widower Stephen Push had been delegated by the dozen 9/11 family groups to testify on their behalf in the first public hearings of the House-Senate Joint Inquiry on Intelligence.

Over the summer, Kristen and "the girls" had made frequent road trips to Washington to build support for their cause: an independent commission to investigate the failures of 9/11. They continued to refuse any traditional organizational structure or title. They remained "just four moms from New Jersey," but in operational terms, that allowed them to be as flexible and fast-moving as a terrorist network. Like those networks, they were part of a leaderless string of family "cells" united by social ties and a messianic zeal for their cause. They used cheap low-tech means—the Internet and e-mail—to cull information and remain in rapid communication with their thousands of sympathizers. And they were ready to "swarm" their opponents on Capitol Hill on a few hours' notice.

Kristen had learned how to rocket down to the Capitol by swinging her

SUV onto the Garden State Parkway shortly after four in the morning. She would pick up Patty Casazza and Lorie van Auken and stop at Mindy Kleinberg's just long enough to tuck her daughter in beside Mindy's mother. The four moms had become expert at changing their clothes while stopped in traffic, so they could hit the Capitol rotunda running. They learned to loiter in the halls where the press hung out, ducking security guards and waiting their chance to buttonhole key opponents as well as supporters. They talked strategy with Senators McCain and Lieberman. They met a few times with Eleanor Hill, the sharp prosecutor who was the inquiry's chief of staff. They even opened a line of communication with the White House.

"George Bush and I get on the phone together," Kristen teased.

In fact, the White House had strenuously objected to the idea of an independent commission like those that investigated the attack on Pearl Harbor and the assassination of President John F. Kennedy. The issue of intelligence lapses and leadership lapses all the way to the top echelons of government was highly sensitive for an administration bent on selling its new policy of preemptive war against Iraq and winning control of Congress in the fall election. The administration had agreed to a joint inquiry by the House and Senate intelligence committees, expecting that much of it would be conducted in secrecy and the hearings would be closed. What the White House didn't bank on was the aggressiveness of the investigations supervised by Eleanor Hill, the former inspector general of the Defense Department under President Clinton. After thirteen closed hearings, the chairman and leaders of the committee decided to hold public, televised hearings. By September, Eleanor Hill was ready to put forward a case that would hold the FBI and CIA accountable.

KRISTEN'S MOMENT

When it was announced that testimony by two family members would open the nationally televised hearings, anonymous insiders at the intelligence agencies were quoted in *USA Today* as sneering, "Who's running this investigation, Oprah? Do they really have to have widows sobbing on the stand?" Even around Middletown, other widows were often critical of Kristen's efforts and expressed discomfort at her assertive manner and media appearances. Kristen ignored the criticism; she never had trimmed her sails according to the prevailing winds.

The morning of the hearing, Kristen stared at her room service tray. She couldn't eat. She padded down the hall of the hotel in her sweats to Patty and Lorie's room. Mindy hadn't been able to come along this time; the anniversary had dealt her son a serious setback. Patty said she couldn't help feeling nervous. They had been warned by Capitol Hill staffers that this would be a major press event. Nationally televised. C-SPAN would cover it. To avoid facing a gauntlet of reporters and cameras, security people had arranged to walk the widows into the Hart Senate Office Building by a back entrance. Patty couldn't help asking Kristen, "Aren't you nervous?"

"You know what, Patty?" Kristen said. "I don't have to look death in the face. If our husbands could face their own death, wait to be burned alive—this is nothing."

Kristen went back to her room and dressed in properly preppy testimony clothes—a white dress shirt and navy pantsuit and heels. Then she took her kit of Aveda aromatic oils back to the girls' room and performed her usual preparatory ritual.

"Let's chakra up." She dabbed the calming oils on their wrists. "This stuff channels your energy. It makes you think clearly, it centers you. This'll work perfectly." Kristen didn't know if it really worked any better than a sugar pill, but she believed in mind over matter and she had convinced the girls that this ritual was essential to their success. "Okay, now let's take a yoga moment. Roll our heads and take a few deep breaths and get centered. Concentrate the chi energy in our core." The girls followed Kristen.

"Okay, let's do it."

They met their security escorts on a street corner and were ushered into a holding room. Waiting there were a few other family group representatives: Ginny Bauer from Middletown; Mary Fetchet and Beverly Eckert of Voices of September 11; Monica Gabrielle and Sally Regenhard of Skyscraper Safety. Kristen's support network took their seats in the front row of the imposing hearing room where the Iran-Contra hearings had been held. When the press was admitted, Senate staffers noticed there were more reporters and photographers than had shown up for appearances by heavyweights from the CIA and FBI. Reporters wanted to hear the story firsthand and learn what the media itself had not been able to find out despite Freedom of Information Act requests. Still photographers went into a frenzy, snapping Kristen and her cohorts.

Kristen took her seat at the long, red-covered witness table. She moved with a sense of purpose, as if she were carrying the weight on her shoulders of all the terrible things that had happened to thousands. Her unruly hair was tied back, her face was without makeup, without a trace of the suntan that

used to characterize her old beach-rat days. She looked up at the raised fir-
mament of House and Senate committee members and their batteries of
staffers. Ordinarily, a few chairs in the front row would be empty, but not this
morning. All nineteen of the members were in their seats, signaling their appreciation of the gravity of the situation. Kristen sat alone.

Lorie slipped Kristen a box of Dots candies, to remind her she was there
to connect the dots. It made Kristen chuckle. Senator Bob Graham, a silver-
haired Florida Democrat, opened the hearing, calling it "our search for
truth." He emphasized the uniqueness of the hearing: "This is the first time
in the history of our Congress that two permanent committees have joined in
a joint bicameral committee to conduct an inquiry." He talked about difficulties that still existed in negotiating with the White House and the intelligence
agencies for documents that would give a complete picture of how terrorist
organizations had moved from a relatively insignificant threat only ten years
before to such a significant threat. The goal of the committee's work, he said,
was to ascertain "what the active consumers of government intelligence
knew, or should have known, about that threat, and how the intelligence
agencies interact with one another." The purpose of testimony from Kristen
Breitweiser and Stephen Push, he said, was "to honor the families."

KRISTEN BEGAN BY thanking the families of the three thousand victims
for the privilege of representing them. Her voice quavered. She was barely
audible. "Mrs. Breitweiser, could you please move the microphone closer to
your face?" she was asked. She felt mortified. She knew her testimony would
be walking a fine line; she intended to take it right to the edge, but it was
daunting. Here she was about to chastise the country's intelligence agencies;
they could ruin her life if they chose to. Realizing the David-and-Goliath position she was in, the thirty-year-old woman rolled her eyes and flashed a
goofy, high-schoolish face. But within seconds she settled down to read her
tightly constructed statement.

"I ask the members present here today to find in my voice the voices of
all of the family members of the three thousand victims of September
eleventh. I would also ask for you to see, in my eyes, the eyes of the more
than ten thousand children who are now forced to grow up without the love,
affection, and guidance of a mother or father who was tragically killed on
September eleventh.

"My three-year-old daughter's most enduring memory of her father will
be placing flowers on his empty grave. My most enduring memory of my

husband, Ronald Breitweiser, will be his final words to me, 'Sweets, I'm fine, I don't want you to worry, I love you.' Ron uttered those words while he was watching men and women jump to their deaths from the top of Tower One. Four minutes later his tower was hit by United Flight 175. I never spoke to my husband, Ron, again."

Kristen's mouth clamped tight and shifted to one side. "I don't know whether he jumped or he choked to death on smoke. I don't know whether he sat curled up in a corner watching the carpet melt in front of him"—her mouth screwed to the side again—"knowing that his own death was soon to come, or if he was alive long enough to be crushed by the building when it collapsed. These are the images that haunt me at night when I put my head to rest on his pillow."

A senior Senate staffer who had arranged many big-name hearings began to sniffle. "You look at this angelic face, this girl who could be your sister, your friend, your neighbor, and it happened to her," she said. "Seeing the other widows in the front row, some sobbing, some poised but dabbing at their noses, you could just feel these senators feeling their pain—and seeing a sister, a wife, a woman on their staff—they made it so real."

In short order, Kristen was on to the meat of her statement, and now she was poised and calm. "September eleventh was the devastating result of a catalog of failures on behalf of our government and its agencies," she stated unequivocally. "Our intelligence agencies suffered an utter collapse in their duties and responsibilities leading up to and on September eleventh. But their negligence does not stand alone. Agencies like the Port Authority, the City of New York, the FAA, the INS, the Secret Service, NORAD, the Air Force, and the airlines also failed our nation that morning. The examination of the intelligence agencies by this committee does not detract, discount, or dismantle the need for a more thorough examination of all these other culpable parties."

This was her main objective—to win the committee's agreement that their investigation could not go far enough.

"An independent blue-ribbon panel would provide a comprehensive, unbiased, and definitive report that the devastation of September eleventh demands," she said. "Soon after the attacks, President Bush stated that there would come a time to look back and examine our nation's failures, but that such an undertaking was inappropriate while the nation was still in shock. I would respectfully suggest to President Bush and to our Congress that now, a full year later, it is time to look back and investigate our failures as a nation.

"We need to have answers. We need to have accountability." She made eye contact with the committee leaders by way of reminding the lawmakers of the most fundamental duty of government. "We need to feel safe living and working in this great nation."

Now she began making a case that the leadership of the country had failed to anticipate a terrorist attack and were now trying to cover up that failure. There was a deafening silence in the room throughout her testimony. The still cameras stopped clicking and reporters stopped writing. They all just listened.

"On May seventeenth, 2002, National Security Adviser Condoleezza Rice stated emphatically, 'I don't think anybody could have predicted that these people would take an airplane and slam it into the World Trade Center . . . that they would try to use an airplane as a missile, a hijacked airplane as a missile,' " Kristen said, eying the panel and coolly reciting a laundry list of historical facts to illustrate that such a possibility had been not only predicted, but predicted by, variously, the Pentagon, the Library of Congress, FBI agents, and foreign intelligence services.

In 1992, the Pentagon had investigated the possibility of an airplane being used to bomb national landmarks. In 1995, Philippine authorities had discovered in Manila the bomb-making lab of Ramzi Youssef, the mastermind behind the 1993 bombing of the World Trade Center. Interrogations of his accomplice, Hakim Mourad, revealed Youssef's plot to blow up a dozen U.S.-owned airliners over the Pacific and discussions of plans to hijack aircraft and fly them into civilian targets in the United States. This terrorist plot was known as "Project Bojinka." Kristen pointed out that "In 1997, this plot resurfaced during the trial of Ramzi Youssef. . . . FBI agents testified that the plan targeted not only the CIA but other U.S. government buildings in Washington, including the Pentagon and CIA headquarters. Youssef's accomplice, Mourad, told U.S. intelligence officials that he would board any American commercial aircraft pretending to be an ordinary passenger. And he would then hijack the aircraft, control its cockpit, and dive it at CIA headquarters."

With the mention of Project Bojinka, Eleanor Hill, the committee's staff director, listened intently. It was extremely significant for several reasons. It had been an early warning that Osama bin Laden was a key promoter of a radical interpretation of Islam, and that his adherents were plotting to inflict mass casualties and attack symbolic targets within the United States, and were discussing plans to use aircraft as weapons. When it came Eleanor Hill's turn to report to the committee, she would add what she had learned from the FBI's criminal investigative files. She had found almost no references to Mourad's plan to crash a plane into CIA headquarters. FBI agents interviewed about Project Bojinka said that those aspects of the plot had not been part of their case against Youssef or Mourad, so they had not considered them "relevant."

Kristen described a 1999 report prepared for U.S. intelligence by an arm of the Library of Congress. It stated, "Suicide bombers belonging to al Qaeda's Martyrdom Battalion could crash-land an aircraft packed with high explosives into the Pentagon, the CIA, or the White House."

The widow's testimony was getting uncomfortably specific. The senators and congressmembers were by now chewing on their glasses, rubbing their chins, some taking notes. Obviously, long before September 11 the American intelligence community had had a significant amount of information about specific terrorist threats to commercial airline travel in America, including the possibility that a plane would be used as a weapon. Kristen now addressed the cover-up:

"On May eighth, 2002, Director of the FBI Robert Mueller stated, 'There was nothing the agency could have done to anticipate and prevent the attacks.' "

She documented that throughout the spring and summer of 2001, intelligence agencies had been flooded with warnings of possible terrorist attacks against American targets. In June of 2001, Condoleezza Rice herself had warned officials—but not the public—"It is highly likely that a significant al Qaeda attack is in the near future, within several weeks." On July 31, the FAA urged U.S. airlines—but not the public—to maintain a "high degree of alertness." Kristen had learned from internal FAA documents that some of the hijackers had actually been randomly selected for prescreening of their carry-on bags. Airport security screeners had passed them through.

Slowly, punctuating her words for emphasis, Kristen said, "Two counterterrorism officials described the alerts of early and mid-summer 2001 as 'the most urgent in decades.' How many lives could have been saved had this information been made more public?"

Senators rocked uncomfortably in their leather chairs.

Kristen didn't let up: "On July fifth, 2001, the government's top counterterrorism official, Richard Clarke, stated to a group gathered at the White House, 'Something really spectacular is going to happen here, and it's going to happen soon.' The group included the FAA, the Coast Guard, the FBI, the Secret Service."

Kristen's eyes, even across the fifteen feet between the witness table and the committee members, sparkled like hard jewels. Her eyes told the story of personal anguish transformed by the alchemy of anger into hard-cut facts. This was no sob story. Kristen was rattling off point after point, and she had the references to back them up.

Eleanor Hill would later comment, "What we found was consistent with what Kristen said. In fact, there was intelligence that terrorists were considering using commercial aircraft as weapons. We also found that nobody in the intelligence community did any kind of assessment of that kind of attack. When we talked to policy makers, they said they didn't even know such a threat existed." Sandy Berger, President Clinton's secretary of defense, would later testify, "I don't recall being presented with any specific threat information or any alert highlighting this threat." Paul Wolfowitz, President Bush's deputy secretary of defense, told Hill's investigators that he had never been told of such a threat. "The point is, they *did* have the intelligence information," Hill emphasized, "but they weren't getting it to the people who needed it in time."

Next, Kristen went after the FBI's shocking record of missteps and myopia. She talked about the Phoenix memo: "When the field agent in Phoenix, Arizona, reported the suspicions of a hijacking plot . . . the FBI did not share the report with any other agency. One must ask, why? In the summer of 2001, while our nation was at its highest state of alert, his memo was flatly ignored. What if his memo was promptly placed on INTELINK, SIPRNET, or NIPRNET?" she asked, throwing in spook-speak she had picked up from reading a policy-level magazine for the intelligence community. "What if other agents had the same suspicions in Florida, California, Georgia, Ohio and Nevada? Could the terrorists have been stopped?

"On August fifteenth, 2001, an alert civilian instructor at a Minnesota flight school called the FBI and said, 'Do you realize that a 747 loaded with fuel can be a bomb?' The next day, Zacarias Moussaoui was arrested. The FBI learned that he had Islamic extremist connections. They also knew that he was interested in flight patterns around New York City, and that he had a strong desire to fly big jets, even though at the time he didn't have so much as a license to fly a Cessna.

"And then what happened?

"The FBI office in Minnesota attempted to get a FISA [Foreign Intelligence Surveillance Act] warrant to search Moussaoui's computer but they were rebuffed. A crucial mistake, because Zacarias Moussaoui's possessions contained evidence that would have exposed key elements of the September eleventh plot."

She knew she was now venturing into highly sensitive, classified territory, raising questions about an internal debate at the Justice Department and the FBI over wiretap surveillance of terrorist groups. She said that officials had acknowledged that their internal debate might have hampered electronic surveillance of terror groups.

"What is not classified is that in early September a Minnesota FBI agent wrote an analytic memo on Zacarias Moussaoui's case, theorizing that the suspect could fly a plane into the World Trade Center. And, tragically, this, too, was ignored."

ELEANOR HILL RECOGNIZED that Kristen was raising some of the very same issues she intended to raise. There hadn't been any precoordination. And obviously, Kristen hadn't had any subpoena power; she had simply compiled and digested every scrap of information publicly available and connected the dots—which nobody else, including the media, had done. Hill had enormous respect for this young woman. "Her testimony was really powerful. What made it so effective was her quiet passion. She didn't try to overdramatize. She didn't need to, because of the strength of what she was talking about."

Kristen went on to raise questions well beyond the mandate of the joint inquiry:

"Why did the New York/New Jersey Port Authority not evacuate the World Trade Center when they had an open phone line with Newark Traffic Control Center and were told that the second plane was bearing down on the South Tower? New York/New Jersey Port Authority had at least eleven minutes of notice to begin evacuations of the South Tower. An express elevator in the WTC was able to travel from top to bottom in one minute's time." Her voice was now edged with contempt: "How many lives may have been saved, had the Port Authority acted more decisively or, rather, acted at all?

"Washington Air Traffic Control Center knew about the first plane before it hit the WTC. Yet, the third plane was able to fly 'loop de loops' over Washington, D.C., one hour and forty-five minutes after the Washington Center first knew about the hijackings. After circling in this restricted airspace—controlled and protected by the Secret Service, who had an open phone line to the FAA—how is it possible that the plane was then able to crash into the Pentagon? Why was the Pentagon not evacuated?

"Why was our air force so late in its response?"

Her closing brought the issues home to the committee members in a personal way: "Undoubtedly, each of you here today, because you live and work in Washington, D.C., must have felt that you were in the bull's-eye on September eleventh. For most of you, there was relief at the end of that day. . . . You were the lucky ones. . . . Please, do not forget those of us who did not share in your good fate."

After an uncomfortable silence, there was a swell of applause. Kristen's testimony brought raves from a Senate staffer who had helped set up the hearing: "All these women had was each other, and their moral standing as citizens who were being victimized by the inattention of the government to their tragedy. Who could deny them?" The usually blasé senior staffer noticed how genuinely the senators were affected by her performance. "They turned into Milquetoast."

Eleanor Hill, too, sensed that the leaders of the committee recognized that Kristen had raised valid points. "Kristen's testimony was very much on point in showing how the American public was not alerted adequately to the immediacy and gravity of the threat from bin Laden, despite all the information that the government had about it prior to 9/11." Hill intended to recommend the creation of a "fusion center," where all the information related to terrorist threats would be brought together in one place, so the dots could be connected, and analyzed, and disseminated to the people who need it in time for it to make a difference (much like the Terrorist Threat Integration Center later proposed by President Bush). Hill appreciated that Kristen had made a powerful case for the necessity of an independent commission to pursue all the unanswered questions. She had laid the perfect groundwork for Hill's own testimony.

Mary Noonan, the chief of staff for Congressman Chris Smith, who had taken on the role of the widows' guide on the Hill, was similarly impressed. "What blew the committee away about Kristen's testimony, followed by three days of Eleanor Hill's testimony, was that neither one did any of the usual political bloviating. They weren't demanding or hostile. But neither did they soften what they had to say with the usual self-glorification and political perfumery that politicians use. It was all substance."

The ultimate measure of Kristen's success was an invitation to meet at the White House—the next day. Her first thought was, *I'm in trouble.*

CRAWFISHING WITH THE WHITE HOUSE

The White House officials, Jay Lefkowitz, a domestic policy adviser to the president, and Nick Calio, a lobbyist for the White House in charge of congressional affairs, handled Kristen with kid gloves. They offered her a soft drink and congratulated her on her testimony. Kristen told the presidential aides she didn't understand why the White House was opposed to an independent commission. "We're not opposed to it," they said in honeyed tones. "We just weren't ready for it." Kristen gloated a little inside: the White House was changing its story.

"Jay was very, very nice," Kristen reported to the girls. "I could be naive, but I think Jay really cares about us and wants to help us. Frankly, after the testimony, we're getting so much recognition, I think the White House sees the writing on the wall."

On the drive back to Middletown, Kristen's cell phone went off. "The White House calling for Mrs. Kristen Breitweiser." She almost laughed. Andrew Card, the president's chief of staff, got on the phone and asked Kristen where she had gotten the Bush quote she had used in her testimony. She couldn't remember. She spent the rest of the frenzied afternoon trying to find it. It turned out that Bush himself hadn't said it; his communications chief, Ari Fleischer, had said it on his behalf. "Oh, oh, now I'm really in trouble," she told the girls. But when Bush came out with his turnaround statement in support of an independent inquiry, he paraphrased the quote Kristen had attributed to him. She called the girls back with a bogus boast: "I basically hooked up the president."

The day after the administration reversed course, the Senate approved a broad independent inquiry by an overwhelming vote of 90 to 8. The House had already voted for a slightly different version. The widows' statements to the press were euphoric. But just as the four moms from New Jersey had thought their June rally would be all that was needed to get the job done, they now naively believed the White House had sincerely embraced their cause. What happened in early October kicked them up another level in their political learning curve.

The White House was making demands that would allow it to control the commission's subpoena power and appoint the chairman. Members of Congress had one foot out the door for a preelection recess. The media lights were turned off. It began to look like the White House strategy was to delay and dilute the very investigation it had publicly endorsed. A hurried meeting was called by senior members of the House and Senate intelligence committees to try to undo the snarls and wrap up the legislation before recess.

The principals agreed on a compromise and made their way to the Senate television gallery where they held a victory press conference—all except for one Republican congressman, Porter Goss. He agreed to the deal and then ducked back to his office, where his phone was ringing. Dick Cheney was on the line. The vice president was not pleased. His orders to Goss were to keep negotiating for the original White House position. That evening, when lawmakers gathered for the final pro forma vote to authorize the commission, Porter Goss dropped the bombshell. People "at a higher level" continued to have concerns, he said, and he was not ready to hold a vote. The senior senators, both Republican and Democrat, were shocked. Senior politicians do not take well to public humiliation. There was yelling.

"It was very clear there was still angst at the White House," Goss later admitted to *The New York Times*. The widows and many lawmakers read it as a sign that the White House was backing out of their endorsement of a commission. The four moms told reporters they were "disheartened" and "deeply disappointed."

"Crawfishing" was what President Bush himself called his signature strategy. Senator Bob Graham, the Florida Democrat who chaired the Senate Intelligence Committee, explained it: "There is a pattern of this White House announcing its support for a general principle, whether it be prescription drug coverage or No Child Left Behind. Then, when it comes down to the actual realization of that goal, they—to use the president's term—crawfish."

Senator Joe Lieberman, the Connecticut Democrat who had sponsored the Senate legislation on the commission, asked openly what the administration was trying to hide. Senator John McCain, co-sponsor of the Senate legislation and an early supporter of the four moms from New Jersey, was more pointed in his criticism: "Every bureaucracy in this town is scared to death of an investigation. Remember, no one has really been held accountable. No one has lost their job, no one has been even reprimanded, nothing has happened as a result of September eleventh. Unless responsibility is assigned, then we can't cure the problem." But McCain was seen by Bush supporters as a Democrat by another name, and neither side had forgotten the bad blood stirred between the two men when they opposed each other for the presidential nomination in 2000.

On Columbus Day, Kristen was breathless. Only a few more days before Congress scattered for campaigning. And if the power balance changed, the families' fight would probably have to begin all over again. While she was standing at the checkout counter at Costco in Middletown, her cell rang—a call from the White House. Later, as she stopped to fill up with gas, she got a call from Congresswoman Nancy Pelosi, one of the four chairs of the joint inquiry. The widows had found Pelosi to be a brilliant strategist and at the same time empathetic to the point that she could present their case as well as they could. But Kristen had to put the congresswoman on hold to take a call from Senator McCain.

"Don't give an inch," the POW survivor counseled.

Next it was the booker from *Hardball* on the phone. Chris Matthews wanted her on his TV show that night. Kristen lit up a Marlboro Light. She had taken up smoking again the day they had told her that her husband's remains had been found. She had finally rinsed the toothpaste off his toothbrush, where it had been waiting for over a year. She had developed ulcerative colitis. Smoking breaks had become the only moments she took for herself to step outside the car, or outside the house, and not hear the phone and not have her child at her leg.

"It's my two-Marlboro moment."

The families had called for a candlelight vigil in the park across from the White House for the next evening. Kristen got on the phone with Patty: "Do we really want to drive to Washington?" There was a sniper loose in the D.C. area, picking off suburban moms just like them as they loaded groceries into the back of their SUV. It seemed like the success of terrorist violence had emboldened all kinds of pathological haters. The widows decided to take the train. The vigil was a dreary affair. A handful of people showed up in a nasty drizzle. When they tried to rest on the wall around the park, police apologetically insisted that they could only remain if they kept walking. The White House canceled its meeting with Kristen. She and the moms decided to stay over and work on House Republicans.

The next day she joined with Stephen Push, whose wife, Lisa Raines, had been killed on the plane that crashed into the Pentagon. Kristen and Steve went to the Cannon House Office Building intending to confront Congressman Porter Goss, point man for the White House obstruction. But according to Steve, "His secretary blocked the door with her body as we approached. She said, 'You can't go in there. He's not there. He's in an intelligence meeting at the Capitol."

Steve wasn't called Push for nothing. "We forced our way in," he said. "Goss was standing right behind the door. He recovered well. He invited us in. He said he was supposed to be at the White House for the signing of the resolution on Iraq. But he stayed with us for an hour. In the end, he agreed with us but said he wasn't going to put the bill through until he got a green light from 'higher-ups.' "

"I'm just a cog in the wheel here," the congressman begged off. "I'm not going to buck the House leadership."

"Directly or indirectly, you're taking your orders from the White House," Steve Push charged. "We want you to buck them. You know it's the right thing to do."

They went on to see Senator Graham. He wasn't there, but his staffer conveyed the same message they had gotten from McCain: "Don't budge."

By now, Steve Push believed he knew why the White House was crawfishing. The legislation gave the commission eighteen months to issue a re-

port to the president and Congress. That would insert an embarrassing political issue into the middle of the 2004 election campaign. At one point, the
president's negotiators suggested they might go along with a commission if
it was limited to one year. Everyone else said that was not enough time. Well,
then, the president's men suggested, what about two years? Or more? So it
was all about keeping the issue of the government's failures on September 11
at arm's length from Bush's reelection campaign.

SHOWDOWN

Okay, let's chakra up." Kristen and the other three moms were back in
D.C. on October 16 for a showdown meeting in Senator Lieberman's
office with all the principals. Kristen dabbed aromatic oil on the girls' wrists.
"They'll always know when the widows are in D.C.—they can smell us coming!"

Crowded into a small conference room were Senators Lieberman and
Shelby, and Congressmembers Pelosi and Roemer, in person; Goss and
McCain were represented by staff. Jay Lefkowitz and Nick Calio were also
there, and surprised to see ten family representatives of victims.

The lawmakers all reported that both the Republican and Democratic
committee members wanted the deal to which they had agreed to go through,
no changes. The only two dissenters were the White House representatives.
Tensions boiled up. The families were asked what they thought. Kristen and
Steve, et al., said they agreed with the congressional members. "What the
White House wants is unacceptable to us. You want to own the committee
and block subpoenas. We don't want either party to be able to block the ordering of subpoenas." Senator Lieberman attempted to avert a showdown:
"Okay, I guess we can schedule a meeting for another day."

But the families had lost patience with the bait-and-switch game. As if
by some extrasensory linkage, they all jumped to their feet in unison and
said, "No! You can't put this off another day. We've been waiting a *year* for
this commission. We can't keep hiring baby-sitters and leaving our children.
This has gone on too long." Kristen and Steve and the other relatives stood
only a few feet from the two White House operatives. "What will it take for
President Bush to agree to the commission?" they demanded. "Why can't we
get this done today? *Why can't you just say yes?*"

"Jay Lefkowitz was visibly shaken, squirming in his seat," according to
Steve Push.

Senator Lieberman appeared to be moved by their passion. Calio said lamely, "We'll get back to you." The families gave a parting shot: "The White House owes us an answer. The ball is in your court now. Everyone else is solidly behind keeping this commission bipartisan."

By November 2, with Congress in recess, there was no movement on a broad independent inquiry. But by now Kristen and the girls had stopped using the negative *d* words—"disappointed" and "disheartened." Instead, they used the *h* words: They were "hopeful" and "heartened." Kristen was newly philosophical: "There's one thing I've learned in Washington. You always have to leave the door open, so people can turn around and change their mind."

After the midterm election, on the morning of November 15, the front page of *The New York Times* spelled out pure triumph: WHITE HOUSE YIELDS ON A 9/11 INQUIRY BACKED BY CONGRESS. It read like a storybook ending to a mission on which Kristen and the other three moms from New Jersey had been embarked for six months.

> *Yielding to intense pressure from families of Sept. 11 victims, the White House tonight agreed to a congressional compromise that would create an independent commission to investigate the terror attacks. The House immediately prepared to pass a bill to establish the commission, and the Senate was expected to do the same on Friday. It will have up to 18 months to hold hearings and prepare a report . . . and is intended to be unflinching in assigning blame for specific government failures.*

The key to the compromise was the White House agreeing to allow Senator McCain, its most bitter critic for stalling, to appoint one of the Republican slots. "We're not crazy about the president appointing the chairman, but our greatest concern was the subpoena power," said Steve. "As long as Senator McCain has one of the picks, and the others are people of integrity, then we're guardedly optimistic."

Senator Lieberman said the panel would finally provide a "clear, clean picture of which government agencies failed and why, in order to prevent a similar attack in future." The panel's inquiry, he said, would be similar to investigations of the Pearl Harbor attack and the explosion of the space shuttle *Challenger.* It would be known as the National Commission on Terrorist Attacks Upon the United States.

Two days before Thanksgiving, Kristen's cell phone rang while she was picking up a turkey for the holiday. It was Jay Lefkowitz, inviting her to the

White House the next day to be present when the president signed the legislation authorizing an independent inquiry. "Sure, if you want to send a car for me, or how about *Air Force One*?" Kristen teased. She wasn't about to sit for twelve hours in the worst traffic of the year, just for a photo op.

Kristen couldn't help smiling to herself. It isn't every day that a girl gets to turn down an invitation to the White House. But the fight wasn't over by any means. The most indelible lesson the girls had learned from their six-month foray into the labyrinth of Beltway politics was this: If your cause is just, you can win—provided you are prepared to make your cause Your Life for as long as it takes. The girls knew by now to expect that their opponents would have more tricks up their sleeves. But for the next few days, they could focus on the simple, doable domestic chores of producing a Thanksgiving dinner. And enjoy being just four moms from New Jersey.

Chapter Twenty-five

LIVES UNDER CONSTRUCTION

A month after the anniversary, offstage at last, the widows and widowers began to feel released for the first time. They could begin thinking about how to design a new life structure for a future on which they had never planned. But the most urgent need at this point was one of the heart: to fill the hole where their loved one used to be.

"Some of the widows are dating," one wag told Karen Cangialosi in October.

"How do you know?" Karen demanded, indignant at the loss of privacy. "Was there an announcement in the newspaper?"

"I heard it at the baseball game."

When the gossip reached Allyson Gilbert as she dropped off the fall FAVOR baskets, she was pleased to hear that the tone of the rumors was not censorious. The men dating the widows had been close to their deceased husbands.

Terry Fiorelli saw she couldn't hold back any longer. The time had come to broach the subject with her support group of her, uh, well, her close friendship with a man. "But how could I tell them?" she worried. "They were in such a different place than I was." The forty-something widow who had been keeping secret company with the widower Kevin Casey for months finally confided in one member, who gave her a terse warning: *Be careful.*

At an early-October meeting of her group, Terry backed into her confession by mentioning an article that was coming out in the local weekly, *Two River Times,* about a 9/11 widow and widower who had gotten together. It didn't take long for her peers to put two and two together.

"You're having sex!" one yelped.

"And we're not," another widow added the Chevy Chase line.

"I'm jealous!" said the first widow.

Terry put her head in her hands while everyone else laughed raucously. When she lifted her head, she was actually blushing. Most of the others murmured their approval.

"Terry, we want you to be happy," said Mary Murphy. "You're giving us all hope!"

A BACKWARD LOVE STORY

Our relationship went the opposite way to normal," Kevin said with a smile. "First we filled the married role; we'll get back to the dating scene later!"

When the widower Kevin Casey met the widow Terry Fiorelli in the waiting room at Catholic Charities, they were two wounded adults merely desperate for someone else who understood what it was like to try to make some limp explanation about "isms" to adolescent kids for whom the disappearance of a parent was entirely personal—a desertion. They didn't need a romantic partner. They both needed another parent.

In the first week Terry was notified that her husband's body had been recovered. That was the trigger that set off her son, Stephen, to smash a hole in the living room wall with his fist.

Kevin's fourteen-year-old son, Matt, was two years older than Terry's son and just as angry. If anything, Kevin's son was even more emotionally shut down. An only child who had been sheltered and indulged by his mother, Matt had lost his world. In a house robbed of a woman's touch, and with no nearby aunts or grandmothers, Kevin was at a total loss for how to offer his son any physical or emotional consolation. Their communication was nil. Kevin tried taking the boy out for dinner to Chili's or T.G.I. Friday's, but the two stubborn Irishmen sat grunting monosyllabically about whether to share mozzarella fingers. "We were butting heads," Kevin said. "When Matthew wanted to break down and cry and be hugged, I'd be more like the coach type of guy, you know, pat him on the butt and say, 'Get out there and hit it hard.' He was afraid to show his emotions. Actually, I was afraid of the same thing." Kevin's hooded eyes cast downward. "I was afraid of crying in front of him."

One Saturday over lunch at Chili's, Kevin brought up a difficult subject.

He hadn't received any remains of his wife, and he confessed he hadn't realized how hard it was to try to grieve when there was nothing to bury and nowhere to go to be with her spirit. He asked the boy if he wished he had something of his mother. The fourteen-year-old kept his eyes locked on the television set over the bar.

"It doesn't matter to me," Matt said. "I don't need it."

Kevin's eyes rolled up behind their lids and he buckled as if he had been punched in the belly. When he looked up again, he spoke to his son in a pained hush. "What do you mean, it doesn't matter?"

The boy's eyes remained fixed on the wall TV, his face a mask of insouciance over the anger he felt at being "abandoned" by his mother. "I'm trying to eat," he said.

Kevin looked defeated.

The only time the boy came out of his shell was at the weekly adolescent counseling group at Catholic Charities. While Kevin and Terry waited for their sons, the two boys became fast friends. Like their parents, the boys needed someone who understood their peculiar pain. "It was pretty fun," Matt said. "Stephen was there in the same group with me. The counselor we went to was a nice guy."

Stephen elaborated, "Like, he asked us a lot about how it made us feel to lose a parent. And how our life was changing."

Kevin felt more alone than ever, and he had no luck with a therapist. "I got really upset, and Matt saw that, saw me sitting by myself. And I think he got afraid for me." At the point of desperation, Kevin called up Terry and confessed he was at a loss for what to do. "She helped me to see I just needed to listen instead of trying to dictate to my son." Terry became Kevin's listening post. Once he trusted in her enough to open up, a swamp of feelings leaked out and became a torrent of words that kept the two on the phone deep into the nights.

The two single parents began doing for each other the most mundane chores that only housebroken husbands and docile wives usually do without complaint. If one was dealing with an adolescent tantrum, the other would take care of the laundry or getting the car fixed. They depended on each other.

"Once we got started getting into it," Kevin said shyly, "we worried about what our parents would think." Grief-stricken themselves, the parents had reasserted their protective roles. Kevin's mother would either fail to give him messages from Terry, or, worse, dismiss the invasion with "Some lady called."

"I was getting defensive about the way I explained it," Kevin said. "Not that I had to prove anything, 'cause once people meet Terry, they know right away what a special person she is. But it's just . . . the guilt."

Terry had the same problem with her father. When Kevin called to see if she was ready for their first date, Terry's father answered the phone. Immediately, the grilling began, and it was worse than the grilling about her first date in high school.

"Who's this Kevin?"

Terry explained how she and Kevin had met in the waiting room at Catholic Charities while their sons were attending a support group.

"Does he drink?" was the father's first question. "Is he a drinker?"

"Dad, we're just going out for coffee."

"Does he smoke? How do you know this guy isn't trying to take advantage of you? He might think you're a rich widow. It's easy for a man to get that idea 'cause you have life insurance. It's a trap."

"Trust me," Terry said firmly. "I'm not going to let anybody take advantage of me." She tried to assure him that Kevin was in just as much pain as she and her father were. He had lost his wife.

"Dad, more than anything else, we're friends to each other."

She knew her father was devastated, so much so that he could not talk about what had happened to his son-in-law. But as the months passed and the ganglia of guilt spread through both families, Terry decided to risk inviting Kevin to her father's house for lunch one Saturday in June. It was a meeting of two territorial alpha males that Kevin would not forget.

Terry's father is a seventy-year-old lung cancer survivor. That is not what he looked like to Kevin when the older man stomped in from working on the lawn to meet this not-so-young man who was courting his widowed daughter. His ropey chest stood out under his sweaty undershirt, his biceps twitched, his height almost equaled Kevin's—and Kevin is a tall, hefty Jersey guy. The two men shook hands.

"I was so intimidated, I didn't know what to do," Kevin admitted later.

Over lunch, the conversation focused exclusively on Terry's missing husband, Steve. Afterward, Terry's father expressed regrets. "I feel bad that we didn't talk at all about Kathy, Kevin's wife. She's got to be just as important to him as Stephen is to us."

That was the first breakthrough. The second one was more physical. Terry's father challenged Kevin to what amounted to a Sheetrocking contest. They would work together on building Terry a bike room. Just how handy was this Lothario? The father barked orders and worked the younger man mercilessly. Kevin passed the test. Their bond began.

That summer Kevin made a radical break with his twenty-three-year record of dedication to his job. He took four months off, using all the days he had accumulated before he woke up to how short life can be. "Back a few years, to get a weekend off with me, you'd have to fight me," he admitted. "But it was important for me to be with Matthew, and to get to know Terry and her kids."

"The first thing we're going to do is go out to the movies!" Terry insisted. She liked to tease Kevin; the last movie he had taken time to see was *Jaws.*

Kevin swung his head back and smiled broadly. "It was wonderful. Playing basketball with Matt every day, taking him to games, going on a cruise together." His romantic times with Terry were spent in the simplest ways. "Just walking the beach together was special."

The unique part, the part that completely sold their kids and their parents, was the way the couple included their lost loves in all that they did and said. Kevin keeps a photograph of Terry's husband beside the picture of his wife. Terry wears her husband's wedding ring on a chain around her neck— "I keep him with me, always"—and next to it she wears a necklace given to her by Kevin. "It's a blessing to find the love of your life just once in a lifetime," says Terry. "I've been twice blessed."

THE WEEK AFTER TERRY'S disclosure to her support group, the women had more probing questions for her.

"How did it feel to kiss a man other than your husband?" one widow asked.

The group facilitator broke in. "I don't know if she has to answer that."

"Yes she does!" insisted the widow, laughing with vicarious longing.

Terry thought to herself, *Haven't you ever kissed a man other than your husband?* Then she realized that some of "the girls" were young and recently married and probably still in romantic love with their husbands. Terry had been married fifteen years. "Well, it's different," she said diplomatically. "You're two different people by now. You're not kissing your husband—he isn't here. I don't close my eyes and think of Steve. I'm way past that."

Karen Cangialosi said approvingly, "The way you two met sounds perfect. And the way you understand each other."

They wanted to know if she and Kevin were going to get married.

"It's too soon," Terry said. "We're each staying in our homes. Our children are young. We can't make any kind of changes for them, they've been through enough. Not that I don't want to get married again," she assured them. "I just . . . I don't know . . . living together, yes. But then, my father, you know, he'd say, 'Fine example you're setting for your children!' I am Catholic and Kevin is Catholic. Right now, we have to take it day by day and concentrate on healing ourselves and caring for our kids."

Cheryl McDonnell listened to this discussion with a hangdog look. She had been thirty-five and just starting out in her first house, a modest three-bedroom on a quarter-acre plot in the Fairview section of Middletown, when her husband's murder had left her stranded with two small children. Her husband, Michael McDonnell, was the young comptroller at Keefe, Bruyette and Woods who had last been seen on the phone getting instructions from the fire department. Cheryl's reality was limited money and no possible way to finish her college degree, not with two little boys constantly threading themselves in and out of her legs. She had let herself go in the last year, preferring to hide inside a big loose T-shirt and jeans, with no makeup and her brown hair swept up into a ponytail.

"Who'd want one of us, with all our baggage?" Cheryl protested. "Any man would have to be crazy."

"C'mon, Cheryl," Karen Cangialosi said, laughing away her negativity. "The widows of Middletown are beautiful, they're young, they're great, they're strong. Any guy would be lucky to have one of us."

"What guy?" Cheryl argued. "There's nothing out there for us. The good ones are gone. You go out to a club or a bar and they're twenty-five years old. Oh, wow, this is promising! I'm like, why am I here? I found somebody to spend the rest of my life with. I was happy. I don't want to go to a bar. I don't want to go on a date. I don't want to care if somebody likes me or they don't like me. I don't care. I *found* the love of my life. I had him. Why is he gone?"

Cheryl was nursing her resentment at the unfairness of being back on the market at all. It was a clash between a glass-half-empty personality like Cheryl's and a glass-half-full personality like Terry's. The motto Terry tried to live by was "There's no such word as *can't*." She also firmly believed, "Our children have to feel they *can* bounce back, even after something as devastating as this. I believe that seventy-five or eighty percent of how well the children do depends on how well the parents do."

Mothers in the group murmured agreement.

"Look at this morning," Terry said. "When my kids and I woke up and went down to the kitchen, ants were everywhere. Crawling up the refrigerator, surrounding the bar. My husband would have been there to take care of it. But my kids and I had to do it. We're the only ones there. Our Christmas tree fell over in the middle of the night. Sure, I cried and called the police.

But we had to set it back up, and then we had a good laugh. See, I have to show my kids that I can handle all these different situations. And they can handle them, too. You have to laugh at it all. I tell 'em, 'It's not the end of the world. Ants. You can get rid of ants. Not a life-and-death situation.' "

Karen Cangialosi shared the same conviction. "God, a year ago I couldn't have done—you name it. I've become a much stronger individual than I ever thought I was. I can even talk to my boys now about football. When I remember how horrible it was trying to get the kids to sleep every night, now they know they're going to be okay. We're getting used to the New Normal."

The widows in the Catholic Charities support group had bonded to the point where they enjoyed socializing together on the outside. "Normally, we wouldn't encourage that," said Maureen Fitzsimmons, "but in this case, it's healthy." Mostly the widows' social occasions consisted of gathering for a barbecue at one of their houses while their collective children played on swings or in the pool. Sometimes they baby-sat for one another while a few caught a movie on a Saturday night.

Mary Murphy voiced a common experience, after the first year: "Nobody's calling me on Friday or Saturday night anymore. All my friends are married. Everybody goes back to their lives. You have to find one for yourself, I guess." Mary had often been told about her grandmother's isolation after she lost her husband in a freak accident when she was about Mary's age. "Even her married friends pulled away," Mary said. "I can see that happening to me down the road. I'm not sure how my married girlfriends view me now." As a potential threat?

"You can't spend the rest of your life just hanging out with the widows from 9/11," Cheryl said.

They all agreed. Some were making an effort to reconnect with friends from their previous lives in school or the workplace. Mary had revived a lapsed relationship with a girlfriend she used to work and vacation with when they were carefree singles.

"One of these days she'll drag me to a singles bar," Mary said. "I'll dip my toe in."

ANNA'S HOUSE

You come into Anna Egan's own house through the kitchen and into the warmth of a fireplace and love seats. She had only left behind her husband's trophy house in Middletown at the end of July, but by the end of summer her new purchase in Connecticut was already a home. Nothing grand about it, not even a window on the driveway side, but that's exactly what she was looking for—a shelter.

In creating a new life structure, Anna had luxuriated in selecting the style of furnishings that expressed her own personality. It was a revelation to her. Entirely different from her husband's taste for the starkly modern. She was given to the cozy informality of an English country cottage.

"I'm rediscovering Anna, and it's like, oh my God, I survived!" she exclaimed, bemused and a little breathless. Michael never liked changes. "But now, there's no more compromising. Sometimes I'll literally turn around in the middle of the room and say, 'Oh, Michael, I know you wouldn't approve, but I like it. How come we never tried this?' "

It took Anna three days to pick out her new bed. "A four-poster—that's me." Feather-filled and so downy and high, she had to buy a step stool to climb into it. And lots of big downy pillows, to hold on to in the night. There were no pictures of her husband in her new bedroom. This was a necessary step in her journey of grieving. One room in which to become accustomed to a world without Michael.

But where to put her husband in her new life? This was another major decision for many of the widows. How to relocate the departed? It starts with the closet.

When it came time to move, Anna had thought she would leave Michael's clothes in the packing boxes. Once she got to Connecticut, she decided she wanted to have him with her—but where? She had an attic room that was going to be all her own. It looked out on the derelict English garden that she was yearning to plant with roses. This would be her room for working, writing, dreaming. She set up her computer and her files and her old record player. She began unpacking Michael's clothes and hanging them in her attic closet. It felt right. This was where she could relive their precious times together.

One day she went through her old record albums. She put on Elton John music from the seventies. "I felt I needed to go back. That's where a lot of my memories are." She drifted back to the Anna who was once a young and beautiful Italian émigrée who loved to dance and sing and met a dashing Englishman who wanted to take her to America. She came across her wedding gown. Suddenly, she had an urge to put it on. It was a little tight, but she slithered in and then danced to Elton and reconnected to Michael on a different plane.

So they could still be together, there in her dreaming room, whenever she chose.

———

IN SEPTEMBER, Anna was ready to give a party. It was a party for her husband's staff at AON. She worried that people might feel uncomfortable coming to visit the poor widow in her little cottage, but her mood quickly shifted once she got into planning her first occasion of pure social pleasure in a year. She also invited friends who had come back into her life from circles that weren't confined to knowing her only as Michael's wife. And kids to play with her retarded son, Matthew.

Ecstatic, Matthew welcomed people as they drove up and invited them to shoot baskets with him. Some played touch football on the lawn while others wandered in and out of the heated tent where Anna had spread a sumptuous buffet. The widow Egan looked like a different person. Her eyes danced. Her hair was a shiny cap of auburn tint and gave her face a gamine shape. Her pocket-sized voluptuousness was filling out and unabashedly displayed beneath a crocheted sweater and hip-hugging pants. She mingled with her husband's staff, including the man who had replaced Michael Egan. No one referred to the tragedy.

Anna proudly led guests on a tour of the new house, pointing out the pictures she had selected and the display of Special Olympics medals in Matthew's bright new room, and finally pointing to the spiral staircase up to the attic and her dreaming room.

"Let me show you Michael's office," she chirped. Anna was halfway up the stairs to her office before she caught herself. "I can't believe I called it that!" she gasped. "Maybe because I moved his clothes into that closet."

As the last guests departed, Matthew sought out his mother. It had been a long time since he'd had to share her with others. They curled up on a chaise in the living room. Matthew laid his head on his mother's stomach.

"I am baby," he said, enjoying the moment of let's-pretend.

It was just the two of them now. The boy claimed all of Anna's time and attention when he wasn't at school. But that, too, was going to change. A couple of months later, Anna had a surprise phone call from her older son, Jonathan, who was now in his sophomore year at Stanford in California. "I'm coming home for Christmas to get all my stuff," he said. She fretted, "Are you dropping out of school?"

"No, I was accepted at Boston College."

Jon hadn't told his mother because he had correctly assumed that she would try to talk him out of disrupting his life on her behalf. Now it was done; he wanted to transfer to an East Coast college so he could be closer to her and Matthew. "I miss you," he said. "And I want to take care of my boy." Matthew, his brother, was now his boy.

By Christmas, the constellations of Anna's life would be dramatically rearranged. She would get Matthew involved with vocational training after school, leaving her time to go on the board of the local chapter of the American Retarded Citizens Association. Her new neighbors, a school psychologist and a lawyer, were both eager to be helpful with Matthew's needs. They invited Anna and Matthew to their annual neighborhood Christmas Eve party, where the husband dressed up as Santa Claus and played the piano for everyone to sing carols.

"It was fantastic," Anna said. "Now we have a new tradition. My neighbors will do the Christmas Eve party, and next year I'll do something for New Year's Eve. I like to make people happy and laugh," she enthused. "And my house, I love it. It's so warm and peaceful. It's me."

AMANDA AND THE FAIRY-TALE BABY

It's so weird that I have a baby!"

Amanda McHeffey gave birth to a baby boy in October, a little more than a year after her brother, Keith McHeffey, was killed and she married his look-alike best friend, Gregg. Amanda was the golden-haired Sleeping Beauty who had lain for weeks on the sofa in a Zoloft swoon after the shock of her brother's death. Her desolated mother, Sherry McHeffey, voiced her own dream often, to both her daughters:

"Why don't one of you have a baby? Just kidding."

But the girls knew their mother was not kidding; she had lost her husband to divorce and her only son to terrorism, all within nine months. Sherry kept saying, "Our family is on a downward slide. Why don't one of you have a baby, just to make things better?"

"You're talking to the wrong person," Amanda would say, brushing off her mother. She was only twenty-one and scrambling to give birth to her own ego. Living at home after college and sliding by in a day-to-day sort of existence, she had been waiting for grown-up life to start. But she had been awakened from her depressed sleep on the sofa by the kiss of Gregg. That was in October after 9/11. From there, the fairy tale rushed to the happy ending for which her mother had wished. Amanda was pregnant by mid-January, married in May, a new mother in October 2002.

"When I was pregnant, I couldn't picture having a baby," Amanda said.

Her mother rushed in to be supportive. "Amanda went from college parties to coming home and a year later, she's a mother—and she has turned out to be a great mother!"

Amanda, still looking like a child-woman, sat on the sofa in her and her husband's fully furnished house and looked in amazement at the six-week-old babe gurgling in his basket on the floor. "It's such a huge adjustment," she said. "Sometimes, in the middle of the night when I wake up from a deep sleep and hear him crying, it takes me a minute to register. *What is that? Oh, I have a baby.* It's all like a dream. *I had a dream I had a baby with Gregg.*"

But now she didn't have to worry about a life plan, she said, relieved. "Unless I decide to work again, which I probably won't. I wouldn't like to work." Her husband was eleven years older with a good job at Prudential in New York. He had a ready-made life structure and she had moved into it, only ten minutes from her mother's house. Amanda's social life now centered around her brother's friends. "They all think about Keith all the time, too," she says. "It's nice to be around people who knew him. You can talk about it. Finally, something good has happened."

Sherry McHeffey looked, in a funny way, like she had regained her own girlishness. She was now a drive-by grandmother, shuttling between her job and her daughter's house once or twice a day, teaching Amanda the rudiments of motherhood and luxuriating in the gift of new life. "I know that Keith would love the fact that Amanda and Gregg are together," Sherry said. "Finally, our family is filling out again."

Chapter Twenty-six

POST-TRAUMATIC STRESS
IN THE YEAR *AFTER*

Surely the holidays would be easier the second year. That was the hope among many of the families. No one was more optimistic than Laurie Tietjen and her surrogate brothers among the Port Authority Police. They planned to keep Kenny's memory alive by continuing the bike drive he had quietly undertaken every Christmas.

THE SHOCK ABSORBER: LAURIE TIETJEN

Forty-seven—that was the magic number of bikes they were expecting to collect this year to give to needy children in Kenny's name. Laurie, his serene blond sister, and Kenny's friends Tom Johnson and Dave Newsham had worked with local police departments to find out which Monmouth County families were in need. The Tietjen family's neighbor held the first annual garage sale to benefit the Kenneth F. Tietjen Foundation, the proceeds to buy more bikes. On a Saturday before Christmas, a flotilla of Port Authority Police vans pulled up in Laurie's driveway with a load of bikes bought from Toys "R" Us.

Laurie was ecstatic, just imagining her brother's delight at a haul five times larger than he'd been able to collect since he started his bike drive as a seventeen-year-old kid. Her mother and father pulled up with pizzas for everyone, but the moment Janice Tietjen stepped out of the car, Laurie knew something was very wrong.

"Ma, what happened?"

"Nothing."

"Ma, something happened."

Kenny's mother broke down. From her mother's throttled utterances, Laurie gathered she had been called by the New York medical examiner's office and notified that more of Kenny's remains had been found. "They gave her very graphic details," said Laurie, "which she didn't need."

This was never supposed to happen. Given the vast number of recovered body parts—more than twenty thousand—the DNA testing was not expected to be completed until December 2004. Families had been sent questionnaires to determine which option they would prefer: to be notified at each and every recovery; to have any further remains disposed of; or to have the medical examiner hold on to any further "finds" until the testing was all over before receiving a final notification. The Tietjens had chosen the last option.

Everyone recalls a moment when the full, gut-searing agony of their loss strikes with full realization. Laurie thought she had reached that realization several times before. The family had held a memorial in October 2001 and a funeral in June 2002 after the final recovery was made—or so they thought. At that point, they had a casket and Laurie knew exactly which parts of her brother were in it. Her flashbacks began after that funeral. She simply spun her wheels faster, going to more 9/11 events and honorary ceremonies and burying herself in paperwork, files which by then had swollen to a stack three feet high.

Laurie's null moment came a few days before Christmas. After her mother had received the startling news, Laurie and two of Kenny's best friends went into New York to collect the most recent remains. Officers Dave Newsham and Tommy Johnson were invited into the makeshift morgue by the medical examiner. When the two cops came out, ashen-faced, they were carrying a stretcher. It was covered with a flag. A stretcher with only a few tiny bumps on it.

Laurie whispered, "Where is everything!"

It hit her hard, she admitted, somewhat abashed. "I probably shouldn't have been shocked, but this was definitely the worst. I was a mess for a while after that."

Laurie told none of her colleagues at work. Like all the other families, she was feeling the pressure to "get on with it." For the next week, her colleagues kept asking, "Why are you so grumpy?" They wanted to forget, or, Laurie sympathized, they just didn't know how to deal with the ongoingness of traumatic grief.

Who among the public would have guessed that the victims' families were getting their loved ones back literally piece by piece? Among Americans lucky enough not to have directly suffered a loss on September 11, it was common to hear impatient comments like "A lot of other people have lost their loved ones in auto accidents or sudden heart attacks—why are we making such a big deal out of these deaths?" How could the public be expected to know about these repetitive tortures? Most of the families had learned to keep the grisly details to themselves.

Shortly after picking up Kenny's remains, Laurie was driving to work past Newark airport when the terror caught up with her. She was watching a jetliner swoop down over the turnpike, low and fat, magnified like a dying shark. Suddenly she thought she saw it slam into the building in front of her. "Real as day! A horrific disaster right in front of me!"

Her heart leapt against her chest like a panicked frog in a jar. "I thought I was having a heart attack."

For Laurie, this was bizarre. "I'm the kind of person, my arm could be hanging off, and I'd say, 'Oh well, it's only a flesh wound.' " But the horrific visions kept happening. Just about every time she drove past Newark airport, which was every day, she was afraid she would freak out. "I'd never had a panic attack before and then, a year and a half later, all of a sudden, anytime I saw an airplane my heart stopped. It's not like I was watching it on TV. I kept getting these vivid images of a plane slamming into buildings right in front of me. I thought, 'What the hell is wrong with me? What am I, crazy?' "

The next invasion of fear happened while she was on a plane. Laurie traveled a great deal in her job, and even after 9/11 she had no apprehensions about plane travel. But on January 8, 2003, she was flying into Charlotte, North Carolina, on a small commuter plane when the pilot aborted the landing. She wasn't fearful when the plane abruptly pulled up nor when it circled for forty-five minutes. The pilot merely said the airport was temporarily closed.

When Laurie's plane finally did land, a business partner met her in tears. "Oh my God, you're alive!" He explained that while her plane was circling, another small commuter aircraft that had just taken off from the same airport rolled left, nose-dived into a hangar, and burst into flames. Laurie immediately called her mother. Janice Tietjen was unnerved. She had heard the news that all twenty-one on board had been killed, and knowing that Laurie was landing at the same airport around the same time, she had died another death, this time for her daughter. "Ever since then, whenever I've flown, I get like—" Laurie gasped for breath.

This is what post-traumatic stress disorder feels like.

POST-TRAUMATIC STRESS DISORDER—WHO, ME?

Just as predicted by the Monmouth County psychologist Monica Endart, trauma as great as that unleashed by 9/11 does not follow a descending course. It percolates. Particularly in affluent communities like Middletown, where the prevalent attitude was "We're doing okay," the full force of the trauma was not expected to erupt, psychologically, until a year or eighteen months after the event.

"Everything we know about post-traumatic stress disorder suggests that it takes a long time for the serious cases to make an appearance in treatment," says one of the foremost researchers in the field, Dr. Rachel Yehuda, professor of psychiatry and director of the traumatic-stress studies division at Mount Sinai School of Medicine. "One of the real problems in our field is that treatment seeking is not a good barometer of how wide the problem is."

Way back in March 2002, when the Tietjens were on tenterhooks waiting to see if any remains of Kenny would be found, they saw a psychologist for the first time. She told Laurie and her parents she thought they all were experiencing PTSD and described some of the symptoms they might expect: flashbacks, panic attacks, inability to concentrate, shortness of breath, chronic fatigue, eating much less or more than usual, or feeling depressed.

"I thought she was a little crazy," Laurie recalled, "because at that point I wasn't having any of those problems. I was just in work mode and taking care of my parents." The therapist urged Laurie to take care of herself, too. She laughed it off. Much too much to do.

Starting on September 11, in the absence of her older brother, Laurie had assumed the role of the family's Shock Absorber. She had awakened her younger sister, Cindy, the next morning and, sitting on the edge of the twenty-five-year-old's bed, said quietly, "We have to be strong for Mom and Dad. Because I don't think Kenny's coming home." Laurie's energy had been totally focused for the first year on taking care of everybody else, affirmed Cindy. "Every piece of information was filtered through her. She gave the rest of us information only if we needed it or asked for it. If she hadn't taken on that Shock Absorber role, I don't know what would have become of us."

For herself, Laurie says, "It was what I needed to do to keep myself sane."

Laurie's story is a classic case of retraumatization. She and her family had done a superb job of coping—up until the assault of news they didn't want. They had developed a way of thinking about their loss that helped them to reestablish some sense of control. They constantly told themselves that Kenny wouldn't have had it any other way; he would have knowingly sacrificed anything to respond to the moment of ultimate disaster; that was who he was. The family created a set of rules for how they would talk about their loss: They wouldn't look on the dark side, wouldn't speak against those who failed to help, wouldn't squander their precious energies fighting with Kenny's angry fiancée. And they had made it clear they didn't want to hear about any more partial recoveries until the final results of DNA testing.

When the medical examiner's office violated their rules, it reactivated the sense of helplessness. And for Laurie, to be confronted with body bits made the horror of her brother's death naked.

When her flashbacks and panic attack occurred, in December 2002, along with them came a whole cascade of other common symptoms. "I'm exhausted all the time," Laurie said. "I can't get out of bed in the morning. The things I had a passion for before don't matter anymore." She had divorced her husband and was busy discarding friends who she felt were only halfhearted. But she found work a solace and seldom missed a day.

The therapist diagnosed Laurie as suffering from PTSD. "She said I had been so wrapped up in other things, this was the first time I was focusing on my emotions and my feelings." Laurie's energies had been depleted by her role as the family's Shock Absorber, but like her brother, she wouldn't have wanted it any other way. A trauma expert familiar with Laurie's story said the probability was that she would recover in a relatively short time and emerge an even stronger person.

The tendency is for people accustomed to being healthy and highly functioning to wait, following a severe trauma, until their marriages are falling apart, their jobs are in peril, or they can barely manage to get dressed in the morning, before they seek professional help. After the Oklahoma City bombing, it took two to three years for some survivors with serious emotional difficulties to seek treatment. "I don't think people necessarily realized that they needed assistance until they got to a nonfunctional point," said Nancy B. Anthony, an Oklahoman who directed the Oklahoma City Community Foundation, which underwrote psychiatric care for survivors and victims' families.

It was no surprise to the small cadre of trauma experts that many serious cases of post-traumatic stress stemming from the September 11 attacks were only beginning to show up between a year and eighteen months afterward. It is predicted that they will continue to surface over the next decade. A study published by the New York Academy of Medicine in fall 2002 predicted the number of New York State residents who could be expected to develop PTSD related to 9/11. Among those in the World Trade Center population who were injured or hospitalized—7,467 people—more than 2,500 were expected to develop PTSD. Family members of those who died, were missing, or had been hospitalized and injured numbered about 17,600, and 34 percent of them, or almost 6,000, were expected to develop PTSD. There were 17,859 rescue and recovery workers. One quarter were predicted to suffer from chronic post-traumatic stress, or over 4,200 people. Dr. Spencer Eth, vice chairman of psychiatry at St. Vincent's Catholic Medical Centers, who has had a decade of experience treating the psychological aftereffects of bombing traumas in New York, believed that number would go considerably higher.

And these twelve thousand–plus mostly delayed cases anticipated by the New York medical establishment were not going to be resolved with a "debriefing" or a few sessions of crisis counseling.

"Critical stress debriefing" is only the most recent palliative the professionals have applied to trauma victims. After 9/11, it was employed with compulsory zeal by some of the law enforcement services. But recent research has demonstrated that debriefing soon after the trauma may inadvertently serve to retraumatize.

"Compulsory debriefing is counterproductive," asserts Dr. Eth. "It might confer some benefit to those most vulnerable to PTSD, but to most others it just reexposes them to reminders of the disaster, and that can tip them over into illness."

The natural early reaction to trauma is to shut down. The mind and body need to conserve energy. Experts say the most helpful strategies in the initial phase promote a sense of safety: being in a familiar place with the people closest to the person; relaxation by whatever means—meditation, massage, music; encouraging action that will enhance the person's ego strength; and treating the physical pain that often accompanies psychological shock. Some people have to shut down for a period of time until they are ready to revisit the trauma and able to engage usefully in processing it.

THE LONELINESS OF SURVIVAL

The people impacted by 9/11 who complained the least and rarely sought help were often those having the hardest time—the witness-survivors. Bob Planer was a prime example. As one of the sole survivors of his department at Keefe, Bruyette and Woods, he had acted on instincts prompted by his survival in the '93 bombing and on the sixth-sense warning from his wife, Paula. He could not have acted more responsibly: asking his colleagues if they wanted to leave with him, and, after the fact, visiting all the wives and arranging for help for the families. Rationally speaking, after a year of intense effort in leading the recovery of his company, Planer had every reason to feel he'd earned a well-deserved rest.

He and his wife made a dizzying set of trips over the Christmas holidays to visit all the branches of their families. Then they took all four children on a trip to the Caribbean. Everyone was excited about scuba diving and maybe trying out parasailing. Luxuriating on a beautiful island with miles of empty beach stretching as far as they could see, the couple congratulated themselves on having erased anything that could remind them of New York. They were contemplating going parasailing as they watched a man on water skis take flight with a sail for wings and soar by overhead.

"See that guy up there?" Bob blurted. "He's about as high as the World Trade Center. That's how it felt for the people who jumped."

"I didn't want to go parasailing anymore," said Paula. "I knew then—it's deep in there with Bob."

The next day, the Planers met a doctor from Lower Manhattan who had worked with the injured at Ground Zero. Bob spent the whole day comparing notes with the man. "I am always interested to hear another story about the World Trade Center," Bob said. "I never have a problem talking about it. It's cleansing."

Paula observed, "It's almost what he needed—to talk about it again."

But was it helpful to keep talking about it? As mental health professionals look at it, this is where survivors often get stuck. Carrying so many sensory cues that seem to be indelibly etched into their memories, almost any stimulus can trigger a memory or a flashback of the event. This can lead to obsessive thinking. The trauma victim becomes obsessed with the event and, like Planer, has an insatiable need to read about it, see documentaries about it, talk about it—reliving it again and again—which is not healthy. A classic example is found in "The Rime of the Ancient Mariner." In the famous Samuel Taylor Coleridge poem, the old sailor invades a wedding feast and tells his tale of being pursued at sea by a bird of good omen, but after he shot the albatross with a crossbow, the mariner's ship was becalmed and he was forever after bedeviled:

> *Since then, at an uncertain hour,*
> *That agony returns;*
> *And till my ghastly tale is told,*
> *This heart within me burns.*

So compelled is the old sailor to repeat his guilty tale, he takes no note of the revulsion of his listeners. Unable to get on with his life, he has turned into a derelict.

Paula Planer admitted the constancy of the trauma for her: "Every day you think about it. It never leaves you. Even when we go out to dinner, if I see one of the widows, I think about it."

The way to escape this obsession, say some psychologists, is through *distancing*. Various techniques are suggested by therapists. Dr. Hilda Kessler, a highly regarded psychologist in Berkeley, California, suggests that a patient look at the incident on an imaginary movie screen. Each time he or she talks about it, the person is encouraged to move back another row or more, until finally he or she is sitting in the back of the theater. Once the person becomes detached from the event in the movie, he or she doesn't *have to* look at it anymore.

A brilliant example of distancing is what Mary Murphy devised as her way to escape reliving 9/11 when reminders at home or in the news became too oppressive. She literally distanced herself and her children by taking to the back roads in their SUV. She got away. The fact that the Planers could not distance themselves from the Trade Center attacks, even by going thousands of miles away to a remote island, felt to them like one more defeat. Bob's way of "curing" himself of the lonely guilt of survivorship had been to throw all his energies into rebuilding the business. Over the fifteen months since the attacks had wiped out 67 out of 220 members of his firm, Bob had worked harder than at any other time in his life. At the end of January 2003, when the Planers curled up in their family room before a fire, Bob announced proudly, "We had a record year at Keefe, Bruyette and Woods, marginally, but a record in the history of the company."

"It was your therapy, too," Paula offered.

Bob's "therapy" had not noticeably diminished his trauma symptoms. The heaviness in his chest was back. He was having trouble sleeping. "Six hours is a great night for him," Paula said.

"I live in trepidation every day," Bob admitted tonelessly. "I still think something is going to happen. And it's going to happen right in Midtown, where I work."

His wife appeared to be suffering from vicarious traumatization. Paula sat on the sofa, pale and drawn, her knees pulled up tight to her chest. "I kept myself so cool and calm all last year," she said. "I got my daughter off to college and got Bob back to work. The minute I knew Bob was out of the dark and my kids were settled, then my ailments began."

"She is fried," Bob said. "I keep after her to slow down."

"Well, we have to get out there and help our neighbors and friends," Paula insisted, "and be there for them the way we were before 9/11." They both believed they could not "waste time" by being depressed. Yet they seemed clearly subdued, neither one showing anything like the physical or emotional élan they had taken for granted before 9/11.

Another central issue that must be addressed by a trauma survivor is: What meaning are you now going to attach to the story?

THIS STORY CAME AS no surprise to mental health experts who were working with people traumatized by 9/11. "The witness-survivors group is the one that keeps expanding over time," said Charles Brown, the administrator of mental health services for Monmouth County. "They defer to the families of victims. If the survivors do inquire about problems they are having, they often pull back and say the same thing: 'How can I ask for any help or even sympathy? I just got scared, but so many other people lost a loved one.' " Exactly the situation with the Planers, who were very likely suffering from PTSD, but who saw themselves as the lucky ones.

In early 2002, Monmouth County set up a resource center at the community college in Middletown, staffed by licensed social workers. The number of people seeking help was constantly increasing. By May 2003, a total of 264 different families had sought help. About one quarter of them had suffered the loss of a loved one, and a number of those were referred to a psychological counselor. An additional two hundred families reported being economically hurt.

After the first anniversary, however, the psychological trauma that had gone untreated in most of the witness-survivors was showing up in their inability to maintain their usual work performance. "Some are phobic, some can't leave their homes," said Brown. "I think what we'll see over time is a presentation of cases that have gone unattended, by virtue of the fact that people didn't seek help or didn't think they were 'worthy' of help, but they're still not sleeping well, or they're drinking or eating more, or their relationships are crumbling."

"Symptoms of stress response after exposure to the Trade Center attack can last a year and still be normal," says Dr. Eth, who directs St. Vincent's participation in Project Liberty, the New York mental health response. He points out, however, that if symptoms persist beyond a year and begin seriously to limit a person's normal activities or lead to depression, they are unlikely to fade away by themselves and are more likely to get worse. In the case of survivors like Bob Planer, he suggested, "the tragedy is not that he has developed symptoms, but that he has deprived himself and his family of the escape from his symptoms."

On the anniversary of 9/11, St. Vincent's was inundated with people who thought they had weathered the '93 Trade Center bombing. Nearly ten years later, they came into the psychiatric clinic very surprised that they weren't "over it." Some hadn't sought treatment, and others might have had short-term crisis counseling. "They had thought they were handling it with support from family and friends, or that an increase in their use of alcohol would be temporary—but when they were retraumatized by 9/11, it all came back," says Dr. Eth.

Of Vietnam veterans who served in combat, 30 percent developed PTSD. Eth says that half of those—some of whom were treated and some who weren't—were still suffering from it twenty years later. PTSD wasn't even a recognized disorder in the early days after the Vietnam War, and most sufferers were treated for physical health problems or suicidal behavior.

"The mental health profession's way of dealing with trauma is still very clumsy, and not substantiated by recent research," says Dr. Kessler. In past trauma studies, researchers never looked at the neurological aspect, only at psychological phenomena. More recently, researchers have tracked the pathways of traumatic fear in the brain and learned how a primitive part of the brain, the amygdala, overrides the cognitive cortexes, or thinking parts of the brain, that would ordinarily separate real threats from false alarms. In the presence of trauma, the amygdala floods the body with stress hormones that jump-start the heart's engine and power up the muscles for flight. It also burns into a substrate of memory every sensory cue attached to the trauma as vividly as burning a CD. Not surprisingly, then, it takes conscious effort and clever strategies to overwrite those memory cues.

Dr. Eth believes the essential ingredient in any form of treatment of PTSD is to assist the person in constructing a verbal narrative of the traumatic experience, but only when the person is ready and able to gain some sense of mastery over the situation. All forms of talking cure are based on this belief: that catharsis comes from putting your internal demons into words.

But September 11 shot holes through many proud banners flown by practitioners of the trauma and recovery centers. When swarms of shrinks descended on Ground Zero, the survivors and rescue workers shrank away from them. The last thing they wanted to do was talk about it. There was nothing whatsoever they could do to change the ghastly situation.

"Denial is your best defense when you can't change the situation," says Dr. Kessler, adding with a slow smile, "That may sound counterintuitive, coming from a psychologist." The point is, when what is making you miserable and terrified cannot be altered or improved by you, better to put it in a steel box. Another psychologist tells patients, "You take it, you put it in the box, you put a lock on it. You put the box down in the basement. And you put a dragon there to watch the box. Then you're free to go on about your business. The dragon will keep watching it, you don't have to. But you have to remember to feed the dragon," she warns. That means, keep the repression going. If it starts to come back up, you push it back down and make sure it stays in the box. A friend who tried the locked box found it too flimsy. One day she had a vision of a huge shipping container being wrapped in steel bands and hoisted by a crane onto a cargo ship. As she watched, the ship sailed out to sea and dropped the container overboard, where she saw it sink to the bottom of the ocean. She never revisited that trauma again.

"Repress Yourself" was the provocative headline of a much-discussed article in *The New York Times Magazine* in February 2003. The author, Lauren Slater, emphasized new research on heart attack patients in Israel, showing that the stiff-upper-lip types who didn't think, talk, or worry much about their near-death experience were far less likely to suffer post-traumatic stress disorder. But the "long-term effects of a repressive coping style" were followed up at only seven months. George Bonanno, an associate professor of psychology at Columbia University Teachers College, described his study of bereaved widows and widowers. The subgroup he defined as "the repressors," he reported, "had less grief over time and had a better overall life adjustment, and this has been consistent across studies."

But before rattled Americans rush to combat the traumatic effects of terrorism by wrapping their brains in duct tape, we should keep in mind that psychology is a nuanced art, and one-size treatment has never fit all. Repression is probably helpful for people whose normal mode is not particularly expressive, but there are many others who *need* to talk it out, or write or paint or compose, before they can understand what they have lived.

Dr. Richard Bryant, a research psychologist at the University of New South Wales, Australia, disparages most current efforts to treat traumatized people. He has systematically tracked people in trauma from their initial responses to their long-term adjustment. His research, he claims, allowed him to identify the vast majority of those at risk for suffering PTSD and demonstrated that early intervention *with those at risk* could prevent the disorder in up to 80 percent of cases. Dr. Bryant's most heartfelt conclusion, however, challenges the current practice of debriefing or mandatory short-term crisis counseling. "The long-held notion that early intervention is the be-all and end-all of treatment for the trauma is nuts," he told a meeting of the American Psychological Association. "Many people in the acute stress phase are made worse by early intervention. Better in the short term to use denial. Or an antidepressant."

With time, many healthy, normally optimistic people are able to find a meaning to attach to the traumatic event that allows them to go on with their lives without the restrictions of psychic numbing, displaced anger, or phobic reactions such as *I can't go into a large city with tall buildings;* or *I can't fly.* And some who were plunged into the dark find they are suddenly able to see.

REUNION OF GROUND ZERO'S FREQUENT FLIERS

Another group at risk of a psychological blow-back from prolonged exposure to the Trade Center site was the behavioral health volunteers from Liberty State Park. Kathi Bedard, the self-appointed Charon who had led the ferry trips for New Jersey families across the river to visit the underworld of Ground Zero, was well aware that fifty-seven straight days of exposure to that desolate place and to the families' shock and raw grief was a setup for secondary traumatization, not only for herself but for the volunteers who stuck it out—those she called her "Frequent Fliers." The volunteers had made an effort to keep in touch by phone and e-mail. As the year 2002 drew to a close, Kathi called for a get-together of her Fliers. She managed to persuade the authorities to open the "chapel" in the old ferry terminal where they had all worked together for three unforgettable months.

As people began arriving from different parts of the country, they moved through the now-deserted terminal like underwater swimmers. Flooded with memories. Some described how their own "movies" of that period began playing on split screens in their minds. Dormant emotions welled up. Hugging and kissing blotted up the tears.

Judy Farrar, a licensed clinical social worker who was in charge of the mental health team for the Red Cross, had come up from Virginia. "It all washes over me—the strong friendships that were forged here," she said. "This was a place where people from all over the country put their own lives on hold so they could come to New Jersey just to help others. This was a city of love, a city of giving."

Bob Bellan recalled how the governor of New Jersey had given him forty-eight hours to set up that "city" for the families of his state. The FEMA emergency services manager had the look of a big, sad buffalo, but he had enthusiastically pulled together a team of creative, flexible people who had come from as far away as Alaska, Hawaii, and Puerto Rico and gained a consensus that their usual therapeutic strategies were probably of no use in that situation. "We developed a companion philosophy," he said. "The call of this place was to provide family members a safe, warm atmosphere where we could guide them to the services they needed. We had to prepare those who wanted to go over to Ground Zero to face the realization that their loved ones were not coming back, and then work with them in a very emotional, compassionate, loving manner to get them prepared to go back home."

All the Frequent Fliers had both positive and negative memories and felt changed by their experiences. Judy Farrar used to be known as somebody who could light up a room and make everyone laugh. "I'm not as light and goofy as I was," she said. But her perception of time and what is meaningful in life was positively affected. "My time now is precious. I'm not going to waste it by working on something I don't believe in. I don't care about the money, I care about using what talents I have to the fullest." Bob Bellan had tried going back to his former job at FEMA but found he couldn't do the same old thing. He retired and sought a new challenge doing emergency management work for local municipalities.

When it came time for Kathi Bedard to speak, she was cheered as "Kathi the Great," followed by lots of jokes and teasing. "I know that I have changed," said the compact woman with restless eyes who once described herself as a "suburban mall rat." She had seen the world she knew blown to bits, but she had also seen what people are capable of at their best, and that had reduced her tolerance for people who do "cheap, stupid, petty things." Her marriage had been put to a strenuous test. Each night when she went home, wrecked, from leading the ferry trips to Ground Zero, her husband would ask, "What happened?" Her tongue would tie up in knots. "I couldn't talk about it. There is no language in the world to describe—" She broke off. "I told him he'd just have to come down."

Fred Bedard introduced himself as "a hairdresser who just happens to be Kathi's husband." They had been married for fifteen years, and he had never seen what his wife, a clinical social worker, did for a living. "She smuggled me in one day, and I was just amazed at what she and all these people do in a crisis," he recounted. "I fumbled all over the place, like Gilligan on a three-hour tour." After helping to guide the families to the viewing platform at Ground Zero, Fred spotted an elegantly dressed older woman about to pass out. "I caught her just before she hit the ground. Me and another guy got her into a golf cart. When she calmed down, she kept asking me who I was. I couldn't answer, I wasn't even allowed to be there." The woman insisted upon knowing what it was that Fred did for a living, why he was so good with people.

"I'm a hairdresser," he said, abashed.

"Oh God," she said, "don't look at my roots!"

Everything about Fred's outlook on life changed after his first trip to Ground Zero, he said. "It took something as horrific as the World Trade Center attack for me to understand who I am. You know what? I'm not afraid anymore." Fred had become a card-carrying member of the Frequent Fliers, returning two or three days a week to help out until the Family Assistance Center closed. "And see that woman?" He pointed proudly to the compact woman with restless eyes. "That's Kathi. That's my wife! Before, I was ready to take up with a twenty-year-old in a red SUV. Now I love my wife to death. I want to get old with her, I want to have sex with her till I'm ninety. We've grown together as a result of this."

Kathi smiled. She said she had been so crazed the year before, she had been afraid her marriage would be a casualty of her work. But like all her Fliers, she vowed she would do it all over again.

Chapter Twenty-seven

THE SECOND CHRISTMAS

It wasn't so much the major holidays that hurt, it was the little private reminders that hit like a mugger when the families least expected a blow. The day the widow met her husband. Or the day they always took the kids in to see the Radio City Christmas show.

Tuesday's Children, a grassroots organization dedicated to making sure that the children of 9/11 were able to continue their family traditions, arranged the second year to send hundreds of families to the Radio City Christmas show. But the founder, Chris Burke, soon learned how volatile the emotional environment remained when he had to pull in extra volunteers just to help make simple phone calls. "What should be a five-minute conversation turns into a forty-minute discussion with multiple breakdowns," he found. "Every phone call is Greek tragedy."

To the surprise of most of the families, the second Christmas turned out to be much harder than the first year's. This time there was no insulation of numbness. This time it was not a first, with everyone and his brother helping to hold them up and walk them through. This time Christmas was just another of the rest of a lifetime of Christmases—without. "They weren't prepared for that harsh reality, and it came as a shock," said Maureen Fitzsimmons, describing the people in her Catholic Charities support groups. "But nobody wondered, 'Am I going crazy?' like they did last year. They were able to identify the Aha! moment and deal with it. These folks have learned that grief is not linear, and that education has helped them enormously."

Many were actively inventing new rituals or seeking escapes.

TAKING OFF THE RING

Karen Cangialosi's hands were buried in a thick black binder full of government instructions for filing with the Victim Compensation Fund. She stopped work for a moment and spread her fingers on the dining room table. Her nails were no longer dry, brittle, and broken. Her nails were long and strong, polished and perfect as ten plastic spoons. But it wasn't her nails she wanted noticed. It was the fourth finger on her left hand. It was ringless.

Whispering so her sons in the next room wouldn't hear, she confessed, "I just took it off last night because I'm going away. We're going to the Caribbean on vacation. I, um, I don't want to lose the ring in the water."

A slow, guilty smile. Okay, she admitted, that was a nice rationale. "The truth is, I don't feel as married as I used to feel."

It was two weeks before Christmas and Karen knew she had to get away. She had called up FAVOR and accepted the vacation offered to her months before: an expense-paid week in the Dominican Republic at the exclusive Punta Cana resort, one of ten vacations donated by an owner, New York attorney Theodore H. Kheel. She was taking the boys out of the country for the first time. Their getaway would come just in time to counter the bittersweet memories evoked the night before, when Karen had gone into New York to a now-annual dinner given by the mutual fund industry in honor of all the people the business had lost on 9/11. She was one of thirty widows surrounded by two hundred men, and she had felt very married. Many of the men needed to share with her recollections of working with her husband. Triggers. She had come home with her head spinning. To a bed still empty.

But the next day she and the boys would step onto a charter plane and put New Jersey and downtown Manhattan and all of those ghosts behind them. The boys sat at the kitchen table dutifully doing a week's worth of homework in advance. Peter admitted daydreaming of palm trees, blue water, beaches, and belly-boarding. Karen just wanted to lie down in the sun. Her companion would be a female cousin who was single.

The pallid Middletown party arrived in Punta Cana at dusk and walked immediately down to the beach. Guests were still snorkeling. Others swayed along the shoreline on horseback. Peter had to do a back bend to see the tops of the tall palm trees. The women pulled off their boots. The languid water tickled their toes. It was the most romantic place Karen had ever seen. She turned to her cousin:

"What am I doing here with you?"

"WHERE ARE THE HUSBANDS?"

That was the question Karen met at every turn. The cute young beach boys were curious, as were other guests who saw the women at dinner: "Where are the husbands?" One man in particular, a French businessman who was there with his young son, kept turning up at the luncheon buffet behind Karen. She noticed he had gorgeous green eyes and thick dark hair. He flirted with her. Karen enjoyed his attentions, but nobody knew she was connected to 9/11 and she was determined to keep it that way. One day the Frenchman motioned to her boys and said, "So, whose children are they? Where is their father?"

"There *is* no father," Karen replied in a pique of frustration, and walked away.

Later, as she lay on the beach, a shadow came between Karen and the sun. The Frenchman. She sat up and said, "I didn't mean to be rude. I just get tired of explaining. . . ." Once she had told him how she lost her husband, he brightened, having thought she was married, and he asked her to dinner.

"He asked me on a date and I brought my kids!"

The Frenchman remained undaunted. He made an effort to entertain the boys and charmed them all by ordering the entire meal in French and Spanish, although they were shocked when he lit a cigarette. He lavished Karen with compliments: Her dress was soigné, her hair was like sunshine. She smiled, pleased that she had painted blond highlights over the gray patches left by the last year. After dinner, Karen took the boys back to their villa. As she settled down her now-twelve-year-old son, she mentioned casually that the Frenchman had asked her to go out later for a drink. "Jeffrey, would it be okay if I went out?"

"Yeah, fine," he said. "Just don't kiss him!"

Naturally, the Frenchman wanted to sleep with her that night. She let it go with a few kisses. "It was nice to have a man pay attention to me." Who better than a handsome Frenchman as costar in the rehearsal for becoming a woman again? And being away, Karen had felt free—her "date" wasn't going to be discussed at the PTA meeting. The next morning, when Karen Cangialosi stepped onto the charter plane to return home, she didn't feel quite as married.

"What I had with my husband I will always have," she said. "That's a part of me. If it was the other way around, I wouldn't want him to be alone. But he would have to find somebody great!" The Frenchman had given her his business card. She didn't intend to pursue it. Her sons had passed judgment:

"He smokes."

THE FAVOR COMMUNITY

Allyson Gilbert had mixed feelings as she made the rounds of her families before Christmas to deliver the last basket.

"We were naive in the beginning," said the cofounder of FAVOR. It was her first volunteer campaign. She and Janet Dluhi had never imagined how consumed they would become, or the powerful ripple effect that their humble outreach effort would have on Middletown. They and the ninety "angels of Middletown" who had joined on as volunteers had demonstrated that even a big sprawling suburb could show the heart of a small town.

"The most striking change in the families is the move by all the women to greater independence," Allyson said. "To go from being reliant on their spouses to becoming the sole decision makers and income managers, as well as household managers—in less than a year and a half—is something impressive to see."

Laura Wilton, another volunteer who, like Allyson, had to juggle her own business and two young children, observed that of the half-dozen families who were "hers," none seemed to be better off financially. She was aware of belt-tightening. But most had been able to maintain the status quo with help from the townspeople, which came in the form of free services, free tuition, and cash donations.

But the FAVOR volunteers had dispensed much more than minimal financial support. They had extended emotional support and selfless friendship. "I thought we'd help out in practical ways, but I never expected that we would create such an emotional bond with our families," said Allyson. *Our* families—that was the tip-off. It had become obvious after the first few months of the FAVOR volunteers' door-to-door visits that it wasn't about the baskets. It was about connection. Human connection.

"To see the families move from shock and devastation to coming back to life again, and to know that you truly helped them from the bottom up, that was an unbelievably wonderful reward for us," said Allyson.

Many people had expressed concern that the women would feel stigmatized as 9/11 widows, that they wouldn't be seen as socially desirable in a very married bedroom community. That fear had evaporated. "The families have felt the warmth and support of the town during this hard time," said Allyson. "Their friends are here, their children have been given a great deal of support. People have let them know they *do* fit in."

Proof of the pudding was the fact that thirty-one of the thirty-three widows and widowers of Middletown proper were staying. That was a tribute to the efforts made by the townsfolk to demonstrate true caring and neighborliness. Only two of the widows had moved away. One was Anna Egan, who had moved back to the state from which she had only recently relocated. The other was a Trinidadian-born widow, who had felt more comfortable moving closer to the islands to raise her mixed-race children.

The volunteers, too, had formed a new network of friendships and common purposes beyond FAVOR. They were almost all mothers who had been sectored off in the different neighborhood schools attended by their children. The tragedy had stretched their world and their worldview. "I think we will have a relationship with the families, and with the volunteers, always," said Allyson. "I've felt a strong sense of community in Middletown for the first time," she marveled. "This collection of seventy thousand people all of a sudden seemed to be like a small town. And it just seems to be getting smaller and smaller!"

THE RUMSON REVELATION

The impact on the Rumson Neck was far more scattered. Craig Cummings was one of the most conscientious of Cantor Fitzgerald survivors. He had first volunteered with the Alliance of Neighbors. Assigned as a "caseworker" for three families, he was expected to question them about their financial situation. "My families didn't want that invasion," he found. "They would never call back."

Cummings suffered further embarrassment when the Alliance virtually shut down after the first few months. "They had too many chiefs and not enough people to do the work," he realized. "Over the holidays this year, the Alliance finally handed out some of its fund—a thousand dollars to each 9/11 family in the county." At the same time, Cummings and the rest of the volunteers received a brush-off letter, "basically saying thanks for your help, but we don't need you as 'caseworkers' anymore."

Craig and Mary Cummings hadn't allowed their disappointment with the Alliance to slow them down. They had been among the first and most tireless angels of Rumson, establishing the Cummings Scholarship Fund and committing to raise the money to meet educational expenses over the next eighteen years for any one of the hundreds of children in Monmouth County who had lost a parent and would need help. They had raised $400,000 and already distributed supplemental monies to ten college-bound kids.

At 7:30 on a Friday night after New Year's, Mary Cummings was dispensing soup and pizza to her four toddlers, who were all tumbling around the TV room with their big Burmese mountain dog. She wasn't convinced that her husband had begun to recover from the trauma of 9/11. He had driven himself in the first months after the tragedy, working virtually around the clock at Cantor to help rebuild the business and to get their scholarship fund off the ground. He scarcely slept. He was spurred on by feeling a new value for life and the truth of the rubric "We are our brother's keeper."

Still, he hadn't regained his equilibrium. "Craig isn't verbal," said his wife. "But what I see is a lot of hyperactivity. He's short-tempered and very closed emotionally. We both go-go-go, and collapse."

Craig came through the kitchen door, apparently upbeat, dressed in a Pebble Beach polo shirt and Docksiders and carrying a carton full of freshly printed handouts for the Cummingses' third fund-raiser, a casino night at the country club. "We're expecting 200 to 250 people tomorrow night," Craig enthused. "That tells you, even with all the press about big life insurance policies, our community hasn't deserted the families."

It had come as a revelation to Cummings that even some of the families of Cantor's highest earners had been underinsured. After a year or two, he calculated, those families wouldn't be able to live in the same house or go to the same schools, unless the wife went to work and made as much money as her husband had.

Some of the women now had boyfriends, observed Cummings. "Their lives are active, they're dating. They don't want to feel like charity cases anymore. Sheila Martello got married right after the New Year. That was a surprise to everyone in Rumson."

The Martellos had moved to Rumson only six weeks before 9/11. Jimmy Martello, who had installed Sheila and their two children in a six-million-dollar home, was one of the big-bonus boys at Cantor. Early on, Sheila had joined with Kristen in bird-dogging Ken Feinberg and insisting that the special master not cap the compensation for high earners like their husbands. She had appeared on TV many times, demanding that the Senate pass the broad tax relief bill for survivors. Martello told Diane Sawyer in an interview on *Good Morning America,* "We're not used to asking for things, we're used to giving, and it is now time for the American government to give to us." Along with Ginny Bauer, Sheila had lobbied until the American government did just that. And once the tax relief bill passed, Sheila retreated into private life. In January, Sheila married a close friend of her dead husband. The wedding was held in semiseclusion in northern New Jersey.

For all his altruistic efforts and fund-raising successes, the sting of surviving September 11 remained a source of chronic pain for Craig Cummings. After a glass of wine, he tapped into the private feelings beneath the surface of his friendly, professional manner.

"I'm doing terrible," he said. "I was under the impression that all I had to do was to get the firm back on its feet and get our scholarship fund off the ground, and after that things would go back to seminormal. But I think about it. Whether it's once a day or fifty times in one day, it's there all the time."

Craig was defensive about the automatic assumption that his problem was survivor guilt. "Me? Guilty of what? I didn't fly the planes into the buildings. I would feel guilty if I was director of the CIA," he said. "I do have a responsibility to help their families—like I'd hope they would help mine. But *guilt* is the wrong word," he insisted. "Doing good makes me feel better. When they won't let you help them, it's uncomfortable."

One of his twin sons crawled onto his knee and Craig's tight-lipped smile spread. "Look, I don't walk around with a doomsday mentality but there's not a day goes by that I don't talk about a dozen people we've lost. It's like a ton of bricks on your back. You can't get rid of it."

After the glass of wine was drained, he waxed rhetorical. "I never thought it would be so long and so constant. When will I ever get away from it?"

IS MURDER MORE UNFAIR TO HIGH EARNERS?

By the second Christmas even Kristen had filed for an award from the Victim Compensation Fund. So had Lorie van Auken, another of the four moms, and Mary Murphy. Terry Fiorelli had filed early and without regrets.

A continuing complaint was voiced against imposing any cap on awards. Some of the higher-earning families complained about inconsistencies in Feinberg's definition of the fund. They used a September 2002 quote by the administrator in *Time* magazine as proof. Though claiming there was no monetary cap on awards, Feinberg said, "I've got to be aware of what is fair not only from the claimants' point of view, but from the taxpayers' point of view." In his original model, he explained, someone earning $1 million a year could conceivably claim $10 million from the fund, and he questioned whether taxpayers should bear the brunt of a $10 million lifestyle.

Later, Feinberg admitted he had imposed a cap. He told *The New York Times Magazine* that the cap reflected his own views, rather than the intention of Congress when it created the act. As Feinberg was well aware, President Bush had hurriedly signed the fund into law at a time when, as former president Jimmy Carter described it, "Congress is so traumatized by 9/11 that it can't think straight."

Typical awards being handed down by the end of 2002 looked like this: If a healthy forty-five-year-old man with two dependent children made $100,000 a year, his widow was slated to received $1.7 million from the fund—minus set-asides. A single thirty-four-year-old trader on the same salary with no children would get around $1.3 million after set-asides.

These numbers did not satisfy some of the very high earners in New York, including seven Cantor Fitzgerald families who filed a class action lawsuit against Feinberg. They claimed that the fund was "arbitrary, capricious and an abuse of discretion." Feinberg's needs-based award calculations, they argued, were unfair to high earners. By using after-tax earnings, Feinberg's calculations lowered amounts substantially.

By the end of May 2003, about 1,700 claims had been submitted out of a possible universe of nearly 3,000 claimants. The striking thing about the awards was how personalized they were. One person who had earned $220,000 received $6 million, while others who were at the same income level were awarded the minimum of $250,000. After all the venting of anger and anguish at the special master, only 75 of the 1,700 claimants had thus far requested a hearing. The median amount for awards—after offsets—was $1.2 million.

This was exactly the number Feinberg had predicted from the start.

THE LATE CRASHERS

As the new year 2003 dawned, those who had started in the support groups fifteen months before were still faithfully attending and wanted to continue. This was the safe haven, the one place where, for fifty minutes every week, they could fully trust that everyone else would listen, hear, and not try to fix it; where they could allow themselves a few moments of regression, where they could cry, "I hated him!" or "I'm so angry at him because he left me!" and get validation, or argument. But there were others who were contemptuous of support groups as an admission of weakness.

Craig Cummings had a bird's-eye view of many of the bereaved families from his fund-raising work. "It's not the widows who are in bad shape as much as the parents," Cummings observed as he made the rounds of Rumson families over the holidays. One of the women, who had lost her son, was in the midst of a bitter divorce, and that was sapping what energy she had left. The other obvious casualties were some of the bereaved men.

"For the first six months, the widowers and the fathers who lost a child were all stoic and appeared as strong as could be," said Cummings. "It was the women—widows and mothers—who were openly devastated and who sought out support and bereavement groups. But six months later, the men fell apart."

The worst off, in addition to the guilt-ridden survivors and recovery workers, were those who had not allowed themselves to grieve. "The people who refused help from the community or support groups were the ones who crashed after the first year," Craig observed, echoing many of the professionals. "The people who realized something major happened in their lives and who sought help are much farther along in their recovery."

A few of the widows showed a brave front for the first year, refusing to be seen in tears. They pushed themselves to accept invitations to parties and invited other widows to go out to dinner or even into New York to a show. Some talked incessantly about finding ways to help others heal and took on a change-the-world fervor. Others still struggling against depression and the temptation to withdraw were intimidated by these publicly active widows. "How can they do all these things?" some of the women in support groups would marvel. "Are they superhuman?"

"Keeping up that facade was a drain," observed a concerned neighbor of one active widow with whom he had worked on ambitious outreach projects. The "superwidow" had been performing an amazing high-wire act. Helping everyone else to heal served to keep the matter of her own traumatic grieving at arm's length. Ultimately, she depleted her energies. She pulled off one last public event and did an about-face—turning on people.

"When the anniversary rolled around, starting about a month before, you couldn't even talk to her," said the sympathetic colleague. "She was getting into fights with her parents and her in-laws. She shut out just about everyone, even really good friends, people trying to help—maybe one day they canceled on picking up her kids. Simple things were magnified a thousand times over." The widow's new strategy, her colleague gathered, was to push the whole subject of 9/11 to the side, as if to say: "I'm over it. I'm going on to my next life."

Chris Burke from Tuesday's Children made a similar observation of the few widows who had directed all their energies outward over the first year and who appeared to be the perfect, keep-your-powder-dry models of successful coping. "They were holding on, but you knew there was a crash coming," he said. "It takes very little for some of the widows to channel their anger in your direction. I hear it every day. They'll lash out at you for the most minor thing. You can say 'Blue,' and they'll explode: ' "Blue"! How dare you say "blue" to me!' "

But eventually, the "perfect" public widows, too, had to pull back and do the messy work of grieving—in private. That was not a side of themselves they wanted others to see.

GINNY BAUER WAS ANOTHER widow who had shunned the support and bereavement groups. As friendly and outgoing as she appeared, she was very private and disliked discussing her feelings. But at the start of the New Year, Ginny looked ten years younger. Her hair was long and soft, the drag on her features had lifted, and she had resumed her place in the social life of Rumson, as popular as ever. Having been an early and active leader of the tax relief fight, she had rediscovered her natural gift as a "good yapper." As the New Year approached, she was restless and excited.

"I am going to go back to work," she announced. "My big process now is trying to figure out what I want to do when I grow up!"

Maybe a lobbyist for good causes. Maybe public relations or customer relations. "I could be a good face for a company," she said with renewed confidence. "Considering that I had never done television before, I think I did a better than adequate job." Ginny had demonstrated in her many media appearances as a citizen-lobbyist that she was a natural at selling whatever she had to sell. She realized that in another year, when her youngest went off to boarding school, she would be rattling around her big house alone. And looking back, she recognized that before her husband's sudden death, they had been at a crossroads.

"Obviously, as the children got older, they wouldn't need me 24/7. I was getting frustrated just being home. I was a good corporate wife. My husband could put me in any situation with his customers, and he knew that I could get along with anybody. So he was looking forward to more opportunities to include me in his business life."

Ginny hadn't been convinced that expanding her role as the ideal corporate wife was her first choice for the transition into middle life. After all, she had been a success in her early life as a saleswoman at Merrill Lynch. Her children, who knew her only as the ever available provider for their wants and needs, used to tease her mercilessly. "Oh Mom, did you get your nails done?" Her husband had tried to correct them, saying, "Don't ever underestimate your mother. She's a very smart woman." But she hadn't done a great deal to demonstrate it, until she was mobilized by the tragedy.

The year before, Ginny had been adamant that nobody was going to make her get a job to support her family. "I felt like it would be unfair for me to have to dramatically change my lifestyle simply because my husband was killed. But as my choice," she said, "it's a different scenario. If the right job comes up, I would jump at it."

Chapter Twenty-eight

———

THE RECOVERING
GROUND ZERO FAMILY

The new burdens of homeland defense and the accumulation of terrorist threats—always anonymous and ambiguous—fell particularly heavily on the Port Authority Police. They hold the keys to the gates of New York City. All the airports, bridges, tunnels, and PATH trains are on their watch, and so are the ports. Even the former night commander of Ground Zero was beginning to get a little punch-drunk from the constant warnings by the feds.

"We're on heightened alert all the time," said Lieutenant Bill Keegan. "It goes on for days, and then it just goes away. We aren't told if they thwarted some real threat, or whether it was some bogus information given to them down in Cuba." Post-traumatic stress was not the greatest problem for Lieutenant Keegan's men, according to Bob Kupferman, a trauma counselor who was working regularly with the men. "What they're grappling with now, as we move into 2003, is *pre*-trauma stress."

Before New Year's Eve, Keegan and the other senior officers were warned there might be an attack on a ship in New York Harbor. Lieutenant Keegan came on duty early that afternoon and drove over to Port Newark. He was startled at what he saw. Normally, the piers along the Hudson at Port Newark and Port Elizabeth—among the largest ports in the country—would be teeming with up to twenty-five or thirty ships. On the afternoon of New Year's Eve, there were no cargo ships in berth anywhere along the Hudson.

"I took the threat more seriously then," Keegan said. He learned that the FBI terrorism task force had ordered the ships tugged out of the harbor and no new ships had been permitted in since the day before. "The cost had to be huge. The port of New York was shut down for almost two days." There were no news reports of this. Later that night a federal official told Keegan, "Look, we're going to stand down on that particular threat." Their information had not been fresh, they conceded, and following up, they had found it was not that credible.

So it went, threat upon threat, alert upon alert, until the credibility of the intelligence officials was becoming somewhat suspect. Lieutenant Keegan's men were canaries in the mine shaft of a national trauma that was only becoming more pervasive. Philip Zimbardo, past president of the American Psychological Association and cofounder of the new National Center on Disaster Psychology and Terrorism at Stanford University, raised the possibility that the Bush administration, hell-bent on going to war against Iraq, could be creating an emotional atmosphere to justify the war by alerting the public to potential threats that most people could do little or nothing about.

KEEPING IN TOUCH

A month before their recovery work ended in May 2002, Keegan had become alarmed. His team's need for help in their personal recovery was being ignored by officialdom, and some of the men's behavior worried him. He heard that St. Vincent's Catholic Medical Centers had assembled a team of highly experienced professionals in stress management and they were working with the New York City Fire Department. He contacted Spencer Eth, vice chairman and medical director at the Department of Psychiatry and Behavioral Health Services, who was also in charge of the World Trade Center services. Dr. Eth invited Keegan to meet with him and his colleague, trauma counselor Don Thoms, a Jersey boy from Freehold, who knew a lot of the Cantor Fitzgerald people from the Middletown area. They hit it off.

When Keegan first invited the St. Vincent's counselors to meet with his men and women, a month before they left Ground Zero, it was an informal conversation over pizza and Cokes in the cramped Port Authority trailer at the site. The men were obviously anxious. They covered it with a lot of posturing, puffing up, teasing, and flirting with the young female social workers. Others were sullen and silent. In the middle of the meeting, a couple of the officers got an emergency call to go investigate a bomb threat. Quips started flying: " 'Scuse me while I go put on my Superman uniform." But the men came back, sat down to eat, and rejoined the discussion.

Thoms, who is administrative director of St. Vincent's Behavioral

Health Services, assured the men that he and his team would design a program around their special needs, ask for their input, and modify their efforts accordingly. He was impressed at how open Keegan's men were. "That was not our experience with every uniformed service," he said. It was entirely different from their reception in the firehouses. "Here come the neck-ups," the firefighters would say jokingly when they saw the clinicians from St. Vincent's. Thoms attributed the difference to the attitudes of their leadership.

"Bill Keegan was very psychologically astute," he said. "I think the openness of his cops has a lot to do with his ability to engage these guys, not in an authoritarian way, but in a compassionate, caring way. And when we got to talk to them on an individual level, or in smaller groups, they were very insightful."

Thoms's primary concern, and Keegan's, was not that the recovery workers were psychiatrically ill, but how to fortify them to face the "returning home" phenomenon. "What was going to happen when they gave up the work that was so meaningful and important to them and went back to being an ordinary police officer, back to being a husband, a father?" Thoms worried. The officers' biggest complaint was that they had no life. "Girlfriends and wives had become very angry because they were never around, and when they were home, they were not likely to be available emotionally or psychologically or sexually," observed Thoms.

"Telling a guy who's been down there for eight months, finding body parts, go home and read a good novel—that's not gonna work—or telling him, take your wife out for dinner—he didn't want to go out for dinner because he knew he'd have to chitchat," Thoms said. "He didn't want to go into a social situation where everyone else was happy when he was not happy." No one outside of their circle really understood what the officers were experiencing. They were constantly asked, "What's it like down there?"

How could they describe what it was like to smell a rotten body and feel excited about that smell, knowing it meant they were going to find human remains? They would say, "Isn't that crazy? I mean, it's not normal." As Keegan's men began to talk, it was clear they were fearful of acting out their anger and sense of helplessness.

One officer blurted, "Listen, am I gonna flip out like one of these rescue people after Columbine or Oklahoma City that killed themselves? You hear about postal workers pushed to the edge suddenly taking somebody out. I have so much anger—am I going to go postal? Kill myself or someone else?"

"One of the reasons we're here is to help you understand the psychological reactions to what you're experiencing," Thoms explained. "So you're not going to be mystified when you get overly upset while taking out the garbage, you know? We'll help you to develop strategies and coping mechanisms where you can manage your anger in a more constructive way. Take a few seconds to understand, 'Now, why did I just snap? What really triggered it?' " The counselors prepared them to recognize the symptoms of a panic attack: "It's not a heart attack, although it may feel that way. What you do is some deep breathing." Thoms summarized: "It's a process of reframing events, strategizing, and operationalizing the new behavior, which is the most difficult. Especially if you're using alcohol or meds to feel null and void. We want to empower you."

"Hey, this was no Joe College couch monster coming around to tell us what life's about," Keegan and the men decided among themselves. This could be as practical as learning how to defuse a domestic violence situation.

When Keegan told his superiors he wanted to commit his men and women to meeting with the counselors from St. Vincent's regularly, for the next year, the idea was not welcomed. "The lieutenant was going out on a limb," Dr. Eth said. "He did not have the support or endorsement of his leadership at the Port Authority. It can work very much to a person's career disadvantage to outshine their superiors and to be as impressive as he is, especially in organizations like police departments, which are very tightly hierarchical and suspicious of outsiders." The corporation finally blinked and let Keegan know that he could do whatever he believed was appropriate for his men and women, but unofficially.

Funding was another obstacle. Project Liberty was an umbrella operation for disseminating FEMA monies for post–9/11 mental health services, but it was confined to residents of New York. "Once you cross the Hudson, it could be China," said Dr. Eth, referring to the famous Saul Steinberg cartoon depicting New York's parochialism. He managed to raise temporary funding privately.

The irony was, FEMA had given Project Liberty the largest ever grant for free federal crisis counseling—$132 million in 2002 on top of its original $22 million allocation. Officials had predicted about two and a half million people would seek out mental health services. But as of April 1, 2003, only 643,710 New Yorkers had taken up the offer. That left roughly $90 million—more than half the money earmarked for free care—unused. Although mental health providers emphasized that many first responders (like the Port Authority Police) were slow to seek help, and witness-survivors and children would be even slower to manifest symptoms of delayed trauma, Project Liberty was due to stop offering help at the end of 2003.

None of the thirty men on Keegan's night recovery team had seen war or combat before September 11, but they shared a bond as tight as men who have been through a war together and left their buddies on the field of battle. After their first few small-group meetings, the men agreed that it was probably good to get together and talk. They welcomed the participation of the down-to-earth trauma counselors from St. Vincent's, Bob Kupferman and Linda Rizotto. Keegan insisted they meet at least twice a month. He kept on them by cell phone.

"Keegan's always bustin' our chops to do the meetings," they said.

A REUNION AT GROUND ZERO

Sixteen months after Lieutenant Keegan's team had come together as the night team at Ground Zero, Keegan invited them all to gather back there to share their thoughts and renew their bonds. It was January 2003, shortly after the New Year. Half of them showed up. Others who had planned to come told Keegan their wives had vetoed their giving up a rare free night to be with the guys.

Officer Brian Verardi pulled up to the Port Authority shack in his truck, followed by Bill Barry, a bulky officer in his early forties with a cheerful smile and a mustache. The wiry young cop and the beefy older officer swaggered toward each other and opened their arms and clamped together. They hugged long and hard.

"That's the way it is with all of us, the midnight crew at Ground Zero," they said.

Verardi, a thirty-year-old who describes himself as "a white kid from Staten Island," was typical of the team members. He was certainly no stranger to human disaster. Assigned as a rookie to East New York, a tough, crime-riddled section of Brooklyn, he had often seen two or three homicides in a night, except they weren't the sort of people considered worthy of mention in the newspaper. "It might be a body tied up in electrical cables and left in the street, or an infant left in the tub to drown while his father went out for cigarettes," Verardi could say, almost casually. "That was worse than what we saw down here, except"—he stopped, choked up a little—"except these were our own."

Bill Barry had been present for most of the recoveries made at night. He introduced his latest news self-mockingly. "I used to be bigger, but I had part of my colon removed." He chuckled. "Whaddayacallit? Diverticulitis." He'd had a few intestinal attacks before 9/11, but mild ones. "It only kicked up after we were pulled out of here." He smiled ruefully. "God bless America." An abscess had blistered his colon and he had been rushed into surgery to have a section removed. "It coulda been because of this." Barry waved an arm toward the floodlit pit behind them. "Yeah, I left my heart and soul in that pit. So what's a little piece of colon?"

Bill Keegan's face was reddened with abrasions from being on duty through a nasty sleet storm on New Year's Eve. Wearing a ribbed turtleneck and jeans, he welcomed the group and shared more hugs. The conversation started, as usual, with grousing about work.

"Everybody else is back to normal," said Keegan. "The bosses went back to eight hours in December. My guys are still working twelve-hour tours. They promised it would end in December. Now I hear May. This reminds you of psychological torture, where they make a promise and yank it away." (The twelve-hour tours were later forecast to continue to the end of 2003.)

"We're being treated like the donkey with the carrot dangling on a stick," groused another officer. "We just keep going."

Kupferman listened carefully. The counselor knew the men needed to be stroked. Back at their old posts, the nickname hung on them by some of their colleagues was "Ground Zero hero." It was a tease, tinged with jealousy. As the strain on marriages had intensified, some of the men had been seeking uncomplicated pleasures outside the home, further jeopardizing the stability of their personal lives. "They didn't like to be bitched at because they weren't home enough or they missed Johnny's baseball game again," the counselor empathized. "And it was all too easy for them to look for stroking from groupies." So pervasive had become these more personal problems, the men were now urged to come in for individual counseling once a week.

Donny Conklin pulled down his wool watch cap. He had worked for eight months on site helping to examine body parts, logging them in and putting them in the cooler truck to be sent to the morgue at Bellevue. He had recently become a new father, but he didn't have much time to enjoy it. "My wife hates the Port Authority now. Everybody's lost their drive. Now we're all sitting around waiting for the next terrorist attacks to happen."

Beyond the frustration and boredom and constant low-grade fear, the men felt the loss of their noble work together. One cop voiced the shared view: "I miss working with the same guys. We'd eat together, go to the pizzeria together, relax together, watch *Blind Date* on TV at two o'clock in the morning. Then go back out to the pit. It was the same guys, same crap every night."

Some had tried to compensate for their new sense of isolation by buying things. Verardi had bought his wife an SUV for Christmas. "I don't know anyone who has done anything extravagant," he said. "Birthday gifts are a little nicer, you take your wife out to dinner a little more. If you can't do it with time, you try and make up for it with money."

A few officers had been swept away by overtime pay, making more money than they'd ever dreamt they would. One bought an H2, a civilian version of a military Humvee. It cost about $50,000 and was all flash. The worry was, would it have to be returned when the overtime stopped?

The single cops were envious of those who already had wives. But more time on the job had produced enough money for many of the single men to buy and furnish a house. The irony was, they had no time to shop for the wife to put in it. They had created the nest and now, as somebody joked, "It needs to be feathered, but where are the birds?"

Once the men got beyond expressing their outer frustrations, Kupferman began trying to draw out their inner fears. "Are you afraid of what may happen next? How prepared do you feel for the next attack?"

"How can you foil someone with a knapsack full of explosives from walking into Times Square or Penn Station?" one officer worried aloud. "Buses blow up every day in Palestine and Israel," said another. "When's it gonna start here?" "We're on heightened alert all the time," said another. "We're almost taking it as the New Normal."

This was the sound of *pre*-trauma stress. Kupferman tried to lighten it up. "Don't worry, you guys are night-shifters. Terrorists work days."

The counselor understood that regaining a sense of control is crucial to healing after trauma. The PAPD men still had no control over how many hours they worked. Their vacations were being suspended for the second year in a row. The Port Authority gave no explanations. The men couldn't tell their families, "Hang tight with me, it'll be over soon." They couldn't promise their wives a summer vacation. They felt overworked, unappreciated, and constantly on hyperalert, while many of their actual working nights were dangerously monotonous. Kupferman worried about the men sitting in a patrol car at the end of a runway at JFK or Newark airport in the middle of the night, when there are no departures. Sitting there with hours to reflect.

"So what's your self-talk?" he probed. "What goes through your mind at those times?"

Rudy Fernandez hovered on the outside of the group, dressed head to toe in black. Rudy was a model police officer. Having graduated from the academy at the head of his class—only a month before September 11—and having piled up a record number of collars in his former employment with the New Jersey Transit Police, Rudy had been given the awesome responsibility of logging in every body part found at Ground Zero on the night shift. Rudy had held himself to the highest standards. He had assured visitors who expressed concern about the unrelieved exposure of the night recovery workers that they were all strong-minded men who would not show the aftereffects of stress and trauma. But that night, sixteen months later, Rudy was brooding.

"I've taken down all my awards and plaques at home," he said. "At my house, now, you wouldn't even know I was a cop." Rudy's thick dark brows dived together, as if shots of pain were going through his brain.

Keegan grew concerned. He knew that Rudy kept his feelings inside. "He's very disciplined, but rigid," Keegan would later comment. "He thinks rigid means strong. He expects himself to be perfect. But the tree that doesn't move in the wind, snaps."

From Kupferman's perspective, the men having the greatest difficulty were those who were single and had very little in the way of a support system. Rudy, for example, was questioning himself about the life choices he had made.

"I've achieved so much," Rudy said soberly. "Or so I thought. Now I look back on my life. And I look at all those lives cut short. Some of the guys we lost never even got married. I look at Donny here, who's just had a baby. Who is really more successful? What's really success in life? To make a record number of collars? Or to be a good father to your children and good husband to your wife?"

Rudy had not been particularly religious before his tour at Ground Zero. "I drew immense strength from my faith," he said. "I happen to believe His divine hand put me down here on September eleventh. And He was with us every day down here," he said. "Just look at the weather. This winter it snows every week. But last winter, while we were on the pile, it didn't snow once." Now, whenever people asked him, "How can you believe in God after what you saw? How did He let that happen?" Rudy said, "I tell them, if God wasn't here that morning, and it happened an hour later, it could have been fifty thousand people who died."

The St. Vincent's counselors had more recently begun seeing the wives and learned that the officers' attempts to make life appear "normal" again were backfiring. It raised the question for the wives: "Well, if it's normal again, why is it still not right? Why can't you come to family gatherings? Or go to Ray's wedding?"

"Homeland security" was not a satisfying answer.

As the night wore on, the men talked about the darker side of their experiences. The replays, the nightmares. "Certain things—like the smell of burning tires—will bring it all right back," said one. "Probably for the rest of my life, when I smell something . . ."

"It's the first thing I think of when I see a red bag," said Keegan. "Even the red plastic bags they use for takeout in a Chinese restaurant."

He was referring to the disposable red bags used in medical settings for hazardous waste. Whenever the men had stumbled upon a cache of body parts, they wanted to grab them right away. But they had to be careful in handling decomposed body parts and wait to get a red bag. A number of the men said their wives reported how they talked about the bags in their sleep:

I need another bag. Here, I'm over here. We need more bags over here. Over here, over here, I need more help!

Kupferman had found the most helpful thing he could do when the officers brought in their wives was to spell out the stark reality for any New York/New Jersey law enforcement officer in the New Normal:

"War has come home. War is on American soil. But now the fighters are not just military people, overseas. They're police and firefighters. And EMS and health care personnel. So, as wives, you need to see yourselves as married to men in battle. And you men, you need to see your wives as feeling lonely and afraid. You both have to be into that war mentality in order to understand what one another might be going through. The blessing is, he comes home every night. So both partners can have back-and-forth communication and be renourished."

The men were of one mind about several things.

Unlike many American men in the last two generations, these men had felt honor. They knew they had never done anything as important and almost certainly never would again. Working every night at Ground Zero from the first week to the last was the best therapy they could have had, to mitigate survivor's guilt. On down days they felt they had failed. But they had *acted.* They had a leader who "let us loose"—gave them an overall plan and let them take control and work together on every recovery. They were men in groups working from the most basic instinct that has served men in groups since the earliest hominids.

And finally, they accepted that now they lived within the world of horror and there was little about it they could control. They knew there were suicide bombers living among them; they had been picked up in Buffalo and Jersey City; maybe they were in Brooklyn, and surely there was a terrorist cell in Manhattan. Bill Barry said, "All we can do is live life to the fullest and make our families the absolute first priority, and hope we're a little better prepared when the next thing happens."

THE FIRST SUICIDE

Nobody saw it coming. Everyone knew Sergeant Tracy Vetter and liked her. The thirty-seven-year-old New Jersey sergeant had worked under Keegan, but now she was assigned to the Port Authority Bus Terminal on Forty-second Street, where she worked with some of the younger guys from Keegan's recovery team. On Saturday morning, March 1, Tracy car-pooled into work with another sergeant, as usual, excused herself to change into her uniform, went to the ladies' room, and shot herself dead.

Sergeant Vetter hadn't even worked at Ground Zero—that was the ominous part.

Keegan's team was shaken. Especially the younger men who, believing they were immortal, had been the most reluctant to show up for their one hour a week to talk with a mental health counselor at St. Vincent's. The lieutenant had heard the same attitude expressed many times: "No big deal, we went through it, we're glad we had a chance to do it, it's over and done, what's the problem?"

Keegan would counter with "I see you were out sick last week, then you took three personal days in a row—that's not a problem?"

"So I just didn't feel like coming back to work."

"You're twenty-four years old, you have seventeen more years to go, and you're already feeling like you don't want to come to work—you don't think that's a problem?"

"We don't have to listen to those neck-ups, they're a pain in the ass."

Keegan would offer another interpretation: "The real reason is, you don't want to be put on the spot because you don't want to talk about it."

The young cops might show up for a couple more weeks, then drop out again: "No big deal."

Keegan would track them down and get in their faces. He knew he was the only person who could look his men in the eyes and speak to what they had experienced in that pit: "So when you found your best friend in pieces and put him in the Stokes basket and laid the flag on top, and you pulled the picture of him out of your pocket and put it on top of the flag, that was no big deal for you? You just happened to be carrying his picture around?"

Why would a Port Authority police officer who hadn't even experienced the work at Ground Zero be driven to suicide? In fact, there was a good deal of empirical evidence that some of the officers who hadn't chosen to work the recovery, or who hadn't been chosen by Keegan's team, were worse off, suffering from guilt and showing signs of depression, marital breakdown, and retreating into isolation. The daytime recovery team had been offered no treatment beyond the two-day stress debriefing mandated by the Port Authority. After Sergeant Vetter's suicide, some of Keegan's message began to get through. He was able to explain his red bag theory:

"We're all carrying around our own red bag of broken emotions from down there. When that bag gets filled up, and you throw in a little relationship problem, or a child problem, or a physical problem, what you would normally be able to handle, you can't. Sergeant Vetter's bag was full. It broke."

Keegan hoped the first suicide might alert his superiors to the need to make the St. Vincent's Trade Center mental health program available to all PAPD officers. He was rebuffed. He and Dr. Eth shared the view that the two-day debriefing the corporation had mandated for those who worked the recovery was next to worthless for the long term. If an officer sought psychiatric assistance officially, through the PAPD, his or her weapon could be taken away. That would strip him of his identity, consign him to a desk job, stigmatize him among his fellow officers, and jeopardize his prospects of promotion. "That policy is a major deterrent for somebody seeking psychiatric assistance," said Dr. Eth, "and it's ineffective, because most of these people have guns at home."

By early spring, the work of the St. Vincent's team with Lieutenant Keegan's men was recognized by the federal government. Funding would be extended through an agency of the Department of Health and Human Services to ensure that all public safety employees could receive mental health support. "They're catching on that this is not some fringe effort," joked Dr. Eth, "we're not all going to join hands and sing 'Kumbaya.' " He was proud that they were starting a program with the NYPD.

The Port Authority remained unresponsive. "The Port Authority has its own way of doing things," Dr. Eth said, sadly resigned. "They don't want to, in essence, acknowledge that their poor response could somehow be implicated in a suicidal tragedy."

Chapter Twenty-nine

———

THE ARC OF RENEWAL

The September widows surprised everyone, and no one more than themselves. Some of those who in the first months had sunk into despair and been barely able to get out of bed had found a toehold of toughness and climbed out of the pits even sooner than some of those who had put up the best fight in the beginning. And some of those who had shown a fighting spirit from the start or who had taken public action, impressing everyone with their apparent energy and élan, had worn themselves out and eventually had to retreat to lick their wounds in private. A year and a half after their traumatic loss, the widows were all in different places along the arc of renewal.

KRISTEN AND THE PERPETUAL BATTLE

Kristen Breitweiser had put off Christmas shopping; she was busy taking on Henry Kissinger. The victims' families were stunned when President Bush appointed the powerful confidant of Richard Nixon to lead the new commission studying the 9/11 attacks. As a wily practitioner of realpolitik with a reputation for operating in secrecy, Kissinger seemed unlikely to push for a no-holds-barred inquiry. Kristen, just past thirty, was too young to know about Dr. Kissinger's role in Vietnam and why, as Nixon's national security adviser, he has been called by some a war criminal for his role in secretly expanding the war into Cambodia. But Kristen jumped onto the Internet to research the clients of Kissinger Associates. She found some suspicious links between his representation of the Unocal oil company and its discussions with the Taliban in the 1990s.

At the time, Unocal and its mysterious Saudi partner, Delta Oil Company, Ltd., were cultivating the leaders of the Taliban to win approval for a thousand-mile pipeline from the Turkmenistan gas fields through Afghanistan to Pakistan. Unocal received assurances from the Taliban that it would support the multibillion-dollar project, which potentially would have rewarded the al Qaeda–supporting government of Afghanistan with $100 million a year. Kissinger was present at the 1995 signing ceremony in New York that sealed Unocal's agreement to build the pipeline. Subsequently, negotiations failed and the project was abandoned.

"I understand a lot of people could be starstruck by who he is," said Kristen. "I'm not. Dr. Kissinger is in charge of a commission that could provide me and thousands of others with answers and closure." She and the other family groups demanded that Kissinger reveal his client list. The diplomat refused and took cover behind President Bush, who gave him an exemption. The families asked for a meeting with Kissinger. The four moms put on their official pantsuits and drove into Manhattan, where they and other family members met with the dour diplomat in the East Side office of Kissinger Associates.

"I think he was surprised by our candor," Kristen said. The widows presented him with a list of questions and immediately went after the conflict-of-interest issue. Lorie van Auken asked if any of Kissinger's clients had ties to Saudi Arabia or Afghanistan or any other Middle Eastern oil state. Kissinger said no. Lorie followed up: "And we would certainly hope that you have no ties to the bin Laden family."

Kissinger remained implacable. He repeated that he had no Saudi conflicts and no Middle Eastern conflicts, but that he would not release the names of his clients. The four moms left the office unsatisfied and the media, hungry for more Kissinger controversy, pumped them for news of the meeting's outcome. That same day, the senior Republican on the Senate Ethics Committee told the White House that all members of the commission were required to comply with the same disclosure requirements. Within twenty-four hours, Dr. Kissinger resigned.

While the fate of the commission hung in limbo until after the Christmas congressional recess, Kristen was thrown back on her inner resources. They failed her. Kristen had spent the past fifteen months living September 11 virtually 24/7. It had become an obsession, a useful obsession in many ways but also one that diverted her from the work of rebuilding the inner security she needed to move ahead in the rest of her life. She harbored more fears than most of the other widows or widowers and seemed always to be suffering from a cold or flu or an intestinal bug, suggesting that the unrelieved stress was compromising the immune system of this formerly sturdy surfer girl.

Kristen, the fighter, was fine so long as she was in battle mode and had her troops around her. The four moms had a passionate cause that contained their anger. They offered one another a solid "family," along with practical help in sharing child care and a built-in social life. "Before we make any big decision, or even small ones, we run it past each other," said Kristen. *Should I buy the boots? Should I hold Caroline back a year in school?* "We're on the phone together all day long. I don't do anything without checking in with them. If we don't hear from one of us for a few hours, the rest of us are, like, 'Oh my God, is everything okay?' "

When the momentum of public battle died down, the private trauma, which Kristen had never dealt with, reemerged and often overwhelmed her. This is the downside of putting all of one's energies into externals, no matter how worthy.

Kristen had intended not to allow herself to slide into depression for the second Christmas. She had been on antibiotics for two weeks before the holidays. "I'm thinking Sun Valley or Florida," she said, girding herself to attempt her first plane flight since 9/11. She had researched the safest airport in the East. Her plan was to drive to Atlantic City. "The FAA center is there, so it's safe," she assured herself. "I'm flying south and taking Caroline. It's going to be marvelous."

But the day before her trip, she began having panic attacks. She paced around her living room all day and night, chain-smoking Marlboro Lights, with the portable phone tucked into her shoulder, talking in relays to Mindy-Lorie-Patty, or calling congressional staffers or reporters. She might not even put down the phone—her lifeline—to answer the door for the FAVOR volunteer or a neighbor. The next morning she canceled her trip.

She spent Christmas and the three weeks after holed up like a hermit. Newspapers piled up in her driveway. A visitor had trouble finding the way to her door after dark. The electricity had gone off, but Kristen didn't care. Inside she said, "It's depressing, but Caroline and I are getting some quality time. The most pressing item on my agenda is making dinner."

Kristen had cut her hair but it didn't make her feel any different. She admitted that she was more fidgety than ever. She couldn't drive over a bridge or through a tunnel without shaking. "You don't feel you can move around freely anymore," she said. These fears were severely restricting her life. But more serious were the inhibitory meanings that Kristen had attached to the trauma.

"I feel like I'm sixty years old," she confessed. As a beautiful young woman on display in public life, she had attracted male admirers, but she had abrasively dismissed them. "I'm not open to bringing new love into my life," she said. "I never wanted to be married, but when I got married, I was really, really happy. And it got taken away from me. I would never want to go through that hurt and pain again." Her tone of voice became more shrill. "There is not a shot in hell that I would ever bring a child into this world. That would be the most reckless, irresponsible thing to do." And finally, in her darkest moods, Kristen would express disaffection for America and talk about possibly moving to Europe. "I do not like what's going on here. I feel like many Americans are asleep at the wheel."

Kristen resolved to see somebody about her panic attacks. She was also distressed that her now-four-year-old daughter was still not speaking quite intelligibly. She said she intended to take her daughter into New York for tests. Before long, however, Kristen's fear shifted instead back to herself and her breast. When she did go into the city to see a doctor, it was for a needle biopsy to alleviate the same fear she had harbored just before September 11. The growth in her breast turned out to be benign.

IT'S NEVER OVER

I do not ever, ever, ever think of the future," Pat Wotton declared, a month into the year 2003. "It's an automatic reaction." But no sooner had she sworn her resistance to letting go of the past than Pat found herself remarking on her own progress. She realized it was exactly a year ago that Detective Capriotti had come to her door with the news that Rod's remains had been found.

"That was one of the bleakest times," she said. "But it's never really over." More recently, the kitchen phone rang one night while she was making dinner for Dorothea and the baby Rodney. The caller ID showed it was from NYME. Pat knew what that meant. A call from the New York Medical Examiner's office.

"Oh my God, you found more of my husband."

The clerk was sensitive. She asked Pat how much she wanted to know. Pat said she didn't want to know exactly what they had found, or when or where. The clerk explained that each body part was assigned a different number, adding, "If I give you all the numbers, you might be real distressed." That was the first time Pat understood the meaning of the word "dismemberment." But she put down the phone, and for the children's sake, she pretended that everything was all right. After dinner she called her brother-in-law and he stopped by so they could commiserate after the children were asleep. "Every time something comes up, I take a step backwards," Pat said. "But my recovery is much quicker." She then proceeded to tell a series of stories that demonstrated considerable progress.

Rather than dutifully go to church on Christmas morning, where she found it depressing to see families all together, she asked the senior parish priest if he would say a private mass for some of the families of 9/11 at one of their homes on Christmas Eve. He refused, saying he had hoped to integrate the widows back into the church family. Although Pat was hurt by being turned down, she didn't give up. She found a retired priest who agreed to give a sermon in their own environment.

It was nothing like the previous year, when Pat had refused Christmas. She hadn't had a tree. She had spent the whole day in a fog. But this year the Christmas Eve service, held in Elaine Chevalier's home on the top of Holly Hill with a view that stretched to the ocean, was intimate. "It was meaningful," said Pat, "it was beautiful." Fifty people gathered for the sermon and lingered afterward to share pasta and wine. It was one of a number of new rituals that Pat was creating.

The biggest decision she had made on her own since 9/11 was to build an addition onto her house. It was Pat's way of setting up her new life structure. She had always been the baby of the family, and since she had not yet been able to find a sense of safety within herself, she felt entitled to return to that role. She was moving her parents in to take care of her and her children and provide a sense of safety.

"I'm sorry it's necessary," she said about prevailing on her parents. "They've been living up here for the last year and a half out of suitcases. Now they've basically given up their lives for me. They hate seeing me sad and alone and struggling."

Between bereaved children like Pat and their parents, the shock of loss often creates a codependency. In Pat's case, her father felt obligated to fill the protective role of her husband. There was good reason. When Pat had become too upset to continue speaking to her trapped husband in the tower, Rod had asked to speak to her father. In the last moments of his life, Rod had said, "Please take care of Pat for me." The father had translated that as his new mission in life.

Pat was fortunate in having found a psychotherapist she could trust. Carol Veizer had been in practice for twenty-five years and was director of the New Jersey Center for the Healing Arts, a nonprofit mental health center in Red Bank. "Counseling as we knew it ended on September eleventh," said the therapist. Among her clients, her staff, and all their family members, twenty-eight people had been directly affected. "We have a community of people who are going to be dealing with time-lapsed recovery. I don't think we have even begun to see the real impact." Although she had studied crisis intervention, Veizer knew there was no paradigm for treating adults or children impacted by 9/11. "The idea in working with victims of crisis is to get them to the past tense, to a place where they can say, 'It's over. It's behind me. Now I can look ahead.' " Carol Veizer fully grasped the fact that for the bereaved of America's worst terrorist event, it will never be over.

Some days Pat would have a session with Carol where she described ways in which she was healing and growing. Then, all at once, she would look at the therapist with her big, sad eyes and begin to weep. "I just want him to come back," she would sob. "Can't you help me bring him back?"

The wise therapist would sit and say nothing. Carol later explained, "There are some things you can't fix. People in deep grief just want to feel that we have really heard their pain. If we try to help or fix it, we rob them of that passage. To have someone you can trust, cry with, confess to, someone who you don't have to feel responsible for, that's the gift we can give."

There is a surreal quality to grieving when there is no body. Carol learned from treating Pat Wotton and other bereaved families in the Middletown area that the absence of a body and a place to grieve allowed them to hold on to the fantasy that their loved one was still not gone forever. "At the point where Pat accepts that her husband isn't coming back to rescue her, she will see that she has to rescue herself and her children," her therapist said. "Then Pat will have to answer their questions about their father and deal with their feelings about what happened to him."

Already, though, it was easy to see that Pat had made tremendous progress. She had found it difficult to be close to her children because it brought up the reality of their murdered father. "But Pat now has a wonderful bond with Dorothea," Carol observed. "Dorothea is trusting and delightful, and gentle with her baby brother." Pat was dressing up more and her recent therapy sessions focused not only on her grief and the events of 9/11. She was no longer a shell. Able now to recall who she was before the tragedy—a very insecure person—Pat was beginning to appreciate the hard-won confidence and competencies she was gaining.

Pat could speak with some insight into her own resistance to moving on. "I still can't allow myself to have a good time. I think it's part of the denial—if I keep depriving myself, maybe he'll still come home." The therapist reminded her, "You can have laughter and pleasure and it doesn't mean you're abandoning Rod."

In February, Pat Wotton's support group asked if she wanted to go with them on a trip to a Caribbean island in May. "Would we have to fly?" Pat asked apprehensively. Of course, that was the point. Pat said she'd think it over. From the first night she began having little panics about flying. She called her therapist. "Don't worry," Carol Veizer assured her. "We can use hypnotherapy to help you get control over those fears."

Pat paid a deposit for the trip. She continued to struggle with her fear of flying without her husband. But she was ready to make plans again.

MOVING ON: MARY MURPHY

Mary Murphy had moved on to grieving for "my boys." These were the men of the mortgage group at Cantor with whom she had worked for ten years, men exploding with young life, men for whom she had been the den mother and who had loved her as a sister, as many as forty-five of them. Such a powerful secondary loss was this, Mary had not allowed herself to think about them until the second Christmas. Suddenly, days before the holiday, she had the urge to go to Ireland. The men had been mostly Irish, and they used to travel together to the famous golf course Lahinch, in County Clare.

"I wanted to be in their atmosphere," she said, and so she flew to Ireland and went to the pubs her boys had frequented and walked the course where they had played, and she said good-bye to them.

Returning home a few days later, she made a new resolution. "I've got to move on. I don't want to stay sad forever." She went out with her friends to a singles bar in New York, just to dip her toe in. "I am a single person. Disgusting as that seems to me, that's who I am now," she said. For the first time, she didn't drive home with the hood of sadness that used to come over her. A girlfriend put a blunt point on the message of the evening's attentions to Mary: "You tell a man that you're a widow with three kids, and he still wants to go out with you, you are already weeding out the scum."

Mary laughed. But now her whole face was animated, and her eyes and her voice, too. She said, "I know now that I will not have to spend the rest of my life alone, if I choose not to."

MOVING ON: GINNY AND SHERRY

In April, Ginny Bauer was named head of the New Jersey State Lottery by Governor Jim McGreevey. It was a high-prestige post with a salary of $103,000 a year—just where she had left off at Merrill Lynch decades before!—and Ginny was thrilled. She would be supervising an experienced staff of 150 and directing the fourth-largest revenue source for the state.

"New Jersey has done so much for me and the other families," Ginny said. "I'm so happy to work for the state and give a little something back."

The state treasurer, John McCormac, extolled Ginny's grace under pressure. "She is a person who, at a time of extreme personal anguish and grief, advocated fiercely for the rights and welfare of other widows and families devastated by the 9/11 tragedy."

SHERRY MCHEFFEY SAILED THROUGH her divorce settlement in a day. "On April tenth, over and done with," she said, laughing as she recalled how positive she had been two years before that she would never survive the abandonment by her husband. Sherry had split the award from the Victim Compensation Fund with her ex-husband. By investing her portion, she will be able to live off the interest it generates and salt away her secretarial salary as savings. Her lawyer assuaged her guilt over receiving money for the death of her son, saying, "Keith would have found a way to take care of you anyway." So all Sherry needed from her divorce settlement was for the mortgage on her house to be paid off.

"In a strange way," she reflected, "September eleventh made it possible for me to waive alimony. The last thing I wanted to have to do was chase down an ex-husband for money. I just want to be free to up and go as I please—it feels good!"

MOVING UP: THE PLANERS

In May 2003, Bob Planer was named to the board of his company. It was a surprise. Keefe, Bruyette and Woods were rewarding him and four other department heads for their efforts in getting the company back on its feet.

"Long overdue," was Paula Planer's comment. But Bob was truly excited. "Most important, I'll have more input in what's going on in the company I care about," he said. The recent scandals in investment banking houses had improved KBW's competitive position. "All the big brokerage houses have had conflicts with their research side, so their research efforts are disintegrating, while ours are getting better every day," Bob said. "We don't have a big investment banking arm, so we weren't tarnished in the slightest by the scandals. We still have a long way to go, but the outlook and opportunities are as great as they've ever been."

He sounded like a man fully back on his game.

Another central issue that must be addressed by a trauma survivor is: What meaning will he or she attach to the story? Paula had supplied an inspirational meaning for herself and her husband: God had spared Bob for a reason; he was meant to do greater things. Bob, too, believed he had to find a way to give back before a third strike took him down. "My goal now is to fully rebuild the company, but I haven't given up the dream of doing charitable work and spending time in a house in Ireland," Bob declared. "September eleventh may have delayed that dream, but it's still out there."

Some people hang on to the trauma wound, reluctant to give up the dubious benefits of the victim role, and thus are unable to move forward. The Planers were beginning to see the much greater benefits of being survivors. "We've come through it pretty well, better than I would have thought," Bob mused in his typically low-key way. "We didn't resort to drinking or drugs. Our children are thriving. We got through it with faith, family, and belief in each other."

DANCING AGAIN: ANNA EGAN

Anna Egan wore bikinis on holiday in Puerto Rico. She had toned up for the trip by consciously eating well and power-walking through the snow over the Connecticut hills. The prespring trip was the first extended pleasure she had given herself since losing her husband. She had been dragging through the icy winter with a lingering flu. In San Juan, it disappeared overnight.

The cure might have been the night she and her son Matthew were sitting at the hotel bar when an encounter made her feel like a woman again. The man on the next stool noticed the boy's curiosity about his tall drink with the umbrella on top. He was a pilot for American Airlines. Anna asked him how he felt about flying since September 11. They fell into easy conversation. First names only.

He asked Anna if she would like to dance. Who knew if he was married? He said no, but pilots are always married. She teased him, "I could ruin your reputation." Matthew loved watching his pretty mother gliding around the dance floor in her long black dress. Anna beckoned to the boy and he joined them on the dance floor. Then Anna danced with Matthew. At eleven o'clock, the boy independently went back to the room. Mom had an hour on her own.

Mmmm, she thought, *I like this. The sparks are coming back. That part of me hasn't died!*

They talked about dating at their age. The pilot told Anna, "You have so much going for you. Just don't let any man take advantage of you." He was a perfect gentleman. "I had a ball, met such interesting people, and I met a wonderful man who made me feel so good about myself as a woman," she trilled to old friends when she returned. "It made me feel whole again."

Anna was already planning to return to Puerto Rico over spring vacation with both of her sons. "I want to throw my eternity ring into the water over there," she had decided. "When Michael gave it to me, it was a promise we'd grow old together. A wonderful promise, but it will never be. It's the beginning of a new life. I need to say good-bye and not forget him. I just want more. Yes, I want to go dancing again!"

She went up to the attic of her new house. "I need to do things differently," she told herself. She moved Michael's clothes out of the closet in her attic and down to the basement along with his old files. Back in her office, her dreaming room, she took out her wedding gown and slipped it on once more. She put on the old Elton John record. And she danced as she had danced on their wedding day.

"It felt good—no crying this time—just nice memories. I looked at Michael's picture and said, 'Thank you, darling, for all the good years.' Then I took off the gown and sealed it up in a vacuum bag and put it in the trunk of mementos for my son Jon."

Chapter Thirty

FOUR MOMS FIGHT FOR
HOMELAND SECURITY

Winter would not give up its grip on the East Coast. The ferries from downtown Manhattan to Middletown crossed the choppy bay toward the headlands of a Jersey coast swallowed in fog. Once docked, homebound commuters were greeted with a deathly serenity. As far as one could see all was white and gray. Rivers scabbed with ice. Every so often, a pool of melt attracted birds who perched on the lip of the ice to drink. The only color in the whole scape was the red, white, and blue of flags, waving bravely from shore.

The clouds of preemptive war were gathering. A virus of fear began spreading across the land. Generations that had grown up on the illusion that American life is risk-free and nothing bad is supposed to happen were suddenly taking their turn on the world stage to live with chronic uncertainty, primed by the incessant pump of TV news to fear what *could* happen, and aware of their own helplessness to prevent it.

The families of Middletown whose lives were shattered on September 11 were in a different place. Some paid little attention to reports of the American troop buildup in the Middle East and the incessant war talk in the media. They tuned out warnings by the FBI director that the American war on Iraq would certainly set off new waves of terrorism on our shores. These families had already known war on their shores. The worst had already happened, and somehow most were finding the resilience of spirit to survive.

MAKING THE SYSTEM WORK

*A*re you up for the next battle?"

Kristen polled her cohorts. President Bush had named a new person to serve as chairman of the national commission to investigate the attacks of September 11. The four moms from New Jersey regrouped and googled Tom Kean, a popular former governor of New Jersey who was now president of Drew University. They couldn't find anything negative about the commission's new leader. On the contrary, Kean had a reputation for integrity, fairness, and open-mindedness. They asked for a meeting with him and found the former governor very receptive. He started out by telling them that friends had suggested he look into the stock trades on the Chicago exchange on September 11. He asked the widows, "Do you know anything about that?"

This excited the four moms. They knew a great deal about that, but nobody had paid attention. On the Chicago Board Options Exchange during the week before September 11, an all-time-record number of put options had been purchased on American and United Airlines—the two selected for hijacking by the terrorists. The investors who placed the put orders were gambling that in the short term the stock prices of both airlines would plummet. Never before on the Chicago board had such large numbers of options been traded in the two airlines. The investors scored a profit of at least $5 million after the attacks. But the names of the investors had never been disclosed, and the $5 million remained unclaimed in the Chicago board account.

"To me, that one piece is key to unraveling this whole mystery," Patty interjected. "With any crime, if you follow who profits from it, you usually find out who perpetrated it. Those trades were criminal. People in the know profited from an attack on the United States."

Kristen connected more dots: Given all the warnings to top officials about al Qaeda's interest in using aircraft as weapons, and given the sophisticated software programs used in real time by the Securities and Exchange Commission in concert with U.S. intelligence agencies to spot trends that might indicate a present or future crime, how could these aberrant trades have gone unnoticed? Who had placed the orders? Why weren't they in jail?

The four moms continued to walk Tom Kean through a forest of other questions. He appeared intrigued and genuinely concerned, a blank slate, and that was good. "The information we gave him was completely, one hundred percent appreciated," said Kristen. "We're ready to give the system another chance."

On January 28, the night of President Bush's State of the Union address, Kristen had a surprise call from the White House telling her to be available at 7:30 P.M. She called back to ask if the rest of the "girls" could be included in the conference call. Yes. Jay Lefkowitz, Bush's domestic policy adviser, called back to notify them that the president was creating a new program to integrate all information about terrorist threats, and he wanted Kristen and the families to be first to know about this historic effort before the president announced it on TV. That sounded good, the women said, but they would really like to have a meeting with the president. They had asked many times before, and always they were put off. Lorie noted that Mrs. Bush had gone to Afghanistan to meet with their women after the war there, but neither Bush had shown the same interest in meeting with wives and mothers of America's terrorism victims. They asked Lefkowitz bluntly, "Do we have your word that the White House will cooperate to facilitate the independent commission?" He said yes.

Kristen and Mindy-Lorie-Patty listened attentively to the president's address. They heard him declare, "Tonight, I am instructing the leaders of the FBI, the CIA, the Homeland Security and the Department of Defense to develop a Terrorist Threat Integration Center, to merge and analyze all threat information in a single location." This promise occupied all of one sentence. What really caught their attention was the dozen times the president referred to September 11 and the way he wrapped it around his vilification of Iraq. He changed the subject from protecting the homeland to a demand that Iraq disarm, or else. Their distilled reaction was: "If he's using nine-eleven as a pretext to go to war with Iraq, and putting innocent American lives on the line, then why didn't he use nine-eleven as a pretext to fix homeland security?" Kristen believed that going to war with Iraq would only increase the threat of terrorism at home.

Several weeks after the State of the Union, when the four moms had a private "meet and greet" in Washington with the members and staff of the independent commission, they asked how they could help. "Get us more money and more press," they were told, "so we can do our job right." The Bush administration was starving the independent commission with a $3 million budget. Patty Casazza summed up the moms' reaction: "We're talking about Washington people who have made it their life to know how to operate in that system, and they're calling on four stay-at-home moms to help them get funding and do their job? It's a joke."

Kristen turned the joke around. Before starting a new round of lobbying trips to Capitol Hill, she asked the commission's vice-chair, former Democratic Congressman Lee Hamilton, and staff director, Philip Zelikow, how much money they needed. When they told her "Eleven million more," Kristen cracked, "Well, President Bush referred to 9/11 twelve times in his address. Let's charge him a million for each time he used it, to fully fund the commission."

HOMELAND SECURITY WAS no joke in Middletown. At a January neighborhood meeting in the Oak Hill section of town, Chief John Pollinger was peppered with questions: "When will smallpox vaccine be available here? Where would we go to get vaccinated? How well are we prepared in case of a bioterror attack?"

"I didn't have any answers," the police chief admitted. "The jitters are coming back."

Pollinger was making a mental effort to confront the New Normal. Later in January, at a meeting of the police chiefs of Monmouth County, he stood up and asked: "Does any police chief in this room know the procedure to use, once the first call has been made reporting smallpox?" No hands went up. Pollinger then dumped some of the worries that were weighing him down: "Imagine people rushing traffic lights, thousands of vehicles jumping meridians, nobody knowing where to go. Where are the vaccination sites? Who's going to manage the crowd? Who does traffic control? If you don't have a vaccination for every single person who shows up, then what? Can you imagine a father being told, we have one for you but not for your kids?"

After hearing the president's address, Pollinger had no doubt that we would be at war with Iraq within a month. But this law enforcement officer, whose wall is covered with pictures of his Republican heroes—Ronald Reagan, George Herbert Walker Bush, Rudy Giuliani—had doubts about the direction in which the younger Bush was taking the country. "You could count me in the sixty-three percent of Americans who are not convinced we should attack Iraq," he admitted. "Show me the proof. We don't attack first. I recognize we have to change that mind-set, but sometimes the president's saber rattling seems to be too personal. His arguments are convoluted and unfocused. They've lost me." The chief saw the administration's attempts to tie Saddam to 9/11 as artificial. "But now we're on a train we can't get off." He was getting more and more jumpy about the lack of preparedness on the home front. "I am convinced there are sleeper cells in New York City." He pointed over his shoulder. "That's only eighteen to twenty miles north of here."

The torturous weeks of waiting for the shoe to drop and the war on Iraq to begin delayed work by the commission. The moms wondered if it was deliberate. TV generals and ex-security officials warned that America's "preventive" bombing and occupation of a Muslim country would serve to feed the recruitment campaign by Osama and unleash greater terrorism. These warnings were dismissed by the coordinated message from the White House that the greater threat was Saddam's arsenal of weapons of mass destruction and ties to al Qaeda, both of which they were certain of uncovering. The moms didn't buy the argument. When the "shock and awe" campaign began raining needlepoint missiles on Iraq, the four moms felt no safer. Like many Americans, they saw the president's obsession with external threats of mass destruction as a distraction from the threat at home, that of terrorists within.

But once the four moms got a letter to the editor of *The New York Times* published, gears moved, and the commission was fully funded. Kristen, Mindy, Lorie, and Patty resolved to work hand in glove with the truth-seekers on the 9/11 commission. But by the time its members got their security clearances and scheduled the first public hearing, for March 31, 2003, the commission had already lost three months of its two-year life.

What's more, we were at war.

A PUBLIC HEARING

On the morning of the first public hearing, the four moms watched in dismay as the scant number of audience seats filled up. Families had been warned that they had to get in line outside by 7 A.M. or forget about getting a seat, although the hearing began at nine. It seemed the hearing had been set up to discourage attendees. It was being held at the United States Custom House in downtown Manhattan, close to the pit where the Twin Towers once stood.

The first testimony was by a Port Authority police officer who recounted in a quivering voice what it was like to dodge one body after another as they dropped from the sky while he was trying to drag to shelter the remains of the first leaper from the Towers. The memory of fire feeding on flesh was rekindled for Patty Casazza when she heard an army lieutenant colonel describe how he escaped from the Pentagon with burns on 60 percent of his body and how doctors had to use maggots to eat the desiccated tissue off his arms.

"This time I was not participating, just listening, and the whole horror swept over me again," Patty said later. "It retraumatized me. The stories." Patty sat beside Lorie, the two women's faces twin masks of tragedy.

Kristen arrived just in time to hear Mayor Michael Bloomberg make a businesslike pitch for more money to defray the costs of his city's massive security operations. He ridiculed the politically inspired formula that assumes many cities are deserving of funds equal to those granted New York, a formula, he charged, that "defies logic and makes a mockery of the country's counterterrorism efforts. New York City has been targeted four times by terrorists," he reminded the commissioners, yet "New York is estimated to get $11 million of the $566 million from the last Homeland Security distribution." Finally, he referred to the "alleged long-term health damage" from the attacks on New York. The mayor did not express concern for long-term damage to the health of the recovery workers or mental health of the survivors or families. His only expressed concern was that "personal injury claims . . . could bankrupt our city." He wanted a federal indemnification plan to protect the city against "the inevitable lawsuits" when it responded to terrorist attacks.

Patty, Lorie, and Kristen huddled together, feeling as though the families were being attacked as litigious. Mindy Kleinberg had been designated to speak for the four moms, now more formally known as the September 11 Advocates. She was severely dressed in black, although wearing her trademark high-heeled wedgies. After describing how she and the youngest of her three children had been skipping home on September 11, oblivious to what was happening in New York City, she questioned how her government and its agencies could have been equally oblivious. She attacked the theory of luck.

"It has been said that the intelligence agencies have to be right one hundred percent of the time and the terrorists only have to get lucky once," she testified. "This explanation for the devastating attacks of September eleventh, simple on its face, is wrong in its value. Because the nine-eleven terrorists were not just lucky once; they were lucky over and over again. With regard to the INS, the terrorists got lucky fifteen individual times, because fifteen of the nineteen hijackers' visas should have been unquestionably denied." Mindy pointed out that most of the hijackers were young, unmarried, and unemployed males—classic overstay candidates. She held up the applications of the terrorists who killed her husband. "All of these forms are incomplete and incorrect," she said. Some of the terrorists listed their destination in the United States as simply "hotel" or "California" or "New York." One even listed his destination as "no."

"How many more lucky terrorists gained unfettered access to this country?" Mindy asked rhetorically. "With no one being held accountable, how do we know this still isn't happening?"

The terrorists' luck continued at the various airports, she narrated. Even though nine of the nineteen were singled out for questioning at ticket counters when they purchased their tickets, they all passed the screening process and slipped through shoddy airport security. "How else would the hijackers get specifically contraband items such as box cutters, pepper spray, or, according to one FAA executive summary, a gun on those planes?" She wound up her lengthy testimony with a summary of her questions: "Is it luck that aberrant stock trades were not monitored? Is it luck when emergency FAA and NORAD protocols are not followed? Is it luck when a national emergency is not reported to top government officials on a timely basis? To me luck is something that happens once."

Mindy looked up and into the faces of ten of the country's appointed guardians. "Commissioners, I implore you to answer our questions. You are the generals in the terrorism fight on our shores. . . . If at some point we don't look to hold the individuals accountable for not doing their jobs properly, then how can we expect the terrorists won't get lucky again?"

At the end of the long day's hearing, Jamie Gorelick, former deputy attorney general of the United States and the only woman on the commission, praised the family members. "I'm enormously impressed that laypeople with no powers of subpoena, with no access to insider information of any sort, could put together a very powerful set of questions and set of facts that are a road map for this commission. It is really quite striking. Now, what's your secret?" Mindy replied soberly, "Eighteen months of doing nothing but grieving and reading articles and connecting the dots."

Former Democratic congressman Tim Roemer, a key author of the legislation that created the commission, added his praise: "You came to every single public hearing that we had on the Joint Inquiry. . . . That had a huge impact on that committee of senators and congressmen. This commission would not have happened if it had not been for you. At a time when many Americans don't even take the opportunity to cast a ballot, you folks went out and made the legislative system work."

WHO'S ACCOUNTABLE?

Such encomiums did little to dispel the uneasy feeling among many of the families that the hard questions raised by their testimonies would be diluted by political considerations. Throughout March and April the moms continued to travel to Washington to meet with the staff of the commission;

Kristen in her husband's sport jacket, Patty in her pedal pushers, Mindy in her orange wedgies, and Lorie in her mules. The staff welcomed their input, but the moms were impatient.

"They want to have this nicey-nice relationship with the White House," observed Patty. "After eighteen months of fighting for this commission, we understand that you don't want to jeopardize relationships, but it's not realistic. You have a White House that doesn't want to cooperate."

This became blatantly obvious when the White House tried to exert executive privilege to deny the commissioners access to transcripts from the closed hearings before the congressional joint inquiry—hearings on the failures of 9/11 that had been held before two of the commissioners. "It's clear the White House doesn't want the information to come out," said Kristen. Soon enough, the moms would have startling proof of the lack of accountability that still left the country vulnerable to "lucky" future terrorists. The CIA had withheld from the congressional inquiry a document under subpoena that would have revealed one of the most glaring intelligence lapses. Two suspected al Qaeda terrorists who wound up as 9/11 hijackers had obtained visas and flown, unnoticed, into Los Angeles in January 2000, a month after the CIA's own Osama bin Laden unit had issued a directive that all suspected terrorists be placed on a federal watch list. One of the terrorists attended flight school and lived, undetected, in an apartment building under the nose of an informant for the FBI. The CIA never notified the FBI to be on the lookout for these suspects.

The families were infuriated to learn that the two top leaders of the CIA's al Qaeda tracking unit had not only escaped being sacked, they had been promoted. And the CIA chief, George Tenet, presumably hiding behind White House protection, had refused to hold anyone at the agency personally accountable. His rationale: "We're in the middle of a war."

Mindy's testimony reverberated: "With no one being held accountable, how do we know this is not still happening?"

But once the war was over, the reservations held by the four moms seemed mild in comparison with assessments of the aftermath by intelligence experts and a growing Greek chorus of lawmakers. Eight weeks after the commencement of military operations in Iraq, Congress was inundated with reports of widespread violence, wholesale looting, economic collapse, power failures, and political chaos. Senior counterterrorism officials reported a spike in recruitment by al Qaeda and an increase in radical fundamentalism all over the world. Moreover, people in many parts of the Arab world who used to love America, including intellectuals who had preached

moderation in the face of rising Islamic radicalism, now spoke of feeling be-
trayed. The war on Iraq was widely interpreted as an attack on all Arabs,
meant to serve the interests of Israel. Others described it as the product of a
"narrow-minded" or even "pathological" American president who "believes
he was chosen by the Almighty to fulfill a Christian mission."

In May, after the terrorist bombings in Saudi Arabia and Morocco, the
first Democratic presidential candidate stepped up to make a charge that the
four moms applauded. Senator Bob Graham said that the Iraq war had done
nothing to make America safer. He charged that al Qaeda had been "on the
ropes" a year before, but had been able to recover because the administration
had diverted military and intelligence resources to Iraq. Senator Graham
claimed that a classified congressional report revealed that "the lessons of
September eleventh are not being applied today." He accused the administration of a cover-up.

"It's nice to see that the Democrats are finally adopting our mantra of the
last year and a half," said Kristen, the formerly unblinking Republican. "I
can't believe Bush has moved up his convention to September 2004 so he
can wrap himself in the anniversary of nine-eleven. How can he use it as a
platform when he hasn't even discussed matters with the families who have
been so affected?"

At the eighteen-month mark—which some experts had predicted would
precipitate delayed stress reactions—the four moms were too busy working
hand in glove with the commission's staff to notice. The first hardball hearing where officials would be questioned was coming up on the eve of Memorial Day weekend. Of the mission of their public life, Kristen was "hopeful."
While driving to a New York hospital to sit vigil with her grandmother while
she underwent heart surgery, Kristen, on her cell phone, brought her private
life up to date. Her ulcerative colitis was back. Bruce Springsteen's drummer
had gotten a variance to build in the nature preserve that was her backyard.
She was terrified she might lose her grandmother, one of the few remaining
members of her family who was still alive and living nearby.

"The only good thing is Caroline," she said. "Her speech is much better
and she's peeing on the potty! She's my little ray of sunshine." Kristen
laughed. "You can quote me on this—everything else is shit."

Chapter Thirty-one

WAKING UP FROM
THE SUBURBAN DREAM

Cruelest is the second anniversary. Two years after a traumatic event is tantamount to the day after surgery. The shock is past, the painkillers have worn off, the visitors have begun to thin out. Everyone begins to focus on recovery. Impatience with the unrelenting sorrow gives birth to the bromides by which the feel-good purveyors successfully commercialize consolation: "Get over it." "It's time to move on." "Put it behind us."

"These clichés do horrible damage," pronounced Oklahoma County's senior assistant district attorney, Richard Wintory, with the vehemence of a final verdict. He knew this from working closely with the families of victims from the Oklahoma City terrorist bombing. "What I saw happen as we passed the second anniversary, the community as a whole—families, friends, even spouses—lose patience. Folks around the survivors don't feel they have to cut them slack anymore. People don't have a template to understand the experience of traumatic grieving that the survivors are going through, so they look to Hollywood or Dr. Phil for their solace, and adopt the American credo of 'Move on.' And this includes the victims themselves. 'Why can't I get past this? Bill or Dave or Sue would want me to move forward.' It accelerates for some a real downward spiral. And this gets a lot worse in the third year. It can become a double-dip depression."

NOSTALGIA FOR CONNECTEDNESS

A curious discomfort with mundane living combined with a heightened fear of dying had crept into the conversation of congregants in the churches and synagogues of the Middletown area. A woman in Rabbi

Levin's temple came up after one Shabbat service and said, "Rabbi, I've been reading about people increasingly worried about the fragility of their own lives."

"That's the point," the rabbi replied. "Are we just feeling more *personally* vulnerable? If we slip back into the status quo ante–nine-eleven, we will only compound the tragedy. Nine-eleven was a wake-up call."

Levin firmly believed that the fall of the Towers had opened doors for a brief period of time. "Some of us did walk through those doors, and some have brought our congregants with us. We can't backslide into the isolation that was." He was troubled by seeing the new sensitivity awakened by the shock of 9/11 replaced by numbness. "Once that happens, the sensitivity is lost, unless"—he sat forward, his eyes blazing with the same passion conveyed by his deep voice—"unless those of us who have been changed by this event move to establish a new platform for a minimal level of connectedness."

Levin wasn't the only cleric in the area to communicate a strong nostalgia for the better angels of congregants' natures that were called out during the heroic phase after September 11. Reverend John Monroe, pastor of the First Presbyterian Church of Rumson, remembered how in the first weeks after the tragedy, every house of worship was packed. "The closeness we felt was the one light in this. For a while we were a community with each other. We would hug and cry and talk about significant things even with people you'd see on the street. And I saw people's lives take turns they might not have taken."

The pastor recalled standing beside the rabbi a few days after 9/11 at a spontaneous candlelight vigil in Fair Haven Fields. Suddenly, the words "blessed are the poor in spirit" had new meaning for Monroe. "The sense of us, in our brokenness, hundreds of people with candles lit, coming together in that field and sharing the fear, the anger, the pain, the uncertainty—those were deep moments. Now, it wasn't happy! But it was wonderful. I remember saying, 'Let's not lose this!' "

That night the rabbi and the reverend became just Harry and John, two men who recognized one another as wanting to do "soul work." Over the following year they had developed a partnership. "On Christmas Eve the rabbi sent some of his folks over to our church nursery to watch our babies so parents could attend the service, and we did the same for his parents on Rosh Hashanah." Similarly, Rabbi Levin had gotten together with Father Jerome Nolan, the Catholic priest whose church was across the street, to exchange teaching one another's children's Bible study classes. "That's a huge step forward," said Levin.

"I do sense, even in this affluent suburb, a deep spiritual hunger," reflected Parson Monroe. "All of us, even if we weren't broken by September eleventh, we're broken by our family hurts or job hurts—unemployment in this area is high now—or we're broken by aging and the loss of independence," he said, his long, pointed nose twitching as it does when his emotions well up. "But we have such a hard time letting down our guard and inviting people into the reality of what we're going through."

SCANT THOUGH THE CONNECTIONS were among Middletowners that had outlasted the heroic phase, one brand-new outreach effort did succeed. Bob Honecker, the senior assistant county prosecutor, was determined to connect with the Muslims of Middletown before the war began on Iraq. He wanted them to know that any retaliation against Muslims would be met with swift action. The first scheduled meeting was scrubbed due to a snowstorm. But two days after American bombs began pounding Saddam's palaces, Honecker turned up on a Sunday night at the Middletown mosque with a retinue of law enforcement officials from the federal, state, county, and local level.

Over a hundred people gathered for prayers in the new *masjid*. Honecker himself had never before been inside a mosque. He watched, fascinated, as the worshipers split between men and women and knelt in tight huddles, each family claiming its own favorite spot. Every age was represented, from elders to babies. With the lawmen permitted to observe their prayer service, apprehension among the congregants ran high. It wasn't within the experience of some of the immigrant Muslims to welcome police into their place of worship; they associated police only with forced entry and arrest.

Honecker opened his presentation by thanking the congregants for allowing him to observe, which had enlightened him about the practice of Islamic religion. Once the meeting was opened up for questions, a fruitful two-hour discussion ensued. The number-one issue for the Middletown Muslim community was safety. Parents expressed concern about their children being targeted in school after 9/11 as "friends of Osama bin Laden." Why, they asked, when in fact their religious beliefs were in total opposition to the acts of Osama? Honecker put it down to ignorance. He asked if the parents were involved with the schools in any efforts to educate students about the Islamic religion.

The congregants shied away from the suggestion. Their cultural habit was to stick together, they explained, rather than involve themselves in the community. Honecker encouraged them to consider becoming more engaged, perhaps offering programs to educate the community about Islamic rituals and religious beliefs—why they dress as they do, pray as often as they do, and the meaning of Ramadan. "When you reach out and educate people and allow them to see you as human beings, rather than as representations of the acts of an evil person like Osama bin Laden, those bigoted and false perceptions are broken down."

The president of the Islamic Society of Monmouth County, Dr. Hassan Elmansoury, voiced his support for this idea. Tension subsided. Refreshments were brought out. Muslim families thanked Honecker and his men warmly for coming out on the night of the Christian Sabbath. In the long history of Middletown as a place of religious refuge since the 1600s, another notch was opened for acceptance of that which seems exotic only so long as it is kept hidden.

REVIVING COMMUNITY

The months spent in Middletown and Rumson had revealed limits to the American suburban dream. It fosters the fantasy that if only we can become rich and successful enough to build a big house and surround ourselves with the privacy of a great lawn and long driveway, we will never need to depend on anyone else. But basing our security on material success requires constant competition. And the facade that must be maintained does not allow for any expressions of vulnerability or need. This leaves us wide open for depression and despair whenever reverses come along, as inevitably they do. When reverses take us down, what we need is family, community, and faith.

Is true community even possible in a sprawling American suburb? Crossing the Oceanic Bridge between Middletown and Rumson, I remembered my first talk with the Rabbi of Rumson, when he told me, "Rumson is an entirely different state of mind from Middletown; there's no connection between these two places, except in your mind." But they had been inescapably connected by tragedy. And after all, there was a bridge between them, physically—why couldn't there be a bridge of caring and neighborliness?

What is community anyway? It's a word we toss around so thoughtlessly, it has lost definition. M. Scott Peck in *The Different Drum* suggests it be restricted to mean a group of individuals who have learned how to communicate honestly with each other, whose relationships go deeper than their masks of composure, and "who have developed some significant commitment to 'rejoice together, mourn together,' and to 'delight in each other.' "

Community is intimate—twenty or fifty or at most several hundred people bound by geography, or necessity, or an intensely shared experience. Certainly September 11 qualified as an intensely shared experience. Pastor Monroe recalled the period afterward, of up to six months, when he felt as though he and his flock were all "dead men walking." What brought him out of it was the spiritual kinship forged by the reverend and the rabbi and the Catholic priest, together with Ophelia Laughlin, the first ordained female Episcopal minister in the area, and other clergy. They had found solace in meeting together in small groups. Monroe was amazed at the sustained impact.

"We as clergy have become so close to one another, I say, 'It's saved my life.' Okay, it's hyperbole, but I wouldn't be nearly as effective a human being or pastor without a place where I can say, 'Hey, gang, I'm drowning, help me here!' " Being a brainy group, the members were serious about decoding Scripture, "but we laugh!" Monroe emphasized. "The frustrations that we can't share with other people, we can share with one another."

The idea surfaced that perhaps these small group meetings, which cut across all religious boundaries, were a template for fostering new connections among the citizens of Middletown and the Rumson Neck. Rabbi Levin shared with Pastor Monroe and Father Nolan and Minister Laughlin a fervent desire to create a place where community really happens. As Monroe described it, "Once you get people together in a small group and they talk and start to trust each other, they start raising the deep questions of life. Then, the sky's the limit."

CONNECTING MIDDLETOWN WITH OKLAHOMA CITY

An idea was born out of brainstorming with the rabbi and the reverend about how to expand the community of those who wanted to work on transforming the trauma into something hopeful. For eight years, Oklahoma City had been grappling with the need to rebuild and strengthen the bonds of community. Middletown was only a year and a half into its post-trauma journey and soon to face the second anniversary. It was suggested that the two could be linked as a community of shared experience.

Oklahoma City's National Memorial has an exhibit devoted to exactly that theme—"A Shared Experience"—highlighting the human response to the terrorist attacks in Oklahoma City, New York City, Washington, D.C., and Shanksville, Pennsylvania. The human response in Oklahoma centered on reaching out, remembering, and educating others. If some of the isolated guardians of Middletown—educators, clergy, mental health professionals, law enforcement officials, and volunteer leaders—could connect with their counterparts in Oklahoma City, they could share their common experiences and impart lessons learned.

Diane Leonard was an obvious family leader in Oklahoma. When Diane's husband, Don, a Secret Service officer, was taken from her by the bombing, she had to battle her way back from insecurity and depression. Notwithstanding, three weeks after the bombing she began working with other families on death penalty reform. A year later, she found herself on-stage with President Clinton when he signed the Anti-Terrorism Bill into law. In the second and third year, Diane saw that many of the rescue and re-covery workers were tortured with guilt and wrecking their lives. These men had resisted help. Diane worked with the police chaplain, Jack Poe, to get a grant from the Department of Justice and set up peer counseling workshops for the men.

It was startling to learn that Diane was still getting calls about rescue workers who were only now speaking up to express their problems and only now willing to accept help. The intensive workshops were still running, eight years later, and they always started out full. Like many other Oklahomans, Diane and Chaplain Poe had responded to 9/11 by heading straight to Ground Zero to offer whatever help they could. Their presence was appreci-ated by the families and survivors with whom they made contact, but the pro-fessionals of New York generally gave them the cold shoulder. The message was: New York knows how to take care of its own.

"When you're trying so hard to be helpful, to be turned away is horribly frustrating," Diane admitted. On hearing the idea for a Phoenix Rising Sum-mit, her enthusiasm was immediate. "We'd be thrilled to be able to give what we've learned in the last eight years to someone else, to shorten or soften their journey."

The directors of the memorial, Kari Watkins and Joanne Riley, were equally receptive. It was agreed that a two-day summit in May at the Okla-homa City National Memorial would be an inaugural effort to develop a long-term, supportive bond between the two communities. Delegates would identify ongoing needs and plan for a return summit gathering, in Middle-town, in connection with the second anniversary of 9/11.

ON THE FLIGHT to Oklahoma City, the delegation of a dozen commu-nity "angels" from Middletown and Rumson passed through a hypnotically beautiful electrical storm. It was tornado season in the Southwest. The plane pitched and rolled. The rabbi chewed his gum. The imam rubbed his feet. The police chief cracked jokes. Laurie Tietjen fell asleep. They were all getting to know one another's defenses against fear.

In the morning the delegation was awed at rounding a busy street corner in the center of downtown Oklahoma City and all at once being enveloped by the serenity of the memorial. Inside the museum they met their counterparts and introduced themselves, each one needing to tell his or her story of the personal connection to a terrorist event. It took less than two hours for the masks of composure to begin to come off.

"My name is John Pollinger," the Chief began in his commanding voice, looking every bit the poster boy for a tough law enforcement official. "I'm the chief of police in Middletown Township. We are proud of the fact that out of three hundred municipalities and cities across the United States, our town has the third lowest crime rate. That is part of the thing that draws a lot of people to our community, because it's safe—" He strangled on the word "safe." "Till one day . . . all those people died . . . and I . . . I couldn't . . . I couldn't do anything about it." He fought to hold back his emotions but they flooded over him. A moment passed while hearts went out to the Chief. "That's why I felt so helpless," he said in a soft, broken voice. "I still have a problem with that. I guess it's for a selfish reason that I'm here . . . it's for me."

Father Nolan was no less naked about his confusion and personal neediness. "I'm still trying to deal with it on many levels," he told the group. "I don't think I've been to Manhattan since nine-eleven. I certainly have not had any desire to go to the site. It's overwhelming to me. I really do have to question, how does this happen? How does a human being do this? What do we do for the people who are left? I don't know. I have to deal with it myself."

Father Nolan's struggle to explain an event that defies our moral understanding was reminiscent of the obsession of Brother Juniper in Thornton Wilder's classic moral fable *The Bridge of San Luis Rey.* The novel begins in 1714 with five pilgrims on foot crossing "the finest bridge in all Peru" when, unthinkably, the bridge collapses and all five plunge to their deaths. Contemporary reactions to the events of 9/11 are not unlike Brother Juniper's reaction to the collapse of the bridge. Convinced the accident had to be "a sheer act of God," the Franciscan missionary sets out to examine in scrupulous detail those five lives, convinced he will learn why they, and no one else among the thousands who might have been crossing the bridge at that moment, were chosen by God either to be destroyed for their wickedness or to be called early to heaven for their goodness. Brother Juniper drives himself mad in the attempt.

Wilder later wrote that he meant the book to be as puzzling and distressing as the news that five of your friends have died in an automobile accident. The underlying assumption of his fable is that any one of us could have been on that bridge when it collapsed—or in those Towers or on those planes or at the Pentagon. But he closed the book with one of the most profound sentences in English literature: "There is a land of the living and a land of the dead and the bridge is love, the only survival, the only meaning."

Laurie Tietjen, who had been sitting with her head bent and her ginger hair falling over her moist eyes, then shared a story that expressed exactly the bridge that Wilder's words evoked. "The first time I went to Ground Zero was maybe two weeks after nine-eleven. I really didn't want to go. Somebody wanted me to go with them. It looked like war. There was still fire everywhere. And there was a very weird smell that I'll never forget as long as I live. I walked away by myself because I was just in shock. And a man came over to me. He put his arm around me. He didn't say anything, just stood there with me. About fifteen minutes. Finally he turned to me and spoke. 'I didn't say anything to you, because I know there's nothing I can say to make you feel better. My daughter died in Oklahoma City.' I will never forget that man as long as I live. He made such a difference that day. He completely understood what I was going through at that time. I would love to track him down and bring back a little of that courage, a little bit of the hope he offered us that day. I just wish I knew his name."

Pollinger moved over to sit beside Laurie. He recalled how it was her brother Kenny's memorial service that woke him up. His new mantra was: "I don't have problems, only distractions." He now keeps a replica of Kenny's police badge framed on his chief's desk and turned toward the visitor's chair, so when he is asked about it, he has another chance to tell the story of how important Kenny's life was to the Middletown community. Amazingly, he'd never met Laurie Tietjen. From then on, he would not leave her side.

The Oklahoma veterans were open about admitting their early mistakes. Ellie Lottenville, an award-winning disaster relief expert with a doctorate in psychology, had volunteered to be on the death notification team. "The first thing I learned is that a Ph.D. doesn't help you in protecting yourself from secondary trauma in disaster work."

"I would like you to take back some protection against your own vicarious trauma," offered Linda Wagner, one of the veteran counselors who worked on Project Heartland for more than five years. A short round woman who exuded warmth, Linda urged her Middletown counterparts to pace themselves, not to make the mistake she and others did by immersing themselves in others' pain, and ending up themselves physically or mentally handicapped. Linda had not only suffered major heart blockage, she now lived with an inoperable brain tumor that slightly impaired her speech and concentration. It did not stop her from reaching out.

At one point she hugged her counterpart, Carol Veizer, the counselor who runs a nonprofit mental health center in Red Bank. Linda took the tree-of-life pendant from around her neck and put it on Carol. "I've been looking for someone to carry this message on," she said.

After a tour through the museum's exhibit of "A Shared Experience," everyone was limp. The participants gladly gathered for a prayer service under the comforting green canopy of the Survivor Tree. The rabbi led a chant of healing straight from the Torah. Voices rang out clear and strong, lifting names of some of the lost. At the peak of song, the rabbi broke into a little dance and others, too, expressed delight. He asked the gathered to embrace each other and cross all supposed barriers.

But it was not that easy.

Laurie had been eyeing with some suspicion the honey-skinned man with a crocheted prayer cap who stood beside the rabbi. The Middletown delegation had brought not only a priest and a rabbi but an imam. It was the first time a Muslim cleric had been included in one of the many ecumenical services at the Oklahoma Memorial. Abdur Rahim Mohammad did not look or sound exotic. A handsome American-born Muslim, he belonged to a liberal wing of the American black Muslim movement. He was a quintessentially American product: an alloy of a South Bronx boyhood and the gangs and drugs that went with it, purified by years of scholarly study of the Koran, who had become a prison chaplain but had never lost his native talent for singing "My Funny Valentine," which he had spontaneously performed at the bar mitzvah of Rabbi Levin's son.

Nonetheless, Laurie Tietjen held resentment toward Muslims, about whom she knew almost nothing, except that it was the label claimed by the suicide bombers who had killed her brother. Before the prayer service, she had confronted the Muslim cleric. "I'm not quite sure how to ask you this question, so I'm just going to come out and ask: Why didn't Muslims stand up after nine-eleven and denounce what had happened?"

Abdur Rahim told Laurie he liked the way her nose crinkled up when she smiled. That put her at ease. She noticed that his smile was especially inviting. He explained that some Muslims did speak up, but there was little media coverage and they were not heard by the general population. Secondly, he said, many immigrant Muslims were afraid of repercussions, and not just from their homelands, but from those Americans who did not want to hear, and would never believe, what the Muslim faith truly stands for.

Laurie listened carefully as this charismatic religious man lifted up hearts under the Survivor Tree. After he spoke, Laurie couldn't wait to give him a hug.

"Would you be willing to come to Middletown to talk to other family members who lost loved ones?"

The imam said nothing would delight him more.

THE TIME BOMB

On the second day, Richard Williams introduced himself as "a survivor." He said he had spent eighteen years as assistant manager of the Murrah Building. "They were my friends and my coworkers, my family. Because this was a federal facility, we had people who went back to work within an hour and never got counseling. Even today, eight years later, some of those people are still coping with their own survivor guilt, their own issues."

He described the damaging effects of a standard debriefing shortly after a trauma. "Our agency put all of us who worked together in a big room and said, 'Okay, everybody tell each other your stories.' To expect people to start healing each other when they're absolutely as sick as they can be, emotionally, well, *that* was the most traumatizing thing any of us had ever experienced. There was guilt. There was animosity. Certain people had been injured, and they resented those who weren't: 'You weren't even *there* that day.' That debriefing probably set some people back a year or two. The agency learned from it and later offered individual counseling."

Assistant district attorney Richard Wintory warned against the emergence of a "hierarchy of suffering" within the victims' community. People can fall prey to competing for levels of grief: "I lost my dad." "Well, that's nothing compared to losing my child." "I was blinded in my left eye." "Sure, but you're alive, my husband is never coming back."

The survivor Williams then told the group about another kind of loss: "I'm here today because of an Oklahoma City policeman. I was dug out of the building and carried out by him. He's my hero. That Oklahoma City policeman is no longer with us. He committed suicide a year later."

That prompted Jack Poe, the Oklahoma County police chaplain, to share what he had learned from their disaster: "Standard debriefings do not work with the police, because our folks carry guns. If they perceive that you're going to tag them as being emotionally unstable, that means you're going to take their gun, and their commission, and you've just stripped them of whatever identity they may have left. Our police suffered in silence a long time to avoid that."

Poe is a big bear of a man with what at first looks like a prizefighter's face. Soon enough, one notices the creases of compassion in his face and the gentleness in his voice. "You talk about any kind of addictive behavior, and we've seen it. Addiction to gambling, womanizing, drugs, alcohol, spending themselves into debt, domestic abuse. If we learned any lesson, it's that it takes a while for the men to integrate this experience. The longer they're on the disaster site, the longer it's going to take. You can't expect a lot of this to surface until three to five years."

A chilling time frame. Laurie spoke up. "I am very, very concerned about the police officers, especially the Port Authority Police, because they have not had any type of counseling since this happened. They've been working twelve-hour days and these guys are hurting like you can't even imagine. Some are already ruining their lives, and they're too proud to admit it or the stigma they think goes along with wanting help. I want to find ways to help them."

When Richard Wintory learned about the response from the PAPD—offering a mere two-day debriefing, and only to those who had worked at Ground Zero for an arbitrary number of days—he became incensed. What about the men who had worked the pile in the first two weeks, or those who had stuck it out for fifty-nine days—were they any less likely to be silently suffering?

"For the PAPD to grade levels of suffering," Wintory said, "it may be done out of ignorance, but it produces an evil effect. I think there is a powerful advocacy role for your Middletown delegates to demand a principled, honorable, comprehensive way to deal with the impact on these responders. It's obscene to me to think New York is investing the time and money in a contingency plan that will allow the city to shut down bridges and tunnels at a moment's notice, but they're not protecting the most important capacity for response, which is not a contingency plan—it's your people."

"You guys are sitting on a time bomb!" Poe injected. He related how his community got around the confidentiality problem. They got the mayor to set aside some of the monies donated to the community foundation, to be held for long-term mental health needs of the first responders. "We drew up a memo of understanding allowing us to designate where the police went for counseling. We set up peer workshops. Once word got out that confidentiality would be assured, they began coming forward. But I can tell you that about three to five years out, confidentiality concerns went out the window. They were hurting so bad, they didn't care who knew—'Just get us some help!' "

THE TRUTH

When Diane Leonard entered the room, she was a breath of fresh air. it wasn't only that the widow was dressed in a floaty floral-print pantsuit and high-heeled sandals, her dark hair arranged like petals around her camellia-white skin. As Middletown delegate Maureen Fitzsimmons whispered, "She projects serenity, and you can't fake that."

"What brought you back?" the group wanted to know.

"Truth." Diane was completely unself-conscious. She told how the event at the Murrah Building had reawakened a previous trauma—the death of her mother, whose body she never saw and whose suicide was never fully explained to her. "I'd had random nightmares about my mother. So I asked to see my husband's body. Everybody begged me not to, even the funeral director. I did see him, and my husband was not whole, but I'm glad I did. It made the event real."

Maureen was struck by the language Diane used. "While some of the other Oklahoma people always refer to April 19 as 'the disaster' and 'the bombing' and 'the trauma,' Diane refers to it as 'the event.' " She didn't need to attach negative connotations to what she has now integrated as an event into the larger tapestry of life.

The day ended with the announcement of a surprise visitor: "Laurie, there's someone here who would like to say hello to you."

In walked a tall, raw-boned Oklahoma man with a big white mustache. He spread open his long arms and, like sister to brother, Laurie Tietjen folded herself into them. The man was Tom Kight, the name Laurie never knew, the man she would never forget, who had held her at Ground Zero.

Tom now had a chance to walk Laurie to the chairs on the Memorial's knoll. The air was windless and warm. Slats of light admitted through the Walls of Time were mirrored in the still water of the reflecting pond. Tom stopped before one empty glass seat, aglow with light. "Say hello to Frankie, my daughter," he invited Laurie.

"It felt as if Frankie was sitting right there with us, and smiling," Laurie said, deeply touched. Here was another lesson: The best way to build bridges from the land of the dead to the land of the living is to tell and retell the stories of those who are gone; that guarantees a measure of immortality. The key is to shift the emphasis from the way the victim died to the way he or she lived.

Tom Kight proudly told the story of how his offspring had lived. Laurie was surprised that this father was still so sad. She held him, saying nothing. As she and Tom walked away from Frankie's chair, Laurie silently promised the daughter that she would keep an eye on her dad. Now the bridge between the living and the dead went both ways.

EVERYONE WHOSE JOURNEY has been followed in this book is, in varying degree, moving on. They are on the other side of the suburban illusion. Living in the New Normal. Their horizon looks very different than it did on that day when the smoke of the burning towers reached like the finger of doom to their doorsteps. Eighteen months later, their horizon shows slants of light.

"We're at a point where we've all decided we have a chance to live," said Karen Cangialosi. "And we're choosing life."

Acknowledgments

As I learned from my mentor, anthropologist Margaret Mead, when a highly significant event opens a fissure in the normal patterns of life, a writer must drop everything and go to the edge, where she will see the culture turned inside out. Although Middletown, New Jersey, was completely unfamiliar to me, I had grown up in a commuters' suburb of New York not unlike Middletown.

The research and writing of this book led me on a journey that for quite a time was lonely and almost unbearably sad, but that I felt compelled to follow until the darkness began to lift. The support I had along the way was crucial. It began with encouragement from Graydon Carter, Douglas Stumpf, and Aimée Bell, my colleagues at *Vanity Fair,* where an early account of the unfolding story in Middletown appeared. The full journey was sustained by the commitment of my brilliant editor at Random House, Robert Loomis.

Anna Szlai was an indefatigable research assistant. Christina Barrett, my editorial assistant, kept me going with her intelligence, maturity, and sweet disposition.

Others whose help in the research process was critical at different points were Rachel Lehmann-Haupt, Sarah Broom, Michael Learmonth, Scott Simonson, Jason Haber, and Heather Baukney. Robert Sind was an invaluable guide to corporate behavior. Kenny Morris, a working actor, managed to transcribe hundreds of taped interviews with accuracy, efficiency, and good humor.

In Middletown I found knowledgeable resources in Maureen Fitzsimmons, Robert Czeck, Mary Lou Strong, and Sherry Villano; New Jersey State Police detectives Jerry Barbato and Jim Bruncati; New Jersey State Police chaplain Reverend Monsignor Philip Lowery; and Riverview Hospital behavioral health managers Tony Trachta, Jim Cunningham, and Mary Anne Ruane. Logistical support and TLC were provided by Linda and Bob Kaufer and a resurfaced grade school pal, Gail Abrams. The staff of the Oyster Point Hotel could not have been more gracious.

In Oklahoma City I was guided by Dr. Paul Heath, Rosemary Brown, and Diane Leonard.

Caryn Carter was always ready and able to help in any capacity at crunch times. Theodore H. Kheel, a lawyer and specialist in conflict resolution whose friendship has been steadfast, guided me in ways too numerous to mention. I am grateful to my agent, Lynn Nesbit, for providing high maintenance. My sister, Pat Klein, was an insightful and enthusiastic reader, as was my dear friend Dr. Patricia Allen. Ella Council, my personal assistant, never failed to keep me nourished in every way. My husband, Clay Felker, not only bolstered me with his usual editorial clarity, he also found ways to revive me from the emotional drain of sharing my subjects' trauma.

Finally, I want to thank the wounded women and men of Middletown for opening their hearts and homes to me.

Index

About the Author

Millions of readers around the world have defined their lives through GAIL SHEEHY's landmark work *Passages* and have followed her continuing examination of the stages of adult life in her bestsellers *The Silent Passage, New Passages,* and *Understanding Men's Passages. Middletown, America* is her fourteenth book. Sheehy is also a contributing editor to *Vanity Fair* and a playwright. The mother of two daughters, she lives between New York and California, and on the Web, where you can visit her at www. gailsheehy.com.

About the Type

This book was set in Times Roman, designed by Stanley Morison specifically for *The Times* of London. The typeface was introduced in the newspaper in 1932. Times Roman has had its greatest success in the United States as a book and commercial typeface, rather than one used in newspapers.